READINGS IN
URBAN
TRANSPORTATION

READINGS IN
URBAN
TRANSPORTATION

EDITED BY

GEORGE M. SMERK

Indiana University Press

BLOOMINGTON / LONDON

Published in Canada by Fitzhenry and Whiteside Limited,
Scarborough, Ontario

Library of Congress catalog card number: 68-14613

MANUFACTURED IN THE UNITED STATES OF AMERICA

C O N T E N T S

Contents

PREFACE

TO THE EXPERT IN THE FIELD OF URBAN TRANSPORTATION, there are probably few things this world needs less than a book of readings on the subject of urban transportation. For that reason, this work is not addressed to those whose knowledge of the subject is profound. Rather it is aimed at those who would like to know just a little more about this most interesting area—the general student of transportation and those laymen who for one purpose or another wish to delve a bit into the whys and wherefores of transportation in urban places. For academic uses, it was planned to supplement general courses in transportation, urban geography, urban administration, and urban planning.

The readings assembled in this book attempt to cover some of the reasons behind the urban transport problem as well as some of the possible solutions. A fair amount of space is devoted to the subject of alternative approaches to solving the problem and to the question of whether such solutions should be based on private automotive transport or on one or more modes of public transportation. There is also a section which deals with the recent role of the federal government in helping to find solutions to the urban transport problem. Some of the important documents concerning recent legislation are included.

G. M. S.

ACKNOWLEDGMENTS

A BOOK OF THIS SORT necessarily depends on the cooperation of publishers, copyright owners, and authors for permission to use their work. The following individuals, institutions, and firms are hereby thanked for their cooperation: The Eno Foundation for Highway Traffic Control, Inc., publishers of *The Traffic Quarterly*, and John C. Kohl for "The Federal Urban Transportation Demonstration Program," and Henry C. Quinby for "Major Urban Corridor Facilities: A New Concept"; *The Journal of Land Economics* for "Subsidies for Urban Mass Transportation"; the British Railways Board for "Urban Traffic Problems and Their Effect on Public Transport," by E. Rockwell, and "Urban Motorways and Urban Congestion," by D. J. Reynolds, both of which appeared in *The British Transport Review;* the American Economic Association, publishers of *The American Economic Review,* and William S. Vickrey for permission to use "Pricing in Urban and Suburban Transport"; the Royal Economic Society, publishers of *The Economic Journal,* and Gilbert J. Ponsonby for "The Problem of the Peak, With Special Reference to Road Passenger Transport"; the Buttenheim Publishing Corporation, publishers of *The American City,* for "No More Off-Street Parking in Congested Areas," by Victor Gruen; the Institute of Traffic Engineers, publishers of *Traffic Engineering,* for "The Importance of Urban Transit and Its Effective Passenger Capacities," by Walter S. Rainville; the Automobile Manufacturers' Association for "Living and Travel Patterns in Automobile-Oriented Cities," by Karl Moskowitz, and "Economics of Consumer Choice in Urban Transportation," by Leon N. Moses, both of which appeared in *The Dynamics of Urban Transportation;* the Graduate School of Business, Indiana University, publishers of *Business Horizons,* for the use of "Free Transit: A Way Out of Traffic Jams?" by L. L. Waters, and "Three Experiments in Urban Transportation," by George M. Smerk; the Connecticut General Life Insurance Company for "The New Highways: Challenge to the Metropolitan Region," by Wilfred

Acknowledgments

Owen; the Institute of Local Government, Graduate School of Public and International Affairs, University of Pittsburgh, for "Transportation and the City," by Wilfred Owen; the Royal Bank of Canada, Montreal, Quebec, for "Our Highways and Our Traffic"; the McGraw Hill Publishing Company, publishers of *Business Week,* for use of the article "Tide Turns for Transit"; and the Kiplinger Washington Editors, Inc., publishers of *Changing Times,* for use of "The Cost of Getting to Work." I would also like to acknowledge with many thanks the editorial work of Mrs. Ellen H. Bernstein of the Indiana University Press.

READINGS IN

URBAN

TRANSPORTATION

PART

I

CONGESTION
IN THE CITY

CHAPTER I

The Decline of Public Transportation

AS WITH MOST OF THE OTHER PROBLEMS OF MODERN LIFE, there is nothing new under the sun about congestion in urban areas. Ancient Rome had such serious traffic jams that all except public vehicles were banned from the downtown streets during daylight hours. In the nineteenth century the streets of London, New York, and other major cities of the world thronged with horse-drawn vehicles; hansoms and growlers vied for space with omnibuses, horsecars, and drays. The Victorian air was blue from the exchange of vituperation between drivers contending for the limited space and was rendered pungent by the universal use of the horse as a source of power. Blue and pungent air is now supplied by exhaust vapor, but the competition for space continues—albeit with more sophisticated conveyances than in times gone by.

The basic cause of congestion remains the same: too many persons or vehicles attempting to use the same space at the same time. The symptom of this disease is not necessarily a complete stoppage of movement; rather it is a general slowing-down and clogging action. Vehicles cannot move smoothly through a congested area any more than air can pass easily through the nasal passages of someone suffering from a severe head cold.

The problem of urban transport congestion today pertains primarily to vehicles. In most American and Western European cities, automobiles provide most of the passenger movement. Increased use of the automobile is not necessarily a problem in and of itself. Only when cars are used to move people in a relatively small area during a relatively brief time span does a problem arise and the automobile become more of a burden than a boon to the city. The automobile is therefore not the villain of the urban congestion problem; the problem focuses upon this type of congestion today simply because that is the kind of congestion we face.

In modern industrialized societies where increasing affluence seems to lead inexorably to increasing automobile ownership and utilization, automotive congestion appears to be particularly difficult to eradicate. Changing patterns of population distribution—from the highly concentrated population of the central city to the relatively thinly populated suburban areas—

[3]

have caused heavier reliance on automotive transportation. These changes have accelerated rapidly in the last two decades. At the same time, the decline in the service offered by public transportation, a subject covered below in substantial detail, provides many urban dwellers with no suitable alternative to driving a car.

The situation demands correction in spite of the difficulties, for the jam-ups of traffic are not merely inconvenient: they are very expensive events which threaten the very substance and fibre of tenable and rewarding urban life. Congestion wastes the time of those entangled. It causes physical and mental wear and tear that reduce productivity at the workplace and prevent the full utilization of free hours. It makes the delivery of goods slower and more difficult, increasing labor costs and adding to the physical wear on vehicles. Police and fire protection are rendered more difficult and expensive since congestion hampers mobility.

Vehicular exhaust fumes from traffic jams pollute the air. Cars unable to move freely clutter the landscape and act as a barrier to pedestrian mobility. Parking lots blight the city center, subtracting even further from the scanty visual amenities present in most American cities. We are almost at a point where the social and economic burdens of urbanization will begin to outweigh the benefits.

Urban Mass Transport at the Ebb

George M. Smerk

THE MODERN CITY AND URBANIZED AREA as we know them today had their beginnings with the industrial revolution. The centralization of production that was brought about by the adoption of machine processes in the middle of the eighteenth century caused a substantial movement of manpower to the old established urban places. It also caused the development of new urban centers, such as Manchester and Birmingham in England, which were established primarily on an industrial base.

The adoption of the factory system brought another significant change —the separation of the workplace from the home. As workers streamed into the cities to work in the mills and factories and offices of the new industrial age, the limitation of early nineteenth-century construction technology precluded building very far up on the vertical scale. Housing had to spread out horizontally.

The need for transport facilities between the place of work and the

[4]

home which would also aid more general urban mobility was met from about 1830 onward by the development of improved means of public transportation. Beginning with the omnibus, working through the stages of the horsecar and cable car, and culminating in the use of electric traction, public transportation substantially increased urban mobility. Not only did the developing public carriers provide greater movement for industrial workers; they also led to the establishment of the financial, commercial, and service hub which came to be the urban core—the downtown area of cities.

Downtown, or the central business district, was thus the creature of the transport provided by the urban public transportation modes. It was the site of the greatest single concentration of humanity during the working hours of the day, and the focus of all retailing and cultural facilities and activities.

The concentration of activity in the downtown section was paralleled along the mass transport arteries by a concentration of population. Housing developed initially within convenient walking distance of public transportation. In areas where the streetcars operated upon streets parallel to one another at distances of a half mile or less, as in Chicago and Philadelphia, housing development was relatively even in its distribution. Toward the outer limits of the city, however, the public transport lines were rarely so close together, and the developed area proceeded primarily along the relatively widespread transport arteries. The gaps between these lines gave a starfish-like pattern to the process of urban development. The space between the arms of the starfish often continued to be used as farmland long after areas on either side had been highly urbanized.

Until well into the automobile age the modern American city was very obviously shaped by public transport, and particularly by the streetcar. The shopping street extending along the carline and the major shopping area at the intersection of two main lines are both good examples of this practice. The signs of this development remain today in older parts of our cities. Students of architecture can usually tell, because of style and construction method, when public transport was extended into a given area, so closely did building follow the availability of transport.

Another factor entered the picture when the electric streetcar was developed. Whereas public transport carried on by means of omnibus, horsecar, or cable car had usually tended to operate in already built-up sections of the city not far from the center, or had extended themselves only gingerly beyond the established limits of the city, the electric streetcar lines pushed far into the outskirts of town. There were several reasons for this. The slow speed of the horsecar and omnibus limited the distance they could cover within a riding time that was acceptable to the public.

[5]

Cable-operated railways were substantially faster, but the cost of construction was so high that they could be operated profitably only on those lines in highly developed areas where traffic was dense enough to warrant the investment. The speed capabilities of the electric streetcar greatly extended the practicable range of operations, however, and the cost of installation was more modest than that of the cable railway.

A force in the physical expansion of cities in this period was the sharp rise in population as people streamed into them not only from abroad but also from the rural areas of the United States. Population pressures at the center of the city caused by these new, usually lower-class, city dwellers gave an incentive to upper- and middle-class residents to move out of the older areas of the city. The street railway companies, spurred on by this shift in population, began the active promotion of housing developments along with the extension of their lines. Many firms were as active in the real estate business as they were in transportation.

A social element helped foster the physical extension of the cities. An early practice of the street railways, going back even to horsecar times, had been service to cemeteries in the outlying parts of the cities. City dwellers made a practice on weekends of visiting the graves of relatives. This practice was aimed not merely at paying respect to the departed but also at enjoying the benefits of a change of pace and of some fresh air and sunshine. The street railway company benefited from the revenues generated by this weekend travel, and they were also able to make fuller utilization of their plant and equipment. The electrification of the streetcars and the vogue for amusement parks, usually operated by the street railway company in a suburban area, added to the cemetery traffic after the early 1890s. Another profitable dimension to the suburban weekend trip lay in the fact that city people traveling on a Sunday through the pleasant outskirts of town were often good prospects for housing lots along the streetcar line. The ride into the hinterlands was a good advertisement for a more suburban form of living which was still convenient to the all-important artery of public transportation. The joys of suburban living could be had with no loss of urban advantages. Thus urban life geared itself in a more or less orderly form to the capabilities and possibilities of public transport.

At the same time, public transportation became more efficient in terms of the space needed to transport relatively large numbers of people. Streetcars could trundle thousands to and from the center of the city and yet occupy only a small amount of space. Naturally there was congestion in larger cities where many lines used the same downtown streets and where horse-drawn vehicles were abundant. In the largest cities, where this congestion eventually became intolerable, the completely grade-separated elevated or subway rapid transit line greatly increased the capacity of a given artery, and in the case of the subway utilized none of the downtown's valuable surface area.

The pattern of ownership and operation of the transport companies changed, too, as cities grew. Initially many separate companies were formed to operate horsecar services; usually a given street or small area was operated by each concern. There was an obvious advantage to the public where competition of closely parallel services spurred improvements in the quality of service and equipment, but this advantage was largely offset by lack of transfer privileges between the separate companies. As cities grew, it was often difficult to complete one's journey on the line of only one railway; transfers were required not only between vehicles but between companies, entailing the payment of another fare.

Inconvenience to the public was matched by management problems that sprang from the attempt to operate, in a competitive atmosphere, a business having most of the characteristics of a natural monopoly. The street railways began to merge, shortly after the Civil War, in order to end the inevitable threat of cutthroat competition. By the time the electric streetcar arrived on the scene, most cities were served by only two or three companies, the products of mergers of many smaller concerns. The street railway was big business. The opportunity presented by the electric car in the burgeoning cities as well as the possibility of monopoly control of a city's public transportation both pushed the drive for further amalgamation. And as the electric car proved practical, there was a need for more capital to convert horse and cable railways to electric traction, a need that could often be met more easily by a single large firm.

Popular enthusiasm for the electric streetcar was feverish. Civic pride, even in towns of modest size, demanded electric streetcars as visible evidence of their progressive spirit. Much the same feeling is present today in the demand for airport construction. By the turn of the century, grandiose schemes for streetcar empires became the order of the day. The fire was fanned by promoters who frequently managed the amalgamation, electrification, and extension of lines in one operation.

As had been the case with the rapid expansion of the railroads a short time before, financing was largely in the form of debt capital. At the time this form of capitalization was resorted to, companies could reasonably expect to pay the interest charges because of their monopoly position. The decades prior to 1900 had been ones of relatively stable costs and constantly increasing patronage. A troublesome factor affecting the large-scale mergers, however, was that all previous debt capital was typically taken over by the newly formed companies. The debt could be quite large since the final merger of all the street-railway companies in one city was based on several previous layers of debt capital from mergers in preceding years. Additionally there was the problem of "watered" capital on all levels. By the time a single corporation came to control public transport there was probably little relationship between the capitalization and the value of the assets—and hence the earning power—of the enterprise.

Cities did not grant the right to operate public transportation services on the public streets free of charge or with complete freedom of action on the part of transport management. Franchises had to be secured in order to operate, and there were definite requirements made of the company. The amount of service to be operated and the fare to be charged, usually not exceeding five cents, were frequently stipulated in the franchise. Street-railway companies were commonly responsible for maintenance of the street between the rails and for some distance on either side; there was a bridge maintenance requirement as well. In some places companies were required to sprinkle the streets for dust control in the summer and to clear them of snow in the winter.

The burdens imposed by franchise terms and by the often overinflated capital structure, with large fixed payments of interest on bonds, was not too onerous as long as public transportation had a monopoly of travel in a city. After the turn of the century, however, problems began to appear. Rising costs of labor, materials, and equipment became a nagging burden. Overextension of operation due to overpromotion or to too sanguine expectations of development and traffic was another problem to many companies. The fare provisions of the franchises limited revenues, while the need to meet regular interest payments on bonds meant that there was a constant drain on those revenues. Often the only way to keep running was to resort to seriously deferred maintenance.

Many companies were facing serious problems by 1910. At about that time, the vision and enterprise of Henry Ford and of other manufacturers were making the automobile generally available to an increasing number of Americans. This competition from private transportation, added to the burdens of an internal nature that were peculiar to the street-railway business, started public transportation on its long downhill tumble.

This first chapter of readings is important in that it points up the reasons for the inability of public mass-transport organizations to meet the travel demands of expanding cities and for the failure of mass transport in most places to play a significant role in urban development after about 1925 or 1930. During most of the past half-century, and particularly since the end of World War II, urban and metropolitan growth has been shaped by private automotive transportation. This is not necessarily a bad thing; but in seeking solutions to automotive congestion, consideration must be given to the fact that auto-oriented suburban growth has helped to distribute the population of metropolitan areas in a low-density pattern. Low population density makes it difficult to operate attractive public-transport services at a profit.

Present thinking leans heavily toward the rejuvenation of mass transportation as an integral part of any solution of the urban congestion problem. To give a solution any hope of success, such mass transport must be an effective and attractive alternative to the private automobile. Financially weak public-transport operations have been unable to do this in the past, and the general image of public transport during the bleak years of auto domination has been so poor that even given attractive services, the public may be reluctant to switch.

Report of the Federal Electric Railway Commission, 1920

THE FIRST READING is taken from a report of the Federal Electric Railway Commission in 1920. A rash of bankruptcies during the First World War brought the deteriorating condition of urban-transport companies to the attention of the public and of the federal government. President Wilson's appointment of a federal commission in 1919 is fair evidence of the national importance attributed to the situation at that time. It is difficult for most Americans in recent years to conceive of the public-transport industry as one so basic to the welfare of U. S. citizens as it was in the first two decades of the century. Only as private automobile congestion has mounted have the public and their elected representatives on all levels of government given consideration once again to the renewed importance of public mass transportation as a factor in urban health and vitality.

To the present-day reader, the most anachronistic feature of the report is its insistence on the necessity of providing urban transport by means of railed vehicles. One should note that this report was written before it was deemed feasible to handle most urban traffic either by motor bus or by private transportation. Indeed it was not until the decade of the 1920s that various highway-related interest groups as well as the general interest of all Americans in highway transportation came to occupy a dominant position on the transportation scene.

What follows is an excellent summary of the distressed condition in which the urban mass-transport industry found itself on the eve of the automotive and metropolitan age. In view of the serious condition of the electric railway industry, on the verge of facing intense automotive competition as well as rapidly changing living patterns, it is small wonder that the principal role in metropolitanization in the following four decades was to be played by the automobile and not by public transportation.

THE PRESIDENT OF THE UNITED STATES:

SIR: THE FEDERAL ELECTRIC RAILWAYS COMMISSION begs leave to present the following report. The Commission was appointed by you in response to a suggestion outlining the need of such a commission in the following letter from two members of your Cabinet, the Secretary of Commerce and the Secretary of Labor:

Washington, D. C., May 15, 1919

DEAR MR. PRESIDENT: The electric railway problem to which your attention has been called on several occasions has recently assumed such serious national proportions as to warrant the prompt attention of the Federal Government. Already 50 or more urban systems, representing a considerable percentage of the total electric-railway mileage of the country, are in the hands of receivers. The communities affected are among the most important—New York, Providence, Buffalo, New Orleans, Denver, St. Louis, Birmingham, Montgomery, Pittsburgh, Memphis, Fort Wayne, Des Moines, St. Paul, Spokane, Chattanooga.

Other large systems are on the verge of insolvency, for the industry as a whole is virtually bankrupt. The continued shrinkage in the value of hundreds of millions of electric-railway securities held by savings banks, national banks, life-insurance companies and by the public at large threatens to embarrass the Nation's financial operations. Furthermore, the withdrawal of this industry's buying power, which is said to rank third in magnitude, involves the unsettlement of collateral industries, naturally entailing labor dislocation that will affect hundreds of thousands of employees.

The return to normal conditions is being hampered and the efforts of the Government to avert strained conditions in finance, labor, and commerce are being less fruitful of satisfactory results than should be expected, if some solution of the electric-railway problem were in view.

What the solution is may, we believe, be evolved by a thorough investigation of general franchise and operating conditions in their relation to rates, including service-at-cost plans, State and municipal taxation, local paving requirements, and internal economies that may be effected.

Report of the Federal Electric Railway Commission, U. S. Government Printing Office, 1920.

We therefore propose and recommend the appointment by you of a Federal board or commission, whose duty it shall be to study and report upon the entire problem, in order that the State and municipal authorities and others concerned may have the benefit of full information and of any conclusions or recommendations that may be formulated. Such a study will, in our opinion, exert a helpful and constructive force in this critical period of the industry's existence and will aid in the readjustment. If you would make such an appointment before June 30 your contingency fund could be used to defray the expenses, which would be about $10,000.

The National Association of State Commissioners has always invited Federal aid in this matter and the recent conference of governors and mayors adopted a resolution recommending Federal consideration of the problem of preventing the financial disaster threatening this industry.

We propose that such a commission shall be made up of one representative of each of the following groups: Treasury Department or War Finance Corporation, Department of Commerce, Department of Labor, National Association of State Commissioners, American Cities League of Mayors, Amalgamated Association of Street and Electric Railway Employees, American Electric Railway Association, Investment Bankers' Association of America.

We respectfully urge your authorization for such a commission, to be followed by your formal proclamation upon the selection of the personnel.

Cordially yours,

WILLIAM C. REDFIELD
Secretary of Commerce

W. B. WILSON
Secretary of Labor

The Commission appointed by you on the 31st day of May, 1919, consisted of the following members, who were to serve and have served thereon without compensation: Charles E. Elmquist, president and general solicitor of the National Association of Railway and Utilities Commissioners. Edwin F. Sweet, Assistant Secretary of Commerce, representing the Department of Commerce. Philip H. Gadsen, representing the American Electric Railway Association. Royal Meeker, Commissioner of Labor Statistics, Department of Labor, representing the department. Louis B. Wehle, General Counsel of the War Finance Corporation, representing the Treasury Department. Charles W. Beall, of Harris, Forbes & Co., New York Bankers, representing the Investment Bankers' Association of America. William D. Mahon, president of Amalgamated Association of Street and Electric Railway Employees of America, representing that association. George L. Baker, mayor of Portland, Oregon, representing the American Cities League of Mayors.

The Commission met on June 4, 1919 in Washington, D.C., and organized by electing Charles E. Elmquist as chairman and Edwin F. Sweet as vice chairman, and subsequently appointed Charlton Ogburn as its executive secretary. At its first meeting the Commission announced that it would attempt to determine the general principles which should govern the regulation, operation and service of electric railways, but that the Commission was without authority to hear and determine specific local controversies, and that it would not undertake in any way to encroach upon the functions of State commissions or of municipal authorities; that the purpose of the Commission was rather to investigate and study the condition of the electric railway industry, including franchises, rates, taxation, and assessments, economies of operation, public relations, regulation, etc.

The Commission gathered its testimony mainly in two ways: First, by public hearings, at which 95 witnesses testified in person and 21 others sent prepared statements; second, by a series of questionnaires sent to every city in which there is a street or intersuburban railway, addressed to the electric railways, the mayors, chambers of commerce, and the central labor unions, and also to all of the State public utility commissions.

The first public hearing was held in New York on June 19, 1919. The next hearing was held in Washington on July 15, lasting two weeks, during which time the witnesses on behalf of the electric railways presented evidence under the direction of the committee of one hundred of the American Electric Railway Association. The next hearing was in Washington beginning August 11, and lasted one week, testimony being offered on behalf of the public, chiefly by representatives of the municipalities and all State public utility commissions. At the last hearing held in Washington, beginning September 29, and lasting one week, testimony was offered by further witnesses representing the public and by witnesses on behalf of labor, represented by the Amalgamated Association of Street and Electric Railway Employees of America. All of these hearings ran through day and night sessions, beginning at 10 a.m. and usually continuing until 10 or 11 p.m., and totaling one month.

Among the witnesses were ex-President William H. Taft, Secretary of War Newton D. Baker, leading bankers, railway managers, economists, mayors, public utility experts, and State public utility commissioners.

The testimony taken embraces 6,195 pages of typewritten transcript.

Three separate questionnaires were later sent out. The first was general, dealing with all phases of the situation. The last two were special, seeking traffic figures, month by month, for the past three years—that is as to the number of revenue passengers, amount of passenger revenue, fare charges, and any occurrence affecting traffic, such as strikes, influenza epidemic and the like.

At the conclusion of the final public hearing the Commission engaged the services of Dr. Delos F. Wilcox to aid in analyzing the testimony gathered and to make suggestions to the Commission with reference to its report. Dr. Wilcox made a very comprehensive analysis of the evidence, containing 823 pages of matter. The Commission regrets that it can not publish this analysis with the proceedings since it represents a complete and masterful study of the whole electric railway problem. Printed with the evidence, however, is a summary of the Wilcox report, prepared by him. The answers to the questionnaires resulted in bringing to the attention of the Commission a great mass of information. All the evidence, exhibits, analysis of Dr. Wilcox and tabulated summaries of information found in the answers to the questionnaires have been considered by this commission.

The final meeting of the Commission was held in Washington July 22 to 27, 1920, inclusive, for the purpose of formulating this report.

Owing to the divergent representation of its personnel, this unanimous report of the Commission necessarily represents decided concessions by some of its individual members.

A complete report of the testimony will be printed, together with this report, and will be placed in the Congressional Library in Washington and other leading libraries in the country, with all regulatory commissions and with the mayors of the leading cities of the United States.

For convenience, we wish, before proceeding to our discussion, to state our principal conclusions and recommendations, which are as follows:

CONCLUSIONS AND RECOMMENDATIONS

1. The electric railway furnishing transportation upon rails is an essential public utility and should have the sympathetic understanding and cooperation of the public if it is to continue to perform a useful public service.

2. The electric railway has been and will continue to be a public utility, subject to public control as to the extent and character of the service it renders and as to the rates it charges for such service.

3. It is of the highest importance that both the total cost of the service and the cost to the individuals who use it shall be kept as low as possible without injustice to those who take part in producing it.

4. The electric railway industry as it now exists is without financial credit and is not properly performing its public function.

5. This condition is the result of early financial mismanagement and economic causes accentuated by existing high-price levels of labor and materials, and of the failure of the uniform unit fare of 5 cents prescribed either by statute or by local franchise ordinances or contracts to provide the necessary revenues to pay operating costs and to maintain the property used in the public service when honestly and efficiently managed.

6. The industry can be restored to a normal basis only by the introduction of economies in operation, improving the tracks, equipment, and service, and assuring a reasonable return upon the fair value of its property used in the public service when honestly and efficiently managed.

7. The electric railways must expand to meet the growing needs of their communities; therefore, the first essential is to restore credit in order to obtain necessary new capital for the extension and improvement of service.

8. Restoration of credit involves a readjustment of relations which will remove public antagonism, provide public cooperation, and insure to the investor the integrity of his investment and a fair rate of return thereon.

9. Effective public cooperation should be exercised by eliminating in so far as is practicable, special assessments for sprinkling, paving, and for the construction and maintenance of bridges which are used by the public for highway purposes.

10. Extensions into new territory resulting in special benefits to the property in that vicinity should be paid for by assessments on such property in proportion to the benefits received, and the amount of such assessment should not be added to the physical value of the corporate property.

11. The great increase in the use of private automobiles, the jitney and motor busses, has introduced a serious although not a fatal competition to the electric railway. These forms of public motor conveyance when operated as public carriers should properly be subject to equivalent regulatory provisions.

12. The full cooperation of labor is essential to the highest prosperity and the usefulness of the industry. The employees engaged in this occupation should have a living wage and humane hours of labor and working conditions. They should have the right to deal collectively with their employers, through committees or representatives of their own selection. All labor disputes should be settled voluntarily or by arbitration, and the award of such a board should be final and binding upon both parties. It

is intolerable that the transportation service of a city should be subject to occasional paralysis, whether by strikes or by lockouts.

13. A private industry should not be subsidized by public funds unless it is imperatively necessary for the preservation of an essential service, and then only as an emergency measure.

14. Unless the usefulness of the electric railways is to be sacrificed public control must be flexible enough to enable them to secure sufficient revenues to pay the entire cost of the service rendered, including the necessary cost of both capital and labor.

15. There can be no satisfactory solution of the electric railway problem which does not include the fair valuation of the property employed in the public service, and where that is done the companies should voluntarily reduce any excessive capitalization to the basis of such value.

16. There is no insuperable objection to a large, wide-open city having exclusive jurisdiction over the rates and services of public utilities.

17. The necessity for scientific and successful regulation of systems, whether large or small, and especially those which operate through several cities and villages and in rural territory, leads to the conclusion that local regulation should generally be subject to the superior authority of the State, whether as a matter of original jurisdiction or through the medium of appeal.

18. Cost-of-service contracts are in the experimental stage, but where tried they seem to have secured a fair return upon capital, established credit, and effected reasonably satisfactory public service. Such contracts may safely be entered into where the public right eventually to acquire the property is safeguarded.

19. The right of the public to own and operate public utilities should be recognized, and legal obstacles in the way of its exercise should be removed.

20. While eventually it might become expedient for the public to own and operate electric railways, there is nothing in the experience thus far obtained in this country that will justify the assertion that it will result in better or cheaper service than privately operated utilities could afford if properly regulated.

21. Public ownership and operation of local transportation systems, whether or not it be considered ultimately desirable, is now because of constitutional and statutory prohibitions, financial and legal obstacles, the present degree of responsibility of our local governments, and the state of public opinion, practicable in so few instances, that private ownership and operation must as a general rule be continued for an extended period.

22. If the reforms incident to public regulation which we suggest in this report should not result in making private ownership satisfactory to the public, such reforms should at least enable public ownership to be established upon a just and equitable basis.

THE STREET RAILWAY IS AN ESSENTIAL INDUSTRY

THE electric railway industry at present is a factor of essential importance in the urban life and, to a scarcely less extent, in interurban relations of the country.

The experience of 75 years, the unanimous opinion of expert witnesses, and of those who are students of transportation problems, and the assumption of the necessity for tracks by inventors working to improve the methods of street transportation alike demonstrate the fundamental and permanently essential nature of the railway—and to the present time of the electric railway—as the most nearly adequate, reliable, and satisfactory system available for transporting the maximum number of people through the streets of our cities with the least interference with the use of these streets for other purposes of public ways.

The Bureau of Census Reports for the year 1917 show the net capitalization as of December 31, 1917, to be $4,869,962,096, which makes this industry one-fourth as important as the steam railroads of the country in point of capitalization. The total mileage in 1917 was 44,835. The net capitalization per mile of track is $109,065. The total revenue for 1917 from railway operations was approximately $650,000,000. These statistics do not include the electrified portions of steam railroads engaged in suburban service. Approximately 40 percent of the mileage is suburban in character.

The number of people with whom the electric railways come into daily contact is shown by the fact that in the year 1917 they carried a total of 11,304,660,462 revenue passengers and 3,202,254,111 transfer and free passengers, as compared with a total of 1,066,638,474 revenue passengers carried by the steam railroads.

In spite of the immense development of the automobile industry the demand for electric railway transportation has increased at a rapid rate. It is estimated that on December 31, 1917, there were 4,643,481 passenger automobiles and that two-thirds of the development of that industry was subsequent to 1912, but the number of revenue passengers carried by the electric railways was approximately 1,800,000,000 more in 1917 than in 1912. During the year ended June 30, 1919, the total number of revenue passengers carried by the local transportation lines of New York City was 2,079,942,604, as compared with 1,402,417,642 carried during the year ended June 30, 1909, an increase of more than 46 per cent in 10 years. On the basis of the estimated population served, the number of revenue rides per capita in New York City in 1909 was 304 and in 1919, 370—an increase of nearly 22 per cent in the riding habit.

In this connection Mr. Henry G. Bradlee, president of the Stone & Webster Corporation, stated in a letter dated October 1, 1919, as follows:

> It would appear that something has been and is still stimulating the street railway business; possibly the automobiles themselves have helped in this direction. People may be acquiring to a greater extent then ever before the riding habit and may be more and more inclined to move about and spend less time in their own home or with their own neighbors. The moving picture is probably also a factor in the situation, but whatever may be the cause, the facts seem pretty clear that the demand for transportation service is still growing apace. This fact, I think, is generally not understood; in fact, I am free to confess that we ourselves were surprised to see the extent of the increased demand for service.

In 1917, the number of employees was 294,826, and it is estimated that the total number of people who were directly and conveniently accessible to electric railway service is about 80,000,000 at the present time. The electric railways have overflowed municipal boundaries and now include a network of interurban lines in many portions of the country, but the fact still remains that the industry is primarily a street railway with its principal function the transportation of passengers within the limits of municipalities.

While the electric railway industry is essentially local, it has certain national characteristics. Its difficulties can not be regarded simply as the isolated problem of a local system repeated hundreds of times all over the country in varied forms and degrees, each problem being independent of all the others. On the contrary, although a local traction system may be separated by hundreds of miles from its nearest neighbor, it is in other ways inseparably connected with all of the others. As a purchaser in the equipment markets of other States it competes with other companies. Its demands for labor and its scales of wages are necessarily felt at once by traction systems everywhere. In procuring its capital its officers have been generally compelled to market its securities to a large extent in other states, among investors who are particularly interested in such classes of investment. The close industrial and financial interdependence of the hundreds of physically unrelated local traction systems, the millions of dollars of capital placed by thousands of investors in plants which manufacture electric traction equipment, and the five billions of electric trac-

[1 7]

tion bonds and stocks to be found scattered all over the country in banks, insurance company reserves, and in private investment, translate the many local problems into a national problem.

FINANCIAL CONDITION OF THE ELECTRIC RAILWAY INDUSTRY

THE investigation demonstrates that the financial condition of the electric railway industry is acute, and that to a very great extent it is not properly performing its public functions.

The record in this case shows that on May 31, 1919, there were 62 companies, having a mileage of 5,912, in receivership, that 60 companies had dismantled and junked altogether 534 miles of railway, and that 38 companies together had abandoned 257 miles of track. Since that date and up to July 1, 1920, there have been 56 additional companies having a mileage of 1,908, which have been thrown into receivership.

The capitalization of the industry, according to the 1917 census report, is represented by $3,058,377,167 in bonds and $2,473,846,651 of stock. For the year 1917 the net income of operating companies was $56,450,930, representing an average rate of return of 2.81 per cent upon the capital stock. In 1918, the evidence shows the net income was reduced to $20,183,413, which represents a return of only 1 per cent. As a whole, there has been some improvement in the industry since the commencement of these hearings, due to the fact that there has been an increase in the car-riding habit since demobilization, and in a great many instances the fare has been increased beyond 5 cents. In spite of this slight improvement, however, the condition of the industry at the present time is serious. A great many companies are unable to properly maintain their track and equipment and to perform efficient public service, to secure funds with which to purchase new equipment, to build necessary improvements and extensions, or to refund maturing obligations.

A large number of factors have contributed to the present plight of the electric railway industry. These may be mentioned:

a) *They were not conservatively financed in their early years, and have not since made good their overcapitalization, except to a limited extent, otherwise than through the process of bankruptcy and reorganization.* In the early days the promoters of electric-railway properties believed that long-term franchises with a 5-cent fare would be permanently profitable. Large sums of money were required to develop the business. In many cases the promoters issued bonus stock to represent their hopes and expectations. This bonus stock did not represent money, service, or property and added nothing to the value of the plant. As a result of this practice, there are many cases where the existing capitalization exceeds the investment in the plant or the value thereof.

b) *Neglect to amortize this excess capitalization.*

c) *Failure to amortize the normal accrued depreciation.*

d) *Payment of unearned dividends and neglect of ordinary mainte-nance.*

e) *Overbuilding into unprofitable territory or to promote real-estate enterprises, involved sometimes with political improprieties.*

f) *A uniform 5-cent fare, which established a constant rate to apply during variable cost periods.* This contract fare has been a source of irritation, resulting in litigation. During normal times many communities sought to have the fare reduced below the contract price. The companies insisted upon adhering to the contract, and they were sustained by the courts. During the recent high-cost period many companies have applied for an increase in fare to enable them to meet operating expenses and fixed charges. In many cases communities undertook to prevent the increase beyond the contract rate. Under the decisions of the Supreme Court of the United States and of the highest courts of a number of states, it is now established that a franchise provision naming a certain rate of fare creates no vested right in any car rider but that such a fare can be properly changed by appropriate legislation and substituted by a higher charge.

As indicative of the fact that the 5-cent fare has not been adequate during the war period, we need only to call attention to the fact that on July 1, 1920, increased fares have been allowed in over 500 selected cities; 10-cent fares have been allowed in 69; 9-cent fares in two cities; 8-cent fares in 30 cities; 7-cent with 1-cent charge for transfers in 26 cities; 7-cent zones in 6 cities; 7-cent in 145 cities; 6-cent zones, with 2-cent transfer charge, in 10 cities; 6-cent for two zones, with 2-cent per zone thereafter, in 13 cities; 6 cents for each two zones in 4 cities; 6 cents cash fare in some cases in 149 cities; 5-cent zones and elimination or reduced rate ticket in 50 cities.

Boston has a 10-cent fare. Chicago, Washington, Cincinnati, Kansas City, Youngstown, and other large cities are on an 8-cent basis.

It would seem that so long as the railways depend upon earning power, and earning power depends upon passenger revenue, the fixed uniform fare is a broken reed for the industry or for the community to lean upon. Perhaps the general sentiment of the electric railways is best expressed by the evidence of Gen. Guy Tripp before this Commission as follows:

We were all living in a fool's paradise in the street railway business when we suddenly woke up—when the war woke us up—to find that no business that could not increase its revenues under any conditions can live or is sound.

Conversely, it may be said that no community should bind itself by contract or otherwise to continue, after normal conditions have been restored, a rate which might be found reasonable during the abnormal period.

g) *Limited franchises which impair credit and toward the expiration of the franchise result in neglect of the maintenance of the property.*

h) *Special taxation and franchise obligations, having particular reference to street paving, street sprinkling, construction and maintenance of bridges used by the general public, general taxation, etc.*

The American Electric Railway Association introduced a chart which showed that the total amount of taxes levied against the properties in 1917 amounted to $45,756,695, of which taxes levied against the personal property was $21,804,619, and on earnings, capital, and other taxes $23,952,076, representing 10.11 per cent of the operating expenses. In 1902 the ratio of taxes to operating expenses was 9.19 per cent. It is thus seen that there is only a small increase in the ratio of expense for this item since last year.

For the period from 1913 to 1918 the expenditures for all taxes, including paving and other imposts, has ranged from $60,000,000 to $65,000,000 corresponding to 10 per cent of the operating revenues. The ratio varies very materially among the different plants.

The evidence on behalf of the companies therefore shows that on the basis of the 5-cent fare the taxes represent about one-half of a cent in the nickel which the car rider has been paying, and that they thus contribute materially to the necessity for fare increases. The argument has been made with considerable force that the car rider should be required to pay for service alone; that he should not, through his car fare, be required to pay for supporting the city's schools, its almshouses and other city institutions. It is contended that the company should be required to pay in taxes to the city only such an amount as would reimburse the city for its actual cost due to the presence of the street railway; and that such a plan of taxation alone would be consistent with the idea that the car fare should be based upon the real cost of rendering the actual service of transportation.

Although there is much force in this idea, and it should be borne in mind by all who are interested in street railway problems, we do not think the time is ripe for recommending its general adoption. The heavy taxation to which the companies are now subject came into being during the period of their prosperity and at a time when they were still essentially private concerns, relatively free from regulation. It was natural that their properties should be taxed in no less degree than the properties of other private corporations.

When a company comes to subject itself to such a comprehensive regulation as renders its property in effect a public instrumentality, then tax exemption begins to be in order. This course has indeed been followed in Cleveland, where as an incident to the passing of the properties under the Taylor Plan of municipal regulation they came to be exempted in large measure from taxation. To the extent that it may become possible in any community under similar conditions to exempt street railway property from taxation, the rider's car fare will come more nearly to represent the actual cost of rendering the service of transportation—in itself a desirable result. But it would seem that the status of the company as a public agency should be well assured before such exemption should be attempted.

i) *Automobile and jitney competition.* For several years prior to the war, and to an increasing extent throughout the war period and up to the present time, the automobile has proven to be a serious competitor of the electric railways rendering local transportation service. Jitneys and automobile buses operating as common carriers have been able in some cases, through the absence of sufficient public regulation, to engage in unfair and destructive competition with the electric railways for the most profitable part of urban passenger traffic. Strong as this competition has been, however, the electric railway industry as a whole has shown a very substantial increase in the riding habit. The operation of jitney buses as common carriers is much more restricted than the operation of private automobiles, but the jitneys have had a definite and intensive effect upon the street railway situation in particular communities, for the reason that they have engaged in direct and in some respects destructive competition with the street cars as public carriers. The experience of numerous communities, even before the extraordinary conditions growing out of the war, made it clear that unrestricted jitney operation, though more or less temporary and precarious in character, threatens the service, credit and solvency of the street railways.

j) *Holding companies and banker control.* About 75 per cent of the public utilities of the country are held, in whole or in part, by so-called "holding companies" which are responsible for their operation. This financing is done in large part through the securities of the parent company, which securities are supported by the securities of the various operating companies. This frequently gives an element of strength to the securities of the parent company, which a single localized operating company could not in all cases present. If it were not for the supporting strength of these parent companies, many of the individual operating companies would have gone under before January 1, 1918.

Through these holding companies the electric railways threaten to become a banker-controlled industry. Those who have the ultimate say in matters of street railway policy from the point of view of investors have been dependent for their profits and their power upon the volume of securities outstanding and the frequency with which these securities have been exchanged or refunded. Holding companies in many instances have been responsible for overcapitalization and have insisted upon drawing from the underlying companies every possible cent that could be secured in order to make a showing on these inflated securities. Hon. Joseph B. Eastman, at present a member of the Interstate Commerce Commission, discussed the question as follows:

> In the third place, a factor of weakness, I think, was the control of the companies in many instances by holding companies organized in the form of voluntary associations, or, to use a more technical term, express trusts. Although the stock and bonds of the street-railway companies themselves were issued under public supervision, these voluntary associations which corralled all their stock were subject to no regulation whatever and issued shares upon an inflated basis, and that had the result of accentuating the desire to draw every possible drop of income out of the underlying companies that could be secured in order to support earnings upon the inflated shares of these voluntary associations.

Through this system of financing and management the utilities have been largely controlled by persons living distant from the community affected by a particular electric railway, whose prime consideration has been to secure a return upon the property. This "absentee" management and control has not been successful in bringing about the proper spirit of cooperation between the local managers, employees and the public. Since the electric railway companies come into immediate daily contact with large numbers of people, it is of the utmost importance, that the industry should gain and hold the respect, confidence, and good will of its patrons. If the local public should invest its money in the stock and bonds of its local utilities there would be an improvement in the relations now existing between the corporation and the public.

k) *Use of regulatory power to compel more and better service.* Through the exercise of this power the companies have been required in many instances to improve their standards of service and equipment; to equip cars with vestibules, for the protection of the motormen; and to give better heating, lighting and ventilation for the comfort and convenience of the passengers. They have also been obliged to install safety devices and make stops at frequent intervals. The exercise of the regulatory power of States and municipalities has undoubtedly added to the cost of the service.

l) *Underlying companies and leased lines.* Consolidations have been brought about through the unification of a number of separate corporations which owned and maintained lines of track within the same city. In many cases consolidations were made upon the condition that these companies should be guaranteed a certain rate of return or fixed sum, which represented a high percentage yield upon the investment. The returns thus secured have been a frequent source of irritation, induced by a feeling that these underlying companies are being paid more than a reasonable return upon the value of their property. Your commission believes that excessive payments to the underlying companies by the operating company have greatly diminished the net operating revenue, and that there can be no satisfactory solution of the street railway problem in such communities until the system has been valued as a whole, and the accounts so kept that the public may know that the rate of fare paid yields no more than fair return upon the value of such property.

m) *Increasing demands of labor.* The wages of street-railway labor prior to the war were generally insufficient from the viewpoint of a living wage, and the increases in wages that have taken place since the beginning of the war period have not on the average been as great as the increase in the cost of living.

At the time of our entry into the war, the average wages of motormen and conductors for companies of 100 miles and over were approximately 31.5 cents per hour. Since the war, there has been a rapid increase in the wages of employees. The National War Labor Board by its awards in the year 1916 established the normal wages for this class of service in different cities, varying from 38 to 48 cents per hour, increasing wages 23½ percent. The awards of the board mark the beginning of the rapidly increasing wages in this class of employment. An exhibit filed by the Amalgamated Association of Street and Electric Railway Employees of America shows the wages for conductors in the principal cities of the United States and Canada as of January 1, 1920. For convenience the exhibit is published as an exhibit attached to this report.

Since that date, new contracts have been agreed to which substantially increase the wages in a number of cities.

n) *The war and the dollar.* The conditions which have been here enumerated tended to break down the credit and stability of the electric-railway industry. The increases in prices of labor and materials entering into the construction, maintenance, and operation of electric railways during the war period have corresponded with the increases in the prices of general commodities and in the wages of labor in all industries. Operating costs became so high that in many cases the revenues were not sufficient to pay even the current expenses of operation. Material and equipment prices reached abnormal heights. The increase over 1915 in railway motors and car equipment show 87 per cent; locomotives, 87 per cent; rotary converters, 75 per cent; transformers, 70 per cent; switchboards, 100 per cent; motor generator sets, 95 per cent; turbines, 100 per cent; pig iron, 106 per cent; steel plates, 141 per cent; copper, 58 per cent; steel castings, 220 per cent; coke, 35 per cent; coal, approximately 100 per cent; asbestos material (which is largely used), 560 per cent; other insulating materials, 125 per cent; magnetic sheet steel, 280 per cent; labor, from 85 per cent to 90 per cent.

o) *Cost of new money.* The destruction of capital incident to the World War and the unprecedented demand of the government and industries for money, resulted in largely increasing the interest rate for loans. More attractive loans are now absorbing money available for investment, leaving the electric railways where, even with credit restored, they would have to compete in the money market with prosperous and unregulated enterprises.

These factors, and more particularly the increase in wages, fuel, material, and supplies, during and since the war period, have brought the electric railway industry to the point where in many instances it may be forced to abandon public service, and, in most cases, to a point where it will be unable to secure new capital to enable it to refund maturing obligations, secure new equipment, and to make necessary extensions and improvements unless some solution of the situation can be found.

Statement of Commissioner Joseph B. Eastman, 1919

THE FOLLOWING TESTIMONY, given by the distinguished public servant Joseph B. Eastman, is interesting in that it focuses on one state. The matters discussed are therefore not couched in the broad and general terms of the conclusions section of the report. While the situation described by Mr. Eastman was not typical of the nation as a whole, since electric railway financing was not as flamboyant in Massachusetts as in other parts of the country, this testimony reveals clearly the problems that could result from overexpansion and excessive promotional zeal, and the threat posed thereby to the subsequent economic health and vitality of the industry.

MR. EASTMAN. Mr. Chairman and gentlemen of the commission, I am very glad to respond to the invitation to appear before this commission,

"Statement of Commissioner Joseph B. Eastman, October 4, 1919," *Proceedings of the Federal Electric Railway Commission,* 1920.

although I should not have sought the opportunity myself, and I am glad to appear because I realize how difficult is the question you have to deal with, and if I can be of any help in aiding you to solve that question I want to do it. My chief fear is that I shall not be of much help, because, although I have spent a good deal of time in the study and consideration of this street-railway question, I never felt satisfied that I had really arrived at any satisfactory solution of it.

I think I ought to state before I begin that I am here solely as an individual and not as a member of the Interstate Commerce Commission. I have not talked the matter over with my colleagues at all; they know nothing whatever of what I am going to say, and they are not in any way responsible for the views I am going to express. The blame is wholly my own.

Whatever qualifications I possess to discuss this question come from experience as a member of the Public Service Commission of Massachusetts. I was on that commission from the fall of 1914 until the end of last year, and during that time we dealt almost exclusively with the street-railway problem. I am somewhat handicapped in speaking to you this morning because of the fact that my experience is confined almost exclusively to Massachusetts and you are considering the entire country. I have some fragmentary knowledge of the situation in other parts of the country. Also I am handicapped that since the beginning of the year I have given little thought to the situation even in Massachusetts, being rather fully occupied with my duties on the Interstate Commerce Commission. I am not familiar, for instance with the statistics of the street-railway operations in that State since the beginning of this year.

I should have liked to have been able to prepare a careful statement on the subject, because that is the kind of a statement that it deserves, but I have been unable to do that; I have not had time; and so I must content myself with certain notes which I have made and the discussion of those topics in a rather random and cursory manner.

Now, I think I ought to begin by setting forth briefly the situation in Massachusetts, because it differs, I think, in a good many respects from the situation in other States. That whole matter, the history of the street-railway situation in Massachusetts, was discussed at great length by Frederick J. McLeod, chairman of the public-service commission, when he appeared before the special street-railway-investigation commission of Massachusetts in November, 1917. That statement of his was afterwards published, and I think it is accurate and it describes the situation fairly, and if you are interested it is well worth your perusal.

But, briefly, there are certain sources of weakness in the Massachusetts situation. In the first place, more street-railway mileage was constructed there in proportion not only to territory but also in proportion to the population than in other States. The last time I saw the figures the discrepancy was rather striking. And naturally enough, much of that mileage was in the country and of a rather inferior type. We have no genuine interurban lines in Massachusetts, although we have plenty of cities which would support lines of that character. The country lines are constructed as a rule not on private right of way but along the highways, just as the street railways are constructed in the city. And that results in slow speed and operation, which enhances the cost and at the same time discourages the traffic. To illustrate that fact—

THE CHAIRMAN: Under the law are they permitted to occupy the streets as telegraph and telephone companies are?

MR. EASTMAN: Yes.

THE CHAIRMAN: Without paying for it?

MR. EASTMAN: Yes. They were given locations in the street through the agency of the cities and towns acting for the Commonwealth. The locations there are revocable locations which do not confer any perpetual right. They can be revoked at any time by the local authorities after one year's time, provided the public-service commission certifies that that is consistent with the public interest. Originally there was not even that proviso; the locations could be revoked at any time and without granting any compensation to the companies.

THE CHAIRMAN: So the companies can be protected against arbitrary action taken by municipalities?

MR. EASTMAN: Yes; they can under the law as it has existed for some years.

Now, to illustrate what I mean in regard to these country lines, take the case of the Bay State Street Railway Company—I believe now called the Eastern Massachusetts, since its reorganization: That operates all over eastern Massachusetts and extends from Newport, R.I., in the south to Nashua, N.H., on the north and has a mileage of very nearly 1,000 miles of track. And although it has a good many urban systems in populous-city centers, it also spreads all over the country districts. And notwithstanding that fact, in 1914-15, when we had that company before us, the average number of car-miles per car-hour was only 8.4, as I recall it, which is a figure which you would not expect in a distinctively urban system.

Now, many of these country lines which were constructed in that way never had a chance of success and probably ought never to have been built. Many of them were practically insolvent from the start and others would have reached that condition if they had been allowed to continue in an independent way. But instead of that—and this is the second point in which our situation is weak—they were taken under the wing of the stronger city company and extensive consolidations were brought upon a share-for-share basis.

THE CHAIRMAN: Before you go into that consolidation can you tell the commission why these lines were built which never had a chance to succeed?

MR. EASTMAN: Well, they were built, I suppose, because of the desire of the country districts to have lines and because of the hope that they would succeed; and also because of the profit which accrued in their construction to promoters of those lines.

THE CHAIRMAN: Did the municipalities contribute to the construction of these roads?

MR. EASTMAN: They did not contribute except in this way, that I think in a good many cases subscriptions were made to the stock by individuals in those towns who hoped to secure benefits from the building of the lines.

THE CHAIRMAN: But there was no public aid or donations?

MR. EASTMAN: There was no public aid or donations. As I was saying, many of these weaker lines were consolidated with the strong lines upon this share-for-share basis. That was regarded as proper in Massachusetts, because it did not result in any increase in the aggregate stock and bonds outstanding. In other words, it resulted in no inflation, in the ordinary sense. But it did have the result of spreading the earnings of the strong lines out over these weaker systems which could not have existed without the help of the stronger lines and upon an independent basis. And that has resulted in greatly weakening many of the city properties. There are very few distinctively city properties in Massachusetts. The Eastern Massachusetts Company, for instance, operates in such populous cities as Lowell, Lawrence, Haverill, Lynn, Brockton, Fall River, Salem, Beverly and others I might name. But at the same time, it spreads out all over the country districts, and the earnings of the city lines are diluted in that way to support the lines which could not exist or thrive upon an independent basis.

That is also true of the lines in Springfield, which extend considerable distances to the west, east and south of the city, out into the country districts. It is equally true of the Worcester company, which has extensive country lines.

About the only company outside of the Boston company of which that is not true is the one located in New Bedford, the Union Company, which is the sole exception to the Massachusetts companies in the matter of prosperity. The Union company, which has confined itself largely within the city borders and has not entered into entangling alliances with outside properties and has been managed by local men and owned by local capital in very large degree, has been much more successful than the others, and up to the present time has been able to preserve the 5-cent fare, although it is now petitioning, I think, for an increase before the public-service commission.

MR. WARREN: It has also reduced its dividend, Mr. Eastman.

MR. EASTMAN: It has?

MR. WARREN: Yes.

MR. EASTMAN: Its dividend for many years was 8 per cent, although under the Massachusetts law much new stock was issued at a premium, the premium going as high as $50 a share.

In the third place, a factor of weakness, I think, was the control of the companies in many instances by holding companies organized in the form of voluntary associations or, to use a more technical term, express trusts. Although the stock and bonds of the street railway companies themselves were issued under public supervision, these voluntary associations which corralled all their stock were subject to no regulation whatever and issued shares upon an inflated basis and that had the result of accentuating the desire to draw every possible drop of income out of the underlying companies that could be secured in order to support earnings upon the inflated shares of these voluntary associations.

In the fourth place, our street-railway companies are entirely separate and distinct from lighting and power property. They are not merged with those properties and operated under one management, as is the case in many other parts of the country. I think it is true, so far as I have the knowledge, that in many cases the superior earnings of the lighting and power properties have been able to support the street railway companies which were united with them, but we have not had that element of strength in Massachusetts and our street railways have had to go it alone.

THE CHAIRMAN: Does the law prevent such consolidations?

MR. EASTMAN: Well, it does not permit it. There is no law authorizing such consolidations. It has, in some cases, been brought about indirectly through the medium of these holding companies, but there is no actual merger of the property.

Now, in the fifth place—and this is true not only in Massachusetts but in all other parts of the country—there has been the ordinary failure to care for depreciation; the need for that was not recognized, and depreciation was not cared for.

In the sixth place, in Massachusetts the cost of coal is, I think, higher than it is in most other parts of the country because we have to bring our coal from rather remote districts. The country itself is hilly, so that it is much more difficult to construct a first-class high-speed interurban line than it is in the Middle West or many other parts of the country; and our cities are old and laid out in many cases with narrow, crooked streets, which also adds to the cost of operation.

In the case of Boston there is a further source of weakness which lies in the enormous investment in rapid-transit structures, subways, tunnels, and elevated lines which have been constructed in Boston to a much greater extent than in any other city except New York, and I think in proportion to the population the expenditure has perhaps been as great in Boston as it has in New York. There was an unusual necessity for such structures in Boston because of the layout of the city and the absolute need for constructing underground highways in the congested central district—congested by physical condition—in order that traffic might be carried through there at a reasonable rate of speed and in reasonable quantity.

As I recall it, about $35,000,000 has been invested by the city of Boston in subways and tunnels. That does not include the amount expended by the company on the Cambridge subway, which cost about $9,000,000 and in addition to that there is a very large expenditure in elevated lines.

In the last place, I might mention that a source of weakness has been that Massachusetts has been the pioneer in the construction of good roads, and well-constructed highways exist all over the State, which has made automobile competition relatively easy.

Now, as counter to that, there have been certain sources of strength, and the chief source of strength has been the supervision over capitalization. The securities of the companies have very largely been issued under the regulation of the public-service commission or its predecessor, the board of railroad commissioners, and that has resulted in much less capitalization per mile than in other parts of the country.

Another allied source of strength was the fact that there was a plentiful supply of local capital which could be secured for investment in these railways and I think they were practically all constructed by that local capital and the investment of that local capital was encouraged by favorable tax laws. In other words, the stock of these companies was not subject to taxation, and for that reason, it became a popular investment for the trust estates and similar investors in Massachusetts who are obliged by law to disclose their holdings and hence have the need of investing in tax-free securities. That resulted in the acquisition and purchase of street-railway stock in many cases upon a bond basis. The security or stock of the Boston Elevated, for instance, was bought by investors on about the same rate of return very largely which they might have secured in investing bonds, and it is very widely held.

That, in a sense it has developed into a sort of weakness, is rather a paradox. At the same time I think it is true. In other parts of the country the exploitation which took place resulted in early smash. That came about in Cleveland, that came about in Chicago, and I think in other larger cities, and they had to begin all over again about the year 1907, and they started in on a depreciated basis and proceeded to rehabilitate the property and they have since had the advantage of that rehabilitation.

Now in Massachusetts, the fact that the securities were regulated and the capitalization was relatively low resulted in prolonging the life of the companies until they began to receive the full effects of accrued depreciation, and they are suffering from that now. If you go back 10 or 12 years, Massachusetts was, I think, receiving as good street-railway service as any part of the country. We used to boast of the street-railway service we received at that time and we were proud of the service which was being given in Boston in comparison with the service which was being given in many other large cities. But at the present time the failure to take care of depreciation, added to the other elements and factors which have entered into the situation in recent years, has resulted in a very weak and undesirable situation.

Coming to regulation, until 1913 the railroad commission in Massachusetts had no mandatory powers. It only had the power to recommend, and for that reason the street-railway companies were free—if they wanted to do so, and except to the extent that they felt bound by agreements with the local authorities—to raise their fares and could do so without the permission of any State commission. Notwithstanding that fact, and notwithstanding the fact that now underlies the situation, they were always in a precarious condition. They did not, as a rule increase their fares. They were rather optimistic of the future. They kept hoping that the increase of traffic would pull them out of their difficulties and it did look at one time as though it might, because traffic was increasing rapidly; population was increasing and traffic was increasing along with it. Of course, the development of the automobile has had a tendency to change that situation. But for some reason or other they did not increase their fares during the period in which they were at entire liberty to do so, except in a few cases. There were certain companies beginning about 1905 which changed from a 5-cent unit of fare and after they had done it the railroad commission considered their situation upon complaint and said they were justified in making that increase.

Now, in 1913 the railroad commission was reorganized into the public-service commission and given full power over the rates, substantially the same powers that the Interstate Commerce Commission possesses over railroad rates. And about 1914 the movement for general increases in fares began in Massachusetts. The first case, or the leading case, under the public service commission, was that of the Middlesex & Boston; and in that case the commission laid down a rule which, I think, was entirely fair and reasonable, but at the same time, it was more favorable to the companies than the commission might have laid down relying upon the precedents of the courts. In other words, instead of taking the basis of reproduction cost less depreciation, the commission took the basis of the amount of money honestly and prudently invested in the property which it was ordinarily able to ascertain very easily because of the fact that the securities had in most cases been issued almost altogether under public supervision.

The commission held that the companies were entitled to a fair return upon the amount of money which they had put into the properties honestly and prudently, and did not deduct from that sum anything on account of depreciation, unless it felt that the failure to take care of depreciation was due to inexcusable mismanagement. There have been cases in which the commission said that companies were entitled to a somewhat lower return. It usually approached the matter in that way, because of the thought that they had paid dividends which they ought not to have paid under the circumstances. And I might say in passing at this time, that notwithstanding the adoption of that rule, which always seemed to me eminently fair to the companies, the commission was generally regarded as hostile and oppressive. That was the very general feeling throughout Massachusetts in regard to the public-service commission. And I may further say, parenthetically, that the experience that I had on that commission did not tend to enhance my opinion as to the intelligence of investors in general. In many cases they bought securities without any real knowledge of what they were buying and when the results of that folly became apparent, they were ready to seize upon the reason that the public-service commission was to blame for their evil situation and—

THE CHAIRMAN: In this Middlesex case did the company ask for a return upon the cost of reproduction new less depreciation rather than investment?

MR. EASTMAN: They did not.

THE CHAIRMAN: Upon what did they ask for a return?

MR. EASTMAN: They asked for a return upon their outstanding securities which were issued under public regulations.

COMMISSIONER SWEET: And they got that, substantially?

MR. EASTMAN: Yes; that is we tried to give it to them. They did not get it, because the fares did not produce the amount. But that was—and I may say that the discussion of what returns the company should receive became very largely academic in Massachusetts.

COMMISSIONER SWEET: They got the ruling from the commission that they wanted in that respect?

MR. EASTMAN: Yes; because notwithstanding the increase which we gave them—and there were repeated increases—they still failed to secure anything like what under our rule we said they were entitled to receive in most cases.

United States v. National City Lines, Inc., 1951

AUTOMOBILE COMPETITION IN THE 1920s and the beginning of the widespread movement of people to the suburbs, away from the lines of public transportation, were capped by the general business decline of the 1930s. Falling revenues and falling ridership coming as a result of general unemployment meant that cost-cutting was necessary if public-transport companies were to survive.

During the Depression the wholesale substitution of buses for streetcars began. In earlier times buses had been used as feeders to streetcar lines and as extensions of lines into sparsely settled suburban territory. As revenues plummeted during the Depression, public-transport concerns were forced to defer maintenance on their cars and right-of-way. Equipment on many weaker lines was soon in a deplorable state, matched only by the catastrophe that was the track itself. To help diminish the fixed costs necessitated by a railway, even heavily traveled streetcar lines began to be replaced by buses. Evidence of the poor economic health of the industry is given by the fact that streetcar services in some towns were frequently terminated by the same cars that had been used to inaugurate electric railway service thirty or more years earlier. Streetcar abandonments stopped during the Second World War, but continued even more rapidly when hostilities ceased.

The switch to buses was heavily promoted by the firms that manufactured these vehicles. It became obvious in some places that the real profit to be gained by a public-transport operation came not in the provision of service to the public, but in providing the vehicles and the supplies needed by those vehicles. An interesting case in point is found in the next reading, which is a court decision in the matter of a public-transport holding company. One should not only note the findings of monopoly and collusion between National City Lines and some other companies, but also realize that such activity had a generally deleterious effect upon urban mass transportation, aiding and abetting the decline of the industry.

United States v. National City Lines, Inc., et al., 186 F2d 562, p. 565.

THE NATIONAL CITY LINES, INC., and others, were convicted in the United States District Court for the Northern District of Illinois, Eastern Division, William J. Campbell, J., of conspiring to monopolize a certain portion of interstate commerce in violation of the Anti-Trust Act, and they appealed. The Court of Appeals, Lindley, Circuit Judge, held that the evidence sustained the conviction.

Affirmed.

On April 9, 1947, nine corporations and seven individuals, constituting officers and directors of certain of the corporate defendants, were indicted on two counts, the second of which charged them with conspiring to monopolize certain portions of interstate commerce, in violation of Section 2 of the Anti-trust Act, 15 U.S.C.A. § 2. The American City Lines having been dismissed, the remaining corporate and individual defendants were found guilty upon this count. From the judgment upon the verdict, the remaining eight corporate defendants and five of the individuals have perfected this appeal. They contend that the count fails to state an offense, that the evidence is insufficient to support the verdict, that a fatal variance between the proof and the charge exists and that the court erred in excluding certain evidence.

The first count of the indictment, with which, in view of the fact that defendants were acquitted thereon, we are only incidentally concerned, charged defendants with having knowingly and continuously engaged in an unlawful combination and conspiracy to secure control of a substantial number of the companies which provide public transportation service in various cities, towns and counties of the several states, and to eliminate and exclude all competition in the sale of motor busses, petroleum products, tires and tubes to such transportation companies then owned or controlled by National City Lines, Inc., or Pacific City Lines, Inc., or of which said companies should acquire control, in the future, all in violation of Section 1 of the Anti-trust Act, 15 U.S.C.A. § 1.

The second count charged defendants with having conspired to monopolize part of the interstate trade and commerce of the United States, to wit, that part consisting of the sale of busses, petroleum products, tires and tubes used by local transportation systems in those cities in which defendants National, American and Pacific owned, controlled or had a substantial financial interest in, or had acquired, or in the future should acquire ownership, control or a substantial financial interest in such transportation systems, in violation of Section 2 of the Act.

It was averred further that the conspiracy to monopolize had consisted of a continuing agreement and concert of action upon the part of defendants under which the supplier defendants, Firestone, Standard,

Phillips, General Motors and Mack, would furnish capital to defendants National, American and Pacific, and the latter companies would purchase and cause their operating companies to purchase from the supplier companies substantially all their requirements of tires, tubes and petroleum products; the capital made available by the supplier defendants would be utilized by National and Pacific, to purchase control of or financial interest in local public transportation systems, located in various states, when the securing of such control and interest would further the sale of and create an additional market for the products of the supplier defendants to the exclusion of products competitive therewith; National and Pacific and their operating companies would not renew or enter into any new contracts for the purchase or use of such products from companies other than the supplier defendants without the consent of the latter; National and Pacific would not dispose of their interest in any operating company without requiring the party acquiring the same to assume the obligation of continuing to purchase its requirements of the commodities mentioned from the supplier defendants, and would not purchase any new equipment making use of products other than those sold by the supplier defendants; as National and Pacific acquired local transportation systems in the other sections of the country, those markets would be allocated to and preempted by a company selling petroleum products in such sections. The count further charged that the agreements and understandings were carried out and effectuated, thereby completing the offense of monopolization of a part of Interstate Commerce. The jury having acquitted defendants upon the first count and having found them guilty upon the second, we are concerned only with the legality of the judgment entered upon that verdict.

We shall follow the pattern adopted by the parties, who have referred to the National City Lines, Inc., and Pacific City Lines, Inc., as the City Lines defendants and to Firestone, Phillips, General Motors, Mack, Standard Oil of California and Federal Engineering Corporation as supplier defendants.

It is undisputed that on April 1, 1939, defendant National City Lines, Inc., had grown from an humble beginning in 1920, consisting of the ownership and operation of two second-hand busses in Minnesota, to ownership or control of 29 local operating transportation companies located in 27 different cities in 10 states. At the time the indictment was returned, the City Lines defendants had expanded their ownership or control to 46 transportation systems located in 45 cities in 16 states. The supplier defendants are manufacturers and marketers of busses, tires, tubes and petroleum products necessarily used by the local operating companies of the City Lines defendants and others. The value of their products introduced in commerce and sold to the City Lines defendants and their operating companies for the year 1946 was over 11 million dollars and, for the period from 1937 to May 1, 1947, over 37 million dollars.

There is no dispute that the City Lines defendants and the suppliers entered into various oral and written arrangements in accord with which the latter purchased preferred stock from the former, at prices in excess of the prevailing market prices, amounting in total cost to over nine million dollars and that the money received from the sales of such stock was used by City Lines defendants to acquire control of or a substantial financial interest in various local transportation companies throughout the United States. The respective supplier defendants entered into separate ten-year contracts with City Lines under which all of the busses, tires, tubes, and petroleum products requirements of the City Lines operating companies were purchased from the suppliers with an agreement not to buy any part of the same from any party competing with them. They provided, in short, that existing purchase contracts of all operating companies with other competitive suppliers should be terminated at their earliest possible moment; that the operating companies would equip all their units with defendant suppliers' products to the exclusion of any products competitive therewith and that City Lines and their operating companies would not renew or enter into any new contracts with third parties for the purchase of such products or change any then existing type of equipment or purchase any new equipment using any fuel or other means of propulsion other than gas.

National City Lines, organized in 1936, as a holding company to acquire and operate local transit companies, had bought, up to the time when the contracts were executed, its necessary equipment and fuel products from different suppliers, with no long-term contract with any of them. Pacific City Lines was organized for the purpose of acquiring local transit companies on the Pacific Coast and commenced doing business in January 1938. American was organized to acquire local transportation systems in the larger metropolitan areas in various parts of the country in 1943. It merged with National in 1946.

Additional facts, while not largely in dispute, are partially controverted, at least in so far as inferences are concerned; however, we think the evidence adequately justified the jury in finding affirmatively that they existed. In 1938, National conceived the idea of purchasing transportation systems in cities where street cars were no longer practicable and supplanting the latter with passenger busses. Its capital was limited and its earlier experience in public financing convinced it that it could not successfully finance the purchase of an increasing number of operating

[35]

companies in various parts of the United States by such means. Accordingly it devised the plan of procuring funds from manufacturing companies whose products its operating companies were using constantly in their business. National approached General Motors, which manufactures busses and delivers them to the various sections of the United States. It approached Firestone, whose business of manufacturing and supplying tires extends likewise throughout the nation. In the middle west, where a large part of its operating subsidiaries were to be located, it solicited investment of funds from Phillips, which operates throughout that section but not on the east or west coast. Pacific undertook the procurement of funds from General Motors and Firestone and also from Standard Oil of California, which operates on the Pacific coast. Mack Truck Company was also solicited. Eventually each of the suppliers entered into a contract with City Lines defendants of the character we have described whereby City Lines companies agreed that they would buy their exclusive requirements from the contracting supplier and from no one else. We think the evidence is clear that when any one of these suppliers was approached, its attitude was that it would be interested in helping finance City Lines, provided it should receive a contract for the exclusive use of its products in all of the operating companies of the City Lines, so far as busses and tires were concerned, and, as to the oil companies, in the territory served by the respective petroleum companies. It may be of little importance, but it seems to be the fact, at least we think the jury was justified in inferring it to be the fact, that the proposal for financing came from City Lines but that proposal of exclusive contracts came from the suppliers. At any rate, it is clear that eventually each supplier entered into a written contract of long duration whereby City Lines, in consideration of suppliers' help in financing City Lines, agreed that all of their operating subsidiaries should use only the suppliers' products. These were not joint contracts; each supplier entered into a separate agreement. Whether the action of the suppliers in this connection was so concerted as to justify the jury in finding that defendants conspired to monopolize that segment of interstate commerce reflected by the purchase and shipment in commerce of busses, tires and petroleum products to the operating companies, we shall discuss more fully later. The facts related present only a sketchy outline of the setup as it was presented to the jury.

The Sufficiency of the Indictment

DEFENDANTS' first point is stated thus: "Count II alleges as a violation of Section 2 of the Sherman Act no more than a conspiracy to monopolize sales to certain specified customers. That allegation does not charge an offense against the United States, since section 2 of the Sherman Act applies only to the monopolization of a geographic market." We have seen that the charge is that defendants conspired to monopolize the sale of petroleum products, busses and tires, to the subsidiary operating companies of the City Lines defendants with the result that competition was done away with in the sale of those products to those customers. But, say the defendants, there is no averment that the purchases of petroleum products, busses and tires by the City Lines defendants constituted a substantial portion of the total market for such products. Though defendants recognize that Section 2 makes it unlawful to conspire to monopolize trade or commerce among the several states, they insist that sales to the City Lines defendants and their subsidiaries do not constitute a part of interstate trade within the meaning of Section 2, for the reason that they amount only to control of a single customer's business. They admit that, if the statute were to be given literal reading, the Government's position would be supportable, for the words "any part" are broad enough to apply to a single customer. However, relying upon Standard Oil Co. of N. J. v. United States, 221 U.S. 1, 31 S.Ct. 502, 55 L.Ed. 619, they argue that the commerce referred to by the words "any part" has both a geographical and a distributive significance not present in the indictment. They admit that it is not open to a monopolist to defend his monopoly on the ground that he controls sales in only a limited geographic area, and that monopolization of the sale of any one product in any one city may be unlawful, even though sales throughout the nation are not controlled, but they insist that the indictment does not charge monopolization of the sale of gas, tires or busses in any state, city or region but only of sales to one customer which are beyond the rule of reason established in the Standard Oil case, 221 U.S. 1 at 61, 31 S.Ct. 502 at 516, 55 L.Ed. 619. They also rely upon Patterson v. United States, 6 Cir., 222 F. 599, certiorari denied 238 U.S. 635, 35 S.Ct. 939, 59 L.Ed. 1499, and United States v. Standard Oil Co., C.C., 173 F. 177, 191, where Judge Sanborn said:

If the second section of the act prohibits every attempt to monopolize any part of interstate commerce, it forbids all competition therein, and defeats the only purpose of the law; for there can be no competition, unless each competitor is permitted . . . to draw to himself, and thereby to monopolize, some part of the commerce.

They argue that requirement contracts with separate customers do not monopolize any part of interstate trade and that this contention is supported by United States v. Columbia Steel Co., 334 U.S. 495, 68 S.Ct. 1107, 92 L.Ed. 1533. Zealous argument is made in support of their contention that, under the decisions upon which they rely, the charge in the indictment is not sufficient to sustain a conviction under Section 2 of the Act. However, in spite of the ardor of counsel, after mature consideration, we are not persuaded of the soundness of the argument.

The indictment charges a concerted conspiracy by the City Lines defendants and supplier defendants to monopolize that part of interstate commerce which consists of all the busses, all the tires and tubes and all the gas, oil and grease, used by the public transportation systems of some 45 cities owned or controlled by the City Lines companies. That, to our mind, is a very substantial segment of interstate commerce, having "geographic and distribution" significance. It is charged that, under the plan of defendants, competing suppliers may not be patronized; that only the suppliers' products and theirs alone will be accepted. It is perfectly obvious that under such averments, that part of commerce which would be reflected in other suppliers furnishing products would be foreclosed and barred. Their competition is completely eliminated and the business of supplying busses, tubes, tires to the public transportation system of the 45 cities is entirely in the hands of the suppliers—in other words, monopolized by them. We conclude that, on the face of the indictment, there is a charge of elimination of competition, of monopolization, as to a substantial segment of interstate commerce, within the language of the Act and as limited by the "rule of reason."

We are impelled largely to this conclusion by United States v. Yellow Cab Co., 332 U.S. 218, 67 S.Ct. 1560, 91 L.Ed. 2010. In the course of that opinion, the court employed language, which, to our minds, is well-nigh conclusive upon the issue of sufficiency of this indictment. On pages 226 and 227 of 332 U.S., 67 S.Ct. on page 1565, 91 L.Ed. 2010, is found a paragraph which we adopt, substituting, however, for the words "cab" and "taxi" therein the words "bus and busses." With that change only, it reads as follows:

By excluding all bus manufacturers other than CCM from that part of the market represented by the bus operating companies under their control, the appellees effectively limit the outlets through which busses may be sold in interstate commerce. Limitations of that nature have been condemned time and again as violative of the Act. Associated Press v. United States, 326 U.S. 1, 18, 19, 65 S.Ct. 1416, 1423, 1424, 89 L.Ed. 2013, and cases cited. In addition, by preventing the bus operating companies under their control from purchasing busses from manufacturers other than CCM, the appellees deny those companies the opportunity to purchase busses in a free, competitive market. The Sherman Act has never been thought to sanction such a conspiracy to restrain the free purchase of goods in interstate commerce.

We can conceive of no logical basis upon which we can distinguish this language from the averments of the indictment here.

In the same case, the Supreme Court proceeded, 322 U.S. on pages 225 and 226, 67 S.Ct. on page 1564, 91 L.Ed. 2010, as follows:

And § 2 of the Act makes it unlawful to conspire to monopolize "any part" of interstate commerce, without specifying how large a part must be affected. Hence it is enough if some appreciable part of interstate commerce is the subject of a monopoly, a restraint or a conspiracy. The complaint in this case deals with interstate purchases of replacements of some 5,000 licensed taxicabs in four cities. That is an appreciable amount of commerce under any standard. See Montague & Co. v. Lowry, 193 U.S. 38, 24 S.Ct. 307, 48 L.Ed. 608.

If we again substitute for the word "taxi-cabs" the word "busses," the language is directly applicable to the case at bar. If, by preventing controlled cab operating companies in four cities from purchasing cabs from manufacturers other than the one favored, opportunity to purchase cabs in a free competitive market is removed and monopolization results, we can see no reason why prevention of 46 controlled bus operating companies in 45 cities from purchasing busses from any manufacturer other than the one favored is not likewise destructive of a free competitive market and an attempt to monopolize that segment of commerce. True, under this indictment, other suppliers may sell to other customers in various cities; but one substantial segment of interstate commerce consisting of supplies to 46 public transportation systems in 45 cities, holding local monopolies, is charged to have been monopolized so far as their purchases of busses, gas, grease, oil and tires are concerned. As the Supreme Court said in the Yellow Cab case:

Likewise irrelevant is the importance of the interstate commerce affected in relation to the entire amount of that type of commerce in the United States. The Sherman Act is concerned with more than the large, nation-wide obstacles in the channels of interstate trade. It is designed to sweep away all appreciable obstructions so that the statutory policy of free trade might be effectively achieved. As this Court stated in Indiana Farmer's Guide Pub. Co. v. Prairie Farmer Pub. Co., 293 U.S. 268, 279, 55 S.Ct. 182, 185, 79 L.Ed. 356, "The provisions of §§ 1 and 2 have both a geographical and distributive significance and apply to any part of the United States as distinguished from the whole and to any part of the classes of things forming a part of interstate commerce."

We do not find anything in United States v. Columbia Steel Co., 334 U.S. 495, 68 S.Ct. 1107, 92 L.Ed. 1533, at odds with the announcements of the Yellow Cab case.

[3 9]

The Alleged Inconsistency of the Verdicts

DEFENDANTS contend that the charges in the two counts were in substance the same and that, inasmuch as the same evidence was relied upon by the government to support each, the verdict of acquittal on Count 1 is inconsistent with that of guilty on Count 2; that, though we have previously held that an inconsistency in verdicts does not as a matter of law prevent judgment from being entered on the verdict rendered, the inconsistency here strips the verdict of any logic or valid reasoning.

We have seen that the language of the first count is entirely different from that of the second, for it charges, first, a conspiracy to acquire control of a substantial number of the companies which provide local transportation service in various cities of the United States—conspiracy to restrain trade by obtaining control of companies conducting transportation systems in various cities. This is a far cry from a charge of monopolization of sales of supplies to such transportation companies. True, Count 1 does include a further charge of conspiracy to eliminate and exclude all competition in the sale of motor busses, petroleum products, tires and tubes to the transportation companies. Thus Count 1 undoubtedly meant to the jury that defendants were charged with restraint of trade in obtaining control of transportation systems plus a conspiracy to restrain competition in sales to those companies. Though it is immaterial, we think it was entirely reasonable for the jury to conclude that the entire charge of the first count had not been sustained. In other words, it seems clear that there is no inconsistency in the verdicts. This thought is fortified by holdings that the same acts and course of conduct may constitute separate violations of Sections 1 and 2 of the Sherman Act. United States v. Socony–Vacuum Oil Co., 310 U.S. 150, 226, 60 S.Ct. 811, 84 L.Ed. 1129; United States v. MacAndrews & Forbes Co., C.C., 149 F. 836, 838; United States v. General Motors Corp., 7 Cir., 121 F.2d 376; United States v. Buchalter, 2 Cir., 88 F.2d 625, 628; Montrose Lumber Co. v. United States, 10 Cir., 124 F.2d 573. At all events, we can see no inconsistency in the jury's finding that there was a conspiracy to acquire a monopoly of the sales to local transportation companies in 45 communities but no conspiracy to restrain trade by securing control of those transportation systems.

However, irrespective of the correctness of our views in this connection, it is clear that inconsistency in verdicts rendered on separate counts of an indictment is not fatal. We so held in United States v. General Motors, 7 Cir., 121 F.2d 376 at page 411, as did the 6th Circuit in American Tobacco Co. v. United States, 147 F.2d 93, 115, where the court said: "But the circumstance that there might be perceived an inconsistency in a possible finding of guilt on the charge of conspiring to monopolize by price-fixing, and a verdict of not guilty on a charge of conspiracy to restrain trade by the same means, would not vitiate the charge or the verdict." To the same effect is the holding in Garrison v. Hunter, 10 Cir., 149 F.2d 844, 845: "Where a defendant is charged by two or more counts in an indictment, consistency between the verdicts on the several counts is not necessary. A verdict of acquittal on one count does not invalidate a verdict of guilty on another count although the same evidence is offered in support of each." The correctness of these decisions, we think, is apparent from such Supreme Court cases as Dunn v. United States, 284 U.S. 390, 393, 52 S.Ct. 189, 76 L.Ed. 356, and Borum v. United States, 284 U.S. 596, 52 S.Ct. 205, 76 L.Ed. 513. We conclude, then, that there was no inconsistency of verdicts and, further, that even if there were an inconsistency, the law recognizes no exception to the rule that such inconsistency is wholly immaterial. We are not persuaded that the verdict of guilty is, by the circumstances of this case, robbed of any presumption ordinarily applied to a jury verdict, for we are concerned not with whether the defendants were rightfully acquitted on Count 1, a wholly irrelevant question, but with whether the evidence is sufficient to sustain a verdict of guilty on Count 2.

SUFFICIENCY OF EVIDENCE

DEFENDANTS maintain that, even though we hold that Count 2 of the indictment sufficiently charges them with an offense against the United States, their conviction must be set aside for the reason that the evidence does not support the verdict. It is their contention that the evidence fails to establish (1) that there was a conspiracy, (2) that the defendants or any of them acted with an unlawful specific intent, or (3) that they shared such intent in an illegal concerted undertaking, but that it discloses only activities lawful in all respects. The government, on the other hand, asserts that the evidence establishes the existence of all the elements essential to a finding of guilty and that, consequently the verdict may not be disturbed by this court on review. This difference presents the difficult crucial question of this appeal. Of course we are not trying this case *de novo;* nor are we called upon to decide whether as triers of the facts we would have found defendants guilty. Our only function is to determine whether the evidence was of such character as to require submission to the jury, or in other words, whether it was the duty of the trial court, as a matter of law, to direct a verdict of not guilty. The proper discharge of this function has made it necessary for us to scrutinize with care voluminous evidence upon which we can only briefly comment, if this opinion is to be limited to a reasonable length.

The first evidentiary question presented is whether the evidence was sufficient to support a finding that defendants acted in concert, with a common design or purpose. The government's evidence, much of it in documentary form, is that, during the period preceding the execution of the contracts under consideration, representatives of the City Lines defendants on several occasions met and conferred with one or more of the supplier defendants; that each of the latter knew that other supplier defendants had executed or were about to execute investment and requirements contracts with one or more of the City Lines defendants, and that these conferences and proposed contracts were the subject of no inconsiderable amount of correspondence among the several defendants, including correspondence between supplier defendants as well as between supplier defendants and City Lines defendants. Thus on February 6, 1938, National City Lines wrote Palmer of Standard of California in reference to its proposed stock subscription contract, that it "must be sent" also to Yellow Truck (General Motors) and sent copies of the letter to Grossman of General Motors, Fitzgerald and Stevens. On March 5, National City wrote Standard, saying that at a conference it was "understood" that the stock of Pacific would be subscribed by Standard and Yellow Truck (General Motors). Copies of the letter went to Palmer, Grossman, Fitzgerald and Stevens. On November 7, 1939, National advised Mack of Yellow Truck's (General Motors) and Standard's investments in Pacific. Before that, on May 10, 1938, National had addressed a letter to the "subscribers to the capital stock of Pacific City Lines," advising them of the exact commitment of each subscriber. A file memorandum tells of a conference on February 2 and 3, 1939, in which the investments of Phillips and "other prospective investors," in return for exclusive supply contracts, were discussed at length. The "others" included Firestone, Standard and General Motors. Copies of the memorandum went to various individuals. A letter of April 19, 1939, from National to Phillips, refers to the agreement of Phillips and "other purchasers" and states that "You are buying the stock at $50 a share, when the market, which is very thin, is about $40," and advises Phillips that "certain privileges of yours under the oil contract are affected by your holding or failure to hold your stock." A copy was sent to Firestone. A letter to Firestone written February 18, 1939, advises that company that Phillips was then making its investigation. Another of February 25 advised Firestone that the Pacific Lines "deal is closed" and that Phillips was "practically ready for closing" and that "two or three other deals" "were very hot." On March 6, 1939, Firestone wrote Phillips concerning its contract with City Lines. On April 12, 1939, Phillips wrote Firestone expressing its belief that "everything has now been mutually agreed upon" and on July 26, Phillips wrote Firestone that "General Motors and Mack Truck are going in for $500,000 each on the same basis as the rest of us." To this Firestone replied that it understood that General Motors, Mack Truck and Standard "were in" and that "we will probably all benefit by the agreement." Many other letters and documents persuasive of concerted understanding were received in evidence.

Although defendants insist that each supplier merely obtained business from the City Lines defendants through separate negotiations, the documentary evidence referred to above and other circumstances in evidence seem to us clearly sufficient to justify the jury in finding that the contrary was true. It is clear that representatives of two or more supplier defendants were in attendance in Chicago and New York at meetings and conferences, out of which grew the investment and requirements contracts. And the fact that copies of a memorandum of discussions held between one of the supplier defendants and one of the City Lines defendants, as well as copies of many of the letters which passed between the contracting parties prior to the execution of the contracts, were sent to representatives of other supplier defendants, coupled with the fact that the latter corresponded with one another relative to the provisions of the contracts, is hardly reconcilable with defendants' contention that their several contracts were negotiated independently of one another but is, rather, convincing that each of the contracts was regarded by the parties as but a part of a "larger deal" or "proposition," to use the words of certain of the defendants, in which all of the supplier defendants were involved. At least the evidence submitted to the jury in this respect was clearly adequate to support its verdict. Buttressing this conclusion is the correspondence exchange between Leonard of Firestone and Riggins of Phillips, in the course of which Riggins informed Leonard that "Roy Fitzgerald advised me that General Motors and Mack Truck are going in for $500,000 each on the same basis as the rest of us" and that he understood that "Palmer got into Chicago on Wednesday and immediately *tried to get in on the deal*" (emphasis supplied) and in which Leonard said, "I have been in New York this week hob-nobbing with Roy Fitzgerald and some of the others who are interested in our proposition" and "Everything seems to be going along very nicely and I do think we will probably all benefit by the arrangement." Of the same import is the statement, in the contract of May 15, 1939, between Firestone and National City Lines, that Firestone's agreement to purchase stock is made "on the representation of National that it will secure the balance of the financing necessary for the completion of a one and a half million dollar expansion program."

Concluding, then, that the record contains the substantial evidence necessary to support a finding that defendants acted in concert rather than independently, it is necessary to determine further whether the evidence justified the jury in finding that they did so with the specific intent outlawed by the Sherman Act. In view of our conclusion that the indictment charges defendants with an offense cognizable under Section 2 of the Act, there would seem to be little doubt as to this issue, for the defendants do not deny the execution of the requirements contracts or that it was their intention to execute them, or that the effect of those contracts is to exclude competitors from selling busses, tires, tubes and petroleum products to the City Lines defendants. Of course, it may well be that defendants did not intend affirmatively to violate the law, but it seems quite evident that they did intend, by making their mutually concerted investments in City Lines' stock conditional on the execution of exclusive requirements contracts in their favor, to join forces in making investments in consideration of the several exclusive contracts and thus, by their united and concerted action, to exclude their competitors from a market composed of the City Lines defendants and their operating subsidiaries, present and future, and, thus, that they intentionally performed acts which inevitably led to violation of Section 2 of the statute.

Defendants argue that the government's evidence discloses two separate and distinct lines of activity, one relating to transactions between the supplier defendants and National, the other encompassing the activities of the suppliers and Pacific; such evidence, they say, not only will not suffice to establish the existence of the single conspiracy charged in the indictment but constitutes a prejudicial variance. They also maintain that the evidence does not establish the existence of a common design or purpose shared by all defendants. However, the fact that one of the supplier defendants was interested only in supplying tires and tubes to both the City Lines defendants and their subsidiaries while another was concerned with only the sale of its petroleum products to the particular City Lines' companies operating in its marketing territory does not negative the existence of a common design to promote, through investments in the stock of one or both of the City Lines defendants, the acquisition by them of more and more local transit companies and, thus, to provide each of the supplier defendants with an ever-expanding market to which it would have exclusive rights as to its particular product by virtue of its requirements contracts. Nor does the circumstance that certain of the supplier defendants had requirements contracts with one but not both of the City Lines defendants absolve those defendants of participation in the conspiracy charged in the indictment or prove that no such conspiracy existed; it was not incumbent on the government to prove that each defendant participated in that conspiracy in all of its ramifications, for, in order that one be found guilty as a conspirator, it need only be shown that, with knowledge of the existence of the conspiracy, he knowingly performed an act designed to promote or aid in the attainment of the object of that known conspiracy. Craig v. U. S., 9 Cir., 81 F.2d 816, 822, certiorari dismissed 298 U.S. 637, 56 S.Ct. 670, 80 L.Ed. 1371, certiorari denied 298 U.S. 690, 56 S.Ct. 959, 80 L.Ed. 1408; Johnson v. U. S., 9 Cir., 62 F.2d 32, 34–35; Marcante v. U. S., 10 Cir., 49 F.2d 156, 157.

EXCLUSION OF TESTIMONY

DEFENDANTS assert error upon the part of the trial court in excluding evidence offered to show (1) the motives and reasons for the actions taken by them and (2) that the business obtained from the supplier defendants for the City Lines was an insignificant portion of the market for tires, tubes and petroleum products. They insist that, though the defendant suppliers were permitted to introduce testimony as to their reasons for making the investments and entering into the supply contracts, they were unduly limited in that they were not permitted to prove customs, background and business practices in general and, that, though the amount of business transacted between suppliers and City Lines was shown, they should have been permitted to prove that it was a small part of the total commerce in such articles. Thus City Lines offered the testimony of a qualified expert to the effect that financing of customers by suppliers had long been a customary and accepted practice in American business. The supplier defendants tendered evidence to the effect that other companies frequently make investments such as they made in the City Lines. Standard offered to show that other buyers had entered into long-term exclusive contracts, that it and the oil industry in general have availed themselves of requirements contracts extensively, that, thereby, they were aided in long range planning for production and refining, and that Standard could have sold the products delivered to City Lines to others at higher prices.

We had thought it well established that evidence of customs and practices in an industry is irrelevant in determining whether there has been an attempted monopolization. This court, in United States v. New York Great Atlantic & Pacific Tea Company, 7 Cir., 173 F.2d 79, 89, said:

> That others engaged in the same practices as the defendants certainly would not exonerate the defendants or tend to disprove their guilt. Certainly trade customs and practices not shown to have been practiced in the same manner as the defendants were shown to have practiced them would not be competent to show that the defendants' practices were not illegal.

We made earlier announcement of this and related rules in United States v. General Motors, 7 Cir., 121 F.2d 376, 406, where we said:

[45]

When persons conspire to impose a direct restraint on interstate commerce, benevolent motives or the activities of third parties do not save them from criminal prosecution for violation of the Sherman law. See United States v. Socony–Vacuum Oil Co., [310 U.S. 150, 60 S.Ct. 811, 84 L.Ed. 1129]. . . . the activities of third parties cannot justify the defendants' violation of law. See Hills Brothers v. Federal Trade Commission, 9 Cir., 9 F.2d 481, 485. . . . evidence of benevolent motives or good intention is immaterial where the operation of the conspiracy, and the specific acts and things done pursuant thereto, necessarily result in a direct restraint of interstate commerce. United States v. Patten, supra, 226 U.S. [525], 543, 33 S.Ct. 141, 57 L.Ed. 333, 44 L.R.A.,N.S., 325.

In both of these cases we think we were fully justified in our holdings by the language of the Supreme Court in United States v. Socony–Vacuum Oil Co., 310 U.S. 150, 60 S.Ct. 811, 84 L.Ed. 1129.

Obviously defendants were entitled to offer evidence as to their intent and motives and this they were permitted to do. They supplied testimony at some length as to their reasons, purposes and motives in entering into the transactions covered by the charge and to prove that the various sales and investment contracts were for the best business interests of City Lines and their operating companies as well as those of the suppliers. Standard was allowed to present evidence as to its policy and the advantages to it of requirements contracts. Indeed, defendants admit that they were permitted to give their individual reasons for making the investment and requirements contracts but insist that they were too narrowly limited in the scope of such testimony. Standard offered evidence which the court received to the effect that it always had other places to sell its products; that it never had more products than it could sell. However, the court refused to permit the testimony to go further, saying that there should be some practical limitation to such collateral evidence.

From an examination of the record, it seems apparent to us that the court, endowed with discretion as to the amount of collateral evidence proper, did not abuse its discretion. This is in line with what the Supreme Court said in United States v. Socony–Vacuum Oil Co., 310 U.S. 150 at 230, 60 S.Ct. 811 at 847, 84 L.Ed. 1129:

While the offer was not wholly irrelevant to the issues, it was clearly collateral. The trial court has a wide range for discretion in the exclusion of such evidence. See Golden Reward Mining Co. v. Buxton Mining Co., 8 Cir., 97 F. 413, 416, 417; Chesterfield Mfg. Co. v. Leota Cotton Mills, 8 Cir., 194 F. 358, 359. Admission of testimony showing the market conditions late in 1934 would have opened an inquiry into causal factors as involved and interrelated as those present during the indictment period. That might have confused rather than enlightened the jury. In any event it would not have eliminated the buying programs as contributory causes to the market rise and stability in 1935 and 1936. And it would have prolonged the inquiry and protracted the trial. As once stated by Mr. Justice Holmes, one objection to the introduction of collateral issues is a "purely practical one—a concession to the shortness of life." Reeve v. Dennett, 145 Mass. 23, 28, 11 N.E. 938, 944. And see Union Stock Yard & Transit Co. v. United States, 308 U.S. 213, 223, 224, 60 S.Ct. 193, 197, 198, 84 L.Ed. 198. . . . In conclusion, we do not think that there was an abuse of discretion by the trial court in the exclusion of the proffered evidence.

The jury's inquiry was not one as to customs or practices or as to what others had done on other times and occasions. The question before the jury was whether what defendants had done amounted to violation of law as charged. The mere fact, if it be a fact, that other suppliers had followed a similar course of conduct by doing what defendants are charged with doing, would in no wise excuse defendants for their acts if those acts were illegal.

That the evidence offered by defendants comparing their total sales to City Lines and their companies and their total sales in the national market was not erroneously excluded is shown by our earlier quotation from the Yellow Cab case, 332 U.S. 218, 67 S.Ct. 1560, 91 L.Ed. 2010. In other words, it was not incumbent upon the government to show that a certain stated percentage of the total commerce was involved in this particular cause. We think the jury could not properly have found other than that the sales of all tires, busses and petroleum products to 46 operating companies in 45 states, aggregating many millions of dollars, constituted a substantial segment of interstate commerce and that evidence comparing this with the amount involved in the total business of the companies was wholly irrelevant. It was not a question of what percentage of the total commerce in such products was but a question of whether a substantial part of commerce was monopolized.

We have considered carefully all the evidence offered and excluded. We think that the court's rulings were fair, and that, having permitted great latitude in admitting testimony as to intent, purpose and reasons for the making of the contracts, the court, in its discretion, was entirely justified in excluding the additional testimony offered.

We believe that what we have said sufficiently disposes of all contentions of defendants without further extension of this opinion. Inasmuch as the charge was sufficient at law, the evidence substantial and adequate

[47]

and the trial without error, as a court of review, we may not properly interfere.

The judgment is affirmed.

The Rail Commutation Problem: The Doyle Report, 1961

THE GROWTH AND EXPANSION OF SOME AMERICAN CITIES, both in population and geographic spread, were sparked by the development of railway commuter service. Where the development of street railways had the effect of extending the closely occupied part of the city beyond the central city area, the commuter railway helped establish satellite towns closely tied to the major population center. The economics and technology of the steam railroad precluded placing stations much closer than a mile or two apart. Growth along these lines of public transport, therefore, did not take the form of solid development; rather it was the development of "nodal" towns or villages surrounding the railway stations with open country in between.

As will be made clear from the reading that follows, service to outlying parts of cities was initially offered by merely stopping regular "through" passenger trains at convenient locations in the suburbs. So great was the demand for these services, however, that in many places it became necessary to operate special suburban trains and eventually to provide completely separate facilities for the movement of commuters. As this service was initially thought of as being a by-product of regular service, and therefore as so much "gravy" for the railway company, the regular passenger fare was cut, or commuted, in order to attract patronage. Hence the name "commuter" for one who shuttles regularly between home and work.

The following excerpt is from the well-known study of National Transportation Policy headed by General John P. Doyle, which is usually referred to as the Doyle Report. The causes for the almost universal railway commuter-service financial losses are investigated in this particular part of the report. The study concludes that most problems of the commuter railways are due to the concentration of traffic at peak periods—encouraged by discount pricing for regular rush-hour commuters, the relatively low fares charged, and the inability of the railway companies to continue to subsidize commuter losses with earnings from freight traffic. While the freight-revenue picture is somewhat more cheerful today than when the Doyle Report was written in 1960, the earnings of freight service in a

The following excerpt is taken from Chapter 7 of "The Doyle Report," *National Transportation Policy,* January 3, 1961.

highly competitive market are still not high enough to warrant the indefinite bailing out of certain highly unremunerative passenger services and commuter operations.

In the final analysis, the community has two choices: One, allow unimpeded growth to create problems, e.g., traffic congestion, then pay the heavy costs of eliminating them; or, alternatively, anticipate the problems, plan wisely to meet them, and minimize the costs by a "pay as you grow" policy. —*Southern California Research Council*

THE FEDERAL INTEREST IN URBAN TRANSPORTATION

OUR investigation of deteriorating railroad commutation services, the task assigned by S. Res. 244, revealed conclusively that the most important forces affecting these services are external to the railroads and largely beyond the control of the managements. It was found that all means of transportation within metropolitan areas are increasingly congested, overburdened and inadequate—suffering greatly from a lack of coordination and long-range planning.

Two of the most fundamental causes of this inadequacy are: (*a*) a majority of commuters from the suburbs, no matter by what means they travel, have never paid the full cost of their home-to-work transportation because of the high expense of providing the required rush-hour capacity; and (*b*) we do not have an element or jurisdiction of government which meets the needs of metropolitan area administration.

The total cost of carrying suburbanites to and from work has risen as fast or faster than the explosive suburban population growth, and the past and present means of financing the deficits of these services through rail freight rates, city property taxes, and gasoline taxes paid by other highway users are increasingly unable to meet the need. This inability is in part due to lack of adequate organizations for financing and directing the growth of metropolitan private and public transport.

The Federal Government has a vital interest in the free flow of commerce in all parts of the United States, in the preservation and propagation of national wealth and tax production, in the provision of the best living and working conditions for the majority of its citizens, and in establishing the facilities and conditions necessary for the national security. To the extent that inadequate urban transportation facilities and the decline of public transport services act to the detriment of these interests, or needlessly increase the total cost of daily economic activities, there is cause for immediate Federal attention. The need for action is pressing because of: (*a*) the great increase in Federal funds expended for urban

[49]

capital improvements such as highways; (b) the necessity to assure the most secure and effective long-term investment of these funds; and (c) the accelerating deterioration of commuter railroad services.

The findings in the following report demonstrate that we are in a period of deepening crisis in metropolitan area transportation and that remedial action is urgent. The surging growth of human and automobile populations in our metropolitan areas is adding to the burden on, and congestion of, transport facilities faster than present improvement programs are giving relief.

The long-range recommendations supported by this report call for changes in organization and process rather than major new spending programs and require only relatively modest increases in the present level of expenditure. However, these modest sums would make the most important possible contribution to the soundness, effectiveness, and longevity of the multibillion dollar Federal and local investment programs. The short-range recommendations, relating only to commuter railroads, are in part changes in procedure and in part an extension of Federal credit for specific immediate needs.

Norman Kennedy of the University of California Institute of Transportation and Traffic Engineering well sums up today's problem:[1]

> America's present concentration of people and resources in urban areas would not have been possible without the mobility and the supply lines afforded by dependable and economic transportation.
>
> But the very technological changes in transportation that have contributed so much to greater mobility now appear to be stifling it. Street and highway traffic congestion seriously hampers the rapid, continuous and flexible interchange of services and goods by virtue of which urban economy and society exist. Capacity needs to be added to urban transportation systems to raise standards of service and to reduce transportation costs. The question is—How?

This committee believes that in many places the "how" could best be answered by giving commuters free mass transportation which would cost less than providing the additional highway and parking facilities needed for their autos. However, this report will not attempt to answer the "how" in terms of systems and hardware but will propose a method for reaching this complex investment decision through joint Federal-local action and will recommend the appropriate Federal actions.

THE RAIL COMMUTATION PROBLEM

COMMUTATION service by privately owned railroads is provided at serious financial losses which prompt railroads to discontinue commuter trains. This action conflicts with the public need for this service. A balanced efficient mass transportation system in our large metropolitan areas must include rail transportation.

The problem of commuter service is an integral part of the policy considerations for the kind and amount of railroad passenger service necessary to serve the public and provide for national defense. Automobile, rail and bus are the major means of transportation in metropolitan areas. Automobile and bus commutation is tied in most directly with highway, street, parking area, and bridge planning whereas rail commutation service is related to the management and regulation of the railroad system.[2]

Automobiles and busses fill critical needs in solving the commuter problem and these means of transportation must be integrated with rail commutation in any total solution of the mass transportation problem of metropolitan areas. The most pressing aspect of the commuter problem is the deterioration of railroad service and discontinuance of trains caused by the steady losses in furnishing this service. These railroad discontinuances conflict with the clear public need for this service.

Since any balanced, efficient mass transportation system in our large metropolitan areas must include rail transportation, the immediate need is to find ways to preserve the present systems until long-range measures can be effective.

The metropolitan areas in which rail commutation plays an important role in moving people between suburbs and the central business district are New York, Chicago, Philadelphia, Boston and San Francisco with a fringe business operated in and out of such cities as Pittsburgh, Washington, and Baltimore. The areas in which railroads are experiencing the most financial distress from commuter service are New York, Boston, and Philadelphia and to a lesser degree, Chicago.

There are three groups of basic causes acting to produce the present acute situation in railroad commutation. They are:

(*a*) Fundamental changes in public habits and desires;

(*b*) Competition has so seriously reduced rail freight revenues, especially in the eastern district, as to eliminate net earnings from rail operations; and

(*c*) The long-time unfavorable price-cost relationships in suburban service are worsening.

Fundamental changes in public habits and desires. A basic cause for the rail commutation problem is the change in habits of personal transportation occasioned by: widespread use of the automobile; the general reduction in the work-week from 6 days to 5 days; and the change in use of leisure time wherein people no longer use the downtown area ex-

[51]

clusively to shop or for entertainment. The general rise in living standards has allowed people to pay more for transportation and thus to secure the actual or fancied conveniences of automobile commuting. The public "buys" a combined price-service package in transportation and the importance attached to these two factors is shifting to service and convenience.

One result of these changes in patterns of living and transportation has been frantic activity by Federal, State, and local governments to build highways, bridges, tunnels, and parking areas to accommodate this automobile traffic. Each such improvement has only accelerated the use made of these facilities by drivers of automobiles which further decreases use of mass transportation systems, and increases traffic congestion.

While total rail commutation traffic has declined from 345 million passengers in 1947 to 221 million in 1957[3] and there have been many reductions in service, the peak hour traffic on the major routes into the center of cities has been stable or increasing.[4] This traffic trend has placed a heavy demand upon the rail commutation system for home-to-work transportation at rush hours, requiring maximum capacity operation for a total of only 20 hours per week. Traffic in the remaining hours has dwindled to a trickle on most systems.

To identify passenger trends in commuter service a study has been made of selected representative railroads for the years 1949, 1955, and 1959 with respect to the number of commutation passengers carried, passenger miles, passenger revenues, average length of haul in miles, and average fare per mile. The results of this study show significant downward trends in total patronage of rail commutation service with certain exceptions in the Chicago area and the Long Island Railroad serving New York City. As examples:

1. In the metropolitan New York area, in the period between 1949 and 1959, the Jersey Central had a decrease in the number of commuter passengers carried of 43.9 percent. The Lackawanna had a decrease of 45.6 percent. The Erie had a decrease of 55.1 percent. The New York Central had a decrease of 47.6 percent. The Long Island had a decrease of 12.2 percent between 1949 and 1954, but an *increase* of 6.6 percent between 1953 and 1958.

2. In the Boston and Philadelphia areas declines of similar degree were experienced by the Boston & Maine, Reading, New Haven, and Pennsylvania Railroads.

3. In the Chicago area, the Burlington had an increase of 52.1 percent in commuter passengers in the 1949–59 period. The North Western had a decrease in passengers between 1947 and 1954 of 2.7 percent, but

an increase of 26.4 percent between 1954 and 1959. The Milwaukee had a decrease in passengers between 1949 and 1954 of 3.7 percent, but an increase of 13.3 percent between 1954 and 1959. The Rock Island had a 10-year decrease in passengers of 24.7 percent and the Illinois Central a decrease of 46.7 percent. The Chicago North Shore, an electric line, is operating under an ICC order requiring a trial 1-year operation before further consideration of a complete abandonment request.

4. In the San Francisco area the Southern Pacific had an increase in passengers of 16.8 percent between 1949 and 1954, but a decrease between 1954 and 1959 of 20 percent.

The single important paradox of this study of rail commutation trends is the experience of three railroads in the Chicago area when compared with three other railroads in the Chicago area and with all other commuter rail carriers. All railroads providing commuter service show serious declines in passengers carried in recent years with the exception of the Burlington, Milwaukee, and North Western carriers in the Chicago area.[5]

Since these carriers are regulated and taxed by the same authority in Illinois, as are the Chicago carriers which are losing passengers, it is apparent that these State policies have not affected the end result significantly. Conversations with officials of the Illinois Central and the North Western, which are the two largest carriers of commuters in the Chicago area and which have opposite trends in patronage, reveal that work rules and labor contracts do not differ materially. Equipment used by each of these two carriers is reasonably comparable in the period ending in 1959. The Illinois Central's average fare of 3.2 cents per passenger-mile is somewhat higher than the 2.8 cents of the North Western but the effect of this differential on the customer is offset by the much shorter average haul on the Illinois Central, 13.7 miles compared with 20.3 for the C. & N.W.

The nonrail differences in the situation of the two carriers seem to be more significant. There is a markedly greater development of multilane and expressway auto facilities on the south side of Chicago than in the western and northwestern areas. The Calumet Expressway was completed during this period whereas neither the Congress Street nor the Northwest Expressways are yet completed. There appear to be higher average family incomes in much of the North Western's area as compared with the south side of Chicago. This difference is reflected in the increasing numbers of persons in the Illinois Central's territory who are said to work in the Calumet industrial area and in the large employment centers to the west and southwest of the central business district. These people cannot conveniently reach their destinations by rail or transit, and since they do not have to enter the central business district they don't suffer from the worst street congestion. Therefore, they drive to work and their patronage has been lost to the Central.

Although the evidence concerning the situations of these two carriers is not conclusive it is a fact that some commuter railroads are experiencing increases in total traffic and in the case of the North Western have realized for the first time full recovery of expenses.[6]

Decline of rail freight traffic and revenue. It is well established that the net revenues from rail freight traffic have made up the passenger service deficit for many years, and were thus literally responsible for continuing intercity and suburban railroad passenger service. The amount of the passenger deficit has increased from $140 million in 1946 to a high of $723 million in 1957. Due to the many train discontinuances and to certain fare increases the deficit has declined to $544 million for 1959. It is clear that very substantial freight revenues were and are necessary to cover the complete cost of rail operations and provide sufficient return to maintain solvency. In 1957, 1958, and 1959 this source of income has declined from the plateau established between 1951 and 1956. The increased size of the passenger deficit caused railroad net income to be immediately and seriously threatened by the recent decline in freight traffic and revenues, and has resulted in extensive efforts by railroad management to reduce and eliminate passenger services including commutation.

The major portion of commuter service is rendered by railroads in the ICC's eastern district. These same railroads also have the highest proportion of passenger revenues, and therefore expenses, in relation to freight revenues. In 1954 passenger revenues amounted to 14.1 percent of total transportation revenues in the United States and 18.4 percent of total in the eastern district. Five years later in 1959 passenger revenues were 12.3 percent of national transportation revenues and 16.8 percent of eastern district total revenues.[7] Thus eastern district railroads have experienced relatively higher expenses and therefore higher operating ratios than companies in other districts. In turn they have been more drastically affected by the recent declines in freight traffic and are the carriers least able to afford it. This has put maximum pressure on the eastern railroads to reduce and discontinue service including commutation. The following table contains indexes showing trends in rail-freight revenues and ton-miles since the Korean war.

As discussed elsewhere in this report much of these declines in rail freight are the result of intense competition between the regulated modes of transport and competition from private and other unregulated carriers. The 1958–59 period has also been affected by a recession and a major

TABLE 1

Class I railroad freight revenues and ton-miles 1956–59, compared with 1953–55 averages [Figures are index numbers]

Years	United States		Eastern District	
	Revenues	*Ton-miles*	*Revenues*	*Ton-miles*
1953–55....	100.0	100.0	100.0	100.0
1956.......	106.2	109.2	107.1	109.8
1957.......	105.9	104.5	105.5	101.9
1958.......	95.7	93.1	88.7	85.2
1959.......	98.6	97.2	91.9	88.7

Source: ICC, statement M–220 for each December.

and lengthy steel strike. The basic nature of freight traffic in New England is changing as discussed in part V, chapter 7, "The Provision of Public Carrier Service in Rural Areas." The only reason for taking note of these problems in this connection is to demonstrate the impact that national problems in freight transportation have upon commuter service in our major cities as long as this service is dependent upon freight revenues for continued operation. Railroad management states that in order to continue operations in the highly competitive freight business they must hold the line on freight rates in the face of rising costs. To do this money-losing passenger services must be eliminated.

Revenue-expense squeeze. The increasing burden of the passenger deficit is due to the fact that unit expenses are rising much faster than unit revenues. This discrepancy is due in part to the difficulty of matching service offered to service purchased, resulting in a decline in the average number of passengers in each railroad car since World War II, and in part to the continuing increases in prices and wages.

The exact amount of expenses directly and indirectly incurred by the passenger service of the railroads is a matter of some controversy. The present methods of separating railroad operating expense between freight and passenger services were devised some years ago and solely for the broad purpose of dividing total expenses between these categories. The methods were not designed to produce acceptable cost accounting data or even to identify the expenses of the various types of traffic moving on passenger trains. The Interstate Commerce Commission took notice of the many criticisms of these practices and undertook a special investigation[8] at the time of the passenger deficit investigation (docket 31954 reported May 18, 1959). The Commission found that: the methods being used were satisfactory and reasonably adequate for the original

[55]

purpose; proposed alternatives were each subject to important criticism; and no convincing showing was made that the existing practices were unreasonable or basically faulty for the purpose for which they were used.

The general dissatisfaction with ICC cost separation is reflected in the demands of the New York and Pennsylvania State Utility Commissions for lengthy cost-finding studies on suburban service costs in connection with New York Central and Pennsylvania Railroad cases. These studies produced relatively small changes in stated railroad suburban operating costs and resulting deficits. However, many questions were raised regarding the soundness of the rather old formulas used to separate railroad expenses, and the lack of original records and other empirical accounting data that are accepted as a necessity in other industries today.

It is clear that the ICC has been remiss in allowing outmoded accounting and costing practices suitable for monopoly regulations to continue. Steps should be taken at the earliest opportunity to revise railroad accounting from the workman in the repair shop on up. Railroad costs should be distributed by type of service from the first compilation forward. Profit-centered accounting is so well established in modern American business of all types that its ultimate application to railroads is beyond cavil. The ICC has regulated rates and fares without adequate and necessary data on carrier costs. The Civil Aeronautics Board has done a much more adequate job of developing cost data for regulatory use.

Except for random information in State commission proceedings there is no specific cost information available for railroad suburban services. However, it is not unreasonable to assume that these services are affected in the same way and by the same forces affecting all reported passenger service costs. Notable exceptions would be dining and sleeping car service. The following table indicates the relative increases in car-mile and train-mile expenses of all rail passenger service.

An important aspect of the structure of railroad costs bears heavily on the revenue–expense relationship in suburban service. Due to high plant investment and relatively inflexible employee work rules railroads have high fixed costs and low variable costs. This means that increased utilization of plant and employees rapidly reduces unit costs. However, suburban service has been marked by maximum capacity operation for 20 hours per week and disappearing traffic in the remaining hours, thus reducing the use of plant and employees. Thus unit expenses are forced up to higher levels unless some way can be found to revive enough off-peak traffic to more than recover out-of-pocket costs, or to lessen the impact of work rules.

[56]

TABLE 2

*Changes in unit passenger service expenses 1949–59—Class I
railroads of the United States*

Year	Expense per passenger car-mile		Expense per passenger train-mile	
	Transporta-tion[1]	Total[2]	Transporta-tion	Total
1949......cents...	23.9	49.6	$2.24	$4.66
1954.......do....	28.5	58.8	$2.82	$5.72
1959.......do....	34.3	67.3	$3.57	$7.02
Percent changes:				
1949–59........	43.5	35.7	59.4	50.6
1954–59........	20.4	16.6	26.6	22.7

1. Solely related rail line transportation expenses.
2. All railway operating expenses except rents.
Source: Association of American Railroads, "Railroad Transportation—A Statistical Record 1921–57," table 23; Statistical Summary No. 44, July 1960.

While unit revenues for all passenger service have increased quite slowly, in fact at a much slower rate than unit expenses as shown in table 3, the trend of unit commuter revenues alone is much better. This should act to relieve the revenue-expense squeeze in suburban service. The experience of the Chicago and North Western indicates this relief is actual. The North Western has been simultaneously improving equipment and service and increasing fares. We note also that the overall passenger operating ratio on the Long Island is less than 100, this being the only important passenger carrying railroad to show this ratio for all services. Two other Chicago railroads informally advised the committee staff that suburban service revenues were very nearly covering fully allocated costs at present. Available evidence indicates that the remaining carriers are covering far less than full costs at present.

Raising commuter fares beyond a certain point has undesirable effects which are discussed in the next section. However, the present levels are not basically unreasonable when compared with unit cost to the passenger for other means of transportation.

Average costs to the passenger per mile in 1958 for various modes of travel were: Intercity rail coach 2.76 cents, suburban rail coach (commuter) 2.57 cents, intercity motorbus (class I) 2.43 cents, rail transit lines (subway and elevated) assuming 5-mile average trip 3.2 cents, motorbus transit assuming 5-mile average trip 3.2 cents or assuming

3-mile average trip 5.3 cents. Estimated private automobile costs vary sharply with the number of passengers. Out-of-pocket costs for one, two and three persons were estimated to be 3.5–4 cents, 1.75–2 cents and 1.17–1.33 cents. Fully allocated private auto costs which are the only costs comparable to public transportation are, in the same order, 10–11 cents, 5–5.5 cents and 3.33–3.7 cents. None of these auto costs include the cost of parking downtown. Rail commutation cost to the passenger was up to 2.75 cents in 1959 but there were undoubtedly increases in some of the other modal costs.

One of the basic causes of the illness in suburban service is that the fares have historically been very low and have probably never covered the costs where suburban traffic has been great enough to require separate trains to serve commuters. This fact has undoubtedly caused much of the neglect of equipment and the poor service which has been frequently described in magazines and newspapers.

The record[9] shows that in the middle of the 19th century the railroads went to great lengths to stimulate development of the suburban areas along their already established lines. In some cases free passes for as long as 3 years were given to those building homes in the new suburbs. The early fares were priced on the theory that commutation was a byproduct of the regular intercity services. At the time of the first ICC investigation in 1911 it was found that these fares had not been changed for 15 to 20 years in most cases and that they were 40 years old in a few instances. Because these original fares, set to promote byproduct short-haul traffic, had become an established part of suburban living and because the railroads still retained a complete monopoly of organized transportation, the ICC allowed increases of only 5 percent in this leading case. In their first decision on commuter fares the ICC stated that commutation was a separate and distinct type of "bulk transportation" service for which only a "reasonable" rate could be expected. The clear inference of this case is that the rate would not necessarily be required by the Commission to cover the expenses.

A few years later (1914) in the first general freight rate increase case, the *Five Percent* case,[10] the Commission considered the available evidence on passenger costs. The general conclusion was that passenger service was far less profitable than freight service and that the rate of 2 cents per passenger-mile for intercity rail coach, required by statute in several States, did not give full compensation. At this time the average commutation rate was about 1.2 cents per passenger-mile and therefore clearly a loss rate even allowing for some cost savings in handling commuter traffic.

Both of these early cases demonstrate that the original concept of commuter traffic was to build up the short-haul patronage on through trains already operated at appropriate times of the day. However, the rapid growth of the new suburbs required a great increase in train operations, equipment, and station investment just to serve the suburban traffic. The Commission acknowledged that what was originally a "byproduct" price was not adequate to cover the full costs of special trains, tracks, and terminals required by that time for suburban service, particularly in Chicago, New York, and Boston.

This very low rate level prevailed for many years. In 1940 the average fare per passenger-mile for commutation was 1.01 cents and many large carriers, the Long Island, New York Central, and the New Haven for instance had fare levels of 0.8 to 0.9 cents. The intercity coach average fare in 1940 was 1.67 cents.

In addition to the very low levels of average commuter fares commutation has been subject to some of the irrational and economically unsound pricing practices too prevalent in transportation[11] and frequently referred to elsewhere in the committee's report. The most economically destructive practice has been the granting of discounts to peak-hour users. This is giving a volume discount to the riders creating the maximum requirement for investment in facilities and operating equipment and causing high labor costs due to prevailing work rules. In most other utility pricing, customers using the service at the peak of demand pay the highest prices and price discounts are used to build business and contribute to fixed costs at times of lower plant utilization. However, the commuter railroads have given the lowest rates to the peak hour customers who are the most expensive to serve and have given the highest rates to the occasional offpeak customer who does not ride often enough to buy a multiple-ride ticket and who is the least expensive to serve. These customers can be served for a very reasonable fare since a large plant is in operation through the middle of the day and the employees must be paid whether they work or not.

It may be too late in urban transportation development to rebuild offpeak traffic through incentive rates but the rate anomaly certainly helped to reduce this traffic which could well have made an important contribution to indirect expenses.

The above commentary on the pricing of rail commuter services is in no sense critical of the original decisions of rail management. At least for the short term they were sensible and logical. However, the growth of suburban service from filling empty seats near large cities—a true by-product—into a large and separate service with its own trains and facilities but without concomitant fare changes illustrates the danger of pricing any transport service as a byproduct except for initial promotional purposes. All types of discount fares in transportation should be rigorously analyzed for contribution to net profits and for relationship to long-term trends at frequent, scheduled intervals.

The following table shows the unit fare trend of the class I railroads for the last 10 years:

TABLE 3

Changes in unit passenger revenues, 1949–59—Class I railroads of the United States (average revenue per passenger-mile)

Year	Commuta-tion	Intercity coach	All travel including 1st class
1949......cents...	1.43	2.41	2.45
1954.......do....	2.03	2.50	2.62
1959.......do....	2.75	2.77	2.95
Percent change:			
1949–59........	92.0	14.9	20.4
1954–59........	35.0	10.8	12.7

Source: Association of American Railroads, "Railroad Transportation—A Statistical Record 1921–57," table 25, Statistical Summary No. 44, July 1960.

. . .

NOTES

1. "Address to the Governor of California's Commission on Metropolitan Problems," June 20, 1959, p. 2.

2. The terms "rail commutation service" and "suburban rail service" will appear repeatedly throughout this report. Each is intended to mean service provided by railroads for passengers moving from suburb to city without regard to whether multiple-ride tickets or single one-way fares are involved, unless otherwise indicated.

3. Association of American Railroads, "Railroad Transportation—A Statistical Record, 1921–57," p. 19; Statistical Summary No. 44, July 1960.

4. See app. A, p. 93, "New Jersey's Rail Transportation Problem," New Jersey State Highway Department, Division of Rail Transportation, Trenton, N.J., for traffic of individual railroad branches.

5. For this purpose the Long Island RR. is not considered to fall within the exception because it is operating under special State legislation.

6. *Business Week,* Feb. 6, 1960, p. 60.

7. Source: Same as table 1.

8. ICC, "Separation of Operating Expenses Between Freight and Passenger Services," Doc. 32141, decided Jan. 27, 1958.

9. ICC, the *Commutation Rate* case, 21 I.C.C. 428, decided June 21, 1911, and *Commutation Fares to and From Washington,* 33 I.C.C. 428, decided Mar. 22, 1915.

10. ICC, the *Five Percent* case, 31 I.C.C. 351, decided July 29, 1914.

11. The port of New York Authority has recently offered book tickets carrying 50-percent discounts to commuting motorists. To the extent these are used at peak hours they represent the same type of unsound pricing, discounts should be used to build offpeak volume.

CHAPTER 2

Automobile Usage and Its Cost

IF ONE WISHES TO ASSIGN AN ARBITRARY POINT to the real beginning of
the automobile age, 1920 is probably as good a date as any. By that time
the automobile was sufficiently dependable to meet a majority of family
transportation needs. It had ceased to be a machine possessed by (or pos-
sessing?) only the rich or the daring. The price of automobiles had gone
down substantially over the years since mass production was introduced,
while quality and reliability had risen just as substantially for even the
most modest vehicle. The quality of gasoline, tires, and other necessary supplies was also steadily improving as the cost of these items was decreasing.
Not only was automotive technology advancing, but the federal government
had begun its programs of highway financing, and state and local governments were rapidly building and improving roads to meet the demands of
the motoring public. Federal highway funds were not available at the time
for use in urban areas, but nevertheless the impetus given by federal action
had stimulated highway construction and motoring everywhere.

Through the decades of the twenties and thirties the quality of the automobile continued to improve and automobile ownership and use spread
rapidly. In the cities it became evident that the auto presented some new
problems as well as some new possibilities. In terms of space occupied it
was most certainly less efficient than the public transportation vehicles
needed to move the same number of people. Signs of congestion had begun
to appear in some places by the late twenties. On the other hand, however,
the flexibility of the private car permitted the development of home-sites
in places remote from public transportation. Clearly, the old dependence
upon public transportation was largely disappearing by the time America
entered the Depression era. More and more people were able to live in
places innocent of the service of public transport agencies. The open spaces
between the starfish-like arms of the city, molded by public transportation,
filled up with auto-oriented community development.

With the automobile age, urban population began to spill in ever-
increasing numbers over the old political boundaries of the city and into
the suburbs. After an understandable lull during the Depression and the

Second World War, the rate of population decentralization and of geographical spread began to accerate wildly when a peacetime footing was reattained. The suburban development engulfed existing towns and villages in the hinterland of major cities, sprawling over a vast area. This sort of urban growth produced no neatly defined organism like the old city of the nineteenth century in the age of the streetcar, but rather an amorphous thing called a metropolitan area. If the older part of the metropolitan area was the creature of the public transport system, certainly suburbanization and metropolitanization were the creatures of the private automobile. They were nourished in part at least by federal policies that responded to public need and demand for more highways and for guaranteed housing loans— the latter under standards and conditions that could usually be met only by housing in suburban locations.

From material in the first chapter of readings, it is obvious that public transportation concerns and agencies found it difficult to meet the challenge of the expanding and decentralizing metropolis. Automotive competition and previous financial difficulties made it almost impossible for them to keep pace. Except for the wartime years, when rationing discouraged motoring, earnings were meager and capital was difficult to attract. Buses largely replaced the street railway lines, both to cut the fixed costs associated with any railway operation and to take advantage of the improved highways that were both leading and following the population to the suburbs.

The extension of bus lines into the rapidly growing periphery of the central city did little, however, to help urban mass transport to prosper. Population was no longer concentrated along the public transport route; instead it was spread out thinly over an extensive area. Fares were increased and service cut back in order to boost revenues and cut costs. Usually this was to no avail. Government policy encouraged the automobile and high-pressure automotive advertising spread the word. Countering the many obvious advantages of private transportation, public transport companies failed to offer an adequate transportation alternative for the American urban dweller. Except in the very largest cities served by a well-developed rapid-transit or railway-commuter operation, the most convenient means of urban travel was by automobile. The result in most American cities was an overwhelming dependence upon the automobile for urban transportation.

The following group of readings explores some of the problems entailed in this dependence. The principal difficulty, as almost any citizen can attest, is that of traffic congestion. This is a condition that has become an integral part of American urban life and one that is both difficult and costly to cure or even to relieve. Congestion is expensive to ignore or to fight. Ignoring it threatens an urban area with eventual decay and ruin because of hampered circulation. Attempting to combat it leads to the frustration of finding and financing the proper remedy.

Statement of Senator Williams of New Jersey, 1962

THE FIRST READING IN THIS SECTION is a speech made by U.S. Senator Harrison Williams (Democrat, of New Jersey) at the opening of the 1961 urban mass transportation hearings before a subcommittee of the Senate Committee on Banking and Currency. Since his election to the Senate, Williams has been a champion of urban causes, particularly urban mass transportation. He is responsible for introducing much of the existing federal mass-transport legislation.

In this speech Senator Williams in effect touches all bases in giving a broad outline of the urban transport problem in the United States. Indeed the speech goes somewhat beyond the title used for this chapter. In so doing it presents a better idea of the magnitude of the problem, however, as well as many of its related facets. Much emphasis is given to the expenditures made and proposed for highways-only programs that—if they were to be carried out—seem to offer little chance for relief of congestion. In making a call for federal aid and leadership for mass transport in U.S. urban areas, Williams sounds the basic theme of coordinating highways and private automotive transport with improved public means of urban travel.

Appended to the Senator's speech is an article from the Newark, New Jersey, *Star-Ledger,* written by Robert P. Kalter. In this short piece, the frustration of tackling urban congestion with highway improvements alone is spelled out in the context of a small area of northern New Jersey.

I THINK THE ADMINISTRATION deserves a great deal of credit for the extensive effort it has made to formulate a genuinely comprehensive program that, for the first time, offers real hope that we may someday find a way out of the daily traffic jams strangling our larger cities and towns all across the country. It also offers real hope to the many smaller cities and towns that have seen their public transportation system, primarily buses, shrink and in many cases disappear, thus depriving a large segment of our population of an essential service.

"Statement of Harrison A. Williams, Jr., A Senator from the State of New Jersey," *Urban Mass Transportation—1962* (Hearings before a Subcommittee of the Committee on Banking and Currency, United States Senate), pp. 52–63.

For a long time mass transportation has been the stepchild of our community facilities. Perhaps we thought that highways and automobiles could somehow serve all needs. Perhaps we thought the railroads could maintain their commuter deficits forever. Perhaps we thought because bus ridership was declining, it was no longer an essential service.

But if I may cite New Jersey's problem as indicative of what is happening around the country, it has been estimated that the State will have to spend at least $3 billion on highways by 1975 just to keep abreast of the traffic congestion that will arise from the expected rapid rise in population and vehicle registration. Yet, New Jersey is going to fall a full $1 billion below this need, at present levels of Federal and State highway funding.

If on top of this shortage, our rail commuter service is allowed to disintegrate and our bus service to shrink, New Jersey's highway needs will skyrocket by hundreds of millions of dollars.

That is why, as the President has stated:

Our national welfare requires the provision of good urban transportation, with the properly balanced use of private vehicles and modern mass transportation.

In other words, it is not a question of "either or," or transit competing with highways. It is a matter of using both to their greatest natural advantage, to supplement one another so that we receive maximum benefits from our investments in both.

I see that both Dr. Weaver of the Housing and Home Finance Agency and Mr. Whitton, the Federal Highway Administrator, are scheduled to testify. I think this is significant because it symbolizes the intimate relationship between transit and highways and between transportation and housing, urban renewal, and other urban development programs.

I think the appearance of these two officials is indicative of a distinctly new and heartening level of cooperative effort that is beginning to emerge.

And we certainly need every bit of cooperation we can get, for as everyone knows who has ever been caught in a traffic jam, if transportation is the bloodstream of an urban society, we are indeed undergoing a serious hardening of the arteries. . . .

Mr. Chairman, if I may, I would now like to discuss in more detail this problem of traffic congestion and what it means to our urban areas.

In an effort to cope with the problem, the country launched the massive $41 billion interstate highway program, with about $20 billion now allocated for urban highway construction. But the realization is growing that, essential as this program is, highways alone are not the answer. The President has therefore called for a long-term effort to preserve and improve essential mass transportation service to help alleviate traffic congestion, especially during rush hours.

Perhaps more importantly, the President has recommended an approach which has been so often disregarded in the past history of urban transportation developments as to seem almost novel and daring.

Very simply, Federal aid for transit and, after an interim period for highways, would be geared to plans for a coordinated urban transportation system that would itself be an integral part of the planned comprehensive development of the metropolitan area.

Traditionally transportation has been the tail that wagged the metropolitan dog. The President proposes instead that we get a vision of what we want our cities and suburbs to be, and build our transportation networks to serve these goals.

What lies behind the emerging urban transportation crisis that has given rise to the President's recommendations?

THE HIGHWAY PROGRAM

FIRST, the highway program. Urban highways are clearly essential to meet a whole variety of needs—national defense, interstate commerce, the afternoon shopper, the traveling salesman, the doctor who must use his car, for the movement of truck freight in the metropolitan area, for countless commercial purposes, for visits to the suburban homes of friends, for weekend vacation travel, and for rush hour commutation of people who, because of the location of their homes or their place of work could never be adequately served by mass transportation service of any kind. In addition, urban highways will be necessary in many smaller and even large metropolitan areas to provide the right-of-way for express bus service where grade-separated transit is not feasible. The existence of the highways, of course, will not guarantee the provision of adequate express bus service, but they will make it physically possible.

But despite the wide range of needs urban highways can and will serve, it is becoming increasingly clear that there is one mammoth problem that highways and automobiles alone cannot hope to meet, except at prohibitive cost or without profoundly changing the face and function of the metropolitan area, and in particular the central city. That is the morning and evening rush hour travel from home to work.

In the first place, urban highway construction is extremely expensive, averaging between $5 million and $20 million a mile in built-up areas. For example, the 15-mile inner loop proposed for the Nation's Capital will cost $300 million. In Philadelphia, a 22-mile highway along the Delaware River will also cost $300 million. In Boston, a 12-mile turnpike into the downtown area will cost $180 million. In New Jersey the average cost of modern highways throughout the State is $6.2 million per mile. And to build the proposed highway, scarcely more than a mile long, across lower Manhattan will cost $100 million. In contrast, this $100 million which will provide just a little more than 1 mile in Manhattan might provide 5 miles or more of highway in the outlying suburbs or around the metropolitan fringe or between cities where in the not distant future these highways will be badly needed and where people will be extremely dependent on their automobiles to get around.

But the per-mile cost of highways in heavily built-up areas is not the only problem. After you build the highway, it then becomes necessary to improve and widen the local street system to handle the cars pouring off the limited access artery. This, plus the highways themselves, creates tremendous problems of family dislocation.

As the President noted in his message, the interstate highway program is displacing 15,000 families and 1,500 businesses every year. This is about the same number as are being displaced by the urban renewal program.

Then there is the loss of parks and trees along the street and other amenities so essential to a liveable urban environment. Air pollution increases, and the city's tax base dwindles as tax-ratable property is replaced by nontaxable concrete and asphalt. And when you get all through, you still have the gigantic problem of finding places for all the cars to park, a job which is not only very expensive, but which also carves away the very commercial and cultural attractions that caused the demand for access in the first place.

To give an indication of downtown parking costs, the $2.46 million civic center garage in Brooklyn, N.Y., provides space for 693 cars at a cost per space of about $3,556. The $4 million Grand Circus Park garage in Detroit holds 1,125 cars at a cost per space of around $3,902. The $4.1 million Auditorium Plaza in Kansas City has room for 1,050 cars at a cost per space of $3,905.

Lastly, there is the question of traffic control costs. Last fall New York City started a program to alleviate traffic congestion in the area of Manhattan south of 20th Street. According to a report in the New York Times, the project

> involves a central control room that receives reports of developing traffic congestion from policemen in 15 radio cars, 15 men on motorcycles and 1 police helicopter.

It perhaps should be pointed out that there are more policemen working to reduce traffic tieups in lower Manhattan than there are people in the entire Federal Establishment working on the problem of improving mass transportation throughout the country.

CARS UP, TRANSIT DOWN

BUT this is not the end of the story, because in the background are two trends which may well turn what is now a very serious problem into a full-scale crisis.

One trend is the rapid rise in automobile ownership. At present there are about 70 million registered vehicles in the United States. In 15 short years this number is expected to rise to well over 115 million, with most of the increase occurring in the metropolitan areas. In fact, in many areas the cars are multiplying faster than the people. In itself this is fine, but it could become a first-class catastrophe if, lacking any mass transportation alternative, it becomes necessary for more and more people to use those automobiles to get to and from work each day.

And this possibility is becoming more and more likely because the other important trend is the equally rapid decline and deterioration of mass transportation service. In fact in the last 10 years, ridership on all forms of mass transportation has declined 38 per cent.

However, it is important to point out that most of this decline has occurred during the offpeak hours and on weekends. Rush-hour ridership has held up very well, and is turning upward in many areas. As a matter of fact, grade-separated transit is beginning to show an absolute increase in ridership and bus ridership seems to be leveling off from its previous decline.

Thus, there is no question that mass transportation can and does provide an absolutely essential rush-hour service.

WHY TRANSIT IS ESSENTIAL

THE reason this service is essential is simply that the alternative costs would be staggering. For example, the American Municipal Association has estimated that if the five cities of New York, Chicago, Boston, Philadelphia, and Cleveland were to lose just their rail commuter service it would cost $31 billion, with 30-year, 4-percent financing, to build the highways necessary to serve a comparable number of people.

In study after study, the same conclusions have been reached.

In Washington, an extensive transportation survey found:

By 1980, under [an auto-] dominant transportation system, 12 to 18 lanes would be required to carry traffic from the Capitol to Wheaton. The inner loop would require 14 lanes. Several other corridors would require more than eight lanes. Not only would the cost be great but excessive damage would be done to residential communities and to the character of the central area of the Nation's Capital. These findings led to the conclusion that, in the absence of substantially improved public transit, the highway system needed to serve the projected traffic volumes is hardly feasible from the engineering standpoint, and is certainly out of the question from the standpoint of desirable regional development.

During Senate hearings on mass transportation legislation 2 years ago a representative of the Georgia Department of Commerce testified:

In Atlanta, the northern portion of the expressway currently has 6 lanes, but has traffic sufficient to warrant 16 lanes. By 1970 this need will have jumped to at least 36 lanes. By no stretch of the imagination is it physically or financially possible to build such a facility.

That is why we must have transit as well as highways, using each to their greatest natural advantage.

Dwight Palmer, New Jersey's highway commissioner, has summed up the problem as well as anyone. He has pointed out that New Jersey's population is expected to increase by 39 percent by 1975, that vehicle registrations are expected to rise by 47 percent.

Just to keep abreast of these rising transportation needs will require "821 miles of freeways extending into every county of the State" plus widening and improvement of about one-half of the existing 1,850-mile State system. He has estimated that this will cost between $2.7 and $3 billion, based on 1956 prices. Yet "if Federal and State funds continue at the present level, we will be about $1 billion short of the amount necessary to construct the required improvements."

As if this weren't bad enough, Commissioner Palmer went on to point out, in his 1960 transportation report to the Governor, that "Should all rail and ferry commuter services be discontinued, State highway programs and budgets would of necessity be increased by many millions of dollars, and to little avail, unless transportation is to move at a snail's pace."

The conclusion is clearly that we need both highways and transit. The problem with transit, however, is twofold.

THE PROBLEMS

IN the first place, private bus, transit, and rail carriers are finding it increasingly difficult to break even, much less make a profit, on a 20-hour-a-week basis. And if they cannot break even, they cannot stay in business. The railroads are especially burdened with heavy capital costs for facilities and equipment. But even bus companies are plagued by similar problems, as illustrated by the difficulties of the Fifth Avenue Coach Line in New York City, which is similar to the problems faced by bus companies in hundreds of other cities across the country, large and small. Caught in the squeeze of rising capital and operating costs, and declining patronage, the private carriers, bus and rail, must resort to raising fares, trimming service, and deferring maintenance—which simply drives away more riders and accelerates the downward spiral.

The only solution to this downward spiral is the injection of public funds to bridge the financial gap standing between the transit carriers and the needs of the community.

The Federal Responsibility

But at this point a second problem arises. When State or local governments begin searching for an answer to a particular traffic problem, they are faced with the overwhelmingly powerful economic fact that in most cases they need put up only 10 percent of the cost for a highway solution, whereas they must contemplate bearing 100 percent of the cost of a transit solution, whether it involves improving a rail line, buying a new fleet of buses, providing fringe area parking, establishing a downtown distributor system, or whatever.

Obviously this situation is not conducive to the establishment of a balanced urban transportation system, utilizing transit where it is logically needed and using a highway where it is logically needed.

There are, of couse, a number of other reasons why this problem involves a considerable measure of Federal responsibility.

For one thing, the problem of providing adequate mass transportation service has long ago spilled over local political jurisdictions. In fact, it has spilled over a good many State boundaries. Some 53 of our 200-odd metropolitan areas either border on or cross over State lines. The financial difficulties of the State and local governments are even more acute than the jurisdictional difficulties. Most of our cities are faced with rising service costs and declining tax bases. State and local debt has risen 15 times faster than Federal debt since the war.

And finally there is the very great national importance of traffic congestion. It has been estimated that traffic jams cost the Nation about $5 billion a year in time and wages lost, extra fuel consumption, faster vehicle depreciation, lower downtown commercial sales, lower taxes, and so forth. It is also clear that traffic congestion discourages private investment in central cities, and thereby makes the task of urban renewal that much more difficult and costly.

The former mayor of Philadelphia, for example, testified last year that

Philadelphia businessmen told him that they would be willing to invest $500 to $600 million over their present plans if they had some assurance that something would be done about traffic congestion. Officials of a non-profit organization in Washington called Downtown Progress, who are attempting to revitalize the downtown area, have frequently stated that the key to their efforts is the construction of the proposed rapid transit system.

Traffic congestion also adds to the cost of moving freight in the metropolitan area, because trucks have to compete for clogged street space with the automobile. Who knows how many truckdrivers simply park on the outskirts of the metropolitan area and wait until the rush hour is over? Those who do come straight in are faced with incessant stops and starts, which are not only time-consuming but extremely expensive. I understand that some trucking firms have set up depots at the fringe of the metropolitan areas, where truckloads are divided into smaller vehicles which can maneuver more quickly and easily in traffic congestion. This, too, adds to the total cost we must pay for our goods and materials.

Safety is another factor. In fact, it was one of the primary factors that led the president of the Standard Oil Co. of California to endorse the ambitious San Francisco rapid transit program, because use of the highways during rush hours exceeded the limits of reasonable safety. And, of course, the more accidents that occur, the steeper the insurance premiums become.

And last but not least there is the intense irritation and frustration we have all felt when we get caught in a traffic jam. If for no other reason than to provide a little better peace of mind for the automobile commuter, Federal assistance is warranted.

THE FEDERAL PROGRAM

THE President's recommendations for a mass transportation program take the following form:

1. A continuing matching grant program with an initial 3-year authorization of $50 million to State and local governments for the construction and acquisition of mass transportation facilities and equipment such as land, right-of-way, parking facilities, buses, rail rolling stock, signal equipment, stations, terminals, and so forth. The Federal share would be two-thirds of the net project cost; that is, that portion of the cost that cannot be financed by revenues from the system.

2. The grant would be contingent on the development of a program, including planning and organization, for a coordinated transportation system as part of a comprehensive plan for the development of the urban area.

3. An emergency program limited to 3 years of grants on a 50-50 matching basis where there is an urgent need for the preservation or provision of mass transportation facilities, and where the comprehensive program is being actively developed.

4. A $55 million research and development program in the field of mass transportation, with emphasis on new technology; $25 million would be provided by transfer of the existing demonstration grant authority, and $30 million would be provided out of the new primary grant authorization.

5. A provision for the payment of relocation expenses, similar to those under the urban renewal program, for any families and business displaced by a mass transportation project.

6. A continuation of the existing $50 million loan program, which is scheduled to expire at the end of 1962. The loans for equipment and facilities could not be used in conjunction with grant assistance.

WILL PEOPLE RIDE TRANSIT?

AN understandable question arising from the President's recommendations is: "Will people actually ride transit after you have spent all this money?"

There are several indications that the answer is "Yes."

New Jersey has long had its eye on one very simple and inexpensive improvement that could have been undertaken at any time. This would be to reroute the Jersey Central main line passenger service to Newark, over the Lehigh Valley tracks from Cranford, linking up with the H. & M. line into New York. The cost would be less than $2 million, yet the State has held up on the project for fear that the H. & M., in its present state of disrepair, would not be able to handle the additional passengers that this improvement is expected to generate.

In other areas where positive efforts have been made to improve transit service, the results have been very impressive indeed.

The New York subway system, which is undertaking a modernization program, had an increase of 20 million riders last year over the year before.

Several years ago, the Boston & Albany Railroad, down to about 3,000 riders a day on its Highland branch line, was petitioning strenuously to eliminate all its service. The Boston MTA took over the 11-mile line, linked it up with the subway system, turned it into a rapid transit-type operation, provided some fringe area parking, and now the line is pushing the figure of 30,000 riders a day, despite the fact that it does not operate on an exclusive right-of-way.

In 1959, Philadelphia, one of the real pioneer cities in the field of mass transportation entered into a contract with the Pennsylvania Railroad to provide more frequent service at lower fares on a line running out to Chestnut Hill. This Operation Northwest, so-called, proved so successful, increasing ridership 30 percent and reducing by 400 the number of cars coming into the downtown area each day, that similar operations were instituted on other lines, and equally successful increases in ridership occurred. The program has been so successful, in fact, that the suburban counties are becoming interested in joining with the city in extending the new improved service out beyond the city line. All told, the five experimental operations are now carrying 6.2 million riders a year—an increase of 44 percent in ridership over pre-Operation Northwest years.

Chicago can point to two significant developments, the first being the almost unprecedented phenomenon of a railroad making money on its commuter service, although recently the service has begun slipping back into the red with the opening of a parallel highway. The railroad is the Chicago & North Western, under the aggressive and farsighted leadership of its chairman, Ben Heineman, who is providing modern, clean, and courteous service to the commuter and even more important service to the city of Chicago. The second development was the construction of a rapid transit line in the medial strip of the Congress Street Expressway. This line, which is operating at only 25 percent of capacity, is already carrying more rush-hour traffic than the highway itself, which is operating at full capacity at rush hour.

In addition to helping reduce traffic congestion and meet growing urban transportation needs, transit can be a vital tool in helping revitalize our cities.

Toronto is the only city in North America actively engaged in the construction of a rapid transit system at the present time. In 5 years since the opening of the subway line there, assessed valuations long the route rose 17 percent more than in the city as a whole. And this amounted to a difference of $88 million in assessed valuation. With the same tax rate, the tax yield from this increase was $4 million, which was enough to amortize the annual debt service on the project.

But it should be emphasized that the ability of transit to improve property and commercial values is not limited by any means to the downtown areas of the central cities.

TRANSIT VITAL TO SUBURBS

WITH proper planning, transit as well as highways can be as great a boon to the suburbs as to the central city. In can be a vital positive tool to help curb suburban sprawl, which profits no one, and help structure better patterns of suburban development. A good illustration of how this might work can be seen in the Year 2000 Plan for the Washington metropolitan area.

In an effort to curb the present aimless, haphazard, and inordinately expensive sprawl that characterizes current development at the fringe of this metropolitan area, the planners and officials have recommended a so-called corridor plan, with future development radiating out from the present fringe in five or six corridors, separated by wedges of open space. More compact and economical developments in the corridors would be encouraged by placing highspeed rapid transit and highways down the centers of the corridors, like spokes on a wheel, tying the suburbs to the central city. With this kind of development, suburb officials might have some hope of providing necessary school, utility, police, and other community services at considerably less cost than would be possible under a pattern of widely scattered, low-density development. And with these rapid transit and highway arteries, industry locating out in the corridors could be assured of access to a labor market throughout the metropolitan area.

It is important to point out that the bulk of the population increase is occurring and will continue to occur in the outlying portions of the metropolitan area, and it is increasing much too fast for the central cities to cope with anything but a small fraction of it. And with the population increase will come commerce, industry, and public services of all kinds.

This fact, combined with the growing capacity of residential, commercial, and industrial developers to lay out whole new communities in one fell swoop, offers unparalleled opportunities to coordinate transit and highway systems with these land-use developments to create new suburban environments with a vastly higher level of diversity, variety, comfort, efficiency, productivity, and attractiveness than we have ever been able to achieve before.

This is why highways should not be the sole concern of the highway engineers and why transit should not be the sole concern of the transit operator. There is a great challenge here as well to those who are vitally concerned with housing, urban renewal, community facilities, and the urban environment generally to achieve the kind of urban society commensurate with 20th-century standards.

PROBLEM OF THE SMALL TOWNS

MR. CHAIRMAN, my comments so far have been directed primarily to the medium sized and larger sized urban areas. But it would be a mistake to conclude that mass transportation is a problem of concern only to those larger areas. Part of the problem is that the larger cities usually command more national publicity. But I recently came across an editorial from the Fairmont, W. Va., Times. The editorial, commenting on a fare increase by the local bus company, noted that

> more than 100 bus companies have been forced out of business in West Virginia within a little more than 10 years. Only 28 are still in operation, counting both city and suburban lines. Between 1955 and 1959 alone, the number of passengers hauled on West Virginia local lines dropped 35.3 percent.

What has happened in West Virginia has been happening throughout the country.

The American Transit Association, which represents about 80 percent of all the bus and transit service in the United States, compiled statistics showing that exactly 145 transit companies have completely abandoned service since 1954. The figure is much larger for the period going back to the end of World War II. These abandonments have occurred in such cities and towns as Little Rock, Ark.; Alhambra, Calif.; Denver, Colo.; Middletown, Conn.; Pocatello, Idaho; Kankakee, Ill.; Wichita, Kans.; Hannibal, Mo.; Great Falls, Mont.; Tulsa, Okla.; and so on down the list.

In addition, another 150 companies have been sold in the same period, for a total of about 350 companies sold or abandoned since 1954. In some of the cities, the service has been restored, but almost invariably at a greatly reduced level, accompanied by higher fares and reduced wages. In 83 cases no replacement has been made at all.

The American Transit Association estimates that there are about 60 cities of 25,000 population or more which have no public tranportation service at all. Many of our smaller cities and towns are experiencing rapid rates of growth, and they are beginning to taste the bitter fruits of traffic congestion. But growing rapidly or not, these cities and towns all have a sizable portion of their residents who have been seriously inconvenienced by the loss of public transportation service. And, of course, there is always a need for standby or emergency public transportation service.

This legislation is designed to help assist in the solution of mass transportation problems wherever they occur, in large cities or in small, and I believe the legislation will be equally beneficial to both.

I have here a number of clippings which reflect editorial opinion on the question of urban mass transportation which I would like to have included in the record. [One of the articles referred to follows.]

BOTTLENECK ON THE ROADS*

Robert P. Kalter

"BOTTLENECK" is a disease of the rubber tire age. An ailment that's with us the year around, it takes on epidemic proportions in warm weather, when highways are swollen with carefree motorists. The unwelcome spring outbreak is already underway—marked by congestion of the arteries with its paralysislike creep-and-crawl, stop-go driving.

The bottleneck malady kills time, wastes millions of man-hours, burns up millions of gallons of gasoline, robs years of life from auto engines and raises the blood pressure of the man behind the wheel. A "bottleneck," according to the dictionary, is "a narrow or congested way, or condition that retards progress." Highway engineers add that many bottlenecks are danger spots that figure all too frequently in serious accidents.

Some bottlenecks can be eliminated, some made less troublesome, while others defy improvement. Some are always present, some materialize only at rush hours, others are strictly seasonal, and many are fleetingly temporary.

A classic example of the permanent bottleneck can be found at Newark Airport. Here Route 1, a major north-south artery, meets Route 22, a primary east-west highway, and Route 21 (McCarter Highway), which brings traffic to and from the city of Newark. On an average day, 102,300 vehicles use Route 1, north of the interchange. South of the interchange, 68,300 vehicles are tabulated daily. Route 22 adds 63,200 vehicles and Route 21, 40,400. It's been a problem spot since the late 1920's, when Routes 22 and 21 angled off Route 1 in a Y-shape, backing up traffic on Route 1 for miles—in an era when rubber tire travel was still in infancy.

To relieve congestion, the highway department in 1931 redesigned the junction into a circle. Two years later a grade separation was undertaken, permitting southbound Route 1 traffic to pass over eastbound Route 22 traffic. All lanes were widened in 1936 and in 1939 other improvements were completed. The circle was completely redesigned in 1946, when the highways were dualized and through lanes were separated from lanes carrying local traffic. Three overpasses and a culvert were required to complete the million dollar project. In 1951 a slot was added to get Route 1 traffic into Route 21 without interfering with Route 22 traffic. And finally, in 1958 a small cement barrier was installed to permit Route 22 traffic to cut into Route 21 without interference from Route 1 traffic.

No Easy Solutions. Without the improvements, the Newark Airport circle would be impassable virtually around the clock. Thanks to the multimillion-dollar changes, it's a bottleneck only during hours of peak

* From the Newark (N.J.) *Star-Ledger,* April 22, 1962.

use—morning and evening rush hours and on summer weekends when it serves as a feeder for New Yorkers bound for the Jersey shore.

Otto H. Fritzsche, the State highway engineer and a realist in facing up to the headache-producing problems of bottlenecks, sees no easy solutions. "Often the elimination of a bottleneck at a particular location succeeds only in creating another bottleneck—perhaps even one of worse proportions—a mile or two away," Fritzsche said.

Will the new superhighways planned for the State eliminate the bottleneck problem? No, say highway engineers. They'll simply move the bottlenecks to county and local roads—at points where traffic enters and leaves the superhighways. Just look at what happened at the busy interchanges of the turnpike and Garden State Parkway through the north Jersey, the engineers say, and warn that more of the same lies ahead.

But the new superhighways will contribute to smoother, jam-free travel for those who can make use of them. For example, Route 22, according to Fritzsche, "is one big bottleneck from the Newark Airport circle to North Plainfield." Within this giant bottleneck are a number of little bottlenecks which the highway department has been attacking piecemeal for years. Center barriers have been constructed along the jug handles, plain and fancy, in an effort to reduce traffic delays, particularly at peak hours. Yet the highway remains clogged with bumper-to-bumper, snail-paced traffic during morning and evening commuter jams.

Work in Progress. Work is now in progress to eliminate a bad trouble spot used by an average 64,000 vehicles a day—the narrow viaduct over Liberty Avenue in Hillside, where 6 lines of traffic are squeezed into 4 lanes while climbing a relatively sharp hill. A 28-foot-wide deck is being added to provide three full lanes of traffic in each direction. The $573,000 project is scheduled for completion later this year.

Another trouble spot was eliminated at Springfield Road, Union, where a traffic light was shut off last year and an acceleration lane built to lead traffic onto Route 22 from Springfield Road. For years residents and employees of industrial plants in the area had pressed for installation of the traffic signal. It went into operation March 27, 1958—and almost immediately was responsible for tying up westbound traffic on Route 22 as far as a mile back, often jamming a major entrance to the Garden State Parkway.

Irate motorists began a campaign to get rid of the light almost as soon as it went into operation, finally winning out May 30. Cost of the 1,675-foot acceleration lane: $74,338. But Route 22, says Fritzsche, will remain a problem and a source of bottleneck trouble, until completion of the proposed Interstate Route 78, which will parallel it.

One of the most successful examples of removing a bottleneck, according to Fritzsche, can be found at the intersection of Route 1 and Route 18 at New Brunswick. Back in 1932, the average daily traffic count showed 36,000 vehicles using Route 1 and 22,000 using Route 18. A postwar homebuilding boom coupled with tremendous industrial expansion boosted the traffic count in 1959 to 74,000 vehicles daily on Route 1 and 64,000 on Route 18. The existing circle was inadequate for the traffic load and monumental bottlenecks developed. Plans for an elaborate interchange were completed to carry Route 18 traffic over Route 1. The $2,712,000 project, finished in September 1960, effectively broke the bottleneck.

Bottlenecks Remain. Despite all efforts, bottlenecks remain to plague the motorist. The bitter truth is there are just too many bottlenecks.

In New Jersey the problem is aggravated because it is a corridor State serving much of the Nation's north-south and east-west through traffic. Jersey is also a commuter State, compounding the problem at morning and evening rush hours. It is also a resort attraction, which swells its highways during the summers.

For these reasons, preservation and improvement of rail mass transportation looms large in the planning of Highway Commissioner Dwight R. G. Palmer.

No More Offstreet Parking in Congested Areas

Victor Gruen

THE DISTINGUISHED ARCHITECT AND CITY PLANNER, Victor Gruen, discusses here the problem of providing sufficient space for the automobile if present trends of automobile ownership, and the necessity for ownership, persist. Congestion in transportation is usually thought of in terms of the space problems of vehicles moving toward some destination under overcrowded conditions. There is another facet to this problem, however—that of providing room for the vehicles under all conditions. This includes not only space for movement, but also for storage and service. Using New York City as a case in point, Gruen establishes the fact that there is not enough room for both people and automobiles to live comfortably with one another in large numbers.

"No More Offstreet Parking in Congested Areas," *The American City,* September 1959.

NEW YORK CITY'S ZONING SOLUTION, discussed at a hearing before the city's Planning Commission on April 13, very sensibly and realistically is based on a concept of a city that can grow to a population of some 11 million persons and no more. This constitutes a very important, significant and valid planning concept. But the new zoning resolution not only neglects to deal with another new kind of population group, namely the automobile population with its insatiable space needs, but on the contrary practically enforces a new tremendous growth of such automobile population by requiring that off-street parking be provided in all residential districts and in all commerical and manufacturing districts except for the most congested downtown areas.

That the authors of the new zoning resolutions are aware of the dangers is indicated in their summary, in which, under the title of "Off-Street Parking Regulations" they state, "Since 1947 the tidal wave of half a million more automobiles owned by residents of the city has swept New York into the unenviable position of having traffic problems comparable with Detroit and other 'automobile cities.' " They mention later on that today 900,000 persons, about half of the people who are employed outside Manhattan's central business district, now drive to work.

The otherwise excellent preface contains the statement that one of the three basic elements on which zoning controls have to be applied is "the *deference* to the role of the automobile." This is an expression by which I am seriously disturbed. It is my opinion that no planning effort should defer to machines but should defer solely to human beings. If ever we allow the automobile to become our *master* to whom we have to show deference instead of our servant showing deference to us, we are decidedly wrong.

What is not recognized in the new zoning resolution is the fact that a new land use of most destructive qualities has developed: the automobile as means of mass transportation. The new land use which occupies nearly one-half of our total city area now has qualities which makes it much more dangerous to human activity and residential areas than any other use, whether industrial or commercial. It brings with it mortal dangers, fumes, gases, noise; it tears community patterns into shreds. That its danger is recognized by the people at large is witnessed by daily events discussed in our newspapers. Just recently the papers brought the news of the protest of the Murray Hill residents against the widening of 37th Street which would involve the loss of many old trees, some 50 feet high, and thus endanger the desirability of this residential area. A short while ago we read of the decision to close Washington Square Park to traffic—a decision which was due to tremendous popular pressure.

[79]

The separation of transportation areas and car storage areas from human activity areas and residential areas is a much more important problem than the separation of any of the human activity uses or residential uses from each other.

The automobile has an insatiable appetite for space. It needs about 300 sq. ft. when stored in its home quarters; 300 sq. ft. when stored in its place of destination, and 600 sq. ft. on its way. It further needs about 200 sq. ft. for those places where it is sold, repaired and serviced. Thus, an automobile needs 1400 sq. ft. of living space. That is about equal to the living space of a family unit.

As new housing is being built, as the final goal of 11 million inhabitants is reached, and as old housing is replaced by new housing, all 11 million inhabitants of New York will have to have one-car space per family unit. That will give us about 3 million automobiles in New York City. These 3 million automobiles will need, as their living space, 4.8 billion sq. ft. of area, or 120,000 acres, most of which will be ground area. The total land area of New York is 204,000 acres.

If New York wishes to remain urbanized, it must not defer to the automobile. It must change decidedly its present policy of facilitating rubber-wheeled traffic and thereby destroying public transportation. It must construct new and better public transportation facilities. Automobile traffic in urban areas must be discouraged.

I am, therefore, in favor of striking out all requirements for off-street parking facilities in all New York areas and forbidding the construction of parking facilities in areas now overly congested.

New York in most respects is no different from other American urban areas. They are all plagued with traffic congestion and the deterioration of the downtown area on the one hand and by the danger of metropolitan explosion on the other. Nearly every city, in its zoning and planning procedure, has needed to adjust to the Automobile Age by throwing the doors wide open to the automobile; by bringing freeways and expressways right into the city, or routing them straight through it; by providing off-street and on-street parking facilities; by widening streets, and by generally promoting urban sprawl.

Because automobiles consume space at a fantastic rate for their movement, their storage, their handling and their care, the urban core has been loosened to such a degree that some of our downtown areas, seen from the air, seem tremendous parking lots, made inefficient by the few remaining buildings which interrupt them.

Depending on the degree to which the motorization of downtown areas has progressed, city core areas have deteriorated physically and economically more or less seriously. In the cities (Los Angeles, for example) downtown has lost its predominance as the leading shopping and social center, and this role has been inadequately taken by outlying suburban conglomerations.

The plans which our office has developed for cities throughout the country embody the principle of creating compact and densely developed activity areas, including retail areas, office areas, industrial areas, which are kept free on the surface from mechanized traffic. They are established as pedestrian districts of a size and character which make walking convenient, and they are surrounded by traffic areas which are immediately adjoined by car storage facilities. Great stress is laid on improved public transportation, which is either carried underground to various points within the pedestrian areas or for which terminals are provided to bring the user of public transportation near the center of pedestrian districts.

In the case of the New York Zoning Resolution, we oppose those parts which require every new building to provide parking facilities, because in our opinion such requirements would draw automobile traffic to an even higher degree than is the case today into the very midst of human activity and residential areas, and thus destroy community characteristics and the cohesiveness of business areas.

The Cost of Getting to Work

ONE OF THE GREAT UNKNOWNS FOR MOST FAMILIES is the cost of getting to work. This is especially true in that great majority of cases where the journey to work is made via automobile. It is fairly easy to note how much the work trips cost when taken by public transportation; a fare is paid each time a ride is taken or each time a monthly commuter ticket is purchased. With the private automobile, however, the cost of fuel, supplies, repairs, etc., tends to get separated from the daily journey to the workplace. Only if a daily parking fee or tollway charge is paid is any money overtly exchanged to point up the expenditures made on the work trip. Moreover, the use of the family car for other than work trips tends to obscure the cost of any particular trip even more.

The article which follows estimates the cost of the work journey made by various means of urban transport. It also considers how the cost of housing is affected by a choice of location relative to commutation costs.

"The Cost of Getting to Work," *Changing Times,* The Kiplinger Magazine, May 1961. All tables are based on data from the First Federal Savings and Loan Association of Chicago.

[81]

Also discussed is the cost of commuting to the community itself, a factor which today looms large in public policy thinking. The drain on the public purse required by large scale commuting by automobile and the consequent need for substantial expenditures for highways necessarily deflect tax revenues from other uses. The recently increasing emphasis on mass transport is therefore aimed not only at congestion relief but at making the public dollar go further in meeting the many demands upon government.

THE PRICE YOU PAY TO GET TO WORK is a debit against your family's standard of living. It cuts down on the income you can devote to nice clothes, wholesome food, first-rate medical care, insurance, good times, education for the kids—all the good things you are working to provide for yourself and your family.

Yet do you know, really, how much this daily trek back and forth is draining out of your pocketbook? Take the most obvious part of the cost, the sheer time involved. If you work five days a week and spend 48 minutes getting to the job in the morning and another 48 minutes getting home again at night, you are putting in an extra eight hours a week, a full workday for which you get no pay at all. And this day of work—which can be fairly rugged, the way traffic is—actually costs you plenty.

Even if your commuting time is half as long, 24 minutes each way, you still put in your extra day every two weeks and foot the bill. Multiply your hourly rate of pay by the time you spend getting back and forth and you will have one measure of what commuting costs you.

But this article is not about the value of your own lost time. It is about actual dollars and cents, hard cash that comes right out of your pocket to pay for getting to work and back.

It happens that this particular cost-of-living item is a remarkably elusive sum. The total charge is split up among many bills you pay. That makes it easy to overlook. And an expense forgotten is an expense that is out of control.

In the next few pages, you will get an analytical look at your commuting bill. When you see the size of it, you may well discover that you are spending more than you need to. And if the audit does suggest ways to save, you will be giving yourself a raise in pay. The possibilities are worth examining, for the spending involved may run as high as 10% of your annual income.

Two Kinds of Costs

One of the most interesting investigations of how the price of getting to work hits the average family budget has been made by William K. Wittausch, assistant vice-president and economic adviser of the First Federal Savings and Loan Association of Chicago.

Mr. Wittausch points out that there are two kinds of direct costs involved in the commuting bill, fixed and variable. The variable expense is the only kind that most households are conscious of, for it represents the direct, out-of-pocket outlay for shoe leather; fares for bus, train or taxi travel; or car-operating costs and parking fees for those who drive to work.

In his analysis, Mr. Wittausch estimates the annual expenditure in 1959 for each of the available modes of transportation for a typical Chicago family with annual income of $8,000.

He calculates that if the breadwinner of this typical family walked to work, 250 round trips a year, he would spend $20 a year extra for shoes. If he used the bus to get to work, the daily fare would be 50 cents. A railroad commutation ticket would cost $20 a month, commuting by taxi would cost $1.50 a day, and driving a car to work would involve operating and parking costs of $1.75 a day.

These estimates probably are conservative. In some cities you would be hard-pressed to hold your commuting costs to those figures, particularly if you live in a remote suburb and travel daily to a downtown working place.

The distance you travel, of course, will be a big factor in determining your expense, no matter which form of transportation you choose. Mileage is especially important if you drive. If yours is a one-car family and you use that family car to get to work, operating and maintenance costs will be on the order of 4 cents a mile. But if you use a second car, owned primarily for commuting duty, depreciation, taxes and insurance must be added to your commuting bill, and the resulting per-mile expense may be two to three times greater. Parking also is highly variable. In some cities, a day's parking by itself comes close to $1.75, the figure Mr. Wittausch uses for both operation and parking.

Accepting the validity of his estimates as indicators of reasonable minimums, however, the variable costs of commuting for the Chicago family work out like this on an annual basis:

TABLE 1

by foot	$20
by bus	$125
by train	$240
by taxi	$375
by car	$438

But that's only the obvious part of the bill. Another portion of the expense is indirect. It shows up in a place where you might not expect to find it—on the annual real estate tax bill. And this portion of your commuting expense is a fixed charge, the same no matter which form of transportation you use.

Part of your real property tax bill is a commuting expense because some of the tax goes to build and maintain local transportation facilities, mainly streets. The share used for this purpose actually is your payment for the privilege of having unlimited private access to the public streets. In a sense, this charge is much like the fixed monthly base rate in your telephone and electricity bills. The base rate is not a charge for actual use of those services but a charge for access to them.

So it is only realistic to add this indirect, fixed expense into your commutation bill. In the Chicago example, Mr. Wittausch assumes that 5% of the typical family's $8,000 annual income goes to local taxes and that one-fifth of that sum is used to provide and maintain transportation facilities. Thus he allocates $80 a year as the fixed expense of commuting.

Adding $80 to the variable costs, how much does the typical Chicagoan spend a year on getting to work, and what share of his income does it take? This table tells the story.

TABLE 2

	variable expense	fixed expense	total expense	% of $8,000 income
by foot	$ 20	$80	$100	1.3%
by bus	125	80	205	2.6%
by rail	240	80	320	4.0%
by taxi	375	80	455	5.7%
by car	438	80	518	6.5%

As you can see, the choice of a means of transportation can make a big difference in this family's spending pattern. Commuting by car is more than five times as costly as walking to work, two and a half times as costly as traveling by bus. And the savings that can be realized by choosing the least expensive means rather than the most expensive means, $418, is not to be sneezed at. As Mr. Wittausch points out, that sum is as much if not more than most Chicago families manage to add to their savings in any one year.

You can get some idea of the impact of these commuting expenses on other incomes from Table 3. While these figures are generally representative for families in the lower income brackets, they understate the costs incurred by families in the higher brackets, who undoubtedly pay more

TABLE 3

THE LESS YOU MAKE, THE BIGGER THE BITE

The lower your income, the higher your commuting costs are per-centagewise. The slice may be as little as 0.5% of your annual income or it may be close to 9% of it, or even more. These figures—explained in the accompanying article—show how the load can vary.

Annual Commuting Expense in Dollars and Percent of Income					
your income	by foot ($100)	by bus ($205)	by train ($320)	by taxi ($455)	by car ($518)
$ 6,000	1.67%	3.42%	5.33%	7.58%	8.63%
$ 8,000	1.25%	2.56%	4.00%	5.67%	6.48%
$10,000	1.00%	2.05%	3.20%	4.55%	5.18%
$12,000	.83%	1.71%	2.67%	3.79%	4.32%
$14,000	.71%	1.46%	2.29%	3.25%	3.70%
$16,000	.63%	1.28%	2.00%	2.84%	3.24%
$18,000	.56%	1.14%	1.78%	2.53%	2.88%
$20,000	.50%	1.03%	1.60%	2.28%	2.59%

Note that the $6,000 man can give himself a $418 raise (nearly 7%) by giving up driving and walking to work. Or he can save $313 (5.22%) by taking the bus.

The $20,000 man can make the same dollar savings, but they amount to only 2.09% of his income when he walks, 1.57% when he switches to the bus.

in fixed costs through the higher taxes on more valuable homes. A family whose real property tax bill was greater than $400 would have a higher commuting expense than this table shows.

LOCATION MAKES A DIFFERENCE

SINCE it is cheaper to get to work from some places than from others, you actually determine the range of commutation costs you must pay when you choose a home. This fact suggests another way to look at the price of getting to work: Consider it part of your investment in a house.

Suppose that you are shopping for a new home and have found two good possibilities in different neighborhoods. As far as the houses themselves are concerned, one is as suitable and as attractive as the other. And there is no difference in price. Each house sells for $20,000.

But there is a difference in the cost of getting to work from the two locations. From one house, the bus fare is 20 cents each way, 40 cents for the daily round trip. The other house is in another zone and the fare is

40 cents each way, 80 cents for the round trip. How important is this difference in the investment required to buy each house?

The difference may be more substantial than the difference between 40 cents and 80 cents would lead you to suspect. Remember that every additional dollar of daily transportation expense because of location takes $250 per year from your family's budget. That sum is the equivalent of 5% interest on $5,000. So the net effect of the additional commuting expense is the same as adding $5,000 to the price of the house.

Apply that principle to the two $20,000 houses you are considering for purchase and see what happens. In the case of the house in the cheaper fare zone, the 40-cent daily cost would be an annual expense of $100, adding $2,000 to the capital cost of purchasing the house, with commuting costs representing 9.1% of the carrying charge. For the house in the more expensive fare zone, the 80-cent daily cost would be an annual expense of $200, adding $4,000 to the capital cost of the home, with commuting costs accounting for 16.7% of the carrying charge.

All other considerations being equal, then, you would be wise to choose the home in the lower fare zone, not because an extra 40 cents a day will cripple you financially but because one home represents an investment of $22,000 while the other represents an investment of $24,000.

Look at Table 4 and you can see how different commuting costs add to the investment requirements of homes of different prices.

TABLE 4

WHAT COMMUTING COSTS ADD TO THE PRICE OF YOUR HOUSE

If your daily transportation expense totals	$ .40	$ .80	$1.20	$1.60	$2.00
a $15,000 house represents an investment of	$17,000	$19,000	$21,000	$23,000	$25,000
a $20,000 house represents an investment of	$22,000	$24,000	$26,000	$28,000	$30,000
a $25,000 house represents an investment of	$27,000	$29,000	$31,000	$33,000	$35,000
a $30,000 house represents an investment of	$32,000	$34,000	$36,000	$38,000	$40,000
a $35,000 house represents an investment of	$37,000	$39,000	$41,000	$43,000	$45,000

AND WHAT OF TOMORROW?

PROBABLY not many families consciously translate their commuting costs into investment terms. Yet they do put a price tag on the time and space that separates their homes from their jobs. A Long Island homebuilder once demonstrated this by offering the same seven-room ranch house at four locations of varying distances from downtown New York. Those at the close-in location outsold those farthest out six to one, despite the fact that they cost $800 to $1,800 more.

This is common sense, the kind of common sense that causes revolutions. When enough of your friends and neighbors get to making dollar-based decisions on where they will live, the shape of American cities may change. Some experts think that the day is coming when the time spent commuting from the most distant suburbs will cancel out the value of making the trip. At that point, the spread of the suburbs will come to a halt. Instead of growing horizontally, as they have for decades, our cities will start growing vertically.

That day is not yet in sight, though. Today's commuters do not show much inclination to adopt the most economical ways of getting back and forth, much less to give up the joys and trials of suburban living in favor of a return to the city.

The New Haven Railroad, for instance, has calculated that driving a Chevrolet daily from Mamaroneck, N.Y. to Grand Central Terminal costs $1,500 a year, even when the car is depreciated over five years and allowance is made for 5,000 miles a year of noncommuter travel. The New Haven offers the same transportation for $262.80 a year. Yet thousands of commuters persist in paying a tab that represents $1,800 to $2,000 of their before-tax income while the New Haven can't fill its trains.

The extent of our commitment to travel by car is nothing short of staggering. As Wilfred Owen of the Brookings Institution has pointed out in *Cities in the Motor Age,* 11 cents of every dollar spent by consumers for goods and services is spent for transportation and 10 of those 11 cents go for the automobile. All together, we spend approximately 27 billion dollars on cars. We spend more for auto transportation than we spend on doctors, religion, charities, telephones, radio, television, furniture, electricity, gas, books, magazines and newspapers put together.

As for rail travel—well, we spend more on flowers, seeds and potted plants than we do on that.

This preference for commuting by car puts a drain not only on the individual families involved but on the entire community, as the calculations shown in Table 5 illustrate.

Although getting people to go to work by other means would represent savings for all concerned, the trend is toward more and more car travel, with the attendant increasing congestion and growing competition for places to park. So more expressways and more parking facilities are built all the time. Another 75,000 commuters from New Jersey into New York City, for example, would call for ten more tunnels under the Hudson and

TABLE 5

HOW TO CUT THE COST OF GETTING TO WORK

Not every commuter will elect to get to work by the same means. The particular combination of choices the people of any community make will determine how much of the city's wealth goes into mere getting back and forth.

Here, for illustration, are three combinations of commuting choices that might be chosen by Chicago's 2,000,000 families and the annual cost of each combination. Note that converting two out of three of the car riders in combination A to bus and train travel as in combination C would reduce Chicagoans' commuting bill by nearly 25% and free $205,000,000 for other kinds of spending.

method of travel	COMBINATION A number using	yearly cost	COMBINATION B number using	yearly cost	COMBINATION C number using	yearly cost
foot	10%	$ 20,000,000	10%	$ 20,000,000	10%	$ 20,000,000
bus	10%	41,000,000	20%	82,000,000	30%	123,000,000
rail	10%	64,000,000	20%	128,000,000	30%	192,000,000
taxi	10%	91,000,000	10%	91,000,000	10%	91,000,000
car	60%	622,000,000	40%	414,000,000	20%	207,000,000
total cost		$838,000,000		$735,000,000		$633,000,000

All tables are based on data from First Federal Savings and Loan Association of Chicago.

20 more lanes of expressway, not to mention 250 acres of parking in the city. Furthermore, acquiring land for new expressways and interchanges removes it from the tax rolls, so that the community's sources of revenue shrink even as it takes on the added construction and maintenance costs.

The auto's ravenous appetite for urban space, according to some authorities, could reach the point where downtown would consist of nothing but expressways and parking garages. Then, of course, there would be no point at all in getting there.

Before that nightmare comes to pass, we'll probably be obliged to get out of our cars and to commute by rapid transit. The current prize exhibit of what this can accomplish is Chicago's Congress Street Expressway, which has rapid transit tracks down the center of the right of way. One lane of transit track carries more than one and a half times as many people as an automobile lane.

The switch to mass transit won't be cheap, however. The system proposed for San Francisco would cost over one billion dollars, the one proposed for Washington would cost half a billion. So someday your cost of commuting may have to include a healthy charge for subsidizing the transit system you ride.

In a way, the overcharge will be a contribution toward keeping alive the city that gives you a living. Even so, your total bill may not be much more than you pay right now when you figure all the costs. And if you get a fast, comfortable ride to work into the bargain, won't it be worth the price?

Highways and Traffic in Canada

IT IS NO SECRET that the world was never really ready for the onslaught of the automobile and that consequently it has been fighting a purely defensive action against the inroads of that remarkably useful mechanical contrivance for almost seventy years. Victory, sadly enough, has so far eluded us and appears nowhere in sight here in the United States.

In the essay that follows, citizens of the U. S. may draw whatever comfort is possible from knowing they are not alone in the battle to meet the challenge of the automobile. In this reading, the Canadian experience is succinctly sketched; with only a few exceptions, the story is like our own.

On both sides of the border there are great unanswered problems relating to safety, traffic control, and building roads quickly enough and in large enough quantities to meet the demand. Not surprisingly, most of these problems come to focus in urban areas. It is obvious that there are no easy answers to the challenge presented by the automobile, whether one is in Canada, the U. S., or any other country. Whatever may be done to make living in the motor age easier and more felicitous, the cost will be high in money, time, and effort. This is not necessarily a cheerless proposition. Along with the other problems of an increasingly urbanized and congested world, meeting the problems of the automobile represents a great and significant social cause which may help to bring out the best in us.

WE HAVE COME TO ACCEPT ROAD TRAFFIC as a normal condition of our way of life, but we keep running into totally unexpected experiences with it every new year.

There are millions of complicated vehicles proceeding in all directions under the impulse of up to three hundred horsepower. They can travel

"Our Highways and Our Traffic," *The Royal Bank of Canada Monthly Letter,* January 1965.

at a hundred miles an hour, but are lucky if they average forty. They run on roads that are never adequate to accommodate them but which cost as much as waging a war.

The car itself is a blessing, not an evil. It is among the most valuable tools of living that man has invented. It has proven itself an adaptable and efficient servant in the movement of goods and people. The highways on which the cars run are not unproductive. They have immensely increased the total stock of land in active use by bringing it within reach of people.

Submissions to the Royal Commission on Canada's Economic Prospects estimated that by 1975 three out of every four Canadians will live in a city, that every second Canadian will drive a motor car, and that seventy per cent of all travel will be on city streets. Even today, with six million motor vehicles registered in Canada, and a ratio of 4.1 persons per car, practically the only persons who walk any distance regularly are those who seek exercise.

But, as Hon. Dr. F. W. Rowe said in his presidential review of the work of the Canadian Good Roads Association at the jubilee convention: "We may well have reached the point where the benevolence of the automobile is being nullified by its malevolence."

CANADA'S HIGHWAYS

THE story of the development of roads in Canada is told in detail in a book published in 1954 by the Department of Citizenship and Immigration, called *Our Transportation Services.*

The first graded road in Canada was built in 1606 under the direction of Champlain. It was a military road, ten or twelve miles long, through Annapolis County in Nova Scotia. The first road in New France was built by De Courcelles in 1665 from Chambly to Montreal. By the summer of 1735 a carriage could be driven between Montreal and Quebec in four and a half days.

An Act of the first Parliament of Upper Canada in 1793 placed all roads in what is now Ontario under the supervision of overseers who were called pathmasters. The Act also required everyone to work from three to twelve days on the roads using his own tools. The first government appropriation for roads in the province was made in 1804, amounting to £1,000.

There was a revolutionary change in road building in 1835, when the first plank road in North America was built east of Toronto. Two years later the highway from Kingston to Napanee was macadamized.

The Red River cart, a small low conveyance with solid wheels sawed from the ends of trees whose diameter was about three feet, carried the road problem into the prairies. Highway building reached the Pacific when gold was discovered in the Cariboo in 1860, and the Cariboo Road, the "Great North Road," was constructed under supervision of the Royal Engineers.

It is true that up until the beginning of the nineteenth century the speed of travel was no better than that of the ancients, a horse pace. But when improvements started, they came fast. Labert St. Clair points out in his book *Transportation* that every major improvement existing today except the airplane was perfected during the life of Queen Victoria, from 1819 to 1901, and she missed seeing the airplane by only two years.

THEN CAME THE AUTOMOBILE

THE first complete and workable gasoline-propelled car was made by Karl Benz of Germany, and display of a Benz car at the Chicago World's Fair in 1893 was responsible for the start of the automobile manufacturing business in the United States.

By 1907 there were 2,131 motor vehicles registered in six provinces of Canada: Nova Scotia 63; Quebec 254; Ontario 1,530; Saskatchewan 54; Alberta 55, and British Columbia 175. The other provinces had none registered, and Prince Edward Island had prohibited them altogether.

Ontario was the first province to take its highway responsibilities seriously. It passed the Highway Improvement Act in 1901, providing a subsidy of a million dollars a year. Roadway construction has never caught up with the demand. The first modern highway of its kind in Canada, the Queen Elizabeth Highway from Toronto to Hamilton and Niagara Falls, was opened by the Queen in 1939, the year in which Germany had completed 1,900 miles of superhighway, with its twin three-lane strips separated by a hedged and grassed parkway 16 feet wide.

Writhing across Canada, according to the Dominion Bureau of Statistics, are 467,100 miles of roads and streets. They are of every known method of construction, of varying widths, and of many quality standards. The pattern has developed from local needs, handicapped by lack of interest, lack of knowledge, lack of funds, and lack of unity of understanding between the authorities whose areas adjoin. Piecemeal development froze the old pattern of cattle trails and streets.

Today, there are about six million vehicles on these painfully inadequate roads and streets. Farms alone, in the vicinity of which the poorest roads are found, have 360,000 passenger cars and 302,000 trucks.

Canada is the only country with a large car population that has no federal highway authority to plan highways, give advice on standards, and correlate the provincial highway building activities. Indeed, within the provinces responsibility is divided among cities and other municipalities and counties. These small units find the burden heavy, even with provincial assistance, and the problem of co-ordinating their city-to-city or regional exigencies with the all-Canada view too much for them.

In 1961 the expenditures by all levels of government on highways and urban streets amounted to $989 million, a per capita outlay of $54. In the same year the revenue from motor vehicle registrations, motor fuel taxes, and other related charges was $624,291,100.

Many people are saying that a revamping is needed of highway financing as part of the general revision of our highway outlook. The individual vehicle owner is paying by way of license plates, gasoline taxes, drivers' licenses, insurance, and tolls on certain roads and bridges. Through municipal taxes he pays his share of the police force needed to keep transportation going, the construction and operating cost of signalling systems and the paved streets on which the automobiles move and park.

Can these taxes pay for the right kind of highways and streets? Can individual provinces and municipalities, with their great differences in natural and developed wealth, maintain equally the types and qualities of highways needed?

Pay-as-you-go highways may help to solve the problem of rapid transit for through or long-haul traffic, but most of Canada's traffic is congested around cities.

R. A. Draper, assistant managing director of the Canadian Good Roads Association, points out that for the first time in its history Ontario spent more in 1963 on urban than on rural roads.

CITY TRAFFIC

WHATEVER highway design is decided upon must be interlocked with the street programme in the big cities. As experience has shown in Toronto and Montreal, highways near cities become merely high speed extensions of city streets, and are used by thousands of commuters for a purpose nobody intended. *Imperial Oil Review* commented dryly: "When the Russian moon rocket circled its target one morning, stalled commuters were backed up as usual for half a mile at the intersection of highways 401 and 11 outside Toronto. It was painfully evident that while the world was well into the Space Age, this six-year-old section of highway 401 at least had never caught up with the Automobile Age."

Some students of the situation, believing that "traffic" has nothing to do with congestion but means the free movement of people and goods, maintain that any attempt to solve the urban problem by the private car alone is likely to be self-defeating.

Private cars and public transit systems are not competitive but complementary. The major role of public vehicles like buses, trains and the underground trains, is to handle commuter trips to and from downtown business districts along a few main travel corridors. When the city of Washington looked into the matter in 1960 the official report said:

Any attempt to meet transport needs by highways and private automobiles alone will wreck the city—it will demolish residential neighbourhoods, violate parks and playgrounds, desecrate the monumental parts of the nation's capital, and remove much valuable property from the tax rolls.

It has been pointed out that a bus route, subway system or commuter train service can carry as many passengers per day on its right-of-way as a ten-, twenty- or thirty-lane boulevard. This theory takes for granted that provision of convenient, speedy and competitively-priced public transportation will remove motorists from the roads. It is well known that when emergencies arise, such as severe weather conditions or motor trouble, or when parking fees rise too high, many drivers turn gratefully to mass transport.

Meanwhile, the war-time question "Is this trip necessary?" becomes for city motorists "Is this trip worth the travel headache it is going to give me?"

The core of a city attracts magnetically with its jobs and its stores. At the time of the latest census, seventy per cent of all Canadians were living in villages, towns and cities with more than 1,000 population. The Gordon Commission predicted that by 1980 there may be eighty per cent of our people living in urban centres.

This problem of traffic in cities has been with mankind for a long time. Hadrian, who was Roman emperor from 117 to 138, boasted:

I reduced the insolent crowd of carriages which cumber our streets, for this luxury of speed destroys its own aim; a pedestrian makes more headway than a hundred conveyances jammed end to end along the twists and turns of the Sacred Way.

Long before horseless carriages arrived on the scene, streets in many of our cities were nightmares of traffic confusion. The cause of today's traffic jams is not the automobile but our failure over centuries to provide adequate street and highway facilities to keep up with the developing means of transportation. Today, we are face-to-face with the realization of a force that is hostile to the flourishing of cities as they are presently laid out. Victor Gruen said pungently in the Summer 1964 issue of *Horizon:* "If we continue full speed ahead on the dead-end road of over-motorization we will lose our cities after killing their hearts."

SAVING OUR CITIES

THE first principle of a modern plan for traffic is to separate the long distance or through traffic from local traffic. The American Automobile Association has said that from one-half to three-quarters of the automobiles in the downtown area have destinations elsewhere and are simply passing through because no convenient alternate route exists. It is short-sighted of business firms to insist upon having through arteries pass their doors. Through traffic discourages local and nearby people from driving downtown to shop.

There needs to be enlargement of the capacity of the city arteries themselves. Main streets should accommodate four streams of traffic excluding curbside parking, with as few intersections as possible. Residential streets should be designed for the slow traffic of vehicles approaching buildings on them. They should be designed to discourage through traffic and should never be used, as is now commonplace in the panic to relieve immediate congestion, as short cuts from artery to artery.

What would be the effect of a correlated system of urban freeways and streets? Properly planned, it could make the urban environment more attractive, strengthen the downtown centre, widen the range of employment opportunities for urban residents, assist in stabilizing and guiding land-use patterns, and improve regional accessibilty for the movement of people and goods in both peak and off-peak travel hours.

Such planning, looking far ahead and not merely to next year's tourist traffic, seems to be the only way out of the traffic jam. It will no longer serve to apply the Emperor Hadrian's cure: to reduce "the insolent crowd of carriages." As a speaker on a TV programme said: "All efforts to separate machines from man are doomed to failure, because deep in human nature there is the irresistible urge to drive a car, and to drive it right to the door of the building for which he aims."

Many schemes are being tried to accommodate the driver who can't quite make it to the door, but can get within easy walking distance of it. Large parking areas are needed in business sections to eliminate all curbside parking, even if the heart of the city comes to present an aerial view similar to that of a bombed-out European city after the Second World War.

This can be accomplished in part by taking over dilapidated buildings of no historic or aesthetic value and razing them. Some cities are establishing parking places on the outskirts of the business section and running buses from there to downtown. Several cities on this continent have constructed huge underground parking garages, with public parks on the roofs. Others require that all new downtown buildings include parking space in basements. The traffic-stopping practice of daytime truck deliveries has been forbidden by some planners, while others have provided conveniently-placed spaces for taxis and have forbidden cruising. Newly developed sectors might be required to provide alleys for delivery of goods and for the collection of garbage.

TRAFFIC CONTROL

AUTOMATED highways and automated automobiles are on the drawing-boards. A Cape Town man, Stanley W. Deane, has invented an apparatus which, when set over a stretch of road, automatically reduces the gasoline flow of every car so as to cut the car's speed to that required, say twenty miles per hour. But it is much too early to predict that motorists will soon switch to automatic controls upon entering certain freeways. Traffic must still be controlled by signs and signals, and by the men at the wheels of cars and trucks.

Much of our national travel time is spent in negotiating a myriad of traffic lights, reading hundreds of traffic-control signs, and watching alertly for often obscure direction signs. Every province, city and county has its idiosyncracies.

It is becoming generally recognized that there is no room for decoration or irrelevant information on road signs. First of all the driver must notice the sign, then he has to read it, then he has to act on it. If, while travelling at the rate of sixty miles an hour he takes his eyes off the road for just three-tenths of a second to learn that the population of the village he is approaching is 1,255, he has covered nearly thirty feet of highway without seeing it.

The Committee on Uniform Traffic Control Devices for Canada set forth the purpose succintly: "The main purpose of highway traffic signs is to aid in the safe and orderly movement of traffic." Warning signs are needed to alert drivers to hazardous conditions either on or adjacent to the road. Guide signs are primarily to direct through traffic. Information signs tell about special regulations which apply only at specific places or at specific times. Pedestrian signs are for the protection of people on foot.

Because of the increasing range of traffic circulation it is of great importance that there be national standardization of these signs. Representatives of all the provinces and eleven major cities approved a manual in 1959 designed to standardize traffic signals and signs and pavement markings to make them the same all over Canada. The project was sponsored jointly by the Canadian Good Roads Association, the champion of good roads in Canada for the past fifty years, and the Canadian Section of the Institute of Traffic Engineers.

The manual, which has more than three hundred illustrations of signs and symbols, recognises that Quebec, because of its bilingual character, has special problems. That province has found it of considerable advantage to adapt international signs which speak mostly through pictures, a universal language.

Pavement and curb markings suffer under the disadvantage of being hidden by snow, but when they are visible they are of help in guiding traffic and preventing accidents. Line markings to delineate the pavement edge, or, in instances where the shoulder is paved, to separate the shoulder from the travelled line, have been found of value. One advantage is that when travelling at night the motorist tends to keep over to the right, thus avoiding the danger of sideswipe collisions. In Ohio, the placing of edge-lines on test sections of two-line rural roads reduced accidents by nineteen per cent and deaths by thirty-seven per cent; in Kansas, accidents were reduced twenty per cent and fatalities fifty-nine per cent.

SAFETY

LIFE cannot be freed from all danger. There would be some highway deaths even if everybody obeyed the law, observed the warning signs, and drove carefully. "But," said the *Montreal Star* in a survey a few years ago, "—this is the terrifying thing about the ten-month record now published —in 15,998 reported accidents out of 19,946 a traffic violation of some kind was a contributory cause."

The solution is education of drivers to the rules of sane and safe driving. They cannot depend upon the car, with all its built-in safety devices. Someone said sagely: "There were just as many careless drivers forty years ago, but the horse had more sense."

Few drivers pause to think how casual is their education in driving a car compared with the requirements in some other countries. To pass the Soviet driving test you have to be approved by a panel of physicians, including an eye specialist, a cardiologist, and one who tests reflexes. You have to work out traffic problems with model cars. You have to prove that you can take apart and mount an engine. All of this is in addition to showing that you can start and stop the engine, back into an alley, park without hitting cars fore and aft, and that you have read the local by-laws.

Canada is paying an annual toll of $300 million in damage, 3,000 deaths, and more than 60,000 injured because drivers out-drive their eyes, take their eyes off the road, fail to keep their cars in fit condition, do not pay attention to safety signs, drive on rough roads as if they were on pavement, keep up a fast pace on newly-wet highways, stop suddenly, cross railway lines bumper to bumper, turn without warning, neglect thinking ahead so as to be prepared, and to prepare others, for a change of position or direction.

There are, roughly, five approaches to the problem of reducing highway deaths: improve the highways, educate adults, educate juveniles, apply the law, improve the cars. Many organizations are attacking on all these fronts.

There is also the pedestrian to be thought of, although it might not be believed by anyone reading the planning report for the rebuilding of downtown Los Angeles: "The pedestrian remains as the largest single obstacle to free traffic movement."

Some things can be corrected when pampering of the violator, whether motorist or pedestrian, ceases. If signals and regulations are to be useful they must be strictly observed, but that the law is deliberately and wantonly disobeyed is apparent to the most casual observer.

The Future

THE state of modern traffic, and the certainty that it will expand, obviously call for larger, more forward-looking study on all levels of government. Painstaking research, imaginative thought, and strategic planning are required, and these must be accompanied by efficiently-directed hard work. The temptation to settle for second-best or temporary relief measures is strong, but should be restricted.

Our highways are not merely driveways for vacations, but an economic force of great importance. In many areas of Canada, economic progress depends on adequate roads. Trucking is big business: it has stimulated trade, given quick and expeditious service to suburban areas, assisted in the decentralization of industry, and contributed to the building up of attractive small communities.

For as far as we can see with certainty into the future we have a society that is based on the wheel. A city roads commissioner told a Toronto audience last year his vision of people travelling in rocket containers the size of telephone booths, dialling their destination and relaxing while the controlling computer took over direction and speed. But we must live through the intervening years by making sane and civilized use of motor vehicles.

There is a feeling of urgency about starting at once to make the best of our remaining time on wheels. If we wait until we see the flames instead of accepting the testimony of the smoke, what will the loss be?

People sometimes are heard to say that there are no great causes left. But here is a great cause waiting for its champions.

CHAPTER 3

The Problem of Peak-Hour Demand

URBAN TRANSPORT IS FACED WITH DIFFICULT PROBLEMS springing in large part from some of the customs and institutions of our society. One of the most difficult problems is the factor of largely standardized working hours, and its corollary, sharply peaked demand. The instance of this peak demand associated with the trip to and from work is the one that occasions the most urban transportation difficulties.

Since the downtown section of most cities is still the largest single concentration of workers in a metropolitan area, it is in the downtown area itself—and in the major transport arteries leading to and from this core—that most congestion in the morning and evening rush hours takes place. But of course the downtown no longer has a monopoly of journey-to-work congestion; this is a problem faced by any place where workers are concentrated in a metropolitan area.

Since transport in a free society must gear itself to the travel demands of the public, urban transportation of all types must be carried on under very trying conditions. The most visible effect of peaked demand is of course traffic congestion: the streets are jammed with automobiles, long lines of cars inch their way onto already crowded express highways, buses and trains are jammed to the doors.

Not quite so visible as the actual physical fact of congestion, the tremendous demand placed on all types of transport facilities for only about four hours each working day is a very expensive business. It is perhaps most obviously expensive to those who participate in it; the physical and mental wear and tear of congestion is one of the more exquisite forms of torture in modern life. For the companies concerned, much of the cost of providing and operating urban transport facilities is in large part due to the need of meeting the heavy twice-a-day burden of the work journey.

The transport facilities and service which must be provided during peaks typically far exceed what is necessary at other times. For instance, urban arterial highways require extra lanes to cope with peak traffic. Such lanes would not be needed if traffic moved in a more regular pattern throughout the day.

The problem is particularly troublesome and expensive for mass transport agencies. Public transportation firms with fixed facilities, such as rapid transit or commuter railway lines, require a physical plant expansive enough to meet peak demand. Moreover, the mass transport firm must invest in sufficient equipment at least to attempt to handle peak demand, plus extra facilities to store and maintain that equipment. It is not surprising that much of the financial difficulty of public transport firms arises from the fact that so much of the plant and equipment must stand idle so much of the time. A new air-conditioned bus—depending on its size—costs approximately $25,000 to $35,000; a new rapid transit car or commuter railway coach may cost in excess of $100,000. When such expensive hardware is used only about twenty hours a week, it is very difficult for a privately owned firm to justify the investment or, indeed, to operate at a profit.

Labor is another expensive problem. Union contracts usually call for a full day's pay whenever an employee is called to duty. In off-peak hours it is often almost impossible to utilize fully the manpower needed to handle rush hour traffic. As a result, men are frequently paid for hours they do not work.

The inability to utilize facilities, equipment, and manpower more fully is further aggravated by the decline of off-peak traffic. Not only has daytime traffic declined, but evening and weekend travel to the urban core for entertainment or recreation has fallen perceptibly in the last twenty years. Television tends to keep people at home. The pattern of increased suburban living has acted to concentrate off-peak travel in suburban locations, encouraging a type of traffic that is especially prone to the use of the private automobile.

Our lives revolve around institutionalized work hours. Making changes in the pattern is bound to be a most difficult, if not impossible, project.

The Problem of the Peak, with Special Reference to Road Passenger Transport

GILBERT PONSONBY

PEAK DEMAND IS A BURDEN to both our highway and our public transport agencies. It is especially troublesome to private-enterprise public trans-

"The Problem of the Peak, with Special Reference to Road Passenger Transport," *The Economic Journal*, March 1958.

portation firms (or, as is often the case in Great Britain, publicly owned firms with a mandate to operate at least at a break-even point, if not at a small surplus) because—unlike highway departments—such operations must deal with such things as business revenues and costs.

Gilbert Ponsonby of the London School of Economics writes of the problems faced today by transport firms caught in the squeeze between costs and revenues as a result of the peaking of traffic. This piece should be read carefully by those who wonder why the local bus company went bankrupt when the vehicles were so crowded at 5:15 in the afternoon.

ALTHOUGH THE PROBLEM OF THE PEAK is common to most branches of transport, it is more especially associated in the public mind with suburban passenger transport, and it is with that aspect of the problem that this article is mainly concerned. In so far as it is a "problem" at all, it is overwhelmingly an economic one. By this I mean there are seldom any technical difficulties in the way of relieving conditions of serious congestion. Supply the technicians with sufficient land, labour, capital and materials, and they would be only too glad to provide all the "capacity" we ask for, whether in the form of additional track capacity or vehicles. But land, labour, capital and materials are relatively scarce and therefore expensive, and are likely to remain so for some time to come. The "problem" therefore is to decide, first, how far we should go by way of using these valuable resources in order to meet peak demands for transport services, and second, in what form and at what prices such services should be provided.

I

BEFORE coming to these problems let us examine precisely why it is so expensive to provide "adequate" passenger-carrying facilities when demand is heavy yet transient. Quite apart from the fact that the resources required may be expensive in themselves, the fundamental cause of high average costs is the fact that whereas in the provision of these facilities a number of costs must be incurred and commitments entered into, the magnitude of which depends essentially upon the capacity for which provision is to be made, the opportunities for recovering sufficient revenue to cover such capacity costs and commitments are confined to a very short period of time. Hence, if the services are to pay their way, there must inevitably be either acute congestion in the vehicles themselves (earning much per vehicle-mile), or queues (enforced staggering), or high fares, or a mixture of them all. To provide extra bus services, for example, at the peak along a particular route may require the provision of extra buses, garage accommodation, drivers and conductors, and all the other requirements of providing additional capacity. Assuming these extra costs must be covered by revenues earned, the latter must be sufficient to cover not only those variable costs of operation which depend on vehicle-miles worked, such as petrol, oil, and some wear and tear, but also such time or capacity costs as interest and depreciation on the capital expenditure involved, rent and rates on extra garaging accommodation, vehicle licenses and insurance, and the full costs of employing additional drivers and conductors. The crux of the matter being that in so far as the demand for the services to be provided is confined to a very brief duration, virtually all the revenue required to meet both time and variable costs may have to be earned during that short time. In short, the opportunities of spreading the burden of time or capacity costs between a large number of hours, passengers, or vehicle-miles are strictly limited. To put it another way, *it is not possible to achieve the economies associated with the intensive utilisation of capital or labour,* with the result that average costs and therefore average earnings per vehicle- or passenger-mile must of necessity be high. An additional cause of high costs per passenger-mile is the serious lack of "balance" of traffic which often accompanies the provision of daily suburban transport services for passengers travelling to and from their work.[1] In cases where garages are at the centre of the city, there is the relatively empty journey out into the suburbs to bring the workers in. Where garages are in the vicinity of the dormitory areas, there is the relatively empty journey back. Thus, average loadings tend to be reduced and the need for high average earnings per seat-mile occupied correspondingly urgent.

An example of such a combination of circumstances arises when a Local Authority builds a housing estate some miles out from a big centre of employment to which tenants must travel daily to work. For in this case the commuters in question tend to be all of the same income group and therefore to start work at about the same time. In addition, if, as has normally been the case, they belong to lower-income groups, there is little surplus purchasing power available to permit much off-peak pleasure or shopping travel on the part of those who don't actually go out to work themselves; the more adequate the shopping facilities provided locally, the less the likelihood of there being profitable off-peak traffic. Finally, if the area of the housing estate is designated "residential," there is no backward or "return load" traffic made up of those coming into the area for employment. In these circumstances, so different from those which obtain in Central London for example, it would seem that, in the absence of subsidy, either queues must be long and passengers thereby forced to spread themselves over a longer period than their first preference, or costs and fares per passenger-mile are bound to be at a high level.

II

As regards the financial limits within which the operator must keep, *it will be assumed throughout that any service provided has got to pay its way*. Thus, although the buses in question may be earning very different amounts at different times of the day, total and average earnings have got to cover total and average costs. But it will also be assumed that the operator does not want to do more than this. Thus, should he find himself earning more than what it costs to provide the service as a whole, then he will either provide additional services at the peak, or reduce fares, or both. Similarly, if costs are not being covered, then some adjustments in service or fares will be made. Finally, unless otherwise stated, it will also be assumed that there is only one operator responsible for working the route, who, whilst enjoying some measure of monopoly, is not interested in earning more than whatever his total costs (including interest on capital) amount to.

III

LET us start by considering a case in which there is a somewhat exclusive demand for passenger services between 7.30 a.m. and 9.30 a.m. in the morning and again between 4.30 p.m. and 6.30 p.m. in the afternoon. It is "exclusive" in the sense that there is virtually no demand for the services outside those hours, whatever inducements (say, by way of lower fares) are offered to encourage such traffic. In this case, the total cost of providing the whole service has got to be met from the revenues earned in the 4 hours when there is this sharp demand. This simple case is illustrated in Fig. 1, which shows what are the costs and earnings of an individual bus (one of several) serving the route in question. Along AB is measured and marked a period of 10 hours from 4 a.m. to 2 p.m. Given a uniform m.p.h., A to B can also be taken as measuring *potential* vehicle-miles operated. (Similar conditions are assumed to exist during an afternoon peak from 4.30 p.m. to 6.30 p.m.)

Up the vertical scale AC is measured both the level of costs incurred and revenue earned per vehicle-mile. The level of actual earnings is represented by the line $RPTP_1S$. As regards costs, running costs per vehicle-mile, *i.e.*, those costs which vary directly with vehicle-miles operated, such as fuel, lubricants, tyre-wear, and some maintenance and depreciation (that due to wear and tear) are taken as being 1s. The maximum amount that can be earned per vehicle-mile at any one time is assumed to be approximately 7s. 6d., that is 60 passengers travelling at 1½d. per mile. In this first case (Fig. 1) that sum is being earned during much of the peak period between 7.30 a.m. and 9.30 a.m. The bus in question started work or left the garage at 6.30 a.m. Up to 7 a.m. it was running very light from garage towards the district in which the peak demands arise, and was necessarily earning less even than variable costs. (Running to and from garage usually involves some "service" mileage for which earnings are virtually nil.) From 7.0 a.m. to 7.30 a.m. it was starting to gather substantial traffic, and was actually earning more than variable costs. A corresponding decline in traffic took place at the end of the peak between 9.30 a.m. and 10.30 a.m., the pattern of the afternoon peak being roughly similar to that of the morning.

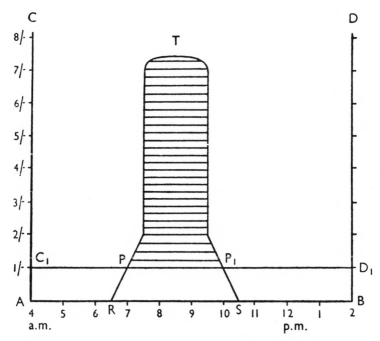

FIGURE 1 *All overheads have to be earned between 7 and 10 a.m. These earnings are represented by the shaded area* PTP_1.

Let us assume that in these circumstances the service as a whole "just pays," but no more. That is, gross revenues are sufficient to cover all the costs necessary to justify the continued operation of the service both in the short and long run. But that, were additional buses put on with a view to relieving that measure of queueing and congestion that in fact existed at the peak periods on this route, the extra gross revenue that would be earned by reason of a somewhat more "adequate" service would definitely *not* cover the extra costs involved. Thus, if the management is under an obligation to make the service pay, however bad congestion may appear to be, no such relief could be given to the situation. The public is asked to grin and bear it! Short of running the services at a loss (which we have ruled out), maybe that is the price that must be paid for the provision of services on such a scale yet for so short a time.

But there is one possible course of action which even in such circumstances should not be forgotten. I refer to the possibility of in some way changing the "quality" of the service provided (and of course the price paid for it too), suchwise that the position as described above may be said to become "relieved." Although this question may appear to be somewhat of a digression from the main argument of the article, it seems desirable at this stage to raise the very important question of what is the most appropriate combination of money-price per passenger-mile on the one hand, and the quality or adequacy of service given on the other. For just as adequacy of service can always be increased if there is an assurance that the public is prepared to pay for it, so fares can be reduced or at least "held," so long as quality of service is maintained at a sufficiently restrained or austere level.

IV

It may well be that in the very overcrowded circumstances described above, a 10% rise in fares would have little or no effect on the numbers travelling, so intense is the demand for facilities. Then, if such an increase was imposed without in the first instance adding to the services, the service as a whole would be more than paying its way, and the undertaking would be in a position to increase the adequacy of the services provided at the peak by putting on extra buses till such time as the undertaking is again no more than covering costs. A new equilibrium would have been reached. Fares would be higher, but the adequacy of service provided improved. It is quite possible that this new combination of fare and quality of service would be more in line with what the public most prefers. Should the introduction of the new combination of higher fare with better service, for example, lead to a larger total number of persons using the service than heretofore,[2] *there is a presumption that a more preferred or cheaper (in the broad sense) service had in fact been provided*. There may also be circumstances in which a more austere service (more standing room but less seats) coupled with a low fare-level may similarly prove a more "popular" proposition. Assuming, however, that the undertaking in question has been reasonably correct in assessing the public's preference in this respect—that it has neither provided a too high quality of serving having regard to its great cost nor too low a quality having regard to the physical discomforts involved—the problem of how much capacity to provide and at what price presents no special difficulties.

In so far as there is now a tendency in public policy both to make individual services pay their way and to fix charges more in relation to costs than heretofore, there would seem to be good reasons for charging a higher level of fare in circumstances similar to those described above, where demand was so restricted over time, than where demand is not so restricted.

V

HAVING started by assuming circumstances most inimicable of all for the economic provision of either comfortable or cheap public-transport facilities at peak periods, some modifications will now be introduced. Let us suppose that a demand for services outside the peak period develops. Now any additional *net* revenue[3] earned outside the peak is an additional contribution to the time or capacity costs, which we have assumed have got to be covered by revenues earned from the service as a whole. To the extent, therefore, that additional net revenue can now be earned in the off-peak, to that extent can the peak be relieved of the necessity of carrying the whole burden of the overheads in the shape of discomfort or high fares. Fig 2 illustrates this different set of circumstances.

In contrast to Fig. 1, the public demand for transport, instead of petering out altogether by 10.30 a.m., is well maintained throughout the middle of the day, revenue earned per vehicle-mile at noon being round about 2s., giving a net revenue of 1s. per mile, the assumed level of costs special to off-peak operation being 1s. The amount of "net" revenue now being earned *additional* to that earned in the first instance (Fig. 1) is shaded. Having assumed that in the difficult circumstances illustrated in Fig. 1 the service was neverthelesss just paying its way, it follows that in these new circumstances the service must be more than doing so. The undertaking is now therefore in a position either to add facilities to the peak period, thus reducing over-crowding and the length of waiting queues, or reduce the level of fares, or both. It follows from this that, from the point of view of an individual undertaking's capacity to meet peak demands to the greatest extent possible, no opportunities of earning additional *net* revenue in the off-peak periods should be missed.

This brings us to the important question as to precisely what extent should an undertaking work into the off-peak period, whether we look at it from the point of view of a single operator in search of additional contributions towards his overheads or several competitors all interested in making both ends meet. (The question is really fourfold in that it raises the four separate but similar questions: first, at what time should a service start up in the morning; second, when should it (if at all) close down after the morning peak; third, when should it start up again in the afternoon; and lastly, when should it be withdrawn in the late evening.)

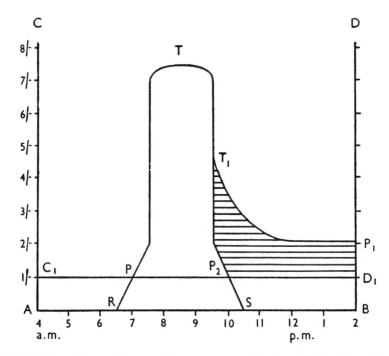

FIGURE 2   *Substantial contributions to overheads, additional to those earned in Fig. 1, are here earned between 9:30 a.m. and 2 p.m. These* additional *net earnings are represented by the shaded area* $T_1P_2D_1P_1$.

The short and simple answer to this question is that so long as revenue is at a sufficiently high level to cover those costs special to the off-peak periods which vary with vehicle-miles worked, in the case under review 1s., then continued operation into the off-peak is justified. But if vehicles are worked into the off-peak periods suchwise that those avoidable costs are not covered, then losses are being incurred. *Hence the importance from a practical point of view, first, of knowing precisely what is the level of an undertaking's cost which vary with vehicle-miles operated—that is, the level of cost that must be exceeded if any net revenue is to be earned in the off-peak; and second, of knowing whether such costs are in fact being covered by revenue earned.* For if mileage is being operated outside the peak, revenue from which does not cover the extra costs incurred, then losses are being incurred and, on our assumptions about overall profitability, additional burdens are being placed on the peak services themselves and those who use them. If alleviating pressure at the peak is our main concern, the broad aim should be to continue operation into the off-peak, so long as revenue exceeds the extra costs of such operations, but no further. Similar considerations should decide the times at which services should start in the early morning and continue into the evening. In every case the criterion should be, does the extra mileage worked bring in revenue at least as much as the extra costs incurred? The term "broad aim" is purposely used, as it is not suggested that in practice an arithmetically accurate adherence to the principle can always be achieved. For example, as already mentioned, there is usually the need to run almost empty to and from garage. Or again, it may be good business to maintain a degree of regularity throughout the middle of the day greater than what a strict adherence to revenue-cost considerations would suggest. It also costs something to withdraw a service for a short time.[4] It is nevertheless true to say that the nearer to the "ideal" any operator can keep, the better position he will be in to provide additional or reasonably adequate facilities at the peak, which is the problem with which we are here concerned. These "ideal" points for starting and stopping are shown as P and P_1 in Fig. 3, which again represents a single peak period.

Along AB is measured time as in Figs. 1 and 2. CD represents the level of costs which vary with vehicle-miles operated. The line $RPTP_1S$ represents the level of revenue per vehicle-mile that can be earned on the route in question at the times stated along AB. It will be seen that operation before 7 a.m. or after 10 a.m. would incur losses (marked in vertical shading), whereas between 7 a.m. and 10 a.m. surpluses are being earned (marked by horizontal shading).

Two further observations seem worth making at this stage. First, although we have assumed the operator in question to have been in a more or less monopolistic position, the proposition in question has equal significance in competitive situations. For in a situation in which there are a number of financially separate operators whose profit margins are small, no *one* operator could afford either to go substantially beyond the points P and P_1 in Fig. 3, and thus incur losses, or to stop working substantially short of them, and thereby forgo opportunities of earning net revenue. In either case he would be putting himself at a financial disadvantage in relation to his competitors. Indeed, one might go so far as to say that the more competitive the situation, the nearer to the points P and P_1 would each operator be constrained to commence and terminate operations. It has sometimes been argued that private operators working for profit are only interested in the peak hours, in which they are said to "skim the cream of the traffic." It would appear from above, however, that it is as much to their interests to go into the off-peak periods as any publicly controlled monopoly. Not that they would ever wish or be willing to go farther than where they cease to cover their variable costs. It hardly needs saying that the problem facing all large undertakings is not so much a matter of the withdrawal of all services at P_1 or none at all, but rather of how much "thinning out" of services is to be undertaken in the particular circumstances of the case. There would, of course, be a tendency to withdraw the vehicles with relatively high variable costs and low earning power (usually the older vehicles) rather than those with the lowest variables and highest earning power (usually the newer vehicles).

Second, there is the question whether we *want* any of our publicly controlled services to operate into the off-peak to the extent of incurring

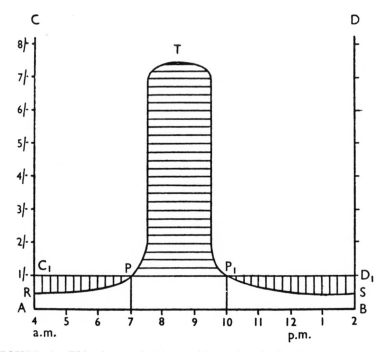

FIGURE 3   *This shows when it would pay best both to start operation in the morning (at P, i.e., 7 a.m.) and to cease operation after the peak (at P_1, i.e., 10 a.m.). The losses that would be incurred were operation to be undertaken before 7 a.m. or after 10 a.m. are marked by the areas C_1RP and P_1SD_1 and shaded vertically.*

expenditure uncovered by revenue and therefore of making losses. The consequences of doing so are clear. By running off-peak services beyond the points P and P_1 in Fig. 3, an undertaking is inevitably adding to the burden to be borne at the peak. By making losses in the valley hours, it is imposing the requirement of earning correspondingly higher amounts at the peak. It is in the public interest so to "subsidise" the off-peak traveller, the shopper, the theatregoer and what some would regard as the less urgent types of pleasure travel at the expense, in terms of higher fares and/or more acute congestion, of the journey to work? My own feeling is that there is no general case for such a subsidy. Nor, however, should those who make use of the off-peak services be denied the benefits of the (sometimes) very low costs involved in providing them.

It is not intended here to go deeply into the question of charging differently as between peak and off-peak periods. Enough has already been said about costs to show that the marginal cost of providing extra bus-miles at the peak is likely to be enormously greater than the marginal cost at other times. The problem is, however, complicated by the fact that money-price is not the only factor in the market, as the absence of over-crowding in the off-peak may in itself be a strong incentive to avoid rush hours. There do seem to be circumstances, however, in which some price differential is fully justified. One of these is when off-peak services can be made to be profitable only by charging a level of fare lower (or higher) than that charged at the peak. In this case the differential should, by making the operation of off-peak services profitable, benefit the peak-hour traveller by relieving him of the full burden of overheads. Another case may be when a price-differential can, by smoothing out or steadying the general flow of traffic, ensure that both a higher load factor and a higher utilisation factor are obtained, thus reducing average costs and therefore the average level of fare. But perhaps the strongest justification of all for inter-temporal differentials is based on the facts that whereas to provide extra bus-miles at the peak involves the provision of extra capacity in terms of extra buses, crews, garage accommodation and so on, extra mileage in the off-peak may cost little more than the cost of fuel, lubricants and a little depreciation.

VI

So far we have assumed that there is a fairly clear division between variable costs (those that vary directly with vehicle-miles operated) and overhead or capacity costs (those that go on in time, irrespective of mileage worked), and that most operators know pretty accurately how large their variables are. We have further assumed that they are much the same as between different undertakings. But in respect of one item of cost we are certainly not justified in making the last assumption. I refer to the wages of drivers and conductors. Should we, when examining the problem of the peak, regard them as a variable or an overhead cost? The short answer to that question is that it all depends upon the terms on which crews are engaged. In so far as a man is engaged and paid for a guaranteed minimum period of 7½ or 8 hours worked consecutively, then, *so far as that 7½ hours is concerned,* the item of wages is very much an overhead cost. No matter whether a crew is on the road for 7, 5, 4 or a couple of hours, under many agreements wages must be paid for the full 7½ or 8 hours. So that, since some peak demands are of so much shorter duration than the time for which crews are thus engaged and paid, for our purpose and under such agreements wages must be regarded as an overhead. On the other hand, if a driver is self-employed, or can be engaged during the peak only or on an hourly basis, then the item of wages at once becomes a relatively variable cost. And since wages are by far the largest single item of cost in the operation of public-service motor vehicles, the matter is of first importance.

Possibly the best way of appreciating the significance of what precisely the terms of engagement are to an undertaking's capacity to meet a sharp peak load, is to compare two extreme cases, in one of which a firm is committed to pay its crews for a guaranteed minimum period of 8 hours worked continuously, but in the other it can engage men on an hourly basis.[5] (It will be noted that in both cases there are still those absolutely variable costs such as fuel, tyre-wear and so on. If these latter are not covered by revenue, then losses will be incurred in either case.) Let us assume that the level of revenue that each firm can earn by serving a particular route is the same. This level is represented in Fig. 4 below by the line $RPTP_1S$.

Revenue begins to exceed "absolute" variables at about 6 a.m., the peak being reached between 7.30 and 9.30 a.m. By 12 noon, however, revenue again falls below such variables.

Let us now consider how these two operators react to such a situation, faced as they are with identical conditions both as regards their prospects of earning revenue, and their "absolute" variables. Let us start by examining what is likely to be the policy of the operator who can hire labour by the hour (Operator I) and to whom therefore (except for periods less than an hour) wages are virtually a variable cost. As regards his time of starting, he will not necessarily start at 6 a.m., *i.e.,* when revenue starts to exceed "absolute" variables. For he will ask himself the question whether the revenue earned between 6 a.m. and 7 a.m. will not only cover "absolute" variables but also the extra wages to be paid by starting at

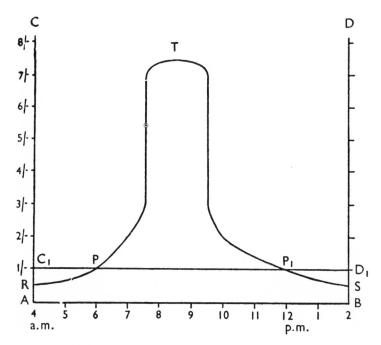

FIGURE 4   *This shows the level of revenue earnable* (RPTP$_1$S) *and that of "absolutely" variable costs* (C$_1$D$_1$) *with which both types of operator mentioned in the text are faced.*

6 a.m. instead of 7 a.m. Since to him wages are among his variable costs, he will not be interested in coming into service until revenue covers not only "absolute" variables but wages also. Similarly, when it comes to withdrawing services with the passing of the peak, to justify his operating between (say) 10 a.m. and 12 noon, revenue must be sufficient to cover the extra costs thereby incurred, costs which he could avoid if the service was not so continued. Thus, as shown in Fig. 5 below, Operator I would be neither interested in coming into service from 6 a.m. to 7 a.m. nor continuing his service between 10 a.m. and 12 noon, for in neither of those 3 hours would the extra revenue earned exceed the extra costs which he would have to incur. Should he do so, or were he compelled to do so by law, he would be making losses to the extent of the shaded areas *EGP* and *P$_1$HF* in Fig. 5. It is to his interest to work from 7 a.m. to 10 a.m. only.

Let us now turn to what Operator II would do in these same conditions of demand, committed as he is to the payment of wages for a minimum of 8 hours at a stretch or not at all. In this case, once the crew

[111]

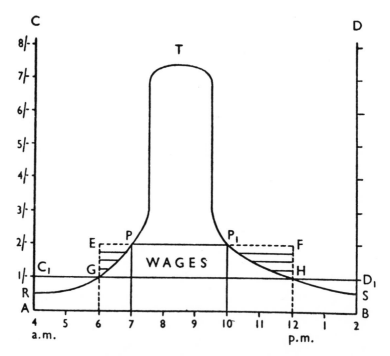

FIGURE 5   *Showing times at which it would pay Operator 1 to start (at* P, *i.e., 7 a.m.) and stop (at* P_1, *i.e., 10 a.m.), and the losses (repre-sented by shaded areas* EGP *and* P_1HF) *he would incur were he obliged to start at 6 a.m. and continue until 12 noon.*

signs on at (say) 5 a.m., it is available for work, apart from rest or meal times, for 8 hours, *at no extra cost to the undertaking.* Within the 8 hours concerned, the management is clearly interested in earning anything over and above "absolute" variables towards this "overhead" of wages. So that it will be interested to start operations whenever the level of revenue earned exceeds such variables. Operator II's case is illustrated in Fig. 6 below.

It will be seen that at 6 a.m. the level of revenue $(RPKTLP_1S)$ passes the level of absolute variables (C_1D_1), so that it will be about then that he will start. And as regards withdrawing services after the peak, it is worth his while to continue operation after 10 a.m. and until 12 noon, since earnings remain well above his absolute variables until that time. To work beyond noon would, however, incur loss, so he would tend to cease operation at noon. Thus, whereas it is to Operator I's interest to operate from 7 a.m. to 10 a.m. only, it is to Operator II's interest to operate from 6 a.m. to 12 noon.

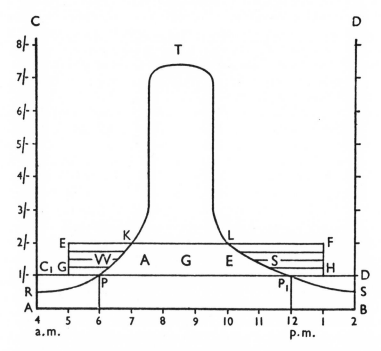

FIGURE 6   *Showing the times at which it pays Operator II to start (at* P *or 6 a.m.) and stop (at* P_1 *or noon) operation, and the amounts by which he is less well off than Operator I (represented by shaded areas* EGPK *and* LP_1HF).

As regards the relative profitability of these services to the two kinds of operators concerned, the crucial question arises which of the two is doing better from a financial point of view, faced as they are with precisely the same demand conditions. Comparing the fortunes of the two operators as depicted in Figs. 5 and 6, it will be seen from Fig. 5 that Operator I's net earnings are represented by the area PTP_1. He incurs costs between 7 a.m. and 10 a.m. only, these costs being made up of his "absolute" variables plus wages for that period. His gross receipts being represented by the whole of the area lying below the line PTP_1, his net earnings are represented by the area lying below the line PTP_1 but above the line PP_1, that is the area TPP_1.

The case of the second Operator, as shown in Fig. 6, is very different. Since he is on the road for 6 hours instead of only 3, both his variable costs and his earnings are more than those of Operator I; whereas his wages bill is for 8 hours. Indeed, if we assume for the sake of simplicity that the rates of pay per hour are the same in both cases, their wages bills are in the ratio of 8:3. Costs incurred in respect of absolute variables are double those of the second Operator, since they are incurred for 6 hours instead of only 3. But his earnings are also greater to the extent of the two areas lying below *PK* (between 6 a.m. and 7 a.m.), and below *LP*$_1$ (between 10 a.m. and 12 noon), which areas represent the extra revenue earned by reason of starting earlier in the morning and continuing longer into the off-peak than Operator I.

So far as overall "net" results are concerned, it will be seen that the first Operator has done much better for himself than Operator II. It will be seen that in the peak period, from 7 a.m. to 10 a.m., they are both earning and (in a sense) costing the same. But if one compares their respective positions during the periods on either side of that peak, it is clear that Operator I is in much the more enviable position. For he has neither incurred any costs nor earned any revenue. Operator II, on the other hand, has incurred both running costs and substantial wage costs. *But such additional costs are quite unmatched by revenue earned.* Indeed, compared with Operator I, Operator II has incurred costs in excess of revenue to the extent of the two shaded areas in Fig. 6. Thus, Operator I is doing much better from an overall "net" point of view than Operator II.

The significance of the above is obvious. It shows that where peak demands are sharp and substantially shorter in time than 7½ or 8 hours, operators in a position to engage labour on terms similar to Operator I are much better able to meet those demands than operators in the position of Operator II. There might be conditions of demand, for example, in which Operator I could make a particular service pay, whereas Operator II could not do so. Or again, if, in the circumstances described above, Operator II, in spite of his high costs, was in fact just making both ends meet, it follows that Operator I must have been doing much more than this, and therefore, on our earlier assumption that neither operator is interested in earning more than his total costs, would be in a position to provide a more ample or cheaper service to the public at the peak than would Operator II.

VII

IF by "solution" we mean that every worker wishing to travel in the rush hours can at an acceptable fare be provided with a seat to himself, then there is clearly no solution in the foreseeable future. In most modern societies it would seem that there will always be circumstances in which travel at peak periods by public transport will involve some queueing and a good deal of standing. But within the limits set by the requirement that the services in question must pay their way, one may well ask in the light of the above analysis by what means we can at least be sure of making the best of an admittedly difficult situation. In this connection I think the following points are worth making:

1. As was pointed out in Section I, the underlying difficulty of providing "adequate" facilities at peak periods stems from the brevity of time during which all time or capacity costs associated with providing such facilities have to be recovered. It followed from this (Section V) that it is in the interests of peak travellers that no opportunities should be missed of earning "net" revenue outside the peak. For to the extent that this can be done, the peak is relieved of the necessity of earning those time or capacity costs associated with providing the service as a whole. No less important, there followed the injunction that it is very much against the interests of travellers at the peak that losses should be incurred at off-peak periods. For thereby the burden to be borne by the peak, so far from being relieved, is that much increased. Hence, from a practical point of view, the vital importance of knowing not only the magnitude of the variable or avoidable costs incurred by providing these off-peak services, but also whether they are being covered by revenue.

2. Those responsible for providing public passenger services should within the limits set by making all services pay their way at all times strive to provide that combination of quality of service and level of fare which most nearly conforms to public taste. The issue as to whether the public prefers so much provision of service (in terms of adequacy, frequency, speed and so on) at a given level of fare, or some other amount of service at a different level of fare, should always be a matter for consideration. As to what combination of quality of service and money-price should be given, a safe rule might be whatever combination evokes the greatest *volume* of travel. For this is tantamount to saying the combination which the public most prefers, *i.e.,* regards as "cheapest" in the widest sense.

3. Finally, there is the problem arising from the facts that the duration of demand for the services of the crews of passenger vehicles is often substantially less than the consecutive period for which such crews are engaged and paid for, and that where the guaranteed 7½- or 8-hour day worked continuously has been adopted, this may lead to much comparatively "light" running outside the peak and may prevent those undertakings committed to such arrangements from providing certain services at a profit at all. It goes without saying that anything that would have the effect of reducing this degree of "indivisibility" in a unit of supply (7½ hours worked continuously) would reduce the costs of providing services for periods of less duration. According to circumstances, it is suggested that the following three possibilities might be carefully examined. Each

in its way might help to provide more adequate or less costly services at peak periods.

First, should not the terms of agreement between employers and the Unions which govern the proportion of "split shifts" (3–4 hours in the morning and a similar period to meet the evening peak) permitted be somewhat relaxed? Second, should not the possibility of employing drivers and conductors during the second half of their 7½-hour shift on something quite other than driving and conducting, be seriously considered? And these alternative jobs in the valley hours need not necessarily be in connection with the provision of transport. Thirdly, why not offer terms of employment whereby at least a limited number of employees could be employed for one shift of 3½ or 4 hours per day only, and be paid accordingly? "Half-time" jobs are a real attraction to some, especially to women whose employment as conductresses is now so widespread.

NOTES

1. On some routes in London (where generally speaking the volume of off-peak travel is substantial), the balance of traffic in peak hours is so bad that the average loading in peak hours is no better than in off-peak hours when the flow, although in no direction so large, is better balanced.

2. The existence of notoriously crowded public services always deters some from using those services, encouraging the use of cycles, cars and taxis, walking and residence in other districts.

3. That is revenue surplus to running costs as defined above.

4. In other branches of transport many and varied considerations may arise. At a slack time of the year when shipping freights are at a low level it may be better for a tramp vessel to accept quotations that actually fail to cover current operating cost than go to the heavy expenses involved in laying up a vessel for a few months, which nowadays may include the difficulty of getting a suitable crew together again. A small accounting loss is better than a large one.

5. A middle case is that of the "split shift" when crews can be engaged for 4 hours in the morning and 4 hours in the evening.

CHAPTER 4

Pricing in Urban Transportation

T HE ESSENCE OF THE URBAN-TRANSPORT PRICING PROBLEM today is that charges to users bear little relation to the cost of providing transport service and facilities. Current pricing policy is one of the many knotty problems that make it difficult to arrive at solutions to the urban transport situation.

An excellent example of this is found in the user-charges levied for the use of urban highways. Motorists pay for the use of highways through licensing fees to the state, wheel-tax assessments to municipalities, excise taxes to the federal government on automobiles and automotive parts, and fuel-tax charges to state and federal governments. Whether the receipts go into local, state, or federal coffers, in recent years these charges have in total equaled—or, in the case of the federal Highway Trust Fund, even exceeded—the expenditures for highway construction, maintenance, administration, and operation. State and local receipts are not always earmarked for highway use, nor are they distributed in proportion to the contribution of given areas. Available revenues have consequently not always equaled the demand for highway funds in particular urban areas. General tax revenues have often had to be used for construction and other purposes on state and local levels of government. Urban taxpayers are subsidizing the motorist. On the whole, however, the average charges levied on motorists cover the average cost of highways.

But the use of averages for both costs and revenues raises problems of its own. An average does not differentiate, for example, between the quality of highways and the cost involved in providing and maintaining them. Urban highways are generally much more expensive to construct and maintain than are roads in outlying and rural areas, yet the motorist pays the same user-charge regardless of the cost or quality of the highways he uses. Expensive segments of urban highways, urban freeways, and superhighways, which may cost anywhere from $4 million to $100 million per mile, offer the motorist highly superior facilities at the same price as a gravel-surfaced county road. And since fuel use is often less per mile on superhighways, the motorist may actually pay less through the fuel tax for using a top-grade highway than he would for a less expensive highway. This bargain pricing is a form of cross-subsidy that encourages the use of improved highways and thus attracts traffic and congestion to busy urban areas. The lack of some means to charge for highways in relation to their costs will usually make an improved urban highway obsolete before the ribbon-cutting ceremony is finished. The tough question is how to levy charges in relation to cost without having the cost of collection itself become burdensome.

With regard to mass transportation, pricing policy in the United States has been plagued by two principal factors: the use of flat fares and the granting of discounts for peak-hour travelers. The flat fare—a set fee no matter what distance is traveled—is typical of urban-transit pricing, although this system is generally not used by commuter railways. The merit of the flat-fare system is that it is easy to collect and does not require the use of a conductor. An extra man is necessary where fairly complicated systems based on distance of travel are used, as in Great Britain and most European countries.

The fault of the flat fare is not only that the fare often bears little relation to the cost involved, but that it tends to discourage the short-haul, occasional rider because of the high average charge levied per mile traveled. For example, at a flat fare of 25¢, a person riding ten miles pays an average fare of 2.5¢ per mile, while another person riding only a mile pays an average of 25¢ a mile. The latter is a pretty steep price for public transportation. The gradual increase in the basic flat fare since the end of World War II—due to increased costs faced by transit companies—has served to discourage the short-distance rider who traveled at off-peak hours from using public transportation. This has tended to accentuate the imbalance in demand between peak and non-peak hours, thereby exacerbating the burden of peak demand.

Another pricing practice that has encouraged travel at the peak hours is the custom of granting discounts for peak travel. Commuter railways are most guilty of this. Monthly commutation tickets, good for anywhere from 46 to 54 rides, may levy a charge on a per-ride basis amounting to as little as half the regular one-way fare. Since only daily commuters, typically those going to and from work, can take advantage of such attractively reduced rates, there is a very strong incentive to use the train for peak-hour journeys. Because there is no reduction in off-peak fares, there is consequently no price incentive for occasional riders to use the mass-transport facility during midday and evening hours. The peak-hour discount in fares is not so pronounced on urban transit lines as it is on commuter railways. Urban transit lines usually charge less per ride through the sale of tokens or tickets, however, which also encourages the regular peak-hour rider while doing little to encourage other riders.

There is probably little that can be done, except over a fairly long period of time, to change the fare system that encourages peak-hour use. We have become accustomed to it. Such pricing has a long history in English-speaking countries, dating back to the first half of the nineteenth century when special fare concessions were made during certain hours of the day to enable low-income workingmen to use public transport facilities —mainly the omnibus—to travel to work. Somewhat later Parliament passed laws requiring that trains with special, low "workingmen's fares" be operated regularly. The business notion of quantity discounts has strong appeal, even when the economics of the situation make it more expensive to supply service to encourage peak demand than to supply service at any other time.

Currently the major issue in urban-transportation pricing concerns the use of price as means to gain more effective use of transport facilities. Much emphasis has been given to the use of price as a rationing mechanism for the use of highways. This follows from the idea that a major breakthrough on the congestion problem can evolve only from less use of the private automobile and from greater use of mass transportation.

The other side of the coin involves pricing to make mass transport more attractive. Various schemes have been put forward, including ideas for free mass transportation. It seems to be assumed that a subsidy is necessary to pay the total cost of improved mass transportation. Much of this assumption stems from the idea that patrons will not willingly pay the full cost of improvements as reflected in fares. This is obviously a matter of considerable delicacy. Mass transportation has generally been considered such a poor alternative to the use of the private automobile that winning increased patronage is a very difficult job indeed. With substantially higher rates to pay for improvement, it may be impossible. More enlightened, perhaps, is the idea that the real challenge to mass transport is to provide a better rather than a cheaper ride. Since the end of congestion depends upon diminished use of the private automobile, any alternative—including subsidized or free mass transport—appears desirable that will achieve this end at a cost less than that of providing ever more facilities for the private automobile. Thus while subsidized mass transportation is still a debatable issue, the growing realization that the urban taxpayer is already subsidizing the motorist has considerably mitigated opposition to public support of mass transport. While Americans will remain touchy on the subsidy issue for a long time to come, the idea that it may take less sauce for the mass-transport goose than for the highway gander has definite appeal.

Pricing In Urban and Suburban Transport

WILLIAM S. VICKREY

THE ARTICLE BY PROFESSOR WILLIAM VICKREY of Columbia discusses the complex issue of how pricing might be used to improve utilization of transport facilities as well as to reduce waste in their use. He concludes that the current pricing policy for public mass transportation and for the use of streets is not only cumbersome but wrong in that it tends to stimulate use of the facilities at the time of day when it is most expensive to provide them. The devices that he mentions for collecting charges from motorists for the use of streets are particularly interesting.

Whether it would ever be possible to adopt Vickrey's suggestions is debatable. Nevertheless, anyone interested in the problems of improving transportation within our metropolitan areas should read and reflect upon what he has to say.

I WILL BEGIN WITH THE PROPOSITION that in no other major area are pricing practices so irrational, so out of date, and so conducive to waste as in urban transportation. Two aspects are particularly deficient: the absence of adequate off-peak differentials and the gross underpricing of some modes relative to others.

In nearly all other operations characterized by peak load problems, at least some attempt is made to differentiate between the rates charged for peak and for off-peak service. Where competition exists, this pattern is enforced by competition: resort hotels have off-season rates; theaters charge more on weekends and less for matinees. Telephone calls are cheaper at night, though I suspect not sufficiently so to promote a fully efficient utilization of the plant. Power rates are varied to a considerable extent according to the measured or the imputed load factor of the consumer, and in some cases, usually for special-purpose uses such as water heating, according to the time of use. In France, this practice is carried out logically by charging according to season and time of day for all consumption but that of the smallest domestic consumers; rate changes at the consumers' meters are triggered by a special frequency signal actuating a tuned relay which connects or disconnects auxiliary registers.

"Pricing in Urban and Suburban Transport," *American Economic Review*, May 1963.

But in transportation, such differentiation as exists is usually perverse. Off-peak concessions are virtually unknown in transit. Such concessions as are made in suburban service for "shoppers tickets" and the like are usually relatively small, indeed are often no greater than those available in multitrip tickets not restricted to off-peak riding, and usually result in fares still far above those enjoyed by regular commuters who are predominantly peak-hour passengers.

In the case of suburban railroad fares, the existing pattern is even contrary to what would be most profitable in terms of the relative elasticities of demand. Both on a priori grounds and on the basis of the analysis of the historical experience recently made by Elbert Segelhorst in a forthcoming Columbia dissertation, it is clear that the price elasticity of the off-peak traffic, at current fare levels at least, is substantially higher than that of peak-hour traffic. If, for example, the average suburban family spends $300 per year for commuting and peak-hour trips and $50 per year for occasional off-peak trips and the commutation fares were increased by 5 per cent, causing a 1 per cent drop in this traffic, while off-peak fares were reduced 40 per cent, with a 30 per cent increase in traffic, gross revenues per commuting family would go up from $350.00 to $350.85, with operating costs if anything reduced slightly, since nearly all costs are determined by the peak traffic level. The riding public would on the average be substantially better off: the above typical family, if it maintained the same pattern of usage, would pay only $315 + $30 = $345 instead of $350 as formerly, and any adaptation that it chose to make to the new rates would represent a further benefit, since the alternative of no change would still be open to it if it preferred. Things may not work out quite this neatly in practice, but the potential for substantial gains from even more drastic revisions in the rate structure is certainly there.

Fare collection procedures are sometimes urged as an excuse for not going to a more rational fare structure, but here there has been a deplorable lag behind what a little ingenuity or modern technology makes possible. There would be relatively little difficulty in devising apparatus for collecting subway fares on as elaborate an origin, destination, and time basis as might be desired, simply by dispensing a coded check at the entrance turnstile against the deposit of an interim fare, this check being deposited in an exit turnstile which will then either refund any excess or release only on the deposit of the remainder of the fare. Bus fares represent a problem that has yet to be satisfactorily solved, but considering the vast waste of the time of operators and passengers through delays caused by present fare collection methods, a concerted attack on this problem should yield high dividends. For commuter railroads, the possibility exists of issuing machine-readable subscriber's cards, with passengers making a record of their trips by inserting the card in a register at the origin and destination stations and being billed according to the time, origin, and destination of the trips actually made by the subscriber, his family, and guests. Something like this seems to be in the offing for the new San Francisco system, which in many respects is more of a commuter service than an urban transit system. Actually, it is not even necessary to enclose the stations in order to use such a system: proper registering at the stations can be enforced by dispensing a dated seat check to be displayed during the trip and deposited in registering out at the destination.

Even short of such mechanization, existing ticketing arrangements are needlessly clumsy, involving in many cases a duplication of effort between station agent and conductor and fairly elaborate accounting and auditing procedures. The New York Central has recently taken a step forward in this respect by arranging to mail monthly commutation tickets to patrons and receive payment by mail. Gross delinquency appears to be running appreciably less than the saving in ticket agents' time, and the net credit loss is undoubtedly much less than this, since many who fail to return or pay for their tickets in fact do not use them, as when they die or move away. Another wrinkle worth trying would be the use of a universal form of multiride ticket, to be sold by ticket agents or conductors at a flat price of $5.00 or $10.00, validated for bearer and those accompanying him, with a liberal time limit, for a number of rides or trip units depending on the stations between which it is designated to be used by appropriate punches at time of sale. An off-peak differential could be provided in conjunction with this type of ticket by providing that two units would be charged for an off-peak ride as against three units for a peak-hour ride. The ticket itself, for a typical suburban route, need be no larger than an ordinary playing card. Accounting would be greatly simplified, conductor's cash fare transactions would be both simplified and greatly reduced in number, and the use of the service would become much more convenient for passengers. Such a ticket would provide a more effective off-peak differential than the shoppers' type of ticket, since those who are either going or returning during the peak or are returning at a later date cannot usually avail themselves of such tickets.

But while suburban and transit fare structures are seriously deficient, the pricing of the use of urban streets is all but non-existent. Superficially, it is often thought that since reported highway expenditures by the state and federal government are roughly balanced by highway tax and license revenues, the motorist is on the whole paying his way. But what is true on the average is far from true of users of the more congested urban streets. Much of the expenditure on such streets is borne by city budgets supported slightly if at all by explicit contributions from highway sources, in most states. More important, much of the real economic cost of providing the space for city streets and highways does not appear in the accounts at all, being concealed by the fact that this space has usually been "dedicated" to the public use at some time in the past. It is extremely difficult to make close evaluations from the scanty and scattered data available, but very roughly it appears to me that if we take the burden of all the gasoline and other vehicular taxes borne by motorists by reason of their use of city streets, this amounts to only about a third of the real economic cost of the facilities they use. In current terms, the high marginal cost of increased street space becomes painfully apparent whenever a street widening scheme is evaluated. Even in terms of long-range planning, urban expressways cost many times as much as expressways in rural areas built to comparable specifications, and while the flow of traffic may be greater, this is not enough to come anywhere near amortizing the cost out of the taxes paid by the traffic flowing over the urban expressways. Even when tolls are charged in conjunction with special features such as bridges or tunnels, these seldom cover the cost of the connecting expressways and city streets. And except where the street layout is exceptionally favorable, such tolls usually have an unfavorable effect on the routing of traffic.

The perversity of present pricing practices is at its height, perhaps, for the East River crossings to Long Island and Brooklyn. Here the peculiar political logic is that the older bridges are in some sense "paid for," and hence must be free, while tolls must be charged on the newer facilities. The result is that considerable traffic is diverted from the newer facilities that have relatively adequate and less congested approaches to the older bridges such as the Manhattan and the Queensboro bridges, which dump their traffic right in the middle of some of the worst congestion in New York. The construction of the proposed expressway across lower Manhattan from the Holland Tunnel to the Manhattan and Williamsburgh bridges would be at least less urgent, if not actually unwarranted, in view of its enormous cost, if, as would seem possible, traffic could be diverted from the Manhattan Bridge to the Brooklyn-Battery tunnel by imposing tolls on the Manhattan and other East River bridges and reducing or removing the toll on the tunnel. (The delusion still persists that the primary role of pricing should always be that of financing the service rather than that of promoting economy in its use. In practice there are many alternative ways of financing; but no device can function quite as effectively and smoothly as a properly designed price structure in controlling use and providing a guide to the efficient deployment of capital.)

The underpricing of highway services is even more strongly pronounced during peak hours. Even if urban motorists on the average paid the full cost of the urban facilities, rush hour use would still be seriously underpriced; moreover, this underpricing would be relatively more severe than for transit or commutation service. This is because off-peak traffic on the highways and streets is a much larger percentage of the total than is the case for either transit or commutation traffic; and therefore in the process of averaging out the costs, much more of the costs properly attributable to the peak can be shifted to the shoulders of the off-peak traffic than can be thus shifted in the case of transit or commutation service. The effect of this is that while the commutation fare problem is chiefly one of the overpricing of off-peak travel, and to a minor extent if at all one of underpricing of peak travel, the problem of the pricing of automobile travel is chiefly that of remedying the underpricing of peak travel, and to a relatively minor extent if at all of the overpricing of off-peak travel. These two relationships combine to give the result that even if motor traffic and commuter train traffic each on the whole fully paid their way on the basis of a uniform charge per trip, the proportion by which the peak-hour motorist would be subsidized by the off-peak motorists would be far greater than the proportion by which the peak-hour commuter is subsidized by the off-peak commuter.

A quantitative indication of the seriousness of the problem of peak-hour automobile traffic is derivable from some projections made for Washington, D.C. Two alternative programs were developed for taking care of traffic predicted under two alternative conditions, differing chiefly as to the extent to which express transit service would be provided. The additional traffic lanes required for the larger of the two volumes of traffic would be needed almost solely to provide for this added rush hour traffic, the less extensive road system being adequate for the off-peak traffic even at the higher over-all traffic level. Dividing the extra cost by the extra rush hour traffic, it turned out that for each additional car making a daily trip that contributed to the dominant flow, during the peak hour, an additional investment of $23,000 was projected. In other words, a man who bought a $3,000 car for the purpose of driving downtown to work every day would be asking the community, in effect, to match his $3,000 investment with $23,000 from general highway funds. Or if the wage earners in a development were all to drive downtown to work, the investment in highways that this development would require would be of the same order of magnitude as the entire investment in a moderate-sized house for each family. It may be that the affluent society will be able to shoulder such a cost, but even if it could there would seem to be many much more profitable and urgent uses to which sums of this magnitude could be put. And even if we assume that staggering of working hours could spread the peak traffic more or less evenly over three hours, this would still mean $8,000 per daily trip, even though achievement of such staggering would represent an achievement second only to the highway construction itself. At 250 round trips per year, allowing 10 per cent as the gross return which a comparable investment in the private sector would have to earn to cover interest, amortization, and property and corporate income taxes, this amounts to over $3.00 per round trip, or, on a one-hour peak basis, to $9.00 per round trip, if staggering is ruled out. This is over and above costs of maintenance or of provision for parking. When costs threaten to reach such levels, it is high time to think seriously about controlling the use through pricing.

It is sometimes thought that pricing of roadway use would apply chiefly to arterial streets and highways and that it would have no application to streets used mainly for access, which should allegedly be paid for by property taxes on the abutting property to which access is given. But the relevant criterion is not the function performed, but the degree of congestion that would obtain in the absence of pricing. To be sure, there would be little point in levying a specific charge for the use of suburban residential side streets or lightly traveled rural roads, since the congestion added by an increment in traffic is virtually nil in such circumstances and the wear and tear usually negligible. In effect, at these levels of traffic the economies of scale are such that marginal cost is only a small fraction of the average cost. But this does not hold for roadways used for access at the center of a city. A truck making a delivery on a narrow side street may cause as much congestion and delay to others as it would in many miles of running on an arterial highway. Even in the case of a cul-de-sac that is used exclusively for access and carries no through traffic, a firm with frequent deliveries will make access more difficult for his neighbors; only by specific pricing of such use can the firm requiring much access be differentiated from firms requiring relatively little, and encouraged to locate where its activities will be less burdensome to the remainder of the community; or to receive and ship goods at times when less congestion is generated. Some of the worst traffic congestion in New York occurs as a result of the way access is had to firms in the garment district; restrictions on truck size and exhortations have produced only minor improvement. It seems likely that a suitable charge for such use of road space would be more acceptable than an arbitrary and drastic ban, and that with a definite financial incentive methods might be found to avoid the creation of congestion.

But talk of direct and specific charges for roadway use conjures up visions of a clutter of toll booths, an army of toll collectors, and traffic endlessly tangled up in queues. Conventional methods of toll collection are, to be sure, costly in manpower, space, and interference with the smooth flow of traffic. Furthermore, unless the street configuration is exceptionally favorable, tolls often contribute to congestion over parallel routes. However, with a little ingenuity, it is possible to devise methods of charging for the use of the city streets that are relatively inexpensive, produce no interference with the free flow of traffic, and are capable of adjusting the charge in close conformity with variations in costs and traffic conditions. My own fairly elaborate scheme involves equipping all cars with an electronic identifier which hopefully can be produced on a large-scale basis for about $20 each. These blocks would be scanned by roadside equipment at a fairly dense network of cordon points, making a record of the identity of the car; these records would then be taken to a central processing plant once a month and the records assembled on electronic digital computers and bills sent out. Preliminary estimates indicate a total cost of the equipment on a moderately large scale of about $35 per vehicle, including the identifier; the operating cost would be approximately that involved in sending out telephone bills. Bills could be itemized to whatever extent is desired to furnish the owner with a record that would guide him in the further use of his car. In addition, roadside signals could be installed to indicate the current level of charge and enable drivers to shift to less costly routes where these are available.

Other methods have been devised in England, where the country can less well afford the vast outlays demanded by our rubber-tired sacred cow, and where street layouts are such as to make provision for large volumes of vehicular traffic both more costly and more destructive of civic amenities. One scheme suggested for use in a pilot scheme for the town of Cambridge involves the use of identifiers to actuate a tallying register, the rate of tallying being governed by impulses the frequency of which would vary according to the degree of traffic congestion existing in the zone in which the car is reported to be. Another extremely simple and low-cost but less automatic device would consist of a meter installed in each car so as to be visible from outside, which could be wound up by the insertion of a token sold at an appropriate price—the token being subject to inspection through a window and being destroyed when the subsequent token is brought into place. The driver can control the rate at which the meter runs down by a lever or switch which simultaneously displays a signal which will indicate to outside observers the rate currently being charged. The driver is then required to keep this signal set to correspond with the rate in effect in the zone in which he is driving as indicated by appropriate wayside signals. Extremely simple methods of varying the rate at which the meter runs down have been devised in

England, which for the time being I must treat as confidential. The rate can appropriately be a time rate rather than a distance rate, since the greater the congestion the greater is the appropriate charge, so that no connection to the wheels is needed and the whole meter can be extremely compact, rugged, and cheap. The chief difficulty with this method is the likelihood that drivers will "forget" to turn the rate of the meter up promptly on entering a higher rate zone, but given a reasonable amount of policing this difficulty might be overcome after an initial period of habituation.

A slightly more elaborate version of this method would call for the changes in the meter rate to be actuated automatically in response to signals emitted from wayside equipment at the boundaries of the various zones. This would probably raise the cost to something above the level of the response block method. On the other hand, both this and the previous method are somewhat better adapted to serving to assess charges for parking as well as for moving about within an area, so that the cost of servicing and installing parking meters could be properly credited against the cost of the new system.

Another version would call for the meter to be run down by pulses emitted from cables laid along the roadway, with the pulse rate varied according to traffic density and other factors. Alternatively, the cables could be arranged to emit continuously and located across the roadway—the number of cables turned on at any one time being varied according to traffic conditions. Reliability of operation can be assured by using two alternative frequencies in alternate cables successively. The cables need not be spaced evenly, but for economy in operation may be placed in groups so that they can be energized from a single source. With either of these methods, any failure of the meter to operate could be checked by requiring the meter to be placed in plain view and arranging for a visible signal to be changed cyclically as the meter is actuated.

Adequate methods for enforcement of each of the schemes seem available which are reasonably simple, with the possible exception of the manual system, where minor negligence might be difficult to check and lead to major negligence. With identifier methods, the registering of the proper vehicle number could be checked by having a few of the detector stations equipped with apparatus to display the number being registered, which could be compared with the license plate by observers. Errors due to malfunction, as well as most fraudulent tampering, would show up as a matter of course during the processing of the records, as each record showing a car entering a zone must match the immediately succeeding record for that car leaving that zone. Cameras can also be arranged at some locations to take pictures of cars not producing a valid response signal. With meters, arrangements can be made to hold used and muti-lated tokens in a sealed box; these could be inspected and their number compared with a non-resettable counter with a capacity not likely to be exceeded during the life of the car, as a part of an annual safety inspection program.

Ultimately, one would expect that all cars in an entire country would be equipped with meters or electronic identifiers. Initially, however, it would be necessary to make some provision for cars from other areas. Cars in transit or making infrequent visits to the congested area could be given the freedom of the city in a spirit of hospitality. Cars making a longer stay or more frequent visits would be required to equip them-selves—say at cordon points established along the major arteries entering the controlled area. Unequipped cars would be prohibited from using the minor streets crossing the boundary of the controlled area. Such provisions would be particularly easy to enforce with electronic identifier methods: unequipped cars passing major control points would set off a camera; unequipped cars using routes prohibited to them would set off an alarm signal, facilitating their apprehension. With a meter system, checking on unequipped cars would have to be largely a manual operation and would probably be considerably less rigorous. Actually a similar problem occurs at present in enforcing provisions against the use of out-of-state license plates in a given state for longer than a limited period.

Such charging for street use could have a far-reaching impact on the pattern of urban transportation and even on the patterns of land use, by promoting a more economical distribution of traffic between various modes, the various modes being used in accordance with their suitability for the particular trip in the light of the costs involved, instead of, as at present, being chosen to suit the preferences and whims of the individual regardless of the impact on others. Motorists will no longer be man-oeuvered into the position of being forced to pay for a luxury that they can ill-afford. Mass transportation will have an opportunity to develop in line with its inherent characteristics, eventually developing a quality and fre-quency of service that will in many cases be preferred even to the spuri-ously low-priced private car transportation that might be provided in the absence of a system of specific charges. Traffic-generating activities will tend to be located more rationally in relation to real transportation costs. For example, appropriate transportation charges might have been suffi-cient to have inhibited the construction of the Pan-American subway-jammer over Grand Central. Rapid vehicular transportation within congested areas, not now available at any price, will be generally available for meeting emergency and high priority needs where the cost is justified. Traffic will be routed more efficiently, so as to provide a smoother functioning of the roadway system as a whole. The levels of charge required to balance marginal cost and marginal benefit in the short run will provide a much more definite and reliable guide than is now available as to where and to what extent the provision of additional facilities can be justified. One can cite, for example, the extra half hour that the airlines have to allow during rush hours for the trip from East 38th Street to Idlewild, in spite of the fact that this route is almost entirely over grade-separated expressways.

One effect of such charging would be to change the relative attractiveness of different forms of mass transportation. Under present conditions, buses are involved in the same traffic tangle as the private car and are often further handicapped by their inferior maneuverability. It is then difficult to make a bus service sufficiently attractive relative to use of a private car to attract a sufficient volume of traffic to make the frequency of service satisfactory. In order to give the transit facility a chance to compete with the private automobile, it becomes necessary to provide some sort of reserved right of way. With buses this in theory takes the form of a lane reserved for them, but in practice this faces formidable problems in dealing with intersections and pickup points, and at best means that the lanes thus provided are likely to be underutilized, since it is seldom desirable to schedule just enough bus service to fully utilize a whole lane of capacity. These difficulties provide a strong argument for going to the very substantial expense of a rail rapid transit system.

With street use controlled by pricing, however, it is possible to insure that the level of congestion is kept down to the point at which buses will provide a satisfactory level of service, and rail rapid transit systems will be required only where a volume of traffic arises that will warrant their high cost on the basis of superior service and operating economies.

But while the most dramatic impact of street use pricing would be to permit the economical allocation of traffic among the various modes, it would be of great importance even in cases where intermodal substitution is not a factor. Even in a community entirely without mass-transit service, street pricing could have an important function to perform. For example, traffic between opposite sides of town often has the choice of going right through the center of town or taking a more circuitous route. Left to itself, this traffic is likely to choose the direct route through the center, unless indeed the center becomes so congested as to make it quicker to go the longer way around. In the absence of pricing, one may be faced with the alternatives of either tolerating the congestion in the center of town, or if it is considered mandatory to provide congestion-free access to the center of town, of providing relatively costly facilities in the center of town adequate to accommodate through traffic as well. With pricing it becomes possible to restrict the use of the center streets to those having no ready alternative and provide for the through traffic on peripheral roadways at much lower cost. Without pricing, bypass routes, though beneficial, often attract only part of the traffic that they should carry for the greatest over-all economy of transport.

Pricing of street use can in the long run have significant effects on the whole pattern of development of urban communities and on property values. While on general principles one can hardly imagine this impact to be other than beneficial, it is a little difficult to discern the net direction in which it would tend—for example, whether the concentration of activity at the center would increase or decrease. In order to gain insight into this problem I have been toying with a model which attempts to incorporate the essential element of choice of route, but in spite of drastically simplified structure and assumptions this model has so far resisted an analytical solution and will probably have to be worked out by simulation and successive approximations on a large electronic computer.

The model is as follows: Consider a community with a system of streets laid out in a circular and radial pattern; for simplicity, assume that the mesh of this network is small enough to be negligible; that is, we can travel from any point in a radial and in a circumferential direction, but not at an angle. Thus any trip must be made up of radial segments and circular arcs. In effect, we assume perfect divisibility of road space, or that the capacity of a street is directly proportional to its width. In the neighborhood of any given point at a radius r from the center, a proportion of $w(r)$ of the area is devoted to streets, the remainder being devoted to business activities that generate one unit of traffic for each unit of net area; i.e., one unit of gross area originates and terminates $(1 — w(r))$ units of traffic. The traffic originating at any one point has destinations distributed at random over the remainder of the business area; i.e., any tendency of related businesses to group themselves close together is neglected. The average cost of transportation per ton-mile (or passenger-mile) is given by some functional relation in which the density of traffic per unit roadway width is an argument. For example, we may put $x = A + B (t/w)^k$, where t is the volume of traffic in tons per hour and w is the width of the roadway in feet, A, B, and k being constants. A may be thought of as the operating cost of the vehicle, where the volume of traffic is negligible, the second term being the additional costs experienced due to delays resulting from congestion; k is the elasticity of this congestion cost, which can be thought of as being proportional to the number of added minutes required to cover a given distance as compared to the time required in the absence of conflicting traffic. A relation of this form was found to fit data from the Lincoln tunnel extremely well up to close to the point where a queue begins to accumulate, with a value of k of about 4.5, so that the marginal congestion cost is some $k + 1 = 5.5$ times the average congestion cost per vehicle. In other words, according to this data, an individual who has to take ten minutes longer to make a given trip than he would if there were no interference from other traffic causes 45 vehicle minutes of delay in the aggregate to other vehicles with whose movements he interferes. Unfortunately, comparable data for the more interesting case of travel over a network of city streets could not be found, but something of this order of magnitude is generally to be expected.

It can readily be shown that optimum allocation of the street space in a given small area between radial traffic and circular traffic calls for the space to be allocated in proportion to the traffic so that the average and marginal costs are the same in both directions. We can thus combine the circular traffic and the radial traffic and speak of the relation of costs to traffic in terms of aggregate ton-miles of traffic in both directions per acre of street area. Thus the cost per ton-mile, can be taken to be $x = A + B$ $(t/w)^k$, with x in cents per ton-mile, t in ton-miles per gross acre of land, and w the fraction of the land devoted to streets, in the particular neighborhood.

Given the density of traffic as a function of r, it is possible to determine the least-cost route for any given trip on an average cost basis in which the shipper bears only the delay costs experienced by him, and alternatively on a marginal cost basis where he must pay in addition a toll corresponding to the delay his trip imposes on others. By imposing the condition that the traffic distribution thus generated shall be one which produces the cost structure leading to the traffic distribution, one gets a differential equation which in principle can be solved to give equilibrium traffic patterns. The cost of this equilibrium traffic pattern can then be integrated over the entire area to give the total cost of transportation, and this can be done both for the marginal cost case and the average cost to get the total saving in transportation cost over a given street network brought about by the pricing of street use.

Unfortunately, the differential equation that results is of the second order and third degree, and I suspect does not admit of an analytical solution in terms of well-known functions. The next step is recourse to solution of specific cases by successive approximations.

As a by-product of this calculation, one could then also derive the equilibrium rentals that would be paid by businesses at various distances from the center, on the assumption that rental differentials would correspond to the differentials in the costs of transportation borne by the business; because of the symmetry of origins and destinations, it would make no essential difference whether shipping costs were borne entirely by shipper, entirely by consignee, or shared between them.

A further step in the analysis would be to take total cost as determined by the distribution $w(r)$ of land between business and transportation uses at various distances from the center and treat this as a calculus of variations problem of choosing the function $w(r)$ so as to minimize the total cost of transportation. In this way one could compare the pattern of land allocation that would be optimal without pricing to that which would be optimal with pricing. Considering the complexity of the problem, I hesitate to make any guesses as to the nature of this difference, except to speculate that it is likely to be somewhat surprising to many of us.

I will wind up by laying before you one final piece of unfinished business, which is the problem of developing criteria for determining how much of the area in a particular neighborhood should be devoted to transportation, given the pattern of rents in the area. Conventional cost benefit analysis, if employed here at all, would tend to take the form of comparing the rent which private business would pay for the space with the reduction in transportation cost which would result from increasing the area used for transportation and decreasing the effective density of traffic. But in connection with the present model, this rule fails to yield optimal results. Let us imagine, to make things a little more explicit, that a Comprehensive Transportation Authority stood ready to rent or lease land, to be converted from or to transportation use, to or from private business, at a price reflecting the marginal productivity of land area in a particular location in reducing the total cost of carrying out a given number of ton-miles of traffic within a given neighborhood. In terms of our cost formula, the rental would be given by the partial derivative of total cost per unit area xt, with respect to changes in the proportion of total area devoted to transportation, w, the density of traffic t remaining unchanged. Thus:

$$-\frac{e(xt)}{eW} = \frac{-e}{ew}(At + Bt^{k+1}w^{-k}) = + kBt^{k+1}w^{-k-1}$$

A business will then move to a higher rent location only if the saving in transportation costs borne by the particular business is greater than the difference in rent. However, since transportation costs are in this model borne in part by the firms with which a given firm deals, only half of the change in the transportation costs of the goods he receives and ships resulting from his change in location will be felt directly by the firm making the change, so that on the whole a firm will fail to move unless the saving in the costs of the shipments to and from the firm is twice as great as the net increment in the costs of transportation resulting from the reapportionment of the space devoted to transportation. In other words, the conventional cost-benefit analysis in terms of going rents has a strong tendency to leave business uneconomically dispersed and to result in too much space in the center of the city being devoted to transportation.

This conclusion is derived from an admittedly highly simplified mode, which neglects such factors as the clustering of interrelated firms, the wide variations in the ratio of land to transportation requirements of various activities, and the possibilities for creating additional space by construction of multistory buildings, or for that matter, multilevel highways. But the model can plead not guilty to the charge of having ignored the journey to work and other passenger transportation, for, input-output analysis style, we can regard labor as the product of the household sector, and, Clayton Act to the contrary notwithstanding, as an article of commerce with a peculiarly high transport cost. The essential difference between this model and classical space economics models such as those of Von Thunen is that the latter imply a well-defined shadow price for each commodity at each point in the space, with transport taking place only between points where the price differential balances the transportation cost, whereas the present model allows for crosshauling and a certain amount of particularism in the relations between economic units. The real world presumably lies somewhere in between these two extremes. Study of journey-to-work patterns seems generally to reveal a situation a fairly long way from the Von Thunen extreme, with a great deal of cross-hauling of labor of roughly comparable skill. According to this, a cost benefit analysis can justify devoting land to transportation only when the savings in transportation costs yield a return considerably greater than the gross rentals, including taxes, that private business would be willing to pay for the space. This in turn means that an even greater preference should be given to space economizing modes of transport than would be indicated by rent and tax levels. And our rubber-shod sacred cow is a ravenously space-hungry, shall I say, monster?

Subsidies for Urban Mass Transportation

GEORGE M. SMERK

THE GENERAL ATTITUDE TOWARD SUBSIDY in the United States is a most human one. While we tend to resist subsidy on the grounds that it en-

"Subsidies for Urban Mass Transportation," *Land Economics,* February 1965.

courages wastefulness and that it is opposed to our basic belief in free enterprise capitalism—an institution that, while vaguely defined in most minds, has become sanctified as the source of our prosperity and moral fibre—most of us seem willing to accept a subsidy cheerfully if it is somehow disguised. What follows is a discussion of the use of subsidies to provide improved mass transportation. An important element in the argument is that such a policy may be less costly than continuing on the present course of subsidizing the motorist.

ONE OF THE PRIME STUMBLING BLOCKS to the improvement and increased use of mass transportation in our cities is the difficulty of making it pay for itself out of the farebox. Indeed, in most cities, because of the highly peaked nature of the demand for mass transport during rush hours requiring a large investment in plant and equipment which lies mainly idle during non-peak hours, it may be impossible for public transport systems to cover their full costs and at the same time offer service of the quality and quantity needed.

This is an especially irksome problem in the United States, where most urban mass transport is in the hands of privately owned railroads and transit companies or public agencies that are required by law to be self-supporting. The formidable competition of the automobile, draining away potentially profitable off-peak traffic, further adds to the woes of these companies. Poor earnings or outright deficits offer little inducement for new private investment in urban mass transport firms. As a result, these firms are withering at a time when the useful service they can perform was never more vitally needed and when the retention and expansion of that service may be the crucial element in cutting the Gordian Knot of congestion and urban decay. Therefore, because of the importance of mass transport, it seems desirable to give some consideration to the use of subsidies for the maintenance and expansion of public transport systems.

The question of subsidies is always a prickly one in the United States. Under certain conditions, however, subsidies may not only be desirable but may be the only way at hand to correct a detrimental situation. The funds so granted may be applied through government ownership of certain transport assets with operating deficits made up from the general tax fund or by allowing assets to remain in private hands with government reimbursing the firm for losses.[1]

Public ownership, control, or subsidies to private firms appear most desirable under one or more of the following conditions. (1) When external economies and diseconomies are large. External economies abound from the provision of transport. In other words, there are many gains and costs which are not realized in pecuniary terms by the enterprise in question, since by its very nature transport confers substantial benefits upon non-users. Likewise there are substantial costs of transport borne by non-users. It follows, then, that it is most desirable to recognize and consider the social benefits and costs related to urban transport in addition to strictly pecuniary factors. Assuming operation of public transport to reflect the general interests of the public, transport output therefore seems most justifiably geared to a point of equality between social costs and benefits rather than strict and sole adherence to the forces of the market as expressed in purely pecuniary terms.

(2) When non-assignable, or indivisible costs, are large in relation to total costs, and call for price discrimination as the only feasible way to recover total costs. These cost characteristics are typical of highway and rapid transit type urban transport facilities. Both have a large proportion of fixed costs, making assignment of cost to specific units of traffic largely arbitrary. Costs may be indivisible because the out-put unit—the bus or train journey—is larger than the sales unit—the passenger journey.[2] Joint costs are also involved due to the round-trip nature of almost all urban journeys. For example, the journey to work necessarily entails a trip back home and traffic lanes constructed to meet peak-demand conditions are also used by traffic during off-peak hours.

(3) When the industry is inherently monopolistic. As far as highways and public transport are concerned, the economies of scale make monopoly inevitable. Highways could not very well be supplied on a competitive basis, hence they are provided by the various levels of government. Likewise, competition between public transport companies, particularly public transit firms with fixed facilities, would require an expensive and undesirable duplication of plant and would normally preclude easy interchange or transfer between different parts of the system.

(4) When public costs of operation are not much different from those of private firms. Public operations have the same costs of operation if labor and materials are bid for in the same market. Nevertheless, private efficiency may be greater because of the spur of hoped-for profits and the measuring rod that profits provide. Where large sums are already sunk in private facilities it may be less costly for public enterprise to "hire" the private firms' operations through lease than to buy out existing firms or to start completely from scratch.

The above public enterprise criteria are generally met by urban mass transport firms and of course highways are already supplied by public enterprise. Assuming that the magnitudes of both costs and gains are at least fairly well-known and the system will be operated for the greatest public benefit, what pricing schemes will be followed?

Referring to Figure 1 as an aid to explanation, S and D are the conventional Marshallian supply and demand curves. MSC represents the

FIGURE 1

PUBLIC ENTERPRISE PRICING

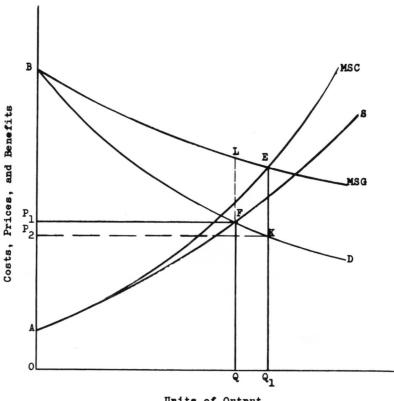

Units of Output

marginal social costs which public enterprise must recognize. The curve MSG reflects marginal social gains. Under conditions of perfect competition, output would be at OQ with a price of P_1. Consumers surplus would equal P_1BF, and in addition there would be gains to non-consumers equal to BFL.

However, as a public monopoly wishing to provide the optimal output from a social viewpoint, the output OQ_1, where marginal social costs and marginal social gains are equal, is the most desirable. To the left of E social gains are greater than costs, and beyond E to the right, costs outweigh gains; therefore, E is the optimal point of production. The question that remains is how to recover the total costs $OAEQ_1$ which are occasioned by this output.

[136]

One possibility would be to set the price at P_2, the price at which output could be sold under competitive conditions. Cost equal to Q_1K could be recovered from users. The remaining costs KE could be recovered by taxing either users or non-users or both. Another possibility is perfect discrimination among all beneficiaries. The highest possible price for each unit of output along the MSG curve between B and E would be charged. Excess receipts $OBEQ_1$ minus $OAEQ_1$ would then be available for some other purpose. Still a third possibility is perfect discrimination among all users along the demand curve to K, where output OQ_1 is reached. Non-consumer gains will be equal to BEK. Some excess receipts may accrue to the public sector depending on whether or not $OBKQ_1$ minus $OAEQ_1$ is positive, negative or zero.

Of the three possibilities discussed above, the second two, those involving perfect discrimination, are unlikely to be useful as a pricing scheme in urban transport. The essential factor of perfect discrimination is that the seller charges the buyer the highest price that he will pay.[3] Buyers will thus pay different prices for each unit they purchase, in line with the notion of diminishing marginal utility of each successive unit obtained. In order to carry out this type of pricing, however, three conditions are necessary: (1) monopoly power; (2) feasibility of establishing contact with the buyers so that the bargains for each unit may be struck; and (3) ability to prevent retransfer among buyers. With regard to urban transport, except for monopoly, great difficulty would be encountered in achieving these conditions. Such pricing is feasible only where there are but a few non-communicating buyers, a condition certainly not met in urban transport.[4]

However, the first possibility discussed above, setting the price at the competitive level and recouping the costs not covered through taxes, has definite merits. As the general public benefits from an increased supply of transport of all types, tax receipts from the general public may with justice be used to make up losses. In general, this is what has been happening in urban areas as far as the supply of highways is concerned. However, social costs are not recovered and a disproportionate share of the pecuniary costs comes from non-users.

An excellent argument can be made for the subsidized operation of mass transport if this requires a lesser subsidy than is at present provided for highways. In Philadelphia, where publicly supported operations of some Pennsylvania and Reading railroad commuter services have been carried on by the city through the Passenger Service Improvement Corporation, the 1960 subsidy for motorists was $50 for each auto registered in the city, but only $2.50 per resident for mass transport.[5] In all Passenger Service Improvement Corporation programs, fares are reduced and service is increased. In essence, the city, through Passenger Service Improvement Corporation, leases the improved quality and quantity of service from the railroads. This is roughly equivalent to producing output OQ_1, charging price P_2, and covering the remainder of the costs through the leased-service arrangement.

Free mass transportation has been suggested as a possible solution to the congestion problem.[6] Where such a scheme went into effect, referring again to Figure 1, output would be set at OQ_1 and the entire cost Q_1E collected through taxes. This assumes that public transport is more desirable than private transport and thus measures should be taken to increase its attractiveness by eliminating fares. There is an implicit assumption that a shift to mass transit would be achieved because motorists view it as a possible substitute for the use of their cars. Considering the substantial quality disadvantage of mass transport compared to private transport, it cannot reasonably be assumed that mass transport is a substitute for the private automobile for the majority of motorists.[7]

If, as is generally supposed, the present patrons of mass transport are really a more-or-less captive group who cannot use an automobile for one reason or another, their demand for transit service is relatively inelastic. Cutting or eliminating the fare would not increase ridership significantly, except perhaps for some off-peak, short-distance riding as a substitute for walking.

Moreover, if to the motorist mass transport is not a close substitute for using his car except perhaps under certain emergency conditions, the demand for automotive transportation is likewise relatively inelastic. Only those marginal motorists who seriously concern themselves with the cost of driving are likely to be attracted and there may not be enough such car-users to relieve the congestion situation to any large extent.

On the other hand, if mass transport could be made more attractive in the dimension of quality so that it is a competitive alternative to the private automobile, the presence of a good substitute for motoring would tend to make the demand for mass transport relatively price elastic and the lack of a specific charge for transit service might result in a considerable shift of demand toward public transport.

Of course, if mass transport were significantly improved in quality, it might be unnecessary to make it free. A partial subsidy, as in Philadelphia, might be all that was needed. Moreover, if public transport could be made attractive enough, and if the great disparity between public and private transport could be lessened, it might be possible to do away with the subsidy eventually. In any case, if the urban problem of congestion is to be alleviated, some sort of subsidy seems necessary. We must decide whether we should continue the relatively high subsidy for the private automobile, or shift to the lower-cost alternative of using public funds to help support mass transport.

NOTES

1. The following discussion grew out of a seminar in Urban Economics at Indiana University. I am indebted to A. M. Weimer, former Dean of the Indiana University Graduate School of Business, and Professor G. W. Wilson for suggesting the general framework used herein.

2. See George W. Wilson, *Essays on Some Unsettled Questions in the Economics of Transportation* (Bloomington, Indiana: Indiana University Bureau of Business Research, 1962), pp. 69–74.

3. See Joe S. Bain, *Price Theory* (New York, New York: Henry Holt and Co., 1952), pp. 416–417.

4. *Ibid.,* p. 425.

5. *IRT News Letter,* Institute for Rapid Transit Bulletin, March 30, 1962, Chicago, Illinois, p. 16.

6. See L. L. Waters, "Free Transit: A Way Out of Traffic Jams," pp. 139-147 below.

7. See John R. Meyer, "Regional Economics: A Survey," *American Economic Review,* March 1963, p. 42; and Leon N. Moses, "Economics of Consumer Choice in Urban Transportation," pp. 162-171 below.

Free Transit: A Way Out of Traffic Jams

L . L E S L I E   W A T E R S

THE FOLLOWING READING IS THE CLASSIC ARTICLE on the subject of free mass transportation. In it Professor Waters argues that transit could be placed on the same basis as police and fire protection—as one of the services provided by the city without specific charge at the time the service is used. One may argue back that even on a free basis, mass transport is sufficiently unattractive in an affluent automobile-owning society to have any great impact on the increased use of mass transportation. Nevertheless, making transit free would save on fare collection costs, if nothing else, and would make loading and unloading a much faster and simpler procedure than they are at the present time.

"Free Transit: A Way Out of Traffic Jams," *Business Horizons,* Spring 1959. The author is indebted to Mr. William Hughes of the University of British Columbia for his assistance in refining this plan for free mass transit.

Furthermore, at a time when there is considerable interest in a radical improvement of mass transport as a means of relieving congestion, other improvements in service, coupled with a lack of specific charge for use, may be sufficient to greatly increase the demand for transit and to decrease automotive congestion.

THE PROBLEM OF URBAN CONGESTION has greatly increased in recent years, and there is little hope that conditions will improve. The population explosion of the last two decades vastly enlarges the dimensions of movement of people and their possessions. The impact of the change in birth rate is yet to be felt appreciably on the demand for automobiles. Those born in 1942 are just now qualifying for drivers' licenses, and a few years will elapse before a cumulative effect impinges on the demand for automobiles.

Furthermore, rising incomes enlarge car ownership. Some 67 million vehicles now swarm over our highways and byways; the ratio of vehicles to population stands just under 1 to 3. In wealthier states, it is even higher—in California, the ratio is 1 to 1.9. Here, there is more than one car to a household, and the percentage of families having two or more cars is rising. College students reflect the American or automobile way of life; the two-car student is emerging. The year when 100 million vehicles swarm our roads is not far distant.

Not much imagination is needed to visualize the impasse developing in spite of ambitious national, state, and local efforts. Very few cities will be ready for a 50 per cent increase in the number of vehicles. If road facilities are utilized moderately, congestion seems to increase geometrically for a time as the car population rises arithmetically. Ultimately a standstill is reached. Of course, an increase in vehicles does not necessarily mean a corresponding increase in traffic. A bachelor who owns two cars is not likely to drive both at the same time.

COSTS OF TRAFFIC CONGESTION

TRAFFIC congestion entails enormous costs, both measurable and immeasurable. These include such diverse items as extra wages of truck, taxi, and bus drivers, wear and tear on vehicle parts, bumped fenders, higher insurance premiums, and greater gasoline consumption. Persons who drive to work may have to start half an hour earlier and arrive at their office or bench with jangled nerves and with the bloom off their productivity for the day. The scramble home is time-consuming and vexatious. If eight hours for sleeping and eight for working are subtracted from a typical day, then only eight hours of free time remain, and meals make further inroads. An extra hour coping with traffic cuts heavily into the optional time of millions of our work force. How does one measure the cost? But why bother when it is known to be so great, whether quoted in money or in some unit of disutility.

A cost that weighs increasingly heavy upon our society is the cost in terms of deaths and injuries. Few inventions of man are as lethal as the automobile.

Another cost is the enormous investment in streets, roads, lights, signs, bridges, and related facilities to meet needs for movement. San Diego, for example, has a $400 million plan. This seemingly large amount is for minimum needs only and is merely in line with programs of other cities. The new interstate and defense highway system initially called for $27 billion. Almost one-half this amount was destined to be spent within cities on that portion of the 41,000 miles within the confines of the cities.

Finally, a host of costs are incurred (but in some cases reduced) by the shifts in population and industry growing out of an array of factors, one of which is traffic congestion. Downtown areas grow absolutely but lag in comparison to suburban centers. Many functions previously concentrated in city centers are now diffused in outlying areas. Property values in sections on the perimeter of the city center have declined in many locales.

This may represent progress rather than retrogression, since it has prompted the organization of groups to save the downtown area, to rejuvenate the blighted section around the center, and to formulate master plans for traffic flow.

Causes of Congestion

THE enormous increase in the number of vehicles and their concentration in metropolitan areas have already been mentioned. The space for vehicles has been relatively limited because it has always been easier for our economy to spawn cars than places to put or use them. The volume of pedestrians further slows movement. At the present time, traffic impediments are so great in Manhattan that the average speed of taxicabs is less than that of marching troops. Cars have grown in size so that more space is required for driving and parking. Standardizing the work day has aggravated the congestion of rush hours. Many of our street facilities are more appropriate for a limited number of horses and wagons or buggies than for the present and prospective traffic.

SOLUTIONS FOR CONGESTION

CURES or attempts at cures for traffic congestion may be divided into four categories: (1) Increase the use of present street capacity; (2) Build more streets, expressways, and freeways; (3) Escape to the suburbs; (4) Stimulate mass transit.

The first category is in the sphere of the traffic engineer with his synchronized lights, one-way streets, improved signs, and other means. Prohibition of parking on streets increases the car-carrying capacity of streets, but also forces drivers to cover great distances in search of a parking lot with a vacancy.

Street widening has been costly and in a sense self-defeating. Expressways from outlying areas to the core have enabled even more people to move to a ranch-style home on the fringes of the city. The best and most taxable houses now are beyond the revenue base of the city that has just built the new thoroughfare! Lower-income people take over the vacated city houses. The new traffic artery can now funnel more cars into the center, thereby creating even more need for parking. A new scale of values for land use emerges. Increasing portions of downtown land must be assigned to parking, and as the process continues, essential qualities in the center of town deteriorate. Stores are no longer close to each other, although proximity of stores and services has long been the great merit of a downtown area. Multifloor parking lots are only a partial offset to the decreasing advantage of downtown areas. This does not mean that cities should not widen existing streets or build new ones. Indeed, an enlarged but judicious program must be followed that takes full cognizance of the limitations of streets.

A shift to the suburbs is a common solution. Many firms should be in the suburbs because there is no need for them to be in the center. Others can perform their services more efficiently by going to the people. The new order with the old city center surrounded by satellite shopping areas has much that is commendable; it is in keeping with changes in living desires and modern contrivances. Yet, during the transition, we should try to make municipal arrangements that serve the metropolitan people best in terms of costs of transport and ease of living. Some suburbs have grown so rapidly that their congestion begins to rival that of downtown.

To date, mass transit has not been as helpful as its potential permits. Cities have grown, but patronage of mass transit has declined. People simply have enough money for individual transportation and prefer it, regardless of moderate differences in cost. Patronage of streetcars and bus lines has declined generally. The rate of return for mass transit systems in 1959 will do well to average 1 per cent on a fair valuation of the assets of the remaining private companies. Transit gets municipalized, not because people prefer a bit of communism at the local level, but because no private investor can get a positive return from the business.

Transit companies are plagued by the high costs of operating on congested streets. They raise their fares a bit to cover costs and contribute even more to the attrition of patronage. Net revenue continues to decline, so rates go up again. By the time transit fares get to $.15 or more per ride, short-distance traffic is discouraged, and inequities on a distance basis are accentuated. This in turn leads to adoption of zones, which provide a measure of relief but not enough to yield adequate income to the transit company. Runs are cut in number and frequency so that the quality of service declines even more.

The load of transit companies tends to become more concentrated through standardization of working hours and the decline of the city center as an amusement area. Television keeps people at home, and they drive to the countryside for amusement rather than take a streetcar to a downtown theater. All sizes of cities have the same problem.

Perhaps those that suffer the most are the ones with a population under 100,000, in which transit has been discontinued completely—there are several hundred of these in the United States. Walking, driving, or taking a taxi are the only means of transportation available to the public. In extremely large cities of the East, there is some possibility that the transit companies or municipal operations may show better financial results because the urban congestion is so great that individuals reluctantly are having to admit that they cannot get around in their own vehicles. This stage, however, has not been reached in commuting service where profitable operations cannot be achieved in the foreseeable future. The poor showing of transit companies looks good only in comparison with the results of commuter service.

The case for mass transit is surprisingly strong. The private automobile in a large city is incredibly inefficient as a mover of people. It is bulky, costly to operate, and requires a disproportionate amount of street space for its operation. A typical city car contains only about 1¾ persons. The schedule below shows the capacity of a single traffic lane in passengers per hour by various modes of transport:

Autos on surface streets	1,575
Autos on elevated highways	2,625
Buses on surface streets	9,000
Streetcars on surface streets	13,500
Streetcars in subway	20,000
Local subway trains	40,000
Express subway trains	60,000

Source: *How To Keep Your Community Going Places* (Schenectady: General Electric Co., n.d.), p. 12.

The differences in the table are rather conservative. A bus with a capacity of 50, including standees, can operate in essentially the same area as two automobiles, which together would normally have 3½ persons. The critical problem is how to get people to utilize mass transit. They cannot be forced, and the service is not good in many cases.

Some officials have suggested barring passenger vehicles from the downtown area. Citizens would drive to parking areas in outlying districts and board a mass transit car. The trouble with the idea is that many citizens simply do not want to do it, and such a program might hasten the movement away from the city center.

FREE TRANSIT AS A SOLUTION

A SIMPLE solution with some complex ramifications would be to institute free transit for everyone. Mass transit can provide far more intensive utilization of space than private automobiles. Although service would have to be improved substantially if people were to patronize even free transportation, this could be done. The idea is not wholly new and was considered some years ago in Paris. Downtown business groups have on occasions provided free transportation for shoppers during off-peak hours. Transit companies themselves have experimented from time to time with reduced rates at off-peak hours. Previous suggestions and discussions have, however, been limited in application and did not seem fruitful. A critical review of all aspects of the problem of movement of people in cities gives impressive support to free transportation.

Mass transit facilities are six to forty times more efficient than automobiles. But people like to drive their cars and cannot be forced to take buses. However, if service were rapid, frequent, and free, the story would be different. People would travel all or part of the distance to and from work, shopping, and play, leaving their cars at home or diffusing parking over a broad area. Service would be fast because there would be fewer cars on the street and because passengers need not even walk by single file to pay their fares as they entered the bus or streetcar. The side of the vehicle could be opened for quick entrance and exit.

The idea is in the interests of economic efficiency on the assumption that a direct subsidy to the rider is not so bad as a larger subsidy to the place where he now rides in his car. Ownership of the transit arrangement could very well remain private and the financial arrangements be handled just like a garbage contract in some cities. If the idea sounds daring, this may be all to the good. We have tried all of the obvious cures for congestion and inefficient movement of peoples in metropolitan areas and have ended up with more distress than when we started. This may be the most effective answer proposed to date.

The transit operation, whether municipal or private, would simply start transporting everyone for nothing—by bus, streetcar, subway, or whatever means of public conveyance is available. Changes in patronage might prompt a new mix of the form of carriage.

Operating costs of mass movement would not rise proportionate to the increase in travel because of offsetting economies. There would not be a second person on a bus or a streetcar because no one would be engaged in the collection of fares. This would expedite service to an amazing degree. The same size of fleet could be operated to provide faster service because of the greater speed. As patronage swelled, an increased fleet would be needed, and this in turn would permit even greater speed because of the reduction in the number of private automobiles on the streets. If more people rode mass transit, some slight increase in revenue from advertising might accrue because the signs would be viewed by more persons.

Free transit could be provided either by a municipal operation or by a private company. If private, there obviously would have to be some means developed for remunerating the company. The difficulties here, though substantial, would not be insuperable, and surely could be worked out. Arrangements could be made for competitive bidding on the basis of number of passengers, passenger miles, or some other unit. Perhaps a superior arrangement could be worked out to operate on a cost-plus basis. Various criteria could be developed for extension or curtailment of service to the mutual satisfaction of the city and the private company.

Free transit would be provided not only to and from the downtown area, but wherever the movement of people made for economies in mass movement as compared with individual movement. There is no reason why the service could not be available to outlying shopping areas within the city limits. The problem should of course be approached on a metropolitan basis rather than a city basis—although the obstacles to this in the political sphere are rather formidable.

SOME EFFECTS OF THE SYSTEM

A MAJOR contribution would be made to the problem of congestion. This arises from the greater efficiency of mass transit in hauling people and especially from the diffusion of parking within the whole metropolitan area away from the centers. Many people would leave their cars at home and travel to their destination via mass transit. Others would drive as long as they encountered no congestion and then shift to free rapid

[145]

service. This would diffuse parking from the heart of the city where space is extremely valuable to areas on the perimeter. As transit volume increased, feeder runs could be authorized that would contribute further to movement on a group rather than an individual basis.

Critics of this plan may promptly assail it as another subsidy. No one is more opposed to certain subsidies than I. But it is primarily *because* of opposition to subsidies that the plan has appeal. Subsidies can be reduced rather than increased by utilization of the plan. Unless some concerted plans for a more efficient and pleasant way to move people are developed, there will be nothing in the future of municipal finance more costly than providing streets and parking places for all those who will be driving.

It is hard to determine precisely the magnitude of the savings that could be brought about by free transit. In one city where an $800 million street construction program is under way, the transit company grosses about $20 million per annum. If the capital expansion program could be reduced by one-third because of the new system, the city would save enough to provide free transportation for more than twice the former volume for a decade. Free transit is not a complete substitute for capital expansion for streets; the new scheme would simply reduce the amount that would be required. The older the city and the more inadequate its existing facilities, the greater the merit of the proposal.

The scheme is a daring one—but it needs to be. We have been too restricted by lack of imagination in previous attempts to solve our problem of urban congestion. There is, of course, a question about whether or not agreement can be reached by all those necessarily involved in putting the system in operation. It cannot be started on a limited or experimental basis; a review of all aspects suggests that pilot operations would not be very meaningful. Moreover, the final form would differ from one city to another. The stage we have now reached is the result of the evolution of many years of the automobile. We cannot expect to alter the situation much within a short period of time. Habits are too deepseated. More important, much doubt exists that people are rational in the use of automobiles anyway. Even if service were superb in frequency and comfort, men might still prefer to drive. There is something unusually satisfying from a psychological point of view about sitting at a wheel and commanding several hundred horsepower. Experiments by transit lines have shown that improvement in service and reduction in fares have not resulted in impressive increases in patronage.

Today few drivers know the cost of operating a car and they might well resent having the information, even though driving may be two or three times as expensive as transit. If free transit were available, they might be inclined to take it—much to their advantage and to that of the whole economy.

Even so, we cannot be absolutely sure of the success of free transit. Many years ago, Will Rogers declared: "America is the only nation that will go to the poorhouse in an automobile." Today he would observe that "America is the only nation in which a person would have a problem in going to the poorhouse. Which automobile would he drive?" Free transportation, however, might save his city from going to the poorhouse, and for the few in our affluent society who still must go, some might choose to leave their two cars at home and go by free, efficient, and comfortable mass transit.

CHAPTER 5

Mass Transport or Private Transport?

ALMOST EVERYONE AGREES that there is indeed a transport problem in
American cities. How to solve this problem remains a matter of
considerable debate. Many experts feel that the answer lies in providing
public highways for private automobiles while also creating a greatly in-
vigorated mass transportation system. The ideal, of course, would be to
have each of the general modes—private transport and mass transport—
do the job that it does best. Private transport is blessed by extreme flexibility; it will remain the type of transportation most desirable and most
economical for both individuals and society as a whole for a wide variety
of trips involving metropolitan areas. For trips oriented to the downtown
core, however, especially the journey to work, mass transport, because of
its economical use of space and its ability to handle large numbers of
people, is generally deemed to have the advantage as far as effective use of
space-resources is concerned. It is assumed that, offered service of a high
enough quality, people will gladly leave their cars behind and take the bus,
commuter train, or rapid-transit train. This may be a dangerous or even
foolhardy assumption when one considers the quality of mass-transport
service available today and the image of mass transport that is held by the
general public.

Clearly there is a need for the proper combination of facilities and
hardware and, where mass transport is concerned, for a substantial marketing effort. How this proper combination can be achieved is a straightfor-
ward-enough process, from an economic viewpoint at least.

The most feasible method is benefit-cost analysis, in which the benefits
and costs of a given group of alternative possibilities for a transport corridor or group of corridors are weighed against one another. In this type
of analysis, the social benefits and costs as well as the strictly pecuniary
revenues and costs must be assessed. If a given number of persons are to
be moved along a corridor, the cost of highway improvement, new highway construction, and the construction of new mass transit facilities and
equipment will be weighed against the benefits accruing from the various
projects. The rational economic choice will be the project that provides
the facilities to meet the need with the greatest net benefit.

There is a certain neatness about the use of benefit-cost analysis that is appealing, yet such analysis is not without significant pitfalls. The major difficulty is in placing dollar values on the non-pecuniary benefits and costs to society. It is certainly unwise not to consider such benefits and costs, but it may be just as bad to apply incorrect values.

Another issue that may loom large in the future is the question of the best type of mass transport if public transportation is to perform a larger share of the work of moving people in American cities. Modal capacity, passenger acceptance, and cost to the community are all important factors. Buses operating in the public streets are probably adequate for the needs of many communities of modest size. Where demand is large along certain travel corridors, however, or appears likely to grow sufficiently great to warrant the investment, grade-separated rapid-transit facilities or perhaps commuter-railroad operations may be necessary. Small and large urban area can therefore have their needs quite well served by what are regarded as conventional public transport modes, but there is a rather awkward middle ground between the ordinary bus operation and rapid rail transit that is currently not being filled in a very satisfactory way.

The issue of the proper kind of hardware to do the job becomes important when one realizes that in most urban areas in the United States the size of the population is such that a good medium-capacity transport facility is, or will be, needed. Investing in high-capacity rail facilities will most likely be a great waste of funds; sole reliance on the bus, however, may not provide a mode of transport of the quality necessary to appeal to the urban public. Nothing has been done yet to fill this gap, but suggestions range from lanes in the public streets reserved for bus operation, through special bus highways and streetcar-like light rapid transit, to monorails and other new concepts of transport. It certainly seems likely that there will be room for a substantial variety of new modes and concepts of operation to respond to the need for quality service, passenger appeal, and manageable costs.

Living and Travel Patterns in Automobile-Oriented Cities

KARL MOSKOWITZ

THE UTILITY OF THE AUTOMOBILE in serving the needs of city travelers is greatest in those cities that are well prepared to handle automotive traffic. In such places any mode of transportation other than the private automobile would have a difficult time providing so well and so inexpensively for the needs of most citizens. This point is clearly made by highway engineer Karl Moskowitz in the following article. Mass-transport advocates too often see only the advantage of moving persons by mass transport; they are often blind to the shortcomings. Reading what Mr. Moskowitz has to say will go far in restoring perspective to the matter.

I

I DO NOT KNOW when or where the expression "Auto-Oriented" originated; I first became aware of it when the city council officially declared Sacramento to be "Auto-Oriented," based on a report by Leo Daly & Associates, for whom Larry Smith made the economic studies. (Wilbur Smith and Associates, by the way, made the traffic surveys and freeway route recommendations for the Sacramento study.)

Sacramento is the central city of a U.S. Census Urbanized Area which had a population of 451,920 in 1960—192,000 in the city and 260,000 outside. I live outside, about 7 airline miles from downtown.

I am a resident of this auto-oriented community and a civil engineer. Plain residents are not as different from civil engineers as is sometimes supposed. Engineers employ many ways of searching for the truth. These include collecting, sifting and analyzing data, discovering relationships, and projecting these relationships. They include rational deduction based on the laws of nature, calculating solutions to equations, inventing, building, and testing. But the first thing an engineer does, if he can, is to take a look at what he can see with his own eyes. With this in mind, the first chapter in this essay is going to be the reporting of things I have seen and experienced myself.

Not only do I live in an officially auto-oriented community; but since starting to write this essay, I have come to the conclusion that I am auto-oriented myself.

It was not always that way. Until I was 11 years old (in 1921) there was not even a car in my family. In 1914 we moved to San Francisco from Berkeley, a suburb about 10 miles away, because my father got a job in western San Francisco; and by the then-existing mass transportation, he could come home only on week-ends. Later, he got a job in downtown San Francisco, and we moved back to Berkeley.

My father used to commute on the big red trains and white ferryboats of the Southern Pacific Company. The commute books contained tickets for every day in the month. This meant that on Sunday there was an un-

"Living and Travel Patterns in Automobile-Oriented Cities," paper presented at a symposium on "The Dynamics of Urban Transportation," sponsored by the Automobile Manufacturers Association, Inc., October 23–24, 1962, Detroit, Michigan.

used commute ticket unless my brother or I used it to go to the City. As a result, I got a lot of rides on those trains and ferryboats, and I loved it.

I can still smell the wax and fresh paint of the upper deck (and the linoleum of the steamer "Berkeley") and the steam and cylinder oil and salt spray of the lower deck. I can still see the big connecting rods and crankshaft of the side-wheel paddles and the walking-beam above of the steamers Santa Clara, Alameda, and Oakland (the Berkeley did not have a walking-beam). I can hear the creak of the piling when the boat hit the slip. I can smell the popcorn roasting in the ferry building. I can feel the slick varnished benches on the seat of my pants. It was a wonderful life, and a wonderful way of starting out the day. I was twelve years old at the time.

Ten years ago I took some rides on the Illinois Central between Chicago and the south side, and last year I took some rides on the subway in New York and on the combination subway-elevated in Philadelphia. In Philadelphia there is a station downtown, underneath the hotel where we stayed, which was reminiscent of the Ferry Building in San Francisco forty years ago. For some reason it didn't seem as glamorous at age 51 as it did at age 12.

At the present time, I consider myself auto-oriented because there are two cars in my family of two people. I have a ten-year-old car which I drive 4,000 miles a year to and from work, and my wife has a four-year-old car which she runs errands in and that we use when we go out of town. Every time either of us goes any place, we go by car.

I live in the suburbs, 8.8 miles from where I work. It costs me $317 a year, or $26.50 per month, to commute:

Car depreciation	$ 50
Insurance	58
Garage rent	78
Gasoline	54
Lube, tires, and repairs	37
Road taxes	40
	$317

I set my own time for going and coming. I have a comfortable seat and privacy. I keep dry in rainy weather, and it takes 24 minutes from my door to the door of the office building where I work. When the freeway, which is now under way, is completed, it will only take 18 minutes. It takes up to 5 minutes to get from the ground floor to the fifth floor of the building by mass transportation (elevators), including the wait.

If I cared to give up the flexibility of schedule and about 5 more minutes, I could join with two fellow-workers, ride in a newer car, and cut my costs by about two-thirds. As a matter of fact, for six years I did ride in a pool of five, and my cost then was $75 per year. A fellow across the street who works in the same building that I do *does* ride in a pool of five, each of whom takes the family car once a week. This does not cause him to buy any more cars than he would if he went to work on the train, if there were a train. So his total cost per *week* is 40¢ for a downtown parking space and 97¢ for running expense of his car.

From the window of the room in my home where I am writing this, I can see the homes of five other neighbors, besides the one who works where I do.

One of these neighbors is a brake lining salesman, and his office is a den in his own house. Every times he leaves the house, he goes to a different place; and he puts about 50,000 miles a year on his car. Second is a lumber dealer, whose yard is about four miles west of here. Third is a house builder who is presently working on a house three miles north and one mile east of here. Next month he may be working on a house 6 miles south. Fourth is a civilian employee of a military establishment four miles north. Fifth is a salesman in a hardware store two miles northwest.

As a civil engineer who majored in railroad engineering, I have been trying to figure out where I would lay a railroad that all of us could ride, if we were unhappy about driving. I must confess that my training is inadequate to this task. There is a freeway about four miles from where we live that does not quite go downtown yet. This freeway is paralleled by a railroad that does go downtown and is on a high-speed exclusive right-of-way. The railroad goes to the same places that the freeway goes, including the lumber yard and the military base. All of us use the freeway from time to time; three of us use it daily, but none of us uses the railroad. We wouldn't use it even if there were some trains on it, and the reason why is that we don't want to live on the railroad, although four of us do work near it.

All of us go to work by car, at the time we want to go and in the direction we want to go, and the longest it takes any of us is 24 minutes. About the longest trip a person can take in this auto-oriented urban area of a half-million people is one half hour, from edge to edge of the area.

Many persons who are devoting sincere, detached consideration to urban problems seem to encounter a paradox when they contemplate neighborhoods like the one I live in. This school of thought has been epitomized in the following quotation:

To most individuals, the automobile is a superior means of transportation. It is convenient, it is flexible, it takes them where they want to go.

From the social viewpoint, on the other hand, transit is the preferred form.

My neighbors and I would agree with the part of this quotation regarding the automobile. But why is it necessary to say that the social viewpoint is "on the other hand"? An engineer would tabulate the alternatives as follows:

On the one hand	*On the other hand*
Automobile	Transit
To most individuals	Social viewpoint
Superior means of transportation	?
Convenient	?
Flexible	?
Takes them where they want to go	?

It is not very difficult to fill in the alternatives where the question marks appear. Inferior, inconvenient, inflexible, does not take most individuals where they want to go. The difficult thing to understand is the alternative that *is* filled in: Is "social viewpoint" on the other hand from "to most individuals"? Unless social is spelled with a capital S, as in "Social Notes From Newport and Park Avenue" (where transit may be preferred—for the masses), or as in "U.S.S.R." (where transit is also preferred, for reasons of their own), the social viewpoint must be considered equivalent, not opposite, to the viewpoint of most individuals—the individuals to whom the automobile is superior, convenient, flexible, taking them where they want to go, when they want to go, comfortably and in privacy.

The same school of thought that places the welfare of society on the opposite side from that of most individuals also seems to be very concerned about transportation costs, especially the fact that some of the costs may be "hidden." In this respect, I will guarantee that my six neighbors and I, who from time to time discuss automobile prices, tire prices, gas prices, insurance premiums, and parking fees over the back fence, know a lot more about the cost of driving a car than we do about the cost of running a railroad which some people would ask us to finance. From what we hear, the cost of running a commuter railroad is pretty high, and almost always necessitates getting money from people who don't use the railroad. It would not surprise me if we know more about the cost of driving a car than even the officials who run railroads and set fares know about the cost of transporting commuters, especially on a railroad that doesn't exist at the present time and would have to compete with an existing mass transportation system (highways) that suits most individuals pretty well.

While on the subject of travel performed by my six neighbors and me, I would like to discuss a frequently deplored fact that on the average, an automobile only carries 1.4 to 2.0 persons.

One neighbor rides in a pool of five, and I drive by myself to the office. The average, so far, is 3.0 per car. The man who works at the military base takes a passenger. Now we have 8 in 3 cars, or 2.67 per car. The lumber dealer, the brake salesman, and the builder drive their own cars, solo. Now we have 11 in 6 cars, or 1.83 average. Finally, the hardware salesman's wife drives him to work and returns by herself. To the observer making an occupancy study, this looks like one trip with two persons and one trip with one person, so we now have a total of 14 persons in 8 cars, or 1.75 per car. Actually, however, the last two car trips only accomplished one work trip, so the real average is 12 work trips in 8 cars or 1.5.

We go in 6 different directions at 7 different times, and to me it seems inevitable, not deplorable, that the average occupancy is low. If it is deplorable, about the only solution I can think of is to follow the example of the residents of an island where I spent some time during the war. Each family had four coconut trees and some grass and chickens and a pig, and they made their own soap and used coconut oil for cooking and lamp fuel, and nobody had to go any place.

What *would* be deplorable would be for all of us to be coerced by economic sanction or forced by fiat to live in places decreed by governmental authority, or to work in another place, decreed by the same authority.

One of the reasons why my neighbors and I live where we do is that for a given amount of housing money,* we have more room. We consider this desirable. I have 7,000 square feet of grass, 50 shrubs, five trees, and 1,000 square feet of flower beds on my own lot, and I enjoy them. I may change 2,000 square feet of grass into a swimming pool next spring, but it will still look attractive and will be used and enjoyed.

My neighbors and I think it would be unfortunate if plans were to materialize that would make it impracticable to live the way we do. One such plan might be to make the cost of parking so high, by condemning the now privately owned land on which we park our cars for public purposes that we could not enjoy, that we would have to move.

Another plan might be to use the $120 per year I pay in road-user taxes to finance the deficit of a single-track railroad which would not come to my neighborhood. It is rumored that this imaginary single track railroad would be able to carry 40,000 people in one hour. I cannot imagine where

* My house and lot cost $12,000 in 1951 when the house was new. My monthly payment on the mortgage and taxes is $77.

these 40,000 people would come from or go to, or what this railroad would be used for during the rest of the day, but I do know that I would not be one of them.

I also know that my travel time is less now than it was ten years ago, despite the fact that this area has two and a quarter times as many people now as it did then, and the reason for this is that my user taxes have financed highway improvements. It seems pretty obvious to me that if my highway taxes were used to finance someone else's train ride, these improvements would come to a grinding halt, and that I could look for steadily increasing travel time in the future instead of the steadily decreasing time which will really be achieved because the improvements will continue to be made.

II

How can an auto-oriented urban area solve its transportation problems and provide for future growth?

I have taken an approach to this question which is different from many other attempts in one main way: Instead of trying to decide what will happen when a given city grows, why not take a look at the cities that have already grown?

I would now like to call the reader's attention to Table 1: "Population, Area, and Miles of Freeway—Five Urban Areas in California."

The five urban areas shown in the table were chosen at random, to cover a wide range in population. Freeway planning in these cities has progressed far enough to know just how many freeways are needed, and, as a matter of fact, where they will be located within a small range of adjustment. In other words, Table 1 is based on facts, not conjecture.

In 1959 the California State Legislature enacted a far-reaching law (Senate Bill 480, introduced by Senator Randolph Collier) that established a 12,000-mile freeway system in the State of California. Maps have been drawn which show the freeways that will be required and constructed in all the urban areas in the State by 1980.

All I had to do in order to construct Table 1 was to look at these maps and decide from knowledge of the present status of these five communities how many of these freeways are needed now (1962). There is no crystal-ball gazing involved. I measured the miles and put them down in the table. The miles shown on line 5 would enable residents in all parts of each community to enjoy journey times as portrayed by curve A on Figure 1. (At the present status of construction shown on line 4 of Table 1, some residents but not all get freeway rides; and the typical journey time in most California communities lies somewhere between curves A and B.)

TABLE 1

POPULATION, AREA, AND MILES OF FREEWAY
FIVE URBAN AREAS IN CALIFORNIA

	Santa Rosa	Fresno	Sacramento	San Diego	Los Angeles
1. Population, 1960	38,800	213,400	438,127	836,200	6,488,000
2. Area, sq. mi.*	13	70	147	263	1,520
3. Population per sq. mi.	2,980	3,050	2,980	3,180	4,260
4. Miles of freeways in operation or budgeted (1962)	4.5	9.1	28.8	38.9	242
5. Miles of freeways needed for 1960 population	5.5	23.5	56.9	99.0	515
6. Freeway miles per sq. mi.	0.42	0.34	0.38	0.38	0.34
7. Per 10,000 population	1.4	1.1	1.3	1.2	0.8
8. Proportion of area occupied by freeways	0.020	0.016	0.018	0.018	0.016

* These areas are slightly different from Census Bureau areas. Census Bureau areas apparently exclude enclaves. For the purpose of relating road miles to area, the over-all area must be considered.

One thing that the reader will note as he studies Table 1 is the amazing consistency between communities having such a wide spread in size. Professor Edgar M. Horwood of the University of Washington tried a similar analysis on a national scale and found almost no consistency. I think maybe there are two reasons for this. First, California has been auto-oriented for quite a while and experience helps; second, he was looking at *future* plans, whereas I am looking at *present* plans.

There has been a lot of loose talk and writing about the area consumed by freeways, streets, and parking. The facts as shown in Table 1 are different from much of this talk. In order to provide for between 50% and 60% of all the travel in an auto-oriented community, about 1.6% to 2% of the area should be devoted to freeways. The other 40% to 50% of the travel will take place on conventional roads and streets, which occupy about 22% of the total urban area. This travel will mostly be short trips and really can be looked upon as land-access travel. No trip can begin or end on a freeway.

In the course of investigating areas devoted to travel, I came across a fact which really surprised me, and I imagine will come as quite a shock to some people who have been concerned about land areas consumed for transportation purposes.

In Part I of this essay, I mentioned that I had not always been auto-oriented. The same thing applies to the City of Sacramento. In 1850 Captain John Sutter laid out the City of Sacramento. He could not have been auto-oriented. He was horse- and pedestrian-oriented. He set aside not 1.6%, not 15%, not 22%, but 38% of the area for streets and sidewalks.

The parts of Sacramento that were laid out in the 1900-1930 era have about 21% of the area in streets, and the parts that have been laid out since World War II have about 15%. The over-all average in the city limits is 22%.

This reduction as the auto came into prominence is not a coincidence. In the days when people had to walk, there had to be a lot of streets because they couldn't walk around the ¼ to ½ mile-long blocks that are suited so well to the automobile age. The automobile that makes it possible for the housewife to hop in the car and drive a mile or two to a supermarket instead of trudging a couple of blocks to the corner grocery, also makes it possible to live on long blocks which cut down the number and area of streets. When the auto-oriented housewife wants to exercise, she again gets in the car and drives to the golf course.

The 18% or more of the total area which is thus *saved* by auto transportation will cover the area required for freeways *tenfold*.

Most California communities anticipate doubling in size during the next 20 years. I do not know whether this will happen or not. During the past 100 years, California has a little more than doubled every 20 years. It is getting to be a habit, and a way of thinking, and people would be surprised if it didn't keep on being that way. (Some of us would also be pleased.)

This growth, if it takes place, will create travel. The 1.6% of the urban areas, and approximately 0.2% of the rural areas that will be occupied by the 12,000-mile freeway system will take care of an amount of travel, in vehicle-miles, equal to the total amount of travel that will be added. Instead of wringing their hands about this travel, Californians are preparing for it. We do not foresee being "choked" by transportation problems.

Another frequently heard comment based on imagination instead of fact, is that parking takes too much space. The facts are that one car space in an off-street parking facility takes about 310 square feet, including aisles and left overs. A parallel-parking stall on a street occupies 176 square feet. (This does not mean, to me at least, that on-street parking is desirable.) At 310 square feet apiece, one square mile will provide surface parking for 90,000 cars. To park all of the 3.3 million cars in the Los Angeles urban area simultaneously, off-street at a place other than their home base on one level (as opposed to multi-level parking garages), would require 37 square miles, or 2.4% of the urban area. In Sacramento, which is more typical of communities between 20,000 and 1,000,000 population, all 225,000 cars could be parked simultaneously away from home, off-street, on one level, in 2.5 square miles or 1.7% of the area.

However, all cars are not away from home at any one instant. In fact, less than half of them are, and many of these are on the streets and highways. Also, there are many multi-level facilities. So the actual area devoted to parked cars is more like 0.4% to 1.0%. I do not think this will break a community. In fact, judging by the financial and any other index that can be thought of, it seems as though the communities that do have lots of cars and lots of freeways and lots of parking space are doing much better than the ones that don't.

The heart of the matter of areas consumed is this: If you look at an office building you might see an area with 0% parking. If you look at a shopping center, you note a large amount of parking area in one place. If you look at a downtown area, you note parking areas in many places. If you look at a garage, it is 100% devoted to parking. This is neither good nor bad. It is simply necessary in order to do business. The question is, where do you draw the boundaries of the "area"? In an auto-oriented community, the boundaries are sufficient to encompass the places where the citizens live and work and play. The total area is devoted to all kinds of activities, one of which is parking cars. From the standpoint of distribution of total assets of the community, if the area devoted to parking is one percent of the total area of the community, this is a good indication of its significance.

To round out the statistical aspects of travel in an auto-oriented community, I have prepared Figure 1 showing typical journey times for various lengths of trip.

This chart is pretty much self-explanatory. Among other things, it shows why freeways become more important as the community grows larger. Attention is invited to the fact that a 30-minute journey only goes about half as far in a community without freeways as in a community with freeways. This means that for the same travel time, the freeway community can have four times as much area and four times the population.

In order to aid readers who may not live in auto-oriented communities to interpret the chart, I have plotted the journey time and distance along the Chestnut Hill Line of the Pennsylvania Railroad on this same chart. This information came from a time table I picked up in Philadelphia last year (1961). I assumed that the typical passenger lives within 5 minutes from the station. No allowance was made for his wife's time if she drives down to the station to pick him up. The peak-hour journey time is less

FIGURE 1 TYPICAL JOURNEY TIMES IN AUTO-ORIENTED URBAN AREAS

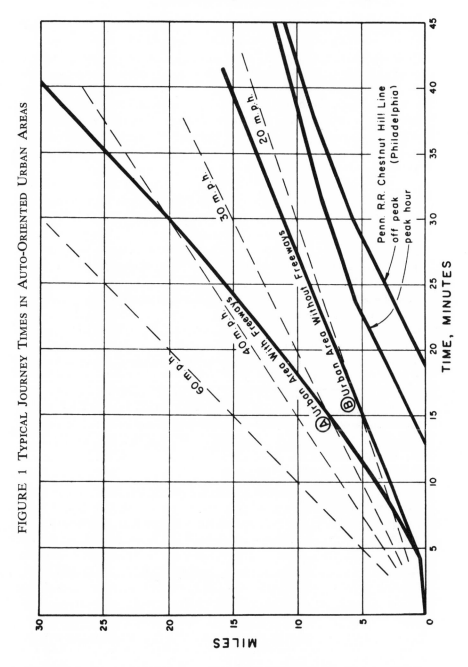

than the off-peak because the average waiting time for the train to start is only 8 minutes during the peak as opposed to 14 minutes during the off-peak.

This comparison also may be of interest to readers who live in auto-oriented communities that are contemplating large investments in commuter railroads, but before drawing any conclusions from it, they should realize that most of them will live more than 5 minutes away from the station, and they will also work more than 5 minutes from the station.

III

Is IT good or bad for an urban area to be spread out, as auto-oriented urban areas are? I guess it depends on the point of view.

Last year I went on a conducted tour with some foreign engineers along the east coast, and we stopped in New York City a couple of nights. We stayed in a hotel on 50th or 51st Street not far from Broadway. They were short of rooms so we had to double up. The room I shared was on the second floor, and it faced a light well about 10 feet across, and it was hot; the air conditioner howled but it did not cool the room. There was just barely enough room for the twin beds in this room, and there was not enough room on the floor for two suitcases. The carpet was dirty and the woodwork needed paint. It cost $18.00 per night. I have no doubt that there are beautiful, cool, clean rooms in some New York hotels, but I also have no doubt that they cost more than $18.00 for two. The meal cost $5.00 and consisted of chicken and peas; the beer cost $1.00 per bottle, and the waiters tried to hike the checks on the foreigners who did not speak English fluently. After dinner, we took a stroll and I noticed that movies cost $2.50. I noticed, too, that drinks were $1.00 and had about ⅝ ounce of whiskey in them.

The next day I noticed that the north-south streets were wide and the east-west streets were narrow. I noticed that even the wide streets were moving very few cars because the drivers were not auto-oriented and did not know how to proceed in an orderly fashion. I also noticed that it took me a half-hour to go and visit a friend down on 8th Street. I went by subway. There are lots of offices in New York, and I don't know how much they rent for; but I think they rent for more than comparable offices in Los Angeles, and I don't think you can get any more work done in them.

The following week, I took my wife on a trip to Los Angeles. We rented a room in a hotel on Wilshire Boulevard for $18.00. This room was a cottage consisting of a bedroom about 16′ x 24′, plus a dressing room the size of the New York hotel room, and a bathroom with a separate shower. The furniture was new and there was plenty of it. The whole room was obviously done by a professional decorator, and had been decorated recently. We had our dog with us. There were a lawn and flowers and trees just outside our three large windows. There was an olympic-sized swimming pool for the guests. There was free parking in a guarded lot behind the hotel. For air conditioning we opened the window, and we needed a blanket.

There is a famous French restaurant on the corner, but we went across the street to a famous American restaurant where we each had a double martini for $1.00 and a dinner built around a 10-ounce steak for $5.00. It was served by a charming girl.

The next day I noticed that the east-west streets were wide and the north-south streets were also wide, and that many cars were moving in both directions because the auto-oriented drivers know how to get the most movement with the least fuss. I noticed that Saks Fifth Avenue and Magnin's had some beautiful shops within walking distance for my wife to kill time in while I went downtown. I noticed that it only took me 14 minutes to go downtown and a half hour to go out to Westwood. In the paper I noticed that the movie that was $2.50 in New York was on view at a nearby drive-in for $1.25; and if I had wanted to go, I would have had a private seat and could smoke and take my dog and babies, if I had any babies.

I noticed that realty companies were building a lot of offices in Los Angeles, and I am informed that the rent for these offices is considerably less than rent in New York, and I noticed that many of them provide parking for the tenants. I do not think the contrast, from the consumer's point of view, between New York and Los Angeles is unrelated to the fact that Los Angeles is auto-oriented. I think that the prices are related to the rent, and I think that the rent is related to the scarcity of land, and I think that the mobility of Los Angeles makes it impossible for land to get as scarce as it is in New York, especially on Manhattan Island.

A lot of people have noticed the advantages of living in Los Angeles. Between 1950 and 1960, the population in the urban area of Los Angeles increased by 2.5 million people, from 4.0 to 6.5 million. This makes it the second largest urban area in the country, exceeding the Chicago-Northwestern Indiana urban area by more than ½ million. The 10-year growth alone was more than the total population of all but four of the other urban areas in the U. S. This does not sound like an ailing community. It sounds instead like a thriving community and I think it is because of, not in spite of, the automobiles there.

There are 3.3 million automobiles in the Los Angeles urban area and more than 200 miles of freeways. The autos and trucks travel about 6 billion miles yearly on the freeways, and another 18 billion miles on the rest of the streets and highways. About 6 billion passenger movements per year are now being made by automobile in the Los Angeles area. To appreciate the magnitude of this number, it may be compared with the 1.7 billion passengers that use the subways and buses in New York each year.

The journey time between typical locations in the metropolitan area of Los Angeles is less now than it was 25 years ago (and, in fact, less than it ever was), notwithstanding that the *increase* in population during that time has been greater than the total population of the Philadelphia-New Jersey urban area is now. Travel time is becoming less every year. Between 4:30 and 6:00 p.m., a 60-mile ride through the whole area along the long axis, from Calabasas to Tustin, takes 90 minutes. During the off-peak, it takes 70 minutes. A 45-minute band from 7th and Broadway in the peak hour encompasses 5.8 million people. During the off-peak, 30 minutes takes you clear out of the urbanized area (and on the east side, into the next one).

I am going to close this essay on living and traveling in auto-oriented cities with a quotation from Life magazine (June 20, 1960):

> Los Angeles, seemingly boundless in size and energy, has taken on the one great attribute it has so far lacked—that of a cohesive city. The tremendous sprawl of Los Angeles across the arid hills and valleys gave it the reputation of being many suburbs in search of a city. The expansion continues. But more and more Los Angeles looks, acts, and sounds like a city.
>
> Imaginative architecture, previously expressed in suburban markets and ranch homes, is forming the heart of downtown from decay into a smart unit of buildings. Home construction on hills closer to the city and the erection of towering apartments have helped consolidate the population. A growing civic pride helped build the $6 million Sports Arena where the Democratic Convention will be held next month. The roar of the civic pride fills the Los Angeles Coliseum when the Dodgers play.
>
> *More important than the Dodgers or civic buildings in giving Los Angeles its new personality are the ribbons of freeway which are gradually tying the city's scattered pieces together.*

Economics of Consumer Choice in Urban Transportation

LEON N. MOSES

VARIOUS MODES OF MASS TRANSPORTATION are often greatly inferior to the private automobile in terms of the quality of service they provide. Pinpointing quality is not as easy as it may seem at first. Nevertheless, discussions of transport quality usually include considerations of such questions as comfort, convenience, frequency of service, flexibility of service (ease of reaching a desired destination), speed, reliability, and accessibility of the service. In addition to the various quality elements there is the factor of cost. In general the public modes of transport are regarded as low in quality, but offsetting this impediment is the generally low cost of mass transport as compared to the private automobile. Conversely, the private car is generally assumed to be a high-quality transport vehicle with relatively high costs.

Some of the more hopeful people concerned with urban traffic congestion feel that automobile users can be enticed from their cars if the price of public transportation is made low enough. The following paper by Leon Moses, based on research conducted in Chicago, reaches a somewhat different conclusion. He argues that significant diversion from the private automobile may be possible only by levying negative charges on public transport—by paying people to ride. An alternative method would be to impose much higher charges on the use of automobiles. All of which bears out the adage that a cheap ride is not necessarily a good ride.

NINETEENTH CENTURY ECONOMIC DEVELOPMENT was in large measure based on the processing of vast quantities of heavy, weight-losing raw materials—coal, ore, timber, etc.—per unit of finished product. The technology of the period gave great impetus to the growth of urban areas in the Middle Atlantic and Lake States that were well located with respect to these raw materials and/or the means—largely rail and water—of transporting them. While by no means identical, the patterns of growth of these cities exhibited certain striking structural similarities.

1. Core or central areas with immense employment densities emerged. These areas dominated the economic, and often the cultural and political, life of the entire city.

2. The cities developed very high population densities. Population tended to concentrate in relatively circumscribed areas around the core and along a few main transport corridors.

3. A zone developed around the core area that was devoted to warehousing and other branches of distribution, as well as to manufacturing, and slum housing.

4. There tended to be large areas of open space between the main railway corridors.

These and other characteristics of cities that grew to immense size un-

"Economics of Consumer Choice in Urban Transportation," paper presented at a symposium on "The Dynamics of Urban Transportation," sponsored by the Automobile Manufacturers Association, Inc., October 23–24, 1962, Detroit, Michigan.

der the influence of nineteenth century technology of production, transportation, and communication dominate current images and definitions of what constitutes an ideal urban area.

Many of the cities that conform most closely to the nineteenth century stereotype are experiencing great difficulty adjusting to mid-twentieth century changes, partly because they are so heavily committed to technological necessities of a past era.

Some of their most severe problems (loss of middle and upper income groups; declining retail sales in downtown areas; erosion of the tax base; decline of mass transportation service and patronage; increased traffic congestion) arise from a conflict between past commitments and present tendencies. The commitments take the form of billions of dollars of social and private investment, particularly in downtown areas; the tendencies referred to are rapid decentralization of population and economic activity within given metropolitan areas, as well as the emergence and rapid growth of new urban centers.

It is commonly believed that the conflict and attendant social and economic difficulties of such cities as Boston, New York, and Chicago are in large measure due to increased automobile ownership and highway construction, and that ways must be found to divert commuters to public transportation.

Various measures have been proposed to accomplish this diversion and ameliorate such conditions as traffic congestion, parking difficulties, decline of mass transportation, etc. Fundamental to any such solution is a knowledge of the factors affecting consumer choice among the various modes. If we wish to divert commuters from their present mode, we must first discover why they have chosen that mode. We must try to determine which characteristics of the alternative modes must be changed so that they are more attractive.

It is the purpose of this paper to examine some of the variables which influence consumer choice in urban transportation. A technique of analysis will be developed which incorporates these variables. With this technique, it is possible to obtain an idea of the magnitude and effectiveness of some of the programs which have been advanced as partial cures for the transportation problems of our major cities.

An individual in an urban area usually makes a number of "trips" each day. For each of these trips, he may face a choice between various modes of travel or combinations of modes. The choice he makes will be that which maximizes the satisfaction or minimizes the discomfort involved in making the trip. The actual decision will be a function of various economic, geographic, psychological and sociological factors which are relevant to this commuter. Although a wide range of things may have an effect on the decision, certain characteristics are usually considered to have the most weight.

One of these is the nature of the trip itself. The location of the origin and destination determine whether in fact there is a realistic choice between two or more modes. A round trip from home to work in an outlying area may involve a route which is not served by public transportation and which is so far that it is prohibitive to walk or bicycle. Mode choice—automobile—is then dictated by these geographic considerations though alternatives such as car pooling may exist.

Similarly, the purpose of the trip may prescribe a certain means of travel. A trip to purchase various bulky or heavy items may have to be made by automobile. In addition, if the trip is one made infrequently, ignorance or inertia may lead to a mode choice which would be non-optimal if the actual alternatives were known.

In this paper emphasis will be placed on the work trip, thus obviating many of the difficulties just mentioned. If a commuter has alternative modes available from his place of residence, it is probable that they will apply to his work trip. Public transportation, especially modes with a fixed roadbed such as rail and elevated, generally focus on employment centers. In addition, it is likely that it will be physically possible for a commuter to take the various modes. Most people carry very little on their work trip—a briefcase or lunch, for example—so that they should be able to ride on any mode that is otherwise convenient. Since the work trip is made so frequently, it is also probable that the commuter will try to learn about his alternative modes and make the optimal choice.

With this emphasis on the work trip in mind, the second group of factors to be considered are the characteristics of the modes. In order to focus on the problem of consumer choice, it will be assumed that place of residence and destination (in this paper this will be place of employment) are fixed and that for the trip under consideration there exist two or more modes which can be taken. In other words, there is a choice between modes which are feasible for the trip in question. Such possibilities as walking or helicopter trips are excluded since the former is economically possible but usually too slow, and the latter, though very fast, is too expensive for all but a very few.

The essential characteristics of various modes facing a commuter are the money costs, the times in route, and the various psychological and physical attributes of a mode which can be called the disutility involved in traveling by that mode.

Each person will weigh these factors differently in arriving at his choice. While one person will spend a great deal just to save a few minutes, another will take a slower and more expensive mode because he "can't stand" traveling on the seemingly superior alternative.

While somewhat paradoxical relative to one another, each of these choices can be "rational" for that particular commuter. Given the origin and destination of his trip, the transportation system, and his own personal characteristics, he may—subject to his income and the attributes of the alternative modes—be maximizing satisfaction.

The model used in this paper to analyze choice of mode for the work trip involves certain assumptions. Some of these have been introduced above but will be repeated here. It is assumed that for the commuter in question there exist at least two feasible modes which he can take for the work trip. The locations of these modes or their routes, and the origin and the destination of this trip are assumed to be constant during the period of the analysis.

It is also assumed that the commuter behaves "rationally": if two modes are the same except for the time en route, he will take the faster; and if they are the same except for the money cost, he will take the cheaper. Initially it is assumed that the disutility of travel is equal on all modes. In other words, if two modes take the same amount of time and cost the same, the commuter will be indifferent as to which one he takes. The implications of relaxing this assumption will be examined below.

The analysis is limited to those commuters for whom travel is a fixed input, though the approach could be used to investigate mode choice where it is variable. We refer to travel as a fixed input when the number of hours a person must spend in travel is independent of the number of hours he works. For example, if a man spent thirty minutes getting to his office, he would have to make the hour round trip whether he worked one hour or eight hours. Travel is a variable input when the amount of income earned depends upon the amount of travel time. Such would be the case for salesmen and household repair men. The fixed input trips are considered the more important here since they form such a large part of the rush-hour travel peaks.

Given our assumptions, the mode characteristics that determine choice are the respective time and money costs. Two questions arise in analyzing choice with regard to these two variables. First, when no mode is dominant (both faster and cheaper), which will be chosen? Second, if a mode choice has been made, what would it require to divert commuters to another form of transportation? The emphasis here will be on monetary means diversion: i.e., price reductions on certain modes and increased tolls on others—rather than changes in time and quality.

Answering the above two questions poses no problem in the case where the modes require the same amount of time. The commuter will pick the cheaper mode since we are at the moment assuming that the dis-utility of a minute spent in travel is the same by the alternative modes. In addition, the minimum amount necessary to divert him from that mode equals the difference in cost between the two modes. That is, if the price of the cheaper mode were raised by that amount or the price of the ex-pensive mode lowered by it, the two would cost the same. The commuter would then be indifferent between them.

It is more difficult to determine a diversion price if, on the other hand, the modes cost the same but require different amounts of time. A given commuter might take the faster mode, but it is difficult to know how much value he places on each minute he saves. Nevertheless, a diversion price can be estimated if work and travel time are equally onerous to the commuter, and if he has freedom to choose how many hours he will work each day.

In these circumstances travel time savings can be valued at the com-muter's wage rate. The rationale for this procedure can be seen from an example. Suppose an individual works eight hours a day at two dollars per hour. He chooses a mode that takes an hour for the round trip in preference to another that requires two hours. How much would this indi-vidual have to be compensated in order to divert him to the slower mode? The answer is two dollars plus one cent. If the worker received two dol-lars, he would be indifferent between the two modes since he would have fifteen hours of leisure, he would spend nine hours in travel and work, and would receive sixteen dollars whichever mode he took.

Differences in cost between two modes can now be introduced. If the faster mode in the above example were also the cheaper, then the com-muter would have to be paid this difference in costs as well as the wage rate differential described above. Similarly, if the faster mode was more expensive, the difference in costs would be subtracted from the wage rate differential to obtain the diversion price.

The approach we have been developing can be expressed in terms of simple algebra. Let c_1 and c_2 be the money costs of the two modes while t_1 and t_2 are the times by these modes and w is the wage rate per unit time. A variable Z can then be defined as follows: $Z = (c_2 - c_1) + w(t_2 - t_1)$.

Under the assumptions specified, Z will indicate which mode will be chosen and what the diversion price will be. If Z is positive then the first mode will be chosen: it costs less, takes less time or both. Similarly, if Z is negative the second mode will be chosen. The absolute value of Z is also the amount which must be paid to switch the commuter from his present mode. In other words, if the commuter were paid this amount to take the other mode, he would be indifferent between the two since he would receive the same amount of income for the same number of hours spent in work and travel no matter which mode he took. The commuter would also be indifferent if the price of his present mode were raised by the amount Z.

In research being done at The Transportation Center, estimates of the value of this variable were made for an actual group of commuters. These individuals were interviewed for a study being done by the Cook County Highway Department. Data were gathered on the time and cost characteristics of their chosen mode, on their next best alternative, and on their annual income. The times and costs necessary for calculating Z were thus available and the wage rate could be approximated. The results so far have concentrated on those people who chose auto, a majority of the cases, though the analysis is equally applicable to those who preferred other modes.

The principal conclusions which can be drawn from our results is that price reductions greater than present fares would be required on each of the various modes of public transportation to divert one-third or more of the commuters who said that the auto was their best alternative.

If the price of automobile commuting were to be raised instead, it would take a one-way increase of about sixty cents or a round-trip increase of $1.20 to divert fifty per cent of the automobile drivers. These figures vary for the various modes but the conclusions can be seen from this summary. Diversion through manipulation of mode prices will be very difficult if our analysis is correct.

This conclusion is reinforced by two characteristics of automobile commuting which have been ignored so far. The first is that often there will be more than one person in each car. The Chicago Area Transportation Study states that there are on average 1.5 persons per car while the American Association of State Highway Officials put this figure at 1.8. If in fact two or more persons are in a car, the diversion price of that *car* will be increased by an amount equal to the sum of the Z's for the riders. In addition, this analysis assumes that the relative times of the two modes are the same throughout the analysis. However, any price change that accomplished some diversion will make it more difficult to achieve further diversion. The reason for this conclusion is that diversion reduces congestion and, therefore, the time required to make a trip for all remaining drivers.

One of the objections that can be raised to the above analysis is that the existence of a standard number of hours has not been taken into account. If there is a standard to which workers must conform, then they are no longer free to choose that combination of income and leisure that is optimal for them. Instead each individual faces a single combination of these variables for each mode, and has a fixed gross income equal to the wage rate multiplied by the standard number of hours. However, the number of hours of leisure that must be forfeited to obtain this gross income, and net income after travel costs, depends upon mode choice.

An illustration may again prove useful. Suppose an individual must choose between two modes. Two hours are required for the round trip by one of them and one hour by the other. The money cost for the faster mode is three dollars, while that for the slower mode is fifty cents. The wage rate is two dollars and the individual is *required* to work eight hours. As a result he has only two choices: fifteen hours of leisure with a net income of $13.00 or fourteen hours of leisure with a net income of $15.50. He can trade one hour of leisure for $2.50 but this is his only choice.

Imposition of a standard number of hours to which workers must conform means that the commuter is probably not as well off in terms of level of satisfaction as he would be if he could choose his hours of work. In this situation, an individual's choice of mode and his diversion price depend upon his preference system between income and leisure, something which cannot be measured.

One individual—call him a leisure preferrer—would devote less time to work if he had freedom to choose his hours. For him, the extra hour of leisure associated with choice of the faster mode is worth much more than the $2.50 he must pay to take it. Another person—call him an income preferrer—would like to work more than the standard number of hours but may be unable to obtain additional employment either in his own or some secondary line of activity. Such an individual might choose the slower mode because of the higher net income associated with it. Thus, when there is a restriction on hours, our Z measure need not indicate the correct mode choice, and it may not produce a correct estimate of the diversion price.

The measure does have value, however, in certain common cases. In urban travel, the automobile is usually faster but more expensive than the various alternative modes which can be taken. When it is known that a person prefers the automobile in this situation, it can be shown that the Z measure is an underestimate of the diversion price for any person who is a leisure preferrer.

This is also true if the automobile is faster and less expensive. It should be noted that with a restriction on hours, the diversion price has two values which are not necessarily equal. The first is the amount which must be charged the traveler for taking his preferred mode so that he is indifferent between it and his next best alternative. The second is the amount he must be paid for taking a trip on the alternative so that it is as attractive as the preferred mode.

In the situation just described, Z is an underestimate of both of these amounts. This is important since we believe that restrictions on hours are much more binding on leisure preferrers than they are on income preferrers. If this is true, then the Z measure, used in the manner described in this paper, would provide a minimum estimate of the amount tolls would have to be raised or fares decreased to divert various percentages of automobile drivers who fall into the most common case: i.e., automobile faster and more expensive.

Until now, the effect of disutility has been ignored. In reality, the disutility of traveling by a certain mode may have an important role in the commuter's decision. There were a number of individuals in the Cook County study who took a mode even though it was slower and more expensive than their "best" alternative mode. Travel by the alternative mode must therefore be so onerous that they are willing to lose income and time to avoid it. In such cases, it is impossible to estimate a diversion price since it might take only a small reduction in the price of the alternative (or rise in the cost of the present mode) to make its time and cost advantages outweigh the greater disutility involved in its use.

The introduction of disutility is more likely, however, to reinforce the conclusions reached above concerning Z. It is commonly believed that the automobile involves less disutility than the other possible modes. This being the case, Z will be even more assuredly an underestimate of the diversion price for automobile drivers. They will have to be compensated not only for the time and money advantages foregone but also for the greater disutility incurred when they switch to another mode.

In summary, this paper has examined some of the important variables which enter into the consumer choice of mode in urban areas. A measure has been developed to indicate which mode a commuter will choose and what the diversion price will be to make him switch to an alternative.

Data available were used to estimate values of this measure for an actual group of commuters who took the automobile. For a majority of such people, those for whom the car is faster, we believe that this measure provides an underestimate of the diversion price even when restrictions on hours of work and disutility of travel are introduced.

The principal conclusion arising from these calculations is that it would be very difficult to divert these drivers through fare reductions on alternative modes. Such a policy would require "negative" prices if it were desired to divert as few as one-third of the drivers indicating any specific mode as their best alternative. It might prove more feasible to raise the cost of automobile commuting, but this would require increases of between one and two dollars per round trip to effect a fifty per cent diversion.

In considering the attractiveness of the two policies so far discussed, it would surely seem more desirable to increase the price of automobile transportation by the amounts indicated than to pay rather large subsidies to individuals in order to divert them to public transportation.

It is appropriate that mention be made at this point that there are a substantial number of very sound economists who urge that the price of automobile commuting also be increased on grounds of economic efficiency. The efficiency argument has it that the price of automobile commuting should be adjusted to its marginal cost and reflect the fact that as the numbers of people increase, the time required to make the trip also increases.

The efficiency argument has a great deal of force and as an economist I accept it. However, city planners, municipal officials, and public administrators whose real concern is not traffic congestion and the inefficient use of highway capacity—viewed as a resource—but the economic future of our mature, central cities, should pause before accepting it.

The assumption most often made in studies that deal with traffic problems is that people will shift to public transportation for the downtown work trip if the cost of automobile commuting is increased sufficiently. There is a third alternative. Substantial increases in the cost of downtown commuting could solve the traffic congestion problem by encouraging a faster movement of manufacturing and business establishments from the core area of the city to suburban areas, or even to the newer, less-well-developed portions of the country.

In economists' language, all of us have been proceeding as if the demand for downtown trips is perfectly inelastic and choice restricted to the various means of getting there. This is incorrect. Transport costs are a significant factor in determining where within a metropolitan area economic growth will take place. If the cost of getting to the downtown area is greatly increased, there is a strong possibility that the core area's traffic problem will be solved by reducing the number of people who work there.

Changes in price are not the only method by which diversion may be carried out. Investments that reduce travel times and the disutility of travel by the alternative modes might prove effective. The Z measure divided by the wage rate would provide an underestimate of the number of minutes by which travel time would have to be reduced in order to carry out various percentage diversions.

Unfortunately, data are not now available on the amount of investment that would be *required* to bring about various reductions in travel time on the alternative modes of public transportation. Until they are obtained, we will not be able to compare the cost and effectiveness of a diversion program based on new investment with one that involves reductions in the price of public transportation.

The Importance of Urban Transit and Its Effective Passenger Capacities

WALTER S. RAINVILLE

MASS TRANSPORTATION CAN PROVIDE a good supply of transportation while using a relatively small amount of valuable land. This is the major argument for increasing the use of the public modes of transport to relieve traffic congestion. Arguments favoring mass transport merely on the basis of its capacity are purely academic if the demand for the service falls off. If strong efforts are made to increase demand for transit, a knowledge of the capacities of the various modes is essential. Anyone concerned with the amount of space necessary to move people by various modes, including the private automobile, is likely to be highly interested in the following paper.

As THE BACKGROUND for a consideration of the importance of urban transit and its effective passenger capacities, let us examine briefly the urban metropolis.

Our census takers, population experts, sociologists, economists and urban planners all point to the bigger and better "metropoleis" (to use the accepted plural) of the future. Despite the drops in population reported for the arbitrarily-delineated central cities themselves, there has been tremendous growth in the surrounding suburban areas and, therefore, in the metropolitan areas as a whole. The dominant population shift is from "farm to city"—or, from rural to metropolitan area.

The growth-process of our urban communities will not be without its growing pains. Problems of area administration, financing, taxation, community services, water supply, housing and urban renewal, traffic congestion and others will increase in numbers, intensity and complexity. Not the least of the "other" problems will be that of adequate transportation for the fluid movement of people and goods—embracing the elements of (1) streets, highways and expressways, (2) off-street parking, and (3) public transit in optimum "balance."

Metropolitan area industry, commerce, education, recreation—all depend upon the adequacy of provisions for free and expeditious movement.

"The Importance of Urban Transit and Its Effective Passenger Capacities," *Traffic Engineering*, May 1961. The original article contained two nomographs, which have been omitted here.

Keeping movement "free and expeditious" will challenge the best—the most dedicated and conscientious—administrative, technical and legal talent available, all working together in concert to achieve a constructive urban program.

CHANGE IN CONCEPT INEVITABLE

THE past few years have seen slow, but perceptible, changes in the thinking of urban planners, administrators—yes, and even politicians—about this problem of free and expeditious movement in our metropolitan areas.

The nation, the general public, our leaders, have all been captivated by the utility and the glamour (or status-symbolism) of the private passenger automobile. Until the recent limited passion for so-called "compact cars" as a change of pace in our rapid march to Automania, the objective of builder, buyer and seller was to "build 'em bigger and fancier"; to stimulate the market for automobiles and all that goes with them in the way of resources—both material and labor. National leaders have blanched with fear at the prospect of a Michigan-based depression resulting from a slackening of the demand for new automobiles. A multi-billion dollar highway program has been spawned to insure that these vehicles will have "a road to run on" when they leave Detroit. Significantly, relatively little has been done—or can be done—about finding a place to PARK them.

Some of our national students and thinkers have long stood aghast at the tremendous waste of our resources—human and physical—involved in the inherent inefficiencies of passenger movement by private automobile in congested metropolitan areas. These lonely watchers are heartened by the slowly-awakening interest of vital thought-forces in the metropolis in approaching the problem in a different way.

It is inevitable that the planners and technicians will come to appreciate and espouse a more efficient use of our material and human resources in effecting the essential movements of persons and goods in, through and around the central city. It is inevitable that they shall discover public transit to be a highly efficient means of effecting passenger movements from the standpoints of conservation of street space and off-street space in the center city, conservation of metals, fuels, rubber and other items of vital importance to our people in time of national emergency or war, and conservation of public and private moneys. It is inevitable that from the foregoing standpoints and others, transit will become increasingly recognized—despite the efforts of the automobile-and-road-builders and their suppliers and adherents—as the preferred means of passenger transport in congested urban areas—preferred from the general, collective, public point-of-view; or, if you will, preferred by the community collectively in its own best self-interest, and notwithstanding the individual preferences and choices of the family units comprising it, which they will gladly set aside in the pursuit of the common good if they are accorded the inspired, dedicated and courageous leadership to which they are entitled in this great country.

In the President's recent special message to the Congress on HOUSING, in speaking of "improving our cities," Mr. Kennedy said, "And they must improve their transportation systems, particularly rapid transit services." Under the heading of "Community Facilities and Urban Transportation," he said "Nothing is more dramatically apparent than the inadequacy of transportation in our large urban areas. The solution cannot be found only in the construction of additional urban highways—vital as that job is. Other means for mass transportation which use less space and equipment must be improved and expanded. Perhaps even more important, planning for transportation and land use must go hand in hand as two inseparable aspects of the same process."

IMPORTANCE OF TRANSIT RECOGNIZED IN 1957 AASHO URBAN HIGHWAY POLICY MANUAL

IN ITS 1957 handbook entitled "A Policy on Urban Arterial Highways in Urban Areas," the Committee on Planning and Design Facilities of the American Association of State Highway Officials had this to say about public transit:

Arterial highways provide for the efficient movement of people and goods, not vehicles alone, and it may be desirable to locate and design highways for use in combination with a transit facility. (page 86)

Public transit may affect not only the geometric design of the arterial highway but its location; thus, provision for public transit should not be an afterthought but an item for consideration in the early stages of design. Thorough analysis is necessary in regard to the origin and destination of transit riders, capacity requirements, and present and future public transportation needs. Hence, the cooperative effort of both highway and transit engineers is necessary to assure proper consideration of all features. (page 140)

Passenger Carrying Capacity. In terms of passengers accommodated, a public transit vehicle, while it is moving, is a more efficient user of street space than a private automobile. The volume of passengers transported depends upon the type of highway, the type of mass carrier, the headway of transit vehicles, and their passenger carrying capacity. (page 141)

The policy manual then goes on to devote a total of some 30 pages to consideration of public transit on major streets, on at-grade expressways, on depressed freeways, and on elevated freeways, along with some dozen illustrations covering bus turnouts and stop facilities at freeway and street levels for various types of interchanges, and including facilities for rapid transit trains in an expressway median strip.

In general—and aside from the omission of certain basic "quantifying" relationships—transit is treated in the AASHO manual as a valued user of the nation's streets and highways, and is commended to the early consideration of the highway engineer as a present and potential element of the urban transportation system.

It is the purpose of this paper to supply some of those important relationships showing the relative "effective passenger carrying capacities" of the private automobile and the various forms of public transit. These should prove of interest and assistance to the highway engineer, the traffic engineer, and the planner.

THE PRIVATE PASSENGER AUTOMOBILE

LET us take the private passenger automobile as a starting point, and look to the Highway Capacity Manual, and at the work of traffic engineering consultants elsewhere, for examples of what this conveyance can do.

Examples are shown in Table 1.

TABLE 1

Vehicle	Type of Facility	Lane Practical Capacity, Vehicles
Automobile	City Street	600 per hour
Automobile	City Street	800 per hour
Automobile	Expressway	1,500 per hour
Automobile	Expressway	2,000 per hour

Let us also examine the results of innumerable central business district cordon counts taken over the years during the heavy hours of movement of retail and office workers, shoppers, etc. These reveal average occupancies of the private automobile, including the driver, ranging from 1.25 to 1.75 rush-hour occupants moving into and out of the C. B. D., with a "usual" average occupancy under such conditions of 1.4 to 1.5 occupants.

Let us add an "extreme" column for an average occupancy of 2.00[1]— seldom if ever attained as an hourly rate during the rush hours to and from the central business district, and construct Table 2 for various average passenger occupancies.

Thus, we get some idea of what the automobile does and can do, as a "private and individual" means of transportation, in moving persons to and from a CBD in rush hours.

TABLE 2

Facility	Lane Practical Capacity, Vehicles	Effective Passenger Capacity			
		@ 1.25	@ 1.50	@ 1.75	@ 2.00
City Street	600 per hour	750	900	1,050	1,200
City Street	800 per hour	1,000	1,200	1,400	1,600
Expressway	1,500 per hour	1,875	2,250	2,625	3,000
Expressway	2,000 per hour	2,500	3,000	3,500	4,000

Table 3 shows the transit bus in peak-hour service.

TABLE 3

Lane Practical Capacities—Transit Bus*

Vehicle	Type of Facility	Vehicles per Lane per Hour	Headway (min.)	Effective Passenger Capacity (Pass. per Hr.–Range)
Transit bus	City Street	60	1.000	3,720– 4,500
Transit bus	City Street	90	0.667	5,580– 6,750
Transit bus	City Street	120	0.500	7,440– 9,000
Transit bus	Expressway	120	0.500	7,440– 9,000
Transit bus	Expressway	180	0.333	10,860–13,500
Transit bus	Expressway	240	0.250	14,880–18,000

* Assumptions: (Range)
    Transit bus—50-seat, loaded to^2 125% 150%
                                    of seats

A COMPARISON OF THE EFFECTIVE PASSENGER CAPACITIES OF THE AUTOMOBILE AND THE TRANSIT BUS

COMPARING Tables 2 and 3, we now have the elements at hand for de-termining a relationship:

(1) A transit bus on a city street operating on a headway of 60 seconds (60 buses per hour) has an effective passenger capacity of 3,720 persons per hour at 125% load factor. The private automobile on a street lane operating at a rate of 800 vehicles per hour and carrying an average of 1.5 occupants has an effective passenger capacity of 1,200 persons per hour. 3,720 divided by 1,200 equals 3.1. Hence, one such lane of buses on a city street has an effective passenger capacity equal to that of 3.1 lanes of automobiles.

(2) A transit bus on an expressway lane operating on a peak-hour head-way of 30 seconds (120 buses per hour) has an effective passenger ca-pacity of 9,000 persons per hour at 150% load factor. The private auto-mobile on an expressway lane operating at a rate of 1,500 vehicles per

hour and carrying an average load of 1.5 occupants has an effective passenger capacity of 2,250 persons per hour. 9,000 divided by 2,250 equals 4. Thus, one such lane of transit buses on an expressway has an effective passenger capacity equal to that of *four* lanes of automobiles.

(3) A transit bus on an expressway lane operating on a peak-hour headway of 20 seconds (180 buses per hour) has an effective passenger capacity of 10,860 persons per hour at 125% load factor. The private passenger automobile on an expressway lane operating at a rate of 2,000 vehicles per hour and carrying an average load of 1.5 occupants has an effective passenger capacity of 3,000 persons per hour. 10,860 divided by 3,000 equals 3.62. Therefore, one such lane of transit buses on an expressway has an effective passenger capacity equal to that of 3.62 such lanes of automobiles . . .

On the basis of the reasonable assumptions of the foregoing "sample" comparisons, it might be said that under these entirely attainable conditions, one lane of peak transit buses can handle as many persons per hour as can be moved by three to four lanes of automobiles. This suggests a lane efficiency of 3 or 4 to 1 in favor of the transit bus.

This is an important relationship for the planner (highway or otherwise) to bear in mind when seeking the solution of urban transportation problems in terms of money and space—especially in view of the added feature that those "bus riders" will not need to have parking spaces provided for them in the congested downtown area.

Rail Rapid Transit

Rail rapid transit systems can and DO carry persons at rates of 40,000 per hour and more to and from central business districts at rush hours. Under today's track, signal, station, platform stairway, ramp, escalator and elevator capacities, it is a demonstrable fact that trains can safely be moved on headways as close as 90 seconds. The technology is available for extending these limitations. But accepting them for purposes of this analysis, Table 4, effective passenger capacities, sets forth the abilities of rail rapid transit on a modest basis . . .

(1) A rapid transit train of 8 cars of "average" size operating on a 2-minute headway has an effective passenger capacity of 28,000 persons per hour. The private automobile on an expressway lane operating at a rate of 1,500 vehicles per hour and carrying an average of 1.5 occupants has an effective passenger capacity of 2,250 persons per hour. 28,000 divided by 2,250 equals 12.44. Thus, such a rail rapid transit system operating over a single track in the prevailing direction has an effective passenger capacity equal to that of 12 such lanes of automobiles.

TABLE 4

Lane Practical Capacities*
*(Subway or elevated, on private right of way, or in center
mall of an expressway)*

Type of Vehicle	Trains per Hour	Headway (min.)	Effective Passenger Capacities (Range)
Rapid)	20	3.0	18,000–24,000
Transit)	30	2.0	27,000–36,000
Train)	40	1.5	36,000–48,000

* Assumptions: rapid transit 10-car train, carrying value—90–120 pass./car.

(2) A rapid transit train of 10 cars of "average" size operating on a 90-second headway has an effective passenger capacity of 48,000 persons per hour. The private passenger automobile on an expressway lane operating at a rate of 1,500 vehicles per hour and carrying an average of 1.5 occupants has an effective passenger capacity of 2,250 persons per hour. 48,000 divided by 2,250 equals 21.3.

The private automobile on an expressway lane at 2,000 vehicles per hour and an average occupancy of 1.50 persons has an effective passenger capacity of 3,000 persons per hour. 48,000 divided by 3,000 equals 16.0. Thus, such a rapid transit system has an effective passenger capacity equal to that of 16 such lanes of automobiles at 2,000 vehicles per lane per hour, or equal to that of 21 such lanes of automobiles at 1,500 vehicles per hour.

The examples chosen suggest a lane efficiency ranging from 12 to 1 to 20 to 1 in favor of the rail rapid transit. Again, as in the case of the transit bus, this is an important relationship for the highway engineer and the planner to keep in mind when considering the transportation needs of urban metropolitan areas—especially in view of the lack of parking requirements for the rail rapid transit passengers in the central business district. Parking lots along the transit route at outlying points can facilitate a desirable "wedding" of the advantages of the automobile where it can best serve (in outlying areas) and rapid transit where it can best serve (in the more congested area), from an overall community point of view.

SOME QUESTIONS ANSWERED

IN the February 1961 issue of *Traffic Engineering* there appeared an item entitled "Let's Analyze It!" This item was carried by the magazine in a "box" to attract attention and, speaking of the relative "effective passenger capacities" of transit and the automobile, it raised the following questions, among others:

(a) But when all is said and done, what good is such a comparison anyway?

(b) Are we interested in what can be done WITH people or TO people, or what people probably WILL do?

(c) And to what degree should this comparison of people passing a point during a single hour be the determinant of the desirability, or even the efficiency, of a facility?

(d) What about Sunday traffic? Freeways often carry more people on week-ends than on weekdays, while transit tracks lie virtually idle.

(e) What about time of trip from end to end? Rail transit can claim high speeds between stops, but what about stops at stations, time lost in waiting for trains, time spent in waiting at transfer points, and time spent in walking from transit vehicles to home or office or store?

Here are some answers to these questions:

(a) *The Comparison:* Such a comparison is important because it draws the attention of the highway engineer and planner, the politician, and the taxpaying public—motorist or otherwise—to the fact that there *is* a more efficient and more economical way of doing the job of moving persons in urban metropolitan areas which *should be carefully investigated* before an open-and-shut decision is made to *attempt* to do the job by building more expressways for more automobiles. . . . It is just as important for people to know these relationships as it is for them to know that the automobile-and-highway alone cannot do the job for the central business district-bound passenger traffic.

(b) *The People:* We must—of necessity—become concerned with what people *should* do (as well as with what they *want* to do), individually and collectively, in the best interests of the urban metropolitan community. This calls for informed, courageous leadership by our elected and appointed public officials at all levels for governmental operation—local, state, regional and national. It calls for showing the public in plain, understandable terms what will happen to our urban society if they are permitted to do as they "*will* to do" with the private automobile, as opposed to the desirable alternatives in urban development which may result from the adoption of a *balanced* transportation program—streets and highways, improved public transit, and additional off-street parking in the proper places—in the optimum combination for a given community's needs.

(c) *The Peak Hour:* There is a practical job to be done each weekday in the metropolitan area—that of moving workers, shoppers, etc., to the central area of activity (as well as elsewhere) and back home again. The bulk of such movements usually takes place over relatively short and congested—but extremely important—periods of time. To gather the necessities and luxuries of life, including the "fishtailed" or even the so-called "compact" varieties, and to pay their taxes in support of the highway and expressway systems, persons must occasionally work to "earn their keep"; and must, if employed in the C. B. D., get to and from work over routes or "throats" which at one point, or along one stretch, become the "heaviest" in terms of persons per hour having to move through. These are the most important points from the standpoint of passenger movement. They are as significant to the transit technician as is the formula for mixing concrete to a highwayman.

Just as you can bail more water in a hurry from a foundering boat with a bucket than you can with a spoon, so you can do a better job of moving people through congested streets to and from the central business district in the rush hour—an extremely important hour in the commercial life of the community—with a public transit vehicle than with a multitude of automobiles. The ratios? One lane of transit buses equals up to *four* lanes of automobiles. One lane of rail rapid transit equals up to *twenty* expressway lanes!

(d) *Sunday Traffic: Idle Transit Tracks:* Fine—we hope the recreation-bound Sunday motorists enjoy their freeways and use them safely! . . . and, that all the fine luxury vehicles using them are in good mechanical condition so that there are no breakDOWNS and tieUPS.

Come Monday Morning, however, the wage-earner must "get back to business" to "pay the freight" on his Sunday recreational activities and to provide his family with the basic necessities and other luxuries of life—such as the taxes he pays in support of his leisure time pursuits. Here, in this most important aspect of family life, the sleeping Sunday rail cars and trackage come to life and handle the passenger traffic needs of this most important hour of the day in doing a job which the private automobile alone would find impossible of accomplishment.

That the transit facilities are not used to capacity off-peak Saturdays and Sundays is an economic fact-of-life which public officials will eventually have to accept—and try to alleviate—in maintaining and improving the public transportation facilities without which the community cannot prosper. The realization must and will become more general through a fact-finding and courageous public educational program that the auto-and-highway alone cannot do the job. Public officials themselves will be forced by the passage of events to tackle this (as now considered) "disagreeable" task in many metropolitan areas in order to preserve the values and advantages, economic and cultural, of a strong central city area.

(e) *Transit Travel Times:* Such elements of time as mentioned by the questioner are admittedly inherent in the use of transit service. . . . Just as inherent, in fact, as certain elements of time involved in the use of the family car in home-to-work movements: unlocking the garage door, backing out into the street; waiting at traffic signals and stop signs en route to and from the expressway; cruising to find a parking space, a parking lot, a parking garage; walking from the hard-won parking space to the office or store. If you are in a car pool, add waiting time for the pool driver to arrive, or, if you are he, waiting for your passengers to finish their morning coffee or shave. Add, when the car breaks down, time wasted in trying to "get it going" before abandoning it (for that trip, of course!) in favor of the bus. Add, in winter, the time spent shoveling the drive or thawing the carburetor, or putting on or taking off chains. Well . . . you can take it from there!

The questioner of the February, 1960, issue asked another one:

(f) Over 300,000 people move over the Hollywood Freeway on a typical weekday. What other transportation facility can make that statement?

Answer:

The New York City Transit Authority could make such a statement if it wished. . . . The Lexington Avenue subway in New York carries far more persons than that on a typical weekday. Some 545,000 persons move over this facility *past the maximum load point* ALONE, not to speak of the thousands of others who use the route in movements which do not bring them past this important "maximum" point of transit schedule design. . . . The Seventh Avenue subway in New York and its counterpart on Eighth Avenue develop quite similar, though perhaps slightly lower, volumes of passenger movement.

So, we will pose a final question for the questioner: "If freeways are the 'hands-down' answer in Los Angeles, why is the Los Angeles Metropolitan Transit Authority spending millions of public dollars in investigation of, and planning for, a rapid transit system for that metropolis?"

NOTES

1. Automobile riding to and from central business districts during rush hours does not, as a matter of observation, "average out" at occupancies of 2.0 or greater. Apparently, most motorists and their families own their automobiles for the "exclusiveness and distinction" they enjoy thereby and do not generally seek to load up their cars with fellow-CBD-bound travelers.

2. Data on peak-hour transit bus operations covering 34 CBD arterial "throats" in 15 cities show an average peak-hour load factor "extreme" range of 120% to 157% of seating capacity, with most observations falling within the range of 125 to 150 per cent of seated load.

Urban Traffic Problems and Their Effect on Public Transport

E. ROCKWELL

THIS ARTICLE BY AN ENGLISH AUTHOR investigates some of the means of improving the lot of public transport in congested city streets, generally through granting specialized or preferential treatment to public vehicles. Such improvements might in some cases be very easily carried out, while in others they would be more complicated. Traffic congestion lowers the quality of the service available from public modes operating in the public streets. The improvements suggested by this author could to some extent overcome this detrimental effect. The suggestions made here might be part of a "first generation" scheme of mass-transport improvement that could be undertaken cheaply and used in an interim period until more effective but more expensive palliatives could be applied.

THE IMPACT OF THE MOTOR VEHICLE on the centres of our historic cities, which were not built for it, has given rise to one of the most intractable problems of our time, directly affecting the daily lives of millions of people. To those called upon to tackle the problem—town planners, traffic engineers, public transport operators—it is therefore important to understand and, if possible, to quantify the relationship between traffic phenomena and central area activities.

This task has been attempted by a Danish expert, Professor P. H. Bendtsen of Copenhagen Technical University, whose book, translated into English, on *Town and Traffic in the Motor Age* was published in 1961 (Danish Technical Press, Copenhagen).

The book (some 160 pages) draws largely on American sources, but many examples of recent European developments are included. It provides a useful synopsis of data concerning traffic to the city centre, parking, and changes in the central area structure under the impact of motor traffic. A brief summary of this material may help to marshal thought on these problems.

TRAFFIC TO THE CITY CENTRE

IN Professor Bendtsen's view, so long as motorization continues to reflect the rising standards of living—and this is likely to continue for a long time

"Urban Traffic Problems and Their Effect on Public Transport," *British Transport Review,* August 1962.

to come—the potential traffic demand created by motorists wishing to take their cars to town will (almost irrespective of economic considerations) always greatly exceed the capacity of the facilities for 'moving traffic' (i.e. the total road capacity) and for 'stationary traffic' (i.e. parking, loading and waiting facilities) which can reasonably be made available in a historically grown town.

It is the scope of these facilities, therefore, which limits the influx of private motor vehicles into the central area.

Experience suggests that the flood of motor traffic using the roads to and within the central area will continue to swell until traffic congestion has closely approached, but not quite reached, the breakdown point at a traffic speed of about 5–6 mph, when further motorists will be deterred from taking their car to town. If the total road capacity is increased by traffic engineering and/or civil engineering measures, yet more motorists will be attracted, and the near-breakdown point will soon be reached again.

All the time, therefore, the city will hover at the verge of a traffic breakdown. It will not, as is sometimes suggested, 'grind to a standstill,' but any abnormal occurrence, even a minor one, may at once lead to traffic jams. (A notorious incident which occurred during the pre-Christmas period a few years ago—a burst water pipe at Holborn, causing enormous traffic dislocation over a wide area—comes to mind.) Even where urban motorways have been built, traffic jams at their approaches are, as in America, a daily occurrence.

If this thesis is valid, it will also govern, to a great extent, the share of public transport in the total commuter traffic to and from the central area. The proportion of commuter traffic using private cars will always reach, and remain at, the level corresponding to the near-breakdown conditions, and the remainder of the traffic will use public transport.

PARKING IN THE CENTRAL AREA

IF it is accepted that the volume of motor traffic to the central area is governed not only by the overall capacity of the street network but also by the terminal facilities available in that area, one might even go further than Professor Bendtsen by putting forward the thesis that the pressure alternately exerted by these two limiting factors will, in the long run, automatically tend to bring about a state of equilibrium. As long as the limitations imposed by road capacity are even more stringent, priority will be given to measures designed to improve road capacity even at the expense of parking accommodation, e.g. by introducing parking meter or similar rationing schemes. If, on the other hand, parking accommodation in the central area is markedly short of the total 'inlet' capacity of the radial roads during the peak hours, the pressure of public demand will eventually force the provision, by public or private enterprise, of additional off-street parking accommodation. Central London may at present still be regarded as being in the former phase; but there are already indications that the increase in road capacity brought about by parking meters and other traffic engineering measures on the one hand, and by structural road improvement schemes on the other hand, may soon, at least for a time, lead to a change of emphasis in favour of the latter phase.

From the results of certain parking surveys and forecasts undertaken in a number of American and European cities, Professor Bendtsen attempts to deduce the laws governing the parking demand, by volume and duration, as a function of the degree of motorization and of the size and 'purchasing power' of the town. One of his conclusions is that, even at an advanced stage of motorization, the demand for parking spaces in multi-storey or underground garages will always be considerably smaller than for ground-level parking spaces. The number of readily sellable parking spaces in such garages is therefore strictly limited (and, in consequence, the rationing of ground-level parking space will remain an effective means of traffic volume control).

CHANGES IN THE CENTRAL AREA STRUCTURE

IT is generally accepted, and indeed obvious, that in the long run, motorization is bound to have a profound effect on the structure of town centres. What is more difficult is to quantify this effect in concrete terms. On the strength of the comparatively few (mostly American) data available, Professor Bendtsen attempts to correlate the motorization trend with the trends of 'downtown' employment, retail trade, office floor area, real estate values, etc. Since these trends are also affected by other factors, the results are not altogether consistent, though certain deductions can be made from them.

The data suggest that, with increasing motorization, central area activities (reflected in the total traffic to the central area) will tend to stagnate. This applies, in particular, to retail trade which will, as traffic congestion progresses, suffer increasingly from the competition of suburban shopping centres. American experience suggests a real danger of 'central area blight,' as new suburban shopping centres come into being, including those erected on virgin land and surrounded by car parks for thousands of cars (the famous 'Northlands' store at Detroit is only one example). It may, however, be some consolation to find, again from American experience, that a new state of equilibrium is likely to be reached eventually between 'downtown' trade and surburan trade, and the old city centre will again begin to thrive. Certain categories of offices and shops will altogether migrate to the suburbs though others, more dependent on central location, will remain.

In European cities, on account of more stringent parking limitations, the stagnation level is likely to be reached earlier than in American cities, probably at a level of one car per 5 or 4 persons. When this happens— and Greater London has already about 1 million private cars in a population of some 8 million—the central area will stagnate or even decline. *That is, unless public transport is allowed to play a greater part.*

This conclusion has now become abundantly clear in the minds of many responsible people, also in the United States, where plans for 'rapid transit' facilities on a large scale are being actively pursued even in such motor-car-dominated cities as Los Angeles, San Francisco and Washington.

In London, where the underground railways already play such a vital part in combating street congestion, the most obvious primary solution lies in the construction of the Victoria Line, which London Transport and the British Transport Commission have sponsored and urged for many years. But although this most valuable increment to London's transport system will have a wholesome effect far beyond its local sphere of influence, especially through the multiple new interchange facilities, its effect on street congestion will not be ubiquitous.

Against a background of rising traffic congestion and increasingly restrictive traffic engineering measures, it is also vitally necessary to give concrete recognition to the importance of public road transport by deliberately granting its vehicles privileged treatment on the roads.

A LONDON TRANSPORT SURVEY

THAT such a policy has already been adopted in many cities abroad is borne out by the results of a recent survey, conducted, at the instigation of London Transport, by the International Union of Public Transport (UITP) which has yielded valuable data from a number of member administrations. These data have been supplemented by data made available by the American Transit Association. Though far from being comprehensive, these data serve to convey a broad picture of the present extent of preferential treatment accorded to public transport.

A study of the measures reported from the 50 cities (including 17 in North America) from which data were available shows a great variety of measures designed to improve public road services in one way or another, ranging from merely administrative measures to minor and major privileges of a traffic engineering character and even to special civil engineering works. A brief synopsis of these measures, broadly in the order of the increasing degree of privilege granted to public transport, is given below.

General Privileges to Roads with Public Transport Services: A fairly general concession is the granting of 'major road' priorities to roads with public transport services. Inasmuch as these roads are generally also those carrying the heaviest traffic volumes, this measure may be said to benefit private transport as much as public transport. Efforts are, however, being made (e.g. in Cologne and Munich) to secure priority rights for *all* roads carrying public transport, even if these roads would not otherwise rank as 'major roads.'

In a similar category are general parking, waiting and loading restrictions on roads used by public transport vehicles. Again, these measures assume a more specific character if they are expressly confined to bus- or tram-stopping-zones, as is the case in a number of cities (e.g. Copenhagen, Lyons).

Preferential Treatment of Public Transport at Intersections: The next step, in order of the degree of privilege accorded to public transport, is the granting of special concessions at intersections, a category which includes a great variety of measures.

A fairly common concession is the priority right of trams at traffic roundabouts (reported, e.g. from Cologne, Hanover, Rome). Priority treatment of buses and trams at police-controlled intersections is also reported (e.g. from Lausanne). General priority right of way for public transport at all non-regulated intersections of equally important roads is decreed by law in Leningrad. Prohibition of turns by general traffic across tram tracks is reported from Zürich, Dortmund, Munich. There are, on the other hand, numerous cases of public vehicles being allowed to make cross-turns filtering through oncoming traffic where such turns are prohibited to other traffic; such cases, affecting buses and trolleybuses as well as trams, are reported from Baltimore, Copenhagen, Geneva, Hanover, Munich, Rome, Seattle and Tokyo. In some cases (Liège, Le Havre) turning trolleybuses are allowed to pass on the 'wrong' side of a traffic island.

Another category of privileges granted to public transport at intersections consists in special arrangements or dispensations in connection with traffic signals. In Aachen, for instance, trams are permitted to start on the amber (preceding the green) signal to allow for their slower acceleration; at Darmstadt, for similar reasons, trams are given separate signals where both the green and red aspects are displayed slightly earlier than for general traffic. In Gothenburg and Lausanne, the phasing of certain traffic signals is automatically influenced through overhead contacts by trams and trolleybuses, respectively. In Munich, special flash-light warning signals are operated by overhead contacts at certain inter-sections to ensure clear passage of trams. In the same town, the phasing of progressively linked traffic signals along certain main roads is so ar-ranged as to favour the trams.

The reservation for public transport vehicles of special marshalling lanes at signal-controlled intersections is a feature encountered in several cities (e.g. Aachen, Krefeld, Lausanne). In some cases, a nearside bus lane may extend from a bus stop to the intersection and even slightly beyond the stop line for general traffic so as to give the bus a starting ad-vantage over other traffic.

Preferential Treatment of Public Transport along a Section of Road: Although the capacity of an urban road network is largely governed by that of its intersections, so that priority treatment for public transport at intersections would already help to utilize road space more efficiently, there is an increasing tendency, in America as well as on the Continent, to extend privileges to public transport vehicles even on the sections of road between intersections.

Here, too, the measures adopted show great variety, ranging from the common continental practice of special rights-of-way for trams and from the ordinary bus-stop bay to the provision of special bus lanes and to the concession for public transport vehicles to run against the flow, with or without special reserved lanes, in one-way streets.

While the provision of special tramway rights-of-way, generally on a reserved centre strip, may be regarded as an altogether special case, there are also cases where the tracks, even where they are embedded in the roadway, are reserved for the exclusive use of trams (e.g. in Brussels and Zürich) or for the exclusive use of trams and buses (e.g. in Rome and Brunswick). In the latter case, trams and buses may share the same stops, using off-centre refuge islands.

The provision of special bays at bus stops is also becoming increasingly popular in this country. In Brunswick, some bus-stop bays are extended to form a kind of 'acceleration lane' to overcome the difficulty, sometimes associated with bus bays, of the buses safely rejoining the traffic stream. From Hanover comes the suggestion that legal priority should be given to transport vehicles emerging from stop bays.

Special Bus Lanes: Perhaps the most striking example of preferential treatment for public transport is the provision of special bus lanes. Al-though of comparatively recent origin, this measure has already found widespread application, especially in America, where there are by now at least 15 cities with special bus lanes, at least during peak hours. 'Before-and-after' studies have proved this segregation to be highly successful in speeding up not only public transport but also the general traffic flow. In Atlanta, for example, it was found that, after the introduction of 'bus only' lanes in Peachtree Street, the speed of private cars increased from 6.3 to 10.5 mph and that of buses from 4.6 to 5.8 mph. A rather special case is the recent introduction of a reserved bus lane across the San Francisco-Oakland Bay Bridge which is reported to have reduced the crossing time for buses from 25 to 13 minutes.

The importance attached to special bus lanes is also reflected in President Kennedy's recent message to Congress, recommending the authorization of an expenditure of 500 million dollars as a first instalment of a long-range programme of federal aid to local authorities for the 'revitalization and expansion of public transport.' This message contains the request for 'favourable consideration of the reservation of special highway lanes for buses during peak traffic hours whenever comprehensive transportation plans indicate that this is desirable.'

The bus-lane issue is, however, by no means free from complications. First, a distinction must be made between different types of bus lanes. These may be kerbside lanes or centre lanes; they may be in full-time operation, or in part-time operation, e.g. during the peak periods only, or even during one peak period only (i.e. an inbound lane during the morning peak only, or an outbound lane during the evening peak only); finally, there is the special case, referred to below, of bus lanes in one-way streets permitting buses to run against the general flow of traffic.

Secondly, the introduction of a special bus lane depends on certain rather restrictive conditions which are seldom met *in toto*. Thus, according to a special report on the subject prepared by a Committee of the American Institute of Traffic Engineers, the provision of a kerbside lane (for buses running in the same direction as the general traffic flow) can only be justified if (a) access of commercial vehicles to abutting property can reasonably be prohibited during the hours of lane operation, (b) if there are at least two other lanes for general traffic in the same direction of travel, (c) if the number of buses per peak hour is not less than 60 but not more than can operate freely on the special lane (an important consideration where there are several routes, requiring 'split stops'), and (d) if the number of bus passengers per peak hour exceeds 1.5 times the number of persons in other vehicles.

In this country, there may not be many stretches of main roads where all these conditions are fulfilled. The most likely candidates for peak-hour bus lanes are certain sections of radial arteries in London where the lanes need only operate in the peak direction, i.e. on one side of the road at a time, and where access to property could reasonably be restricted during that time.

It would be much more difficult to find, at least in London, examples of roads suitable for full-time bus lanes. But the potential advantages of such a measure are so great that it deserves to be given the most careful consideration.

Running against the Flow in One-Way Streets: A special privilege, increasingly accorded to public transport vehicles abroad, is the facility to use a one-way street in the direction opposite to the general flow of traffic. This facility is becoming more and more important with the more widespread application of one-way systems. Though generally beneficial to the handling of vehicular traffic, such systems are often detrimental to public transport passengers—still the great majority of people—inasmuch as public transport vehicles are in many cases prevented from reaching the most important traffic objectives.

That such one-way systems may well be a 'mixed blessing' is well borne out by London Transport's experience with the schemes recently introduced in London. Some of these schemes, e.g. the introduction of one-way working in Tottenham Court Road and Gower Street, have been wholly successful in that the general speed-up of traffic has been so great that the considerable loss in local bus traffic, reflecting a loss of convenience to bus passengers and a loss of revenue to the operator, has been balanced by the advantages gained from the improved running times and regularity of the bus services. In other cases, however, there has been no gain in running time as the gain in traffic speed is off-set by the need to cover great distances; there is therefore no advantage to set against the marked loss in bus traffic.

A case in point is the one-way scheme for Piccadilly–Pall Mall where the stops for westbound buses on the important bus route 9 are now so far away from the main traffic objective (Piccadilly Circus) that the connection of this route with Piccadilly Circus is virtually severed, resulting in a considerable loss in bus traffic. On the strength of the American criteria mentioned above, especially the first, it would hardly be possible to provide an against-the-flow bus lane along the relevant section of Piccadilly, but it might still be possible to adopt the relatively easy remedy of restoring two-way working on a limited section of Piccadilly between the Circus and Duke Street only, which would enable westbound buses to serve the Circus but would still discourage the use of Piccadilly by other westbound through traffic.

Cases of public transport being allowed to use a one-way street in the 'wrong' direction are reported from at least 22 cities. In 16 cities, trams are running against the flow on certain sections of one-way streets. Twelve cities report cases of buses and/or trolleybuses running against the flow. In some of these cases (e.g. at Baltimore and Harrisburg), a special lane has been allocated to the 'wrong-way' buses. In other cases, the buses are simply allowed to 'gate-crash' the one-way street, without being allocated to a special lane. Leningrad states that, where one-way streets exist, public transport complies 'in so far as is practicable,' but where parallel one-way street are separated by a considerable distance, so that the service to the public would deteriorate, public transport vehicles are allowed to operate in both directions. No undue difficulties appear to have been encountered in any of the cities where public transport vehicles have been accorded such privileges.

Streets Completely Reserved for Public Transport: There are also a few cases of short sections of streets being reserved solely for use by public transport vehicles. In Milan, for example, one of two parallel narrow streets in the town centre is exclusively reserved for trams and buses. A similar case is reported from Basle, while in Munich (for buses) and Aachen (for trams) certain sections of roads are forbidden to all except public transport vehicles during certain times of the day.

Underpasses or Overpasses for Public Transport Vehicles: The ultimate in privileges granted to public transport vehicles may be said to be the provision, by the highway authorities, of separate thoroughfares above or below the main street level exclusively reserved for public transport. This category might also include certain tramway tunnels, a well-known feature in a number of cities, which again figure prominently in the plans of several German towns. At least one case, however, is also reported of an engineering structure specially provided for buses, viz. at Vancouver where a special spiral ramp has been built to enable buses to 'jump the queue' of vehicles waiting to cross the Lion's Gate tollbridge.

CONCLUSION

IT would appear even from this cursory and far from comprehensive survey that, in many foreign cities, the importance of public transport as the most effective solution to urban traffic problems is being increasingly recognized by means of practical measures designed to facilitate the movement of public transport vehicles and thus to enable them to perform their vital task of serving the great majority of the public.

It is a matter for regret that up to now the list of cities where such measures have been taken includes virtually none in this country. In some cases, this may well be due to the fact that the transport undertakings or local authorities concerned are not yet sufficiently aware of the issues involved, and of the measures that can be taken to enable public transport to discharge its vital duty to the community in the best possible way. It may be a rewarding task for urban public transport undertakings in this country to examine the possibilities for such measures in their own cities and to advocate their adoption.

Urban Motorways and Urban Congestion

D. J. REYNOLDS

IN THIS COUNTRY WE CALL THEM FREEWAYS or expressways; in Great Britain they are called motorways. In either case they are grade-separated superhighways and in both countries they are the subject of controversy where they intrude into urban areas. At present there are no urban motorways in Britain, although many have been proposed and construction may begin in the not too distant future.

The usual argument favoring these vast public works is that they will tend to relieve traffic congestion in urban areas. This has been the common reason for their construction in the U. S. D. J. Reynolds examines the American experience with expressways and disputes this argument. He points out that unwise construction of superhighways may make the congestion problem even worse, although there may be a tendency to relocate the site of the congestion. In addition to the question of congestion, Reynolds discusses the basic change in the urban fabric that must occur if public policy aims at handling the greatest bulk of traffic by means of the private automobile on greatly improved highways. This serious and far-reaching change involves the structure and density of many British and European cities, which are typically more close-knit than are their U. S. counterparts. Whether such a change would be socially or economically wise is a matter that deserves serious consideration, both in this country and abroad.

ALTHOUGH NO URBAN MOTORWAYS have yet been built in Britain, they are under discussion, and it is important to consider and analyse the case for these roads in full. Their long-term effects are likely to be complex, widespread and difficult to assess.

Rural motorways, despite their technical advantages, have two important defects. They bypass congested and uncongested sections of road

"Urban Motor Ways and Urban Congestion," *British Transport Review,* August-December 1961.

[191]

alike and they often create excess road capacity that cannot be fully utilized for many years to come. The urban motorway, with all the advantages of the rural motorway and more besides, does not generally suffer from these defects, but as a solution to the urban problems of congestion and accidents it has certain drawbacks which must be considered. They arise mainly from the fundamental causes of urban traffic problems in many cities today.

In this analysis an urban motorway will be regarded as a radial route running from the outskirts of the city towards the centre, the type commonly proposed. The ring-road motorway, e.g. a new route around the circumference of the city, is a special case deserving separate consideration.

THE URBAN MOTORWAY

THE case for the urban motorway is generally made out as follows. Additional road space is needed in congested cities. The urban motorway, by avoiding the acquisition and demolition of expensive frontaging property in densely built-up areas, and with a wider choice for its line, and greater freedom to use cheaper or derelict areas and new techniques such as overhead building, is likely to be a cheaper solution than the improvement of existing streets.

In addition, the motorway, by separating opposing streams of traffic, segregating motor traffic from other traffic and avoiding the stopping and parking of vehicles, can be much safer and can secure a much higher capacity to handle traffic volumes, than the same road area added to existing streets.

Although much will depend on individual cases, there seems little doubt of the superiority of the urban motorway over the improvement of existing roads in congested cities. Where doubt on the urban motorway arises is on more general and fundamental grounds. In particular it seems that two basic questions must be asked:

(i) Is the provision of additional road space the appropriate solution to the urban congestion problem?

(ii) Given that additional road space (in particular urban motorways) is to be installed in congested urban areas, what are the full overall effects likely to be?

ADDITIONAL ROAD SPACE

THE case for additional road space to combat congestion is generally assumed rather than stated, for if it is accepted that the purpose of the road system is to accommodate satisfactorily the traffic flows that arise on it the obvious solution to congestion is the expansion of the road system.

Like all assumptions, however, the idea that the general solution to congestion is the expansion and improvement of the road system needs to be questioned, particularly in the case of densely built-up areas. In justification of the road improvement approach it is usually argued that, since road users are heavily taxed and pay more in taxation than the cost of the road system they use, the expansion of the road system to meet their demands is, therefore, appropriate. This argument gives rise to two comments. The first is that the appropriate cost of the road system is usually taken to be the annual expenditure on the maintenance and improvement of the road system. The more normal current cost or price of an existing asset, however, would be its market price or, in the absence of a market, the current value of the road system demanded by traffic, assessed at the marginal costs of road space—i.e. the cost (per unit area) of adding to road width. To define the cost of the road system without including a considerable sum for the use of assets as valuable and as scarce as road space and the road system is unrealistic, and without much further investigation it is impossible to say whether the road user is paying the appropriate cost for the use of the road system.

The second comment is that even if it is accepted that the road user pays the appropriate cost for the road system as a whole, it is not certain that he pays the relevant cost of his road use in all circumstances. There is fairly clear evidence that, including taxation, the average road user pays more than the full real cost of his journeys on rural roads which are uncongested or relatively cheap to improve, and more important, that the road user pays considerably less than the true cost of his journeys on urban roads which are congested or relatively expensive to construct or improve.

Excessive congestion may arise from failure to charge vehicles the full cost of the road space that they occupy, or the costs that they impose on other road users, or a sufficient tax to represent a convenient expression of these values. This is confirmed by experience in congested urban conditions. As a typical case, on main streets in Central London a flow of 1,500 vehicles per hour on a street 40 feet wide reduces speed between intersections from a possible 25 mph to 15 mph approximately.

Assuming conservatively that one additional vehicle-hour costs ten shillings, the cost imposed on other vehicles by a single vehicle is some 5.3 pence per vehicle-mile, whereas the average fuel taxation paid by vehicles is only of the order of 1.65 pence per mile under congested conditions, e.g. a fuel tax of 2s 9d per gallon with a mean fuel consumption of 20 miles per gallon. Similarly, if it is assumed that such a flow continues for 6,000 hours in the year, the taxation paid by traffic is only some £62,000 per mile per year.

Even ignoring the maintenance costs attributable to road use by vehicles, at a rate of interest of about 5 per cent this is enough to pay the annual charges on a road with a capital value of only about £1.2 million per mile. This is well below the value of an existing main street, which at the marginal cost of adding to road width might be valued at up to £10 million per mile on the basis of a street 40 feet wide valued at a marginal cost of up to £50 per sq. ft., such as has been estimated for widenings in Central London. (Widening the Strand near Charing Cross station in 1958–9 is estimated to have cost £25 per sq. ft.)[1] Even allowing for higher traffic volumes on motorways the tax contribution of traffic will still be below that demanded by the costs of urban motorways, which are estimated to be some £3 million to £4 million per mile upwards.[2] For example, 3,000 vehicles per hour for 6,000 hours a year paying tax at the rate of 1.1d per mile (tax being lower because of lessened congestion and lower fuel consumption) would raise £82,500 per mile per annum, sufficient to pay charges on a road costing only about £1.65 million per mile.

Both in principle and in practice, therefore, it appears that the cause of excessive congestion in cities is the failure to charge road users the full cost of their journeys, either in the form of the congestion they impose on other road users or in the cost of the scarce road space that they occupy. If the difficult problem of charging the road user the full costs of his journeys, therefore, can be overcome and traffic flow reduced to that willing to pay full costs, it is possible that the existing road space may prove adequate for the traffic volumes offering. Depending on the importance of the journeys made and the importance of the particular form of transport used it is possible that a small charge will have a relatively large effect in eliminating marginal journeys, i.e. those that are only just worth while even when they do not pay full costs, or in transferring journeys to more space-saving means of transport.

Although it is now fairly common to give serious consideration to the price mechanism as the solution to urban traffic problems, the traditional solution is still sought in engineering and road construction. The ideas expressed above run counter to much established thinking by road authorities[3] and by the public, and are likely to encounter opposition if pressed towards a practical policy. Nevertheless, the failure to charge full costs and the excessive traffic arising from this seem the immediate causes of excessive urban congestion, not lack of road space. In this light, until road transport is paying something like its full real costs in congested areas, the initial case for additional road space looks doubtful.

Mass Transport or Private Transport?

URBAN MOTORWAYS IN CONGESTED AREAS

IN view of the impending spread of vehicle ownership (see *Road Research* 1960, H.M.S.O. 1961) and the public demands for a road system to accommodate increasing traffic satisfactorily, it may be held that one should not be too purist or academic about solutions for congestion, particularly if they are unpopular. If, therefore, the urban motorway seems to offer a reasonable chance of satisfying public demands successfully it should be constructed. It is useful, therefore, to consider whether the urban motorway is likely to achieve the results claimed for it and provide a substantial and sound solution to city congestion problems.

From data on existing traffic flows, origins and destinations of traffic, and estimates of speeds on original routes and on the new or improved routes, it is possible to estimate the effects of new road construction and improvement on existing traffic and to value the benefits to that traffic. The main difficulty arises in estimating the size and effects of the expansion in traffic consequent on road improvements, i.e. the quantity and effects of what is often termed generated traffic. If the new or improved road has the capacity to carry extra traffic volumes with little extra cost or congestion, and if a small reduction in cost of travel will bring a large increase in traffic, then final benefits from improvement are likely to exceed initial benefits considerably. If, however, the capacity of the improved road is limited and if small cost reduction brings large traffic increases, then final benefits are likely to be considerably less than initial benefits. The effect of the improvement is likely to be taken out mainly in the form of an increase in traffic, all traffic enjoying only a comparatively small benefit from the improvement.

Taken in isolation, the urban motorway tends towards the former case (increased net benefit from 'generation' of traffic), while improvement to existing roads resembles the latter (decreased net benefits from 'generation' of traffic). This is a further reason for preferring urban motorways to the improvement of existing streets. However, the urban motorway cannot realistically be considered in isolation, because by its superiority over alternative routes the urban motorway will attract, concentrate and generate traffic and discharge it at one point into the existing road system. If demand is responsive to improvement in travelling conditions, therefore, additional congestion is likely to arise on the existing road system where the motorway traffic impinges upon it, and the full effects of the urban motorway are likely to be similar to those given for the latter case, i.e. seriously decreased benefits from generated traffic (expansion in demand).

It is difficult to estimate how far traffic responds to improved travelling conditions. Even where a suitable example to study arises, e.g. the Cromwell Road Extension on the western approaches to London, the resultant generated traffic is widely diffused. In addition, bound up with changes in the location of industry, housing, etc., it will generally take a considerable time to build up, so that it will be difficult to disentangle from other 'secular' changes in traffic (i.e. changes that would have occurred without road improvement). It is likely, however, that traffic will be very responsive to changes in road conditions in cities, because road improvement will benefit the faster private vehicle more than the slower bus and so generally alter the balance between public and private transport in favour of private transport. Since a large part of passenger travel in cities is carried out by public transport, a relatively small shift from public transport will cause a relatively large increase in private travelling. Thus of the passengers entering Central London between 7 a.m. and 10 a.m. in 1959, 926,000 (75 per cent) were carried by rail (London Transport and British Railways), 223,000 (18 per cent) by bus and 85,000 (7 per cent) by private car.[4] Thus a transfer of only 1 per cent of journeys by public transport to private car in this peak period would lead to a 12 per cent increase in private car journeys, and on the basis of traffic composition an increase of perhaps 5 per cent in total traffic. This process of transfer from public to private transport will tend to be cumulative and continuous, as has been frequently pointed out; for, with falling traffics and revenues, the raising of fares and/or the cutting of services will lead to further shifts to private transport. Although London probably represents the extreme case of dependence on public transport, in particular on rail transport, and of the dangers of a shift from public to private transport, these problems are reproduced to a lesser extent in other cities.

On the whole, therefore, the urban motorway is likely to increase congestion seriously where it discharges (or attracts) traffic on to (or from) the existing street system, although lack of parking facilities may act as a factor limiting the expansion of traffic and terminal congestion. This terminal problem is probably crucial to the effectiveness of the urban motorway, and deserves special consideration.

THE TERMINAL PROBLEM

THIS question seems to have received insufficient attention (e.g. at the Conference on Urban Motorways, London, 1955).[5] For with a very elastic (responsive) demand, additional congestion on the unimproved street system could in principle reduce benefits from the construction of the motorway virtually to zero.

The advantages of the radial urban motorway lie in its high capacity and the resultant attraction, concentration and generation of traffic. If these advantages are not to be largely nullified it is important to disperse this traffic again and to minimize its impact on already congested streets. For the radial urban motorways commonly advocated, this suggests the construction of terminal (motorway) ring roads, attractive parking facilities and interchange facilities to encourage the private traveller to transfer to public transport. Apart from the roundabout nature of the journeys involved in transferring to such a motorway system, traffic being concentrated from a wide area and dispersed again, the cost of these additional facilities must be included in the cost of the motorway system. Costs are therefore likely to be considerably higher and benefits lower than those arrived at by comparisons between the immediate costs of a motorway without terminal facilities and immediate benefits to existing traffic. More important, the motorway system and its terminal facilities will cost the more the closer the system penetrates towards the centre of the city. This raises the question whether net benefits from the system will rise as sharply as costs as it approaches the centre, and the question of the optimum location for the motorway system, i.e. the location where the increment in net benefits from the system equals the increment in its costs. Two possibilities for the optimum location of the motorway system and its terminal facilities suggest themselves. Attractive and spacious parking and interchange facilities will be required. In view of the sharp increase in road construction costs with the acquisition and demolition of real property it is possible that the optimum location for the motorway system and its terminal ring road will be at the outskirts of the city, so that the best system will in fact be largely rural or suburban rather than urban.

The second possibility arises from the older and cheaper rings of property which surround city centres at some distance from the centre, which are often derelict and ripe for redevelopment and which have neither the advantages of a central location, nor the spaciousness of the outer suburbs. Such areas may also contain railways or other continuous rights of way running in the desired directions which might permit construction overhead.[6] A motorway system in such a location would gather more traffic and achieve greater benefits, but would need more terminal space than one on the outskirts and would encounter higher costs. On the evidence above, the traffic volumes which would constitute the justification for this system would not be willing to pay these higher costs. On the whole, therefore, a motorway system penetrating closer to the centre of the city seems the more doubtful alternative, although it is impossible to be conclusive about this.

The essence and logic of an urban motorway system with terminal facilities seem to lie in expansion of the road system and generous accommodation for traffic up to the terminal points or the terminal ring road, with restriction of traffic thereafter. This may be done in a variety of ways. The case for the use of the price mechanism is strong, and there might be a case for extreme measures such as preventing access to existing streets within the ring and thus forcing traffic to use the parking and other terminal facilities provided. It is more in keeping with current policy and thought, however, to attempt to achieve restriction within the ring by means of inducements and subsidies. This suggests subsidized parking facilities at the ring with interchange facilities between private and public transport, with perhaps subsidized rates on public transport for car-parkers only (on production of parking tickets) on the lines of the 'park-and-ride' schemes introduced in the U. S. A. Subsidies do not appear to be sound economics in this situation (see below) but by whatever means it is achieved, a sharp cut-off in vehicle flow within the terminal ring seems essential to ensure the effectiveness of an urban motorway system.

WIDER EFFECTS

THE wider effects and dangers of urban motorways are likely to arise from their tendency to expand demand for travel, and in particular to encourage the process of cumulative transfer from public to private transport outlined above. Unless restrained by restrictive measures this expansion of traffic volumes and its impact on the unimproved road system is likely to set in train a process of road improvement, expansion of traffic, additional congestion, further improvement, etc. with no obvious equilibrium in sight until a large part of the city has been devoted to road facilities at heavy cost and private transport has virtually taken over the role of public transport. A shift towards the phenomenon of the 'exploded city' of the United States, with wide dispersal of the city and its population, will then have taken place, making it difficult to revive public transport to help solve traffic problems, since public transport has obvious difficulty in providing a frequent and economical service to compete with private transport under such conditions.

Again, uneconomic investment in urban motorways or in any city transport facilities (as well as subsidies) aggravates the problems arising from the excessive size of cities, for the optimum size of a city will be the outcome of many economies and diseconomies of scale and size, some of the most important diseconomies limiting city size being the travelling distances required and the congestion encountered. Uneconomic investment or subsidy will therefore encourage the growth of towns or cities beyond their optimum size.

Much of the analysis above is apparently confirmed by the experience in American cities where road improvement and the construction of urban motorways has been carried further than in Britain. Thus in *The Metropolitan Transportation Problem* (Brookings Institute, 1958) Wilfred Owen says of Los Angeles—a city almost entirely adapted to transport by private car and truck:

> The dilemma of Los Angeles is that traffic continues to outstrip the rapid pace set by the road builders. During the rush hours the tremendous jams on the major freeway routes have reduced average speed and intensified accident hazards.
>
> The wide dispersions of origins and destinations and the tremendous area of the metropolis make the provision and use of public transportation service extremely difficult. Yet the nerve-racking negotiation of the freeways in rush hours is an experience that many motorists find increasingly unpleasant, and the question is whether Los Angeles has built too many accommodations for the automobile or not enough.

Again, the decline of public transport simultaneously with the growth of the private car and substantial urban road investment to accommodate it, has been discussed by Gallagher[7] for twenty-two of the largest American cities. The American trend seems now towards the revival of urban public transport by subsidy or massive investment, but according to Gallagher only eight of the cities studied seemed likely to succeed.

In all this the major issue is the provision to be made in cities for increasing volumes of private road transport. Two main equilibrium states for the city can be discerned, the compact city adapted to space-saving public transport but ill-adapted to private transport, and the spacious city adapted to space-using private transport and more spacious forms of living but ill-adapted to public transport. The first was clearly the optimum when the older cities were laid down and built up in the public transport age, the second may be the optimum for the new town or city laid down and built up in the private transport age. The crucial question then is whether the gains from the transition to a spacious city will be worth the heavy cost of redesigning and rebuilding the older city.

The evidence of this analysis suggests that this transition would not be worth while, although the demands of traffic and of road users, who will not be called upon to pay the cost of the transition at all directly suggest that it would. The most logical and economic response to the growth of private transport and the demand for the more spacious living that private transport makes possible, seems to be the urbanization (or suburbanization) of the countryside rather than the more costly alternative of redeveloping compact towns and cities more spaciously. Although this will probably mean a relative decline in the importance of cities and the further spread of urban or suburban development into the countryside, to which strong planning objections can be made (which might be met by careful grouping and substantial decentralization from large conurbations) this seems to be the logical outcome of the growth of private transport and the greater scope it provides for spacious living.[8] Provided that the persons demanding such facilities are willing to pay their full and proper cost which will be low for rural development, no strong economic objection to the process seems possible. The economic objections to the more costly redevelopment of cities on more spacious lines are stronger, for the logic and *raison d'être* of the city seem to lie in its compactness, and the growth of private transport with its demands for space suggests passing the city by in favour of more spacious forms of development, leaving the city to be gradually redeveloped as cheap opportunities arise.

FURTHER KNOWLEDGE REQUIRED

KNOWLEDGE on urban congestion and its fundamental causes and solutions is still rather vague and speculative (although over-simplified analyses sometimes indicate a misleading amount of precision in our knowledge) and much more analysis and understanding of the problem is necessary before costly solutions can be put forward with any confidence. However, many alternative approaches exist for advancing knowledge on this complex subject and there is difficulty in selecting the methods likely to be most fruitful. At one extreme the practical traffic engineering approach, whereby traffic volumes and delays are measured and studied and improvements to deal with them are designed, has much to commend it as a direct attack on the problem. Moreover, as traffic studies are now being extended to cover origins, destinations and directions of traffic it may be possible to use computers to process large volumes of complex data and so to yield meaningful results in terms of road design. This approach has the drawback however of concentrating only on actual and measurable data and effects, giving little attention to generated traffic and other wider potential effects, which, as American experience has shown, can be very dynamic and exercise a potent influence on the final outcome of road improvement schemes. Also this line of attack may become deeply involved in the immediate problems and techniques of measurement to the detriment of effects which cannot easily be measured but which might be important.

At the other extreme can be placed the broad town planning approach, planners having been much alive to the wider effects and dangers of urban road expansion.[9] This approach lays down various *desiderata* for the town or city and considers the problem in terms of such things as balance, harmony, scale, etc.; or more concretely, draws up overall plans to deal with traffic and town planning problems. The drawbacks to this line of attack are its vagueness and even for the plans drawn up there are few clear ultimate criteria whereby one plan can be adjudged sound and superior to another, and most traffic plans must be based on assumptions which may or may not be sound.

Although progress should be attempted on all fronts, the most promising line of attack for the moment seems to be in the middle ground between engineering and town planning. The techniques used should be reasonably precise and disciplined, although not too closely bound up with detail and questions of measurement, and should be capable of bridging the gap (at present wide) between particular detailed effects and wider general effects. It is also desirable that the techniques used should reconcile persons' preferences with the availability of (scarce) resources in order that the analysis should be realistic, rather than concentrating on ideal solutions for which the necessary resources are unlikely to be available, e.g. very comprehensive redevelopment schemes.

In short an economic approach seems to be a useful bridge between engineering and town planning and to offer scope for some advance in knowledge and greater realism in these problems, although this would entail much more than simplified comparisons of cost and benefit on proposed improvement schemes, which in this context are more a tool of engineering than of economics.

In economics two lines of attack seem to be the most promising. First, a better understanding of the forces shaping the spatial economy of towns and cities is required in order to throw more light on the interrelationships between town size and transport facilities and to determine the conditions that must be fulfilled in order that towns and cities attain something like their optimum size and their optimum transport systems. This suggests the building of theoretical models with the dangers of abstraction, but with a determination to stick close to real problems. With the evolution of reasonably simple tools and techniques greater understanding of urban traffic and town planning problems might be achieved.

Second, on a more direct and practical level some experimental application of the price mechanism to towns or cities would be valuable in helping to discover the demand relationships for various forms of transport and to discover whether urban traffic problems can be solved by the price mechanism with little or no damage to urban economies. Apart from the theoretical case for the price mechanism in congested areas, and the fact that urban congestion is unlikely to be solved by road improvement alone the application of the price mechanism involves little real

[2 0 1]

cost (the charges imposed being merely a transfer payment). It is thus a much cheaper, more flexible and quicker instrument for experiments (and solutions) than road construction schemes.

CONCLUSIONS

ON the whole therefore it is concluded that, with the present knowledge (or lack of knowledge) of urban congestion, and of its fundamental causes and solutions, and in the light of American experience, the construction of urban motorways would be a costly and risky 'shot in the dark' which may well do little to solve urban congestion problems and lead to dangerous and irreversible ultimate effects such as the decline of public transport and the phenomenon of the exploded city. There is a considerable onus of proof therefore on the proponents of urban motorways.

NOTES

1. R. F. F. Dawson, 'Traffic Effects of Strand Widening,' *Traffic Engineering and Control,* May 1960.
2. A. C. L. Day, 'Car Ownership and Use,' Annual Conference, Town & Country Planning Association, October 1960.
3. C. T. Brunner, 'Cities—Living with the Motor Vehicle,' British Road Federation, 1960.
4. J. D. C. Churchill, *Journal of the Town Planning Institute,* September–October 1960.
5. Proceedings of Conference on Urban Motorways, British Road Federation, 1956.
6. Alan Day, 'Roads over Railways,' *The Observer,* January 25, 1959.
7. J. S. Gallagher, 'Urban Transport Developments in the U S A,' *British Transport Review,* December 1960.
8. P. Self, 'Cities in Flood,' Faber & Faber, 1957.
9. M. MacEwen, 'Motropolis,' *Architects' Journal,* October 1, 1959.

Tide Turns for Transit

THIS READING presents several basic themes. Overriding all, we have the major problem of the American city caught in the costly and enervating web of traffic congestion and the seeming impossibility of meeting the problem by attempting to handle urban transport almost exclusively with

"Tide Turns for Transit," *Business Week,* October 20, 1962.

automobiles. To this is added the possibility that improvement and expansion of the mass transport systems of our cities may help to reduce automotive traffic and thereby provide much-needed relief. There is also the idea that there is a definite role for the federal government in what at first seems to be a matter of strictly local interest. Finally there is the question of whether or not improved mass transportation will prove sufficiently attractive to the public to effect any significant move away from the use of the private automobile.

FOR THE MILLIONS OF AMERICANS who commute to work by car, battling the daily traffic is an ordeal—nerve-fraying, time-wasting, accident-breeding, and pocketbook-flattening.

The hardening of traffic arteries discourages downtown shopping, promotes blight, causes an enormous waste of productive time, sharply increases police requirements, and slows the movement of goods as well as people.

Today a great debate is raging over how best to unclog city streets and increase the efficiency of urban transportation. Basically, the argument is over how much emphasis to put on freeways and private automobile transportation, how much on mass, public transportation.

Time for a change? In recent years, most urban travel has been given over to the private passenger car. Confronted with the ever-mounting tide of automobiles that welled up with postwar affluence, cities have relied mainly on construction of broad, limited access freeways. A heavy outpouring of federal highway aid encouraged this.

Now, however, there is a growing belief among city managers and planners that the time has come to right the urban transportation balance and to begin reducing some of the emphasis on freeways catering to automobile traffic in central business districts.

Rising trend. Early next month residents in the San Francisco Bay area will vote on a $792-million bond issue for a regional rail rapid transit system to serve more than 30 cities. On Nov. 1, a special agency created by Congress to draw up a mass transportation plan for Washington, D.C., and its nearby suburbs will lay its proposal on Pres. Kennedy's desk. The plan will call for railroad commuting and, eventually, a subway.

Cities that already have extensive rail commuter and rail rapid transit systems—New York, Chicago, Boston, Philadelphia, and Cleveland—are pumping new life into them through rehabilitation and expansion.

Los Angeles and Atlanta—both of which have relied principally on buses or street cars for public transportation—are considering building rapid transit systems.

Other big urban centers—among them Miami, New Orleans, Buffalo,

and Milwaukee—either have under way or are about to begin comprehensive regional studies that are expected to lead to increased emphasis
on public transportation by bus. And in Pittsburgh and St. Louis, public
agencies are contemplating buying up bus and trolley lines within those
cities and their surrounding areas, and pulling them together to form
integrated, areawide systems—a step already taken successfully by a number of other cities.

New capital. This renewed interest in mass transit is expected to lead
to a substantial capital investment over the next decade. In a study made
for the federal government, the Institute of Public Administration, a nonprofit research organization, conservatively estimates the anticipated outlay at $9.8-billion.

But will these plans ever get beyond the point of meriting a big layout
in the Sunday newspaper?

In highway and automobile circles, there is a crack that when it comes
to rapid transit systems, cities do a lot of talking but don't build them;
that even with bus systems, planners envision a lot of improvements that
seldom materialize.

Even if the mass transit systems do materialize—along with more freeways that must inevitably be built—can the public be induced to use
what is obviously the more efficient means of transportation?

CONVENIENCE FIRST

"AMERICAN travel habits haven't a damn thing to do with efficiency,"
declares Robert Livingston, Colorado State Highway Dept. planning and
research director. "All I know is the facts: The number of people per
unit of automobile keeps going down and down and down."

Sad record. If proof were needed that most people prefer convenience
to efficiency, there is no better evidence than what has happened to mass
transportation over the past two decades—the years when motorists were
demanding ever bigger, broader, longer freeways.

Since 1940, the bus and rapid transit industries have lost 28% of their
passengers, have decreased vehicle-miles operated by 17%, and trimmed
employment by 41%. A 92% increase in revenue, through a seemingly
endless series of fare hikes that drive still more people to their autos, has
been outstripped by a 116% jump in operating expenses.

Last year these two industries earned a profit of only 1.9% on gross
revenues of $1.4-billion. Not since 1950 has their profit been as much
as 4%.

This picture is considerably bleaker when the commuter rail situation
is painted in. Service reductions and abandonments have been regular
since World War II; use of equipment a half-century old is not unusual.

The New Haven RR, a major commuter line serving both New York and Boston, is in bankruptcy.

Even so, there are many indications that the present groundswell of interest in mass transit means a real comeback. There will be setbacks: Taxpayers will balk at bond issues, and other financing problems will arise. Road building and auto interests will throw up strong opposition, particularly to rail transit. But in the long run, mass transportation will be revived and revitalized. It has to be.

A look at population and automobile growth trends provides the basic reason: People and cars will proliferate and concentrate in urban areas at such dizzying rates that mass transit must be expanded to ease the crush of automobiles and space-consuming freeways.

Today, roughly two out of every three Americans live in and around cities; by 1980, with the population an expected 250-million, three out of every four will. This vast conglomeration of people will be concentrated in only about 2% of the nation's land area—with most of the concentration in 40 great urban complexes.

Along with the increase and concentration of people in urban areas, there will be a parallel—but more rapid—rate of growth in automobile use. Auto registrations, now 65.6-million, will hit 120-million by 1980—roughly one car for every two persons. Most of these cars will be driven in urban areas. Already 50% of total auto travel occurs on city routes; by 1980, 60% will.

TALE OF FOUR CITIES

As they contemplate the future, those concerned with urban affairs face this question: Can we continue to allow mass transportation facilities to wither away and still afford the price—in both dollars and space—that will be exacted by freeways and parking facilities to accommodate the rising wave of automobiles?

Atlanta's Mayor Ivan Allen, Jr., answers this way:

If we abandon mass transportation and require all those using it to rely solely on the private automobile for moving around, or if we fail to provide for future mass transportation facilities where none now exist, the congestion on our streets and highways and the lack of storage space for our private cars will become so unmanageable that the private automobile will cease to be a convenient and flexible mode of transportation. Instead, it will be an instrument of private torture.

Atlanta's dilemma. Allen says that without public transit by 1970, Atlanta would need a total of 120 expressway lanes radiating out of the city, and 28 downtown connectors—"a physical impossibility if the city is to remain a city."

[205]

As an alternative, Atlanta is contemplating a $215-million rapid transit system utilizing present rail facilities that fan out from its center. Automated trains of single or multiple cars, traveling at an average 45 mph, would operate over 60 miles of track serviced by 32 stations. Passengers would be discharged in a downtown transit center.

The plan is subject to modification, and completion of the system is probably 10 or more years away. But political and business leaders—including Robert L. Sommerville, president of the Atlanta Transit System, which operates the city's existing bus and trackless trolley system—agree overwhelmingly on the need.

Out of the question. In Washington, a 1959 transportation study, looking ahead to the metropolitan area's 1980 traffic, specifically considered the possibility of an auto-dominant system in which the presence of the existing bus network was recognized, but a continuing decline in bus service was accepted.

Under these conditions and allowing for automobile traffic growth by 1980, the study found that 10, 12, and 14-lane freeways in portions of the District of Columbia, as well as one 18-lane section near the central business district, would be required—again a virtually impossible use of urban space. Hence the mass transit plan soon to be sent to the President.

San Francisco's aim. San Francisco is trying to bring to reality a rapid transit system aimed at taking 25% of the automobiles out of its peak rush hour traffic and reducing the need for additional freeways. Currently 48 lanes of highways serve the area's needs. By 1980, however, an additional 72 lanes would be needed in San Francisco, Oakland, and Berkeley, plus an additional 36,000 parking spaces.

To build one mile of freeway requires 30 to 40 acres of space. In San Francisco the density of population is 16,500 people per sq. mi., so that one mile of freeway can displace 800 to 1,000 people—and many businesses. It takes taxable property off the tax rolls, too, though highway advocates insist that increases in surrounding land values more than offset this.

Though the Bay Area tore down an earlier transit system a few years ago, its new rapid transit plan calls eventually for a 75-mile, $1.3-billion network of aerial, subway, and surface lines over which "space-age" electric trains would travel at 70 mph. It would include a four-mile tube sunk beneath the bay from Oakland to San Francisco, and feature 37 passenger stations with parking lots for 30,000 cars.

Los Angeles, too. Even Los Angeles, which also tore down an earlier transit system, and which more than any other city has committed itself to freeway transportation, is turning to mass transit as a supplement. Two-thirds of downtown Los Angeles already is consumed by streets and parking areas; yet without some alternative, more space to accommodate more automobiles will have to be provided. The metropolitan area's 7.3-million population will jump to 11.3-million by 1980.

Already, more than $1.2-billion has been spent on 346 miles of free-way in Greater Los Angeles. By 1980, it's estimated that 1,342 miles of freeway will have been completed at a cost of $4.3-billion.

To conserve what is left of central city space, Los Angeles is con-templating a 22.7-mile, $210-million rapid transit system.

COSTS OF CONGESTION

IN considering the future, then, city officials see a pressing need to keep automobiles and freeways from taking a disproportionate share of space in the central business district—and mass transportation offers the best insurance against this.

Expensive freeways. The high cost of urban freeways is also a big factor. Those that are part of the federally aided Interstate Highway Sys-tem, for example, will consume 45% of the program's total $41-billion cost, though they account for only 13% of the total mileage.

The proposed 13-mile "inner loop" freeway system in Washington carries a price tag of $300-million, roughly $23-million a mile. A 12-mile turnpike in downtown Baltimore cost $180-million, $15-million a mile. And a three-mile stretch of beltway in Cleveland cost $75-million, or $25-million a mile.

Highway builders argue that it is unrealistic to cite such per-mile costs without considering the traffic handled. They point out that the urban section of freeways that are part of the Interstate System will handle close to half the system's total traffic.

Highway groups also point out that highway users pay for the roadway through user charges—tolls and taxes on gasoline, tires, parts, and ac-cessories and excise levies on new equipment.

But freeways also generate other costs: improvements in local street systems feeding into them; additional parking (more and more cities are going into the municipal garage business); expansion of traffic control systems. The expressways feeding New York's newly double-decked George Washington Bridge, for instance, have become so complicated that nearly $1-million worth of signs is required to steer motorists into the correct lanes. Moreover, a network of "escape lanes" has had to be set up for motorists who lose their way.

Urban sprawl. Mass transit gets an additional boost from the growing concern of businessmen and local officials over the fate of central cities. With the trek to the suburbs and the flight of industry and business to peripheral areas, central business districts find it increasingly difficult to maintain themselves as vital cores of urban areas.

This massive decentralization also accounts to a great extent for the plight of public transportation. City populations have moved outward faster than routes could be extended under old regulatory restrictions and meager transportation company earnings. The shift has drastically reduced population densities, so that many routes prove unprofitable even when extended.

Revival of mass transportation could help slow this trend, city planners believe, preserving and enhancing the social and cultural values of both central city and suburban living.

The "Year 2000" plan for the Washington metropolitan area, for example, seeks to curb haphazard sprawl with a corridor plan of future development. A half-dozen corridors, which new mass transportation lines would help develop, would radiate from the present fringe of the city, separated by wedges of open space.

Economic drag. The principal way mass transportation can help in protecting the central city is by removing the economic drag of congestion. Measuring the dollar cost of congestion to a city is extremely difficult, but some efforts have been made.

San Francisco analysts estimate that during the rush hour in three Bay Area counties alone, 150,000 man-hours are now lost to highway congestion on the average work day. In Pittsburgh, it's estimated that a 10-minute delay in traffic means a productive time-loss of $222,000 at basic steel wages. The National Retail Dry Goods Assn. calculates very roughly that the annual cost of congestion in New York City is $1 billion.

GOVERNMENT'S HAND

Two other trends are working in favor of a mass transit revival: first, a growing acceptance of the reality that mass transit, if it is viewed as a public necessity and if it is to operate at fares low enough to attract substantial patronage, must in many cases be subsidized, and second, the federal government's increasing interest in helping cities—both with money and advice—in solving urban transit problems.

The trend toward subsidy stems from the realization that, though fare box revenues often cover operating costs for transit companies, they seldom are sufficient to support a large-scale investment program. And unless equipment is kept up to date, patronage will continue to decline. The reason the fare box is usually insufficient is that mass transportation is mainly a peak-hour operation.

Philadelphia story. Philadelphia is an outstanding example of a city that concluded that maintaining and improving rail commuter service was vital even if the service had to be subsidized.

Through a government agency known as the Passenger Service Improvement Corp., Philadelphia "buys" commuter service from the Pennsylvania and Reading rail lines. This service is tied in with a city-owned subway, and a rapid transit line from Philadelphia to Camden.

PSIC makes up railroad deficits stemming from reduced fares, additional service, and modernization. The reduced-fare operations, started in 1958, have increased use of commuter lines by an average of 43% in the past three years.

Kennedy plan. On the national level, Pres. Kennedy is pressing Congress to approve federal subsidies for expanding mass transportation. The rationale is that the government pays 90% of the cost of city freeways that are part of the Interstate Highway System, and 50% of the cost of urban highways that are part of the primary and secondary highway systems. Therefore, there is a corresponding need to support urban mass transit.

Another argument is that fragmented local governments cannot raise the needed funds. An Atlanta regional planning official says bluntly: "We simply will not have a rapid transit system unless we get some federal aid."

Under the Kennedy plan, federal assistance would be primarily in the form of grants for capital improvements, amounting to two-thirds of the net project cost.

The President has recommended a three-year, $500-million federal outlay as the first installment. Whether or not Congress enacts this, the odds are that it will expand federal aid for mass transportation in some form.

The federal government already has a limited aid program, and the President has taken steps to coordinate it, and any new program, with federal highway activities. For instance, he has instructed the Bureau of Public Roads to consider favorably the reservation of special lanes for buses on federally aided urban highways during peak hours.

Place for buses. This is a recognition of the importance of buses in urban transportation. In medium-sized and smaller cities the only feasible form of mass transportation for many years will be buses. Even in the bigger cities express buses will play a vital role.

The bus offers greater flexibility of routing and scheduling than does rail transit. It can readily adjust to changing needs, and provision for its use can be made from highway-user revenues, thus avoiding high fixed-capital investment.

The great problem is that buses have to operate in the same environment of congestion as the automobile unless they are allotted special lanes. Congestion skyrockets their cost of operation.

Freeways, particularly those with special lanes, are ideal for express buses; but local service is often out of the question because of an absence of pull-out areas.

What can be done with effective bus transportation has been demonstrated in Houston, where transit operator Bernard Calkins bought a declining company with outmoded equipment for $2.4-million in June, 1961, and revitalized it. Calkins is carrying out a $15-million modernization program leading to a fully air-conditioned fleet. He has improved routing, added 30 miles to the system, and substituted zone fares for a one-rate system to raise money for new equipment. The trend of declining ridership in Houston has been reversed.

Aid in planning. Aside from promoting use of reserved lanes on federal-aid highways, the Kennedy Administration has also pushed through Congress a requirement that urban highway development be coordinated with mass transit planning. Under the new law, the Secretary of Commerce will not approve federal-aid road projects in metropolitan areas after July, 1965, unless they are based on continuing, comprehensive transportation planning by state and local governments cooperatively.

Federal funds aid mass transportation through other programs:

One provides $50-million in loans for acquiring, constructing, reconstructing, and improving mass transportation facilities, and $25-million in demonstration grants covering two-thirds of the cost of mass transit experiments. Under the grants, the University of Washington is studying the performance and impact of the monorail from downtown Seattle to the World's Fair. Detroit ran an experiment to find out if bus service improvements would induce people now driving to switch.

Federal funds to aid planning helped finance a $3.5-million study of Chicago's needs, which recently recommended extension of the city's elevated-subway system, 230 more miles of expressways, and moving sidewalks in the Loop. In Massachusetts, under the same program, work has started on a mammoth, $10.2-million study covering 144 communities and towns.

WILL THEY SWITCH?

BUT the question remains: If you build new transit systems or improve old ones, will people ride them?

Dr. Leon N. Moses, Director of Research of the Transportation Center of Northwestern University, studied the question as part of a research program under a grant from the Automobile Manufacturers Assn.

He found that in the Chicago area only 13% to 32% of auto commuters who listed other forms of transit as their second choice would actually shift to these other methods even if they were free (assuming prices were the only variable factors).

To get a 50% diversion to other forms of mass transit, Moses found auto commuters would have to be paid 35¢ a trip on bus-streetcar, 45¢ a trip on elevated-subway, and 15¢ on suburban railroads.

These figures are based on what people think the cost of various forms of transportation is. It can be argued that commuters don't actually count in the full cost of automobile operation (table, below).

AVERAGE COST FOR ONE PERSON TO TRAVEL ONE MILE
(in cents)

Commuter rail coach		2.6
Subway or elevated		3.2
Bus		3.2
Auto	Out-of-pocket cost	Full Cost*
One	3.5 to 4	10 to 11
Two riders	1.8 to 2	5 to 5.5
Three riders	1.2 to 1.3	3.3 to 3.7

* Full cost includes depreciation, insurance, etc., but not downtown parking.

It can also be argued—and often is—that even if they did, a substantial number of people would go right on driving. Lewis Mumford, author and commentator on urban problems, puts it thus: "Since the motor car is treated like a private mistress and not included in the family budget no matter how extravagant her demands, it is hard to dispose of such a sentimental attachment on purely practical grounds."

Dim view. Highway and auto interests take a dim view of the revived interest in mass transit. They particularly abhor the occasional suggestion that highway funds should be used to finance rail rapid transit, or that needed freeway development should be held up while transit plans are being studied.

They make the point that in no major city, including Los Angeles, has an entire freeway system been completed. The freeway pattern for most big cities aim at having through traffic and traffic from one suburb to another avoid downtown areas, by using outer belts. Surveys in large cities, according to the Bureau of Public Roads, show that over 80% of traffic on downtown streets in peak hours is merely passing through to other destinations. Completing bypasses for this traffic will greatly alleviate congestion.

Perennial lag. While this is a convincing argument, mass transit boosters question whether freeway construction will ever catch up with growth in auto travel. And even if it does, they ask, what will threading metropolitan areas with more and wider ribbons of concrete do to the structure of cities?

"This," says Mumford, an avowed mass transit man, "is pyramid building with a vengeance: a tomb of concrete roads and ramps covering the dead corpse of a city."

Major Urban Corridor Facilities: A New Concept

HENRY D. QUINBY

THE TYPE OF FACILITIES AND EQUIPMENT necessary to meet transport demand in urban areas should vary to meet the demands of given routes, lest we be guilty of sending a boy to do a man's job, or vice versa. Where demand is relatively light, it may be quite adequate to rely on the private automobile or conventional city bus utilizing ordinary city streets. Where demand is exceptionally heavy, rapid transit lines or cummuter railways, in conjunction with lesser-capacity modes as feeders and distributors, may be the only practical solution. In the United States, freeways have typically been built to handle intermediate-demand conditions, but a vast multiplication of lanes is usually required if peak traffic is to be handled without undue congestion or drastic slowdowns. The principal complaint against constructing freeways to cope with such demand situations is that they tend to gobble up land at an alarming rate.

The problem of dealing with intermediate traffic loads has up until now been met far more by use of freeways than by reliance on mass transit. The reason, of course, is that there is at present no form of public transport particularly fitted to handle volumes of traffic in the range between the capabilities of the bus and the grade-separated railway. An interesting solution to the problems of meeting conditions of medium demand is made by

"Major Urban Corridor Facilities: A New Concept," *Traffic Quarterly,* April 1962.

Henry D. Quinby. His advocacy of light rapid transit—or "limited tram-lines"—for transport corridors where trips are not longer than 20 miles and when demand is between 10,000 and 34,000 persons per hour, is based on considerations of cost, attractiveness to the patron, preservation of amenities, and relatively intense utilization of valuable land. What he suggests has already been carried out to some extent in Europe, and may provide a practical concept for use in the United States.

THERE HAVE BEEN NUMEROUS APPROACHES to the growing problem of urban highway congestion. These have ranged from the manifold and relatively inexpensive traffic engineering treatments of facilities already in existence to proposals for massive new public works projects often involving tens or hundreds of millions, or even billions, of dollars. Both highway and transit solutions have been attempted, occasionally in coordination with each other, more often not. Yet urban metropolitan vehicular congestion continues to increase.

In the highway field there has been renewed recent interest in intermediate urban solutions which may approach the speed, capacity, and mobility of massive new freeways, but which cost generally far less and disturb fewer existing properties or aesthetic values. Such intermediate highway proposals often feature prominently the at-grade or semi-at-grade expressways. These may make economical use of existing streets and permit peak hour speeds and per-lane capacities of two-thirds or more of those of congested urban freeways. They may also provide more frequent access to the arterial and local street network, and hence reduce point-to-point urban travel times, with less high-volume ramp congestion. Such intermediate facilities may accomplish all this at a fraction of the cost of freeways, and may also permit more thorough coverage of an urban area by vehicular facilities.

In the transit sector of urban transportation as in the highway sector, there are three general levels of application. As in the systems of local streets and arterials, there are the local surface transit systems. Similar to full freeways, there are the completely grade-separated rapid transit lines. Moreover, there is also available an intermediate range of transit facilities. Such facilities include the at-grade or semi-at-grade transit services, which may have reserved rights-of-way or use existing streets and highways for all or parts of their routes, and which operate relatively fast service, often with limited numbers of stops. Each variant of such intermediate transit service has its role of particular value, depending on the range of person-trip lengths served and the speed and capacity required. The variant forming the subject of this paper involves potentially greatly improved service to urban and inner suburban areas of medium and large size cities. It will be most effective along routes or corridors of present or potential traffic concentration, and for person-trip lengths up to maxima of approximately 8 to 20 miles depending on schedule speed.

In both the highway and transit fields, intermediate types of solution have been considered and constructed in the past. In recent years, however, overwhelming emphasis has usually been given to full freeway and grade-separated rapid transit projects. Urban facilities of these types often involve capital costs of between $4 million and $30 million per route-mile. These great costs have resulted in actual construction or programming of relatively few urban route-miles of such facilities, compared with the tremendous needs of our rapidly growing metropolitan regions for internal transportation facilities of greater spatial frequency, speed, and capacity. It behooves us, therefore, to re-examine carefully the possibilities for intermediate types of solution, where urban geographic, topographic, traffic concentration, and trip-length conditions may provide a warrant for them, and where they may have some practical advantages, including the possibility for financing them, over other facility types.

A glance at the historical trends in transit traffic, in urban vehicular congestion, and in the expenditures to alleviate congestion, indicates how serious is the need for some realistic compromise between worsening traffic conditions and the vast proposed and committed expenditures to solve them. Intermediate transit, as well as highway, solutions may be considered in order to improve the prospects for shortening the gap between urban traffic growth and the new facilities we are actually able to build for such growth. In this connection, however, a word of caution is perhaps necessary. Interesting as the prospects for intermediate types of solution may be, they should not, of course, be regarded as having a clear advantage outside the range of applications to which their use is best suited.

INTERMEDIATE SOLUTIONS

INTERMEDIATE types of urban transit solutions already in use include express or limited-stop services generally mixed with other traffic on arterials or freeways, reserved street lanes, operation on private rights-of-way, and the like. Considering the increasing magnitude of the urban transportation problem, these applications have so far been relatively limited in scope and extent. We shall observe that, as applied today, they have their limitations. When brought to bear on the urban traffic problem, such facilities have often failed to attract percentages of peak period trips significantly high enough to be effective in meeting the congestion problem in the corridors.

Express and limited-stop urban bus service must generally pick up and deliver patrons in tributary service areas as well as move expeditiously on freeways. Often, the freeways are not located along the direct axes of such bus routes, and the time saved thereby is lost by slower running and route-lengths longer than minimally necessary to reach freeway interchanges. Still more important, peak period freeway congestion often retards the speed of such service to the slow pace of all other vehicles, which further discourages the attraction and effectiveness of the service. Buses also suffer from common width and length limitations which often result in relatively cramped seats and aisles. In addition, the obnoxious noise and fumes from most types of buses, and the fact that, even with the best springing available, they must travel directly on pavements which are often uneven, definitely do not encourage their use by those who have other choices available.

Reserved lanes have been made available to transit vehicles on certain streets in a few cities. In even fewer cases, buses have separate rights-of-way, with or without grade separation, often because such rights-of-way were inherited from the electric railway lines which they replaced. There has been much recent discussion of, but relatively little action toward, more reserved lanes for buses, either on public pavements or on segregated rights-of-way. In view of the oft-cited need for such action, it is indeed unfortunate that so many valuable former electric railway rights-of-way have been allowed to disappear from efficient transit use in American metropolitan areas.

PRESENT URBAN CONGESTION

WE may pause here to observe what is happening to urban traffic and vehicular congestion without the expanded use of more effective intermediate types of transit solution. This review should not, however, obscure the importance of greater consideration to such intermediate *highway* solutions as the at-grade or semi-at-grade expressway. We may note that, without more effective intermediate transit solutions, and given the limitations of those which have been applied relatively infrequently to date, the actual and potential demand for movement in many critical sections of our major urban areas is growing faster than our real ability to meet such demand. Widespread and serious congestion, especially during broad peak periods, is one result. Another is the shifting of urban economic, land use, and population patterns into forms more nearly compatible with the inadequacies of present circulation networks. Such new urban forms, gradually forced as they are by congestion and insufficient capacity, are often undesirable from the standpoints of community development, living standards, and spatial organization. Generally they may be described as catalysts of the amorphous urban sprawl so increasingly characteristic of most of our larger metropolitan areas.

At the heart of the matter are two principal transportation factors: (a) the necessarily slow evolution of massive "full" solutions; and (b) woefully low present street use efficiencies. Only some 800 to 1,200 people per hour can usually pass a given point in automobiles mixed with other traffic on each congested urban street lane, unless they are signalized rigidly to favor one direction of travel. One lane of buses mixed with other traffic seldom exceeds 6,000 people per hour in such streets. To make stops, these buses constantly interfere with other vehicles by disorderly lane-changing, with front or rear ends encroaching on adjacent lanes, and by their slow rates of acceleration. Present types of the traditional streetcar, well below their potential in carrying capacity, operated in single units by one man, and usually mixed with other traffic in the center and potentially fastest street lanes, leave very much room for improvement where, in fact, they even continue to exist. In almost all cities, streetcars have also been burdened with the cost of maintaining the portion of the roadway on which both they and all other vehicles travel; such expense has been a prime factor in their demise.

TREND TO CHANNELIZATION

IT is more than merely interesting to observe that, even though the traditional streetcar with its fixed path has all but disappeared in America, there are a number of examples and proposals for nearly equally fixed, exclusive bus lanes or bus rights-of-way. "Flexibility" apparently may be susceptible to more than one definition, depending on whether spatial flexibility of route and maneuver, *or* flexibility of speed and capacity is primarily desired. When, however, numerous intermediate stops must be made, as on urban internal transit routes, an exclusive lane of buses seldom exceeds an hourly capacity of 7,500 passengers.

Trends toward the systematic channelization of urban movement are not limited, of course, to transit buses. It is equally interesting to observe, in the control of all vehicular traffic, these tendencies away from the ideal of simple spatial flexibility of movement within the urban grid toward the newer desiderata of speed and capacity flexibilities. Indeed, to drive through the downtown and intermediate areas of our well traffic-engineered larger cities is to be impressed by the degree to which all vehicle movement is channelized and controlled, almost to the extent of a railroad-tracked and block-signaled system. Since the pressing objectives of modern urban traffic engineering are to maximize capacity, speed, and safety, it is only logical that the means employed should lead toward goals of orderly, channelized, and controlled flow.

When, however, urban internal problems become too great for traffic engineering improvements to existing facilities, significantly effective though such improvements usually are, the almost inevitable public and professional reaction has been to look to massive new freeway and/or rapid transit facilities as their *sole* source of salvation. For regional types of trip, generally over 10 miles in length and often over 20, such facilities do provide the principal answer, because regional trips require the proportionally greater trunk line speeds attainable only with such facilities. Regional freeways and rapid transit involve generally reduced capital costs in outer areas. In addition, the large amounts of land required for freeways are obtained with less land-use conflicts in these areas.

PROBLEM IN INTERNAL URBAN PARTS

THE major transportation problems still reside, however, in the great bulk of person-trips made in the urban internal parts of larger metropolitan areas. A significant part of the urban internal problem is that the principal freeways through these areas often can accommodate, and then sometimes inadequately, only predominantly the longer-length regional and outer suburban trips. In the larger metropolitan areas, the urban internal trips are characteristically from 1 to 10 miles in length. For these local trips, there are, as has been suggested, most attractive alternate possibilities in the range of the intermediate types of solution. Because of the great number and concentration of these trips in limited space, the chances that sufficient additional freeways will be built fully to accommodate their demands are clouded, if not put beyond the range of practicability, in most larger American cities. The freeways that can be constructed—over a relatively long period of time—are very often occupied, to the extent of a major share of their capacity within urban areas, by the longer-length regional or outer suburban types of vehicular trip. The record and prospects for completion of freeway and fully grade-separated rapid transit projects built to serve predominantly local, urban internal movements within the larger metropolitan areas are not often such as to encourage optimism that broad success will soon be achieved by these means alone in the urban transportation field. Great cost, often in excess of $20 million per mile, and, for the freeways, amounts of land-taking which many citizens may view with alarm, pose practical deterrents to the possibilities of fully solving the urban internal transportation problems of such areas solely or principally by these massive means.

A New Intermediate Concept

IN the context of the preceding discussion, a new or modified intermediate transit solution is proposed for applicable urban internal transportation problems. The concept involved is one of new, fast, large, three-section articulated transit vehicle operation, termed "limited tramlines." It may be considered as a modified, inexpensive form of rapid transit. A variant of the concept, discussed below, could involve the use of buses. The new types of transit vehicle involved would operate with rather widely spaced stops in selected principal traffic corridors, between the major downtown and other centers and the urban and inner suburban areas of the larger metropolises. The phrase "limited tramline," rather than street railway, purposely signifies the full departure of this concept from the traditional and obsolescent street railway practices of the past.

The limited tramline vehicle would be designed integrally with the traveled way upon which it would operate. Too often in the past, specific transit rolling stock, the way upon which it travels, and the elements which control its movement have not been fully designed in an integrated "systems approach." The result has been that one or more of the components comprising the total vehicle-way-control "system" may be noticeably out of balance with the others.

The traveled way for this intermediate transit solution would take advantage of any potential grade-separated and at-grade rights-of-way which might become available along each principal corridor to be served. However, expensive new grade-separated alignments would be avoided except in cases of extreme necessity. Examples of possible rights-of-way include, among others, railroad lines and former electric railways; available open space; existing or potential center-malls in arterials, expressways, and freeways.

In the core portions of the major central business districts served, the limited tramline would operate preferably in specially reserved malls or lanes of certain streets selected for their suitability, but could, for limited distances, operate in regular street lanes. It is conceivable that the popularity of one or more of the limited tramline routes would be sufficient to warrant some shallow subway or elevated construction along suitable downtown sections, or that some off-street rights-of-way could be made available in the core areas. However, central routing, with a series of downtown station stops spaced from about 600 to 1,000 feet apart, is essential for proper delivery.

Beyond the immediate downtown area, all, or almost all, operation would be on reserved, but not necessarily grade-separated, rights-of-way. Stops would be spaced an average 1,200 feet apart in urban areas and about 1,500 to 2,000 feet apart in suburbs. A principal resource for this operation would be specially prepared or presently available arterial center-mall rights-of-way, with the running surfaces laid in attractive grassy expanses and landscaped with bushes, flower beds, and small trees. Such malls need be only 30 to 34 feet wide at stopping platforms and 22 feet in between. The opportunities to combine a fast, high capacity transit line with a park-like center-mall would enhance both the utility and the beauty of arterials where the limited tramline solution may apply. Alternatively, the limited tramline, once beyond the central district, might run in or alongside potentially available railroad, electric railway, freeway, or expressway rights-of-way, or make use of other available or acquired land space. Although not suitable for application over extensive lengths, limited tramlines could be operated for short distances in mixed vehicular traffic lanes, provided some favorable treatment were given to tramline movements.

Hand-in-hand with the well-engineered spatial relationship of the limited tramline to other traffic is the need for new practices in track construction and maintenance. Present practices in this field have undergone relatively little change for the better part of a century. Reserved trackage not laid in pavement should have a firmer foundation, employing concrete or asphaltic slabs and solid footings in most soils, rather than traditional ballasts. Crossties of new design and materials may be employed. Most crucial of all, the entire rail assembly, including especially the fastening link between running surface and tie or slab, is in need of complete redesign to permit smoother and quieter riding, higher speeds, longer rail life, and far easier maintenance and replacement. Included in these new designs should be triangular or other improved types of laterally braced fastening links to insure good lateral stability in non-paved track areas and permit easy replacement of worn rails. The rails themselves should be entirely redesigned with thicker railhead surfaces to permit longer life and, as a relative innovation, the turning-over of rails for use on 4, rather than just 1 or 2, flange contact edges. All rail joints should of course be welded and rail surfaces periodically ground smooth.

Where street trackage may be necessary, monolithic types of track construction, although still used today, have been obsolete for nearly half a century. Again, tracks should be laid on a well-footed slab situated under the pavement surface. Rails of the new types described above should be bolted to the slab or special crossties by new types of fastening links to permit quick rail turning or replacement. Most important of all, relatively narrow slots should be provided in the street pavement so that rails may be quickly turned or replaced without the necessity for disturbing any of the pavement. The small spaces between rail and pavement should be filled with an appropriately firm, yet conveniently removable, mastic material.

THE LIMITED TRAMLINE VEHICLE

THE traveled way, however, is second in importance to the vehicle itself in this transit concept. The characteristics of the limited tramline vehicle contain the essential key to the significance of this concept. Prominent among these characteristics are the following. The high capacity obtained by each three-section articulated unit economically permits two-man, and hence noticeably faster, operation at most times of day. The limited tramcar may also be operated as a one-man vehicle in hours of lightest traffic. Under two-man operation, the driver only drives the car, while the conductor, seated in the rear of the unit, only collects cash and token fares and, if issued, sight-checks "flash-type" commute tickets. The rear of the unit may consist of up to four entrance doors and a large prepayment vestibule with capacity for up to 50 standees.

The valuable principle of "passenger flow" is introduced: Passengers first enter the vehicle rapidly through four convenient rear doors. After paying their fares to the conductor *while the car is in motion,* they flow forward through the long articulated unit to find seats or standing places. They alight at their respective stops via either two center or two front doors. (At heavy boarding stops, peak period passengers may in addition enter through the two center and two front doors after paying fares to special platform collectors. Also, the driver may possibly sight-check, while stopped, the holders of "flash-type" commute tickets; only such holders would be permitted to enter via the two front doors.)

The most important points are that all fares are paid *while the vehicle moves* and that passengers may quickly enter and exit through a large number of doors, under full supervision. Fare structure, fare collection, and transfer issuing are simplified to expedite passenger flow. These procedures cut stop times to a fraction of those necessary when the driver alone must collect fares, make change, answer questions, and admonish people to "move to the rear of the bus"—all usually accomplished through a single entry door and in pathetically cramped space. The bus driver must then cautiously pull out of the curb lane into mixed traffic while wrestling with the driving wheel. Such ubiquitous, present-day transit practices are obsolete on heavier lines; potential schedule speeds under such primitive conditions are reduced to a shambles. It is no wonder that, in conditions of cramped crowding, unnecessary stop delays, and exasperated tempers, patrons with an alternative mode at the disposal have deserted urban transit systems in droves.

Another important improvement in the limited tramcar concept is high rates of acceleration and deceleration. With empty car weight per lineal foot reduced to 600 pounds or less, it is economically possible to provide regular acceleration rates averaging 3.0 to 4.0 miles per hour per second in the full 0 to 30 miles per hour speed range. Deceleration, with efficient dynamic braking, is equally rapid. Such rates are entirely safe when a careful, smoothly graduated normal starting and stopping program is built into the control mechanism. High acceleration and speed would also be enhanced by powering most, if not all, axles and by the possible introduction of automatic shifting to several different gear-ratios depending on attained speed. Car-borne static frequency changers, now in the process of development, would permit alternating current to be fed directly to the car with consequent reductions in electric line losses, capital cost, and operating expense. New types of a self-optimizing car controller, employing transistors, solid-state switching devices, and computer elements, provide a new conception of tramline electrical systems control.

By means of large, lighted car-borne signs and additional platform notices, boarding patrons in the lightest hours of travel could be directed to the front door entrances, should one-man operation then be desirable. As an additional economy, it is possible that the center section of the three-section articulated unit could be removed during periods of lightest traffic. With modern body, truck, control, and track way designs, and with advanced vehicle springing systems, the limited tramcar would offer a quality of smooth, quiet riding comfort never previously attained on urban transit vehicles.

The limited tramline vehicle would be 88 to 95 feet long and 9 feet wide. It would have a comfortable capacity of from 280 to 330 seated and standing passengers. A comparison of important *typical* values is tabulated on page 222.

A model three-section articulated limited tramline car* running on a reserved right-of-way has a potential hourly capacity of at least 17,000 passengers per track with single units and 34,000 with two coupled together, to be compared with only 800 to 1,200 persons per hour in automobiles in inefficient adjacent lanes. There is compelling justification, therefore, to reserve special limited tramline lanes in streets where conditions make such reservation desirable. These cars have been operating in Düsseldorf, Germany, with conspicuous success since 1957. Their use

* The original article contained five illustrations which have been omitted here.

	Limited Tramline Concept	PCC Street Car	Urban Diesel Bus
Maximum passenger capacity per vehicle	310	125	85
Crew members	2	1	1
Ratio: maximum passengers to crew	155:1	125:1	85:1
Average level acceleration rate in the 0–30 m.p.h. range (in m.p.h.p.s.)	3.5	3.0	1.3
Empty weight per lineal foot (in pounds)	600	800	500
Typical schedule speed, including stops but excluding layovers (in m.p.h.) *	17	11	10
Percent by which tramline speed is greater		55%	70%
Practical capacity of one track or lane (in passengers per hour) *	34,000	11,000	7,000
Percent by which tramline capacity is greater	—	209%	386%

* On a typical major urban corridor route, located in or along major radial arterials; in weekday peak periods; on level, tangent way; including stops but excluding terminal layovers; limited tramline concept potential versus current typical transit practices in mixed traffic for single PCC Cars and diesel buses.

has since spread to many parts of continental Europe. It is emphasized, however, that all the features of the limited tramline concept, as set forth herein, have not yet been fully embodied in any existing system. . . .

DIESEL BUSES

A VARIANT considered under this intermediate transit concept was the use of diesel buses. If the buses were to operate in special reserved rights-of-way, the capital cost of the traveled way involved would not be substantially less than in the tramcar version. If the buses operated along existing pavements, their cost, of course, would be small compared to that of new tracks and wires. However, it is not proposed that the transit vehicles in this concept operate generally for any appreciable length in actual street pavements. Both the bus and tramcar versions of the concept would, therefore, involve separate traveled way cost for the major portions of their routes.

Diesel buses could not be built to the larger length and width dimensions proposed for the limited tramcars, because they would then become unmaneuverable. The fact that the limited tramcar operates at extremely high capacity and entirely in *a spatially engineered and guided line of travel* is a very strong factor in its favor. These economies are especially important when, as is so generally the case, urban land and street space are at a premium. The largest practical articulated buses would at best have little more than half the capacity of three-section articulated tramcars. Diesel buses have an over-all acceleration rate of only two-fifths or less that of the tramline car proposed. Since over a quarter of all present urban transit running time is spent accelerating, the importance of this factor is apparent. Furthermore, paved bus rights-of-way could not be as attractively landscaped as a tracked right-of-way, where grass may be grown everywhere except at the narrow railhead surfaces. For these reasons, the bus variant of the basic limited tramline concept is not considered to be as attractive or practical as the use of railed tramcars.

Inherent in the limited tramline concept is the integration of its operation with that of vehicular movement where, as at street crossings or in jointly used rights-of-way, the two modes are in actual contact. It is proposed that traffic signals along an arterial having a limited tramline be adjusted to give equal, if not preferential, treatment to the mode with the greatest street use efficiency and capacity. Left turns across the limited tramlines would be held to a reasonable minimum. Where such turns were prohibited in the interests of both transit and vehicular movement, motorists would be encouraged to make three right turns around the block instead. Vehicle movement across the main arterial in question would be restricted to major cross streets, at about quarter-mile intervals. The general approach would be to apply evenly all the techniques of modern traffic engineering to achieve maximum tramline and street utility, and maximum carrying capacity for persons and goods.

WARRANTS, CAPABILITIES, AND COSTS

WHAT are the potential warrants to be considered for this intermediate transit concept? Significant to such a determination for each potential route is knowledge of its possible extent and physical geometry, and hence of its prospective schedule speeds. Population, employment, and shopping concentrations along the route, future origin-destination patterns for various types of trip, potential future traffic volumes, and similar data should be determined. A limited tramline route should be warranted with a minimum hourly *rate* of 10,000 potential passengers past the maximum load point in the peak half-hour peak direction. The average weekday ratio of passenger-miles to scheduled unit-miles of peak period passenger capacity should exceed 0.27 and preferably 0.35. Should maximum hourly volumes in each direction exceed 17,000 passengers, there may be warrant, because of their low relative capital cost, for consideration of two limited tramlines appropriately spaced for greater area coverage in the same general corridor. Minimum feasible trip-lengths to be served are one-quarter mile; maximum feasible trip-lengths depend on the schedule speed of the particular line. Limited tramlines, as described herein, should have average schedule speeds ranging from 14 to 30 miles per hour. Operating in the reserved center-mall of an urban and inner suburban arterial thoroughfare with average 1,200-foot station spacings and without grade-separation, a limited tramline should achieve an average schedule speed of 16 to 18 miles per hour. The maximum feasible trip-length to be served under that condition would be about 8 to 12 miles. Were the limited tramline to be located in a full or semi-grade-separated right-of-way similar to the new Highland-Riverside PCC Car line in Boston, schedule speed should be 22 to 30 miles per hour with 2,000-foot-spaced outer stops, thus permitting feasible maximum trip-lengths of from 11 to 20 miles.

The physical geometry, traffic engineering, and capital cost of each proposed route will be matters of great importance. Of the essence is a spirit of realistic evaluation, imagination, and compromise between the needs and abilities of the automobile on the one hand, and of the limited tramline on the other. This spirit is vital to working out tramline route physical geometry, traffic engineering, and cost, wherever urban traffic density and congestion are acute enough to warrant study of this new intermediate solution. For example, it may be necessary to sacrifice some moving and parking lanes in arterials where the proposed tramline is to operate on a paved yet segregated or center-mall right-of-way. Consideration here should be given to the seriousness of the over-all traffic problem in each urban corridor, to the relative costs of alternate solutions, and to the relative capacities and speeds of the limited tramline and regular vehicle lanes.

The paramount advantage of this concept is its low capital cost relative to the speed, capacity, convenience, and comfort which it provides. *Typical* peak period access frequencies, capacities, speeds, and median capital costs of important types of urban transportation facilities are compared in the table on page 225.

While the above examples are illustrative and could vary markedly with individual routes, they are indicative of the relative capabilities and costs of the various major urban facility types. The compelling cost-capacity advantage of the limited tramline solution—when and where properly applied—over urban freeways, subways, and elevateds is apparent. For every effective peak urban person-trip-mile of capacity provided, the typical capital cost is $1,670 for freeways, $440 for subways, and $140 for elevateds. For the tramline it is only $60 in fully modified private rights-of-way, or $30 in arterial center-malls. The values shown for the less effective bus service conservatively exclude any capital cost

Urban Transportation Facilities: A Comparison of Typical Features

Urban Facility Type (a)	Number of Lanes or Tracks (b)	Typical Frequency of Access or Stops (in feet) (c)	Peak Hour Peak Direction Person-Trip Capacity (d)	Peak Hour Peak Direction Typical Speed (in m.p.h.) (e)	Typical Full Capital Cost for One Urban Route-Mile (f)	Cost/ Capacity Ratio (f)/(d) (g)
Automobiles						
Freeway	8	6,000	9,000	32	$15,000,000	$1,670
At-Grade Expressway	8	2,000	6,000	25	3,000,000	500
Arterial	6	600	3,000	20	*	—
Present Transit						
Express Subway	2	9,000	50,000	33	22,000,000	440
Local Subway	2	3,200	50,000	20	22,000,000	440
Express Elevated	2	9,000	50,000	33	7,000,000	140
Local Elevated	2	3,200	50,000	20	7,000,000	140
Freeway Express Bus	2	4,000	8,000	22	*	—
Arterial Limited Bus	2	2,000	7,000	14	*	—
Local Surface Bus	2	600	7,000	10	*	—
Limited Tramline						
—In Available Private Rights-of-Way	2	2,000	34,000	25	2,000,000	60
—In Arterials	2	1,200	34,000	17	1,000,000	30

*Traveled way assumed already available.

for their shared use of freeways, and represent current typical transit practices in mixed traffic on major urban corridor routes.

Peak period movements composed primarily of trips to and from work will continue, as long as cities and congestion exist, to dominate requirements and planning for urban transportation facilities. The relative peak period speeds shown in the table only partly demonstrate the effectiveness of intermediate solutions such as the limited tramline. Even so, its 17 miles per hour typical speed in arterials and 25 via private rights-of-way are to be compared with 20 miles per hour via local subway and elevated, 22 via express bus, 33 via express subway and elevated, and 32 via freeway. The limited tramline stop spacing, however, is much more frequent than in the full grade-separated solutions. It is typically every 1,200 to 2,000 feet, compared with 3,200 to 9,000 feet on urban subways and elevateds and 6,000 feet on urban freeways. In addition, the limited tramline would be located accessibly at street level in the direct corridors of busy population centers. It becomes evident, therefore, that on the basis of true *door-to-door* travel times the limited tramline solution compares very favorably with the other urban and inner suburban transportation facilities. Such travel times are further powerfully enhanced by the relatively low capital cost of the limited tramlines. It becomes an economic matter to build these modern facilities at much more frequent spatial intervals than freeways, subways, or elevateds.

From still another standpoint, that of operating expense per passenger-mile, this concept offers important economies. The first of the two tables above indicates that the ratio of peak period vehicle capacity to crew required is 85:1 for urban diesel buses, 125:1 for PCC Cars, and 155:1 for the limited tramcar. To this may be added a 25-year vehicle service life, a 50-percent or greater improvement in surface transit schedule speed, new economical methods of track maintenance, and the low car weight per lineal foot. The effective operating economies made possible by these advantages immediately suggest themselves.

CONCLUSION

To what extent has the limited tramline concept been developed today? We may see *partial* examples of it in the new articulated cars and reserved tramline rights-of-way in Cologne, Rotterdam, Zurich, Bonn, Copenhagen, Essen, Milan, Frankfurt, Rome, Basel, Amsterdam, and Düsseldorf, as European examples. In America, there is the recent successful opening of the 12-mile Highland-Riverside inner suburban line for PCC Cars into Boston. Cleveland has two limited tramline routes on its Shaker Heights Rapid Transit system, operated again with PCC Cars. Other similar lines operate on extensive reserved trackage in Pittsburgh, Boston, San Francisco, Newark, Tokyo, Lima, São Paulo, and Buenos Aires. In Baltimore, a suburban-interurban electric railway to Annapolis gladly abandoned all passenger service ten years ago but is now actively seeking to reopen its rail service. The PCC Car, developed three decades ago, has not kept pace, however, with more recent developments in transportation technology. It cannot be considered as fully modern a solution as the limited tramline concept, although it is still reasonably well suited for many of the more traditional types of line on which it operates.

It is well to bear in mind that the limited tramline concept, as proposed, is an *intermediate* solution. It serves best for trip lengths of up to 40 minutes or, depending on attainable schedule speeds, up to 8 to 20 miles. Those speeds, when the concept is fully applied, will range between about 14 and 30 miles per hour. Its capacity approaches that of full subway and elevated lines. It is specifically to be noted that this concept is not generally adapted to longer distance regional express freeway or rapid transit movements having trip lengths of 20 miles and more, where average 40 to 50 mile per hour speeds and interchange or station spacings of over 2 miles are usually required.

In addition, there has been a trend in recent decades in the Western Hemisphere toward gradual abandonment of all at-grade types of rail solution for urban transport problems. Such developments have to be taken into serious consideration. Nevertheless, should a realistic engineering and economic analysis indicate attractive possibilities for application of the type of intermediate solution proposed herein, past trends, merely because they are such, should not foreclose further earnest consideration or ultimate adoption of this solution at locations and for movements where it may well be eminently suitable.

In formulating these necessary solutions, let us make the most efficient possible use of available urban land and street space. Let us unite speed, frequency, capacity, convenience, and economy. In most modern processes needless waste cannot and is not tolerated. We may ask ourselves then why especially valuable street space and urban land should be wasted or inefficiently used in cases where this can practicably be avoided. Why should several times *more* money be spent to solve a problem which may when fully analyzed be susceptible of far less expensive and more potent intermediate solutions? Our judgments and our imaginations should be open to effective intermediate urban and inner suburban transport concepts. Of these, the limited tramline concept holds out potently attractive new possibilities.

PART

II

THE FEDERAL
ROLE IN URBAN
TRANSPORTATION

CHAPTER 6

Federal Aid for Urban Highways:
The Commitment and the Challenge

W HEN THE FEDERAL GOVERNMENT initiated its policy of aiding highway development, with the Federal-Aid Highway Act of 1916, it
specifically excluded aid to any area that could be remotely considered to
be urban. This situation continued up to 1944; urban highway construction
and improvement projects had been undertaken during the 1930s, however,
as part of the national government's program to relieve unemployment in
the cities in the depths of the Depression.

In passing the Highway Act of 1944, Congress set in motion an attempt
to upgrade the national highway system in the postwar years. This time
urban areas were specifically included in the provisions in order to insure
the adequacy of circulation in our cities. The Highway Act of 1956, creating the Interstate System, later provided for urban sections of that system. A way of treating the whole problem of transport in metropolitan
areas was included in the Highway Act of 1962. Under this act no federal
aid for highway projects in urban areas of over 50,000 population was to
be made after July 1, 1965, unless the Secretary of Commerce was convinced that the projects were based on continuous and cooperative planning
conducted by the states and the local communities. It thus became a pre-
requisite for highway aid that all aspects of the transportation problem—
including mass transport—had to be considered.

Following are excerpts from the Highway Acts of 1944, 1956, and 1962
which related to urban areas.

Highway Act of 1944

An Act

To AMEND AND SUPPLEMENT the Federal-Aid Road Act, approved July
11, 1916, as amended and supplemented, to authorize appropriations for

Highway Act of 1944, Public Law 78–521.

[2 3 1]

the post-war construction of highways and bridges, to eliminate hazards at railroad-grade crossings, to provide for the immediate preparation of plans, and for other purposes.

Be it enacted by the Senate and House of Representatives of the United States of America in Congress assembled, That, when used in this Act, unless the context indicates otherwise:

The term "construction" means the supervising, inspecting, actual building, and all expenses incidental to the construction or reconstruction of a highway, including locating, surveying, and mapping, costs of rights-of-way, and elimination of hazards of railway-grade crossings.

The term "urban area" means an area including and adjacent to a municipality or other urban place, of five thousand or more, the population of such included municipality or other urban place to be determined by the latest available Federal census. The boundaries of urban areas, as defined herein, will be fixed by the State highway department of each State subject to the approval of the Public Roads Administration.

The term "rural areas" means all areas of the State not included in "urban areas."

The term "secondary and feeder roads" means roads in rural areas, including farm-to-market roads, rural-mail routes, and school-bus routes, and not on the Federal-aid system.

SEC. 2.

For the purpose of carrying out the provisions of the Federal Highway Act, approved November 9, 1921, as amended and supplemented, there is hereby authorized to be appropriated the sum of $1,500,000,000 to become available at the rate of $500,000,000 a year for each of three successive post-war fiscal years. . . .

SEC. 3.

The sum authorized in section 2 for each year shall be available for expenditures as follows:

(a) $225,000,000 for projects on the Federal-aid highway system.

(b) $150,000,000 for projects on the principal secondary and feeder roads, including farm-to-market roads, rural free delivery mail and public-school bus routes, either outside of municipalities or inside of municipalities of less than five thousand population: *Provided,* That these funds shall be expended on a system of such roads selected by the State highway departments in cooperation with the county supervisors, county commissioners, or other appropriate local road officials and the Commissioner of Public Roads: *Provided further,* That in any State having a population density of more than two hundred per square mile, as shown by the latest available Federal census, the said system may be selected by the State highway department with the approval of the Commissioner of Public Roads without regard to included municipal boundaries: . . .

(c) $125,000,000 for projects on the Federal-aid highway system in urban areas.

SEC. 4.

After making the deductions for administration, research, and investigations as provided in section 21 of the Federal Highway Act of 1921, the sums authorized shall be apportioned as follows:

(a) The $225,000,000 per year available for projects on the Federal-aid highway system shall be apportioned among the States as provided in section 21 of the Federal Highway Act.

(b) The $150,000,000 per year available for projects on the secondary and feeder roads shall be apportioned among the States in the following manner: One-third in the ratio which the area of each State bears to the total area of all the States; one-third in the ratio which the rural population of each State bears to the total rural population of all the States, as shown by the Federal census of 1940; and one-third in the ratio which the mileage of rural delivery and star routes in each State bears to the total mileage of rural delivery and star routes in all the States: *Provided,* That no State shall receive less than one-half of one per centum of each year's allotment under subsection (a) and this subsection.

(c) The $125,000,000 per year available for projects on highways in urban areas shall be apportioned among the States in the ratio which the population in municipalities and other urban places, of five thousand or more, in each State bears to the total population in municipalities and other urban places, of five thousand or more, in all the States as shown by the latest available Federal census: *Provided,* That Connecticut and Vermont towns shall be considered municipalities regardless of their incorporated status. . . .

SEC. 5.

(a) The Federal share payable on account of any project provided for by the funds made available under the foregoing provisions of this Act shall not exceed 50 per centum of the construction cost thereof other than costs of rights-of-way, and as to costs of rights-of-way shall not exceed one-third of such costs: . . .

. . .

SEC. 7.

There shall be designated within the continental United States a National System of Interstate Highways not exceeding forty thousand miles in total extent so located as to connect by routes, as direct as practicable, the principal metropolitan areas, cities, and industrial centers, to serve the national defense, and to connect at suitable border points with routes of continental importance in the Dominion of Canada and the Republic of Mexico. The routes of the National System of Interstate Highways shall be selected by joint action of the State highway departments of each State and the adjoining States, as provided by the Federal Highway Act of November 9, 1921, for the selection of the Federal-aid system. All highways or routes included in the National System of Interstate Highways as finally approved, if not already included in the Federal-aid highway system, shall be added to said system without regard to any mileage limitation. . . .

. . .

SEC. 14.

This Act may be cited as the "Federal-Aid Highway Act of 1944."
Approved December 20, 1944.

Highway Act of 1956

An Act

To AMEND AND SUPPLEMENT the Federal-Aid Road Act approved July 11, 1916, to authorize appropriations for continuing the construction of highways; to amend the Internal Revenue Code of 1954 to provide additional revenue from the taxes on motor fuel, tires, and trucks and buses; and for other purposes.

Be it enacted by the Senate and House of Representatives of the United States of America in Congress assembled,

TITLE I—FEDERAL-AID HIGHWAY ACT OF 1956

SEC. 101. SHORT TITLE FOR TITLE I.

This title may be cited as the "Federal-Aid Highway Act of 1956."

SEC. 102. FEDERAL-AID HIGHWAYS.

(a) (1) *Authorization of Appropriations.* For the purpose of carrying out the provisions of the Federal-Aid Road Act approved July 11, 1916 (39 Stat. 355), and all Acts amendatory thereof and supplementary

Highway Act of 1956, Public Law 84–627.

thereto, there is hereby authorized to be appropriated for the fiscal year ending June 30, 1957, $125,000,000 in addition to any sums heretofore authorized for such fiscal year; the sum of $850,000,000 for the fiscal year ending June 30, 1958; and the sum of $875,000,000 for the fiscal year ending June 30, 1959. The sums herein authorized for each fiscal year shall be available for expenditure as follows:

(A) 45 per centum for projects on the Federal-aid primary highway system.

(B) 30 per centum for projects on the Federal-aid secondary highway system.

(C) 25 per centum for projects on extensions of these systems within urban areas.

(2) *Apportionments.* The sums authorized by this section shall be apportioned among the several States in the manner now provided by law and in accordance with the formulas set forth in section 4 of the Federal-Aid Highway Act of 1944, approved December 20, 1944.

. . .

SEC. 108. NATIONAL SYSTEM OF INTERSTATE AND DEFENSE HIGHWAYS.

(a) *Interstate System.* It is hereby declared to be essential to the national interest to provide for the early completion of the "National System of Interstate Highways," as authorized and designated in accordance with section 7 of the Federal-Aid Highway Act of 1944 (58 Stat. 838). It is the intent of the Congress that the Interstate System be completed as nearly as practicable over a thirteen-year period and that the entire System in all the States be brought to simultaneous completion. Because of its primary importance to the national defense, the name of such system is hereby changed to the "National System of Interstate and Defense Highways." Such National System of Interstate and Defense Highways is hereinafter in this Act referred to as the "Interstate System."

(b) *Authorization of Appropriations.* For the purpose of expediting the construction, reconstruction, or improvement, inclusive of necessary bridges and tunnels, of the Interstate System, including extensions thereof through urban areas, designated in accordance with the provisions of section 7 of the Federal-Aid Highway Act of 1944 (58 Stat. 838), there is hereby authorized to be appropriated the additional sum of $1,000,-000,000 for the fiscal year ending June 30, 1957, which sum shall be in addition to the authorization heretofore made for that year, the additional sum of $1,700,000,000 for the fiscal year ending June 30, 1958, the additional sum of $2,000,000,000 for the fiscal year ending June 30, 1959, the additional sum of $2,200,000,000 for the fiscal year ending June 30, 1960, the additional sum of $2,200,000,000 for the fiscal year ending

June 30, 1961, the additional sum of $2,200,000,000 for the fiscal year ending June 30,1962, the additional sum of $2,200,000,000 for the fiscal year ending June 30, 1963, the additional sum of $2,200,000,000 for the fiscal year ending June 30, 1964, the additional sum of $2,200,000,000 for the fiscal year ending June 30, 1965, the additional sum of $2,200,-000,000 for the fiscal year ending June 30, 1966, the additional sum of $2,200,000,000 for the fiscal year ending June 30, 1967, the additional sum of $1,500,000,000 for the fiscal year ending June 30, 1968, and the additional sum of $1,025,000,000 for the fiscal year ending June 30, 1969. . . .

(e) *Federal Share.* The Federal share payable on account of any project on the Interstate System provided for by funds made available under the provisions of this section shall be increased to 90 per centum of the total cost thereof, plus a percentage of the remaining 10 per centum of such cost in any State containing unappropriated and unreserved public lands and nontaxable Indian lands, individual and tribal, exceeding 5 per centum of the total area of all lands therein, equal to the percentage that the area of such lands in such State is of its total area: *Provided,* That such Federal share payable on any project in any State shall not exceed 95 per centum of the total cost of such project. . . .

(1) *Increase in Mileage.* Section 7 of the Federal-Aid Highway Act of 1944 (58 Stat. 838), relating to the Interstate System, is hereby amended by striking out "forty thousand," and inserting in lieu thereof "forty-one thousand": . . . .

Highway Act of 1962

SEC. 9.

(a) CHAPTER 1 OF TITLE 23, United States Code, is amended by adding immediately following section 133 the following new section:

§ 134. *Transportation planning in certain urban areas.*

It is declared to be in the national interest to encourage and promote the development of transportation systems, embracing various modes of transport in a manner that will serve the States and local communities efficiently and effectively. To accomplish this objective the Secretary shall cooperate with the States, as authorized in this title, in the development of long-range highway plans and programs which are properly coordinated with plans for improvements in other

Highway Act of 1962, Public Law 87–866.

affected forms of transportation and which are formulated with due consideration to their probable effect on the future development of urban areas of more than fifty thousand population. After July 1, 1965, the Secretary shall not approve under section 105 of this title any program for projects in any urban area of more than fifty thousand population unless he finds that such projects are based on a continuing comprehensive transportation planning process carried on cooperatively by States and local communities in conformance with the objectives stated in this section.

The New Highways: Challenge to the Metropolitan Region

WILFRED OWEN

RARELY HAS ANYONE SUMMED UP the metropolitan transportation problem and its solutions more succinctly than Wilfred Owen. In the following paper he points out the problems to which even a rich nation is susceptible when its urban transportation systems begin to break down. The joys of life are muted and both urban and suburban slums grow apace as a result of haphazard transport development.

The Highway Act of 1962 was designed to alleviate the problem. The challenge described here by Owen has still not been fully grasped, although the situation is certainly not as bleak as when this piece was written. What follows falls midway between what was and is, and what might be. The "might be" is far off, but at least a few steps have been taken in the right direction.

THE PROBLEM

THE metropolitan areas of the United States are the focal points of America's life. They account for the majority of its people, industry, and intellectual and social accomplishments.

In the past five years these areas have accommodated an astonishing 97 percent of the nation's total population growth. Today they are reaching out for fresh land at the rate of a million acres a year.

"The New Highways: Challenge to the Metropolitan Region," a booklet published in 1958 by Connecticut General Life Insurance Company, based on "The Metropolitan Transportation Problem," by Wilfred Owen, published by the Brookings Institution.

But the central city is in serious trouble, and the surrounding metropolitan area is facing difficult problems. Heavy concentrations of people and industry and obsolete patterns of development have spread blight and decay over great areas of urban land. One-third of the urban population is housed where miserable living conditions prevail, unchecked by adequate laws or proper enforcement of existing laws. For the masses of our people, cities have become disagreeable to live in and work in, and difficult to move around in.

Open space in our explosively expanding metropolitan areas has all but disappeared, and with it the light and air and opportunities for recreation that a nation with wealth and leisure time should be able to enjoy.

Many of our great cities are hardpressed financially. They are confronted with enormous problems in maintaining essential public services.

Traffic has reached almost intolerable limits. For many people the journey to work has made a mockery of better working conditions and has cancelled the advantages of shorter hours on the job.

Modern transportation has enabled large numbers of people to concentrate in cities. It has supplied the food and materials necessary to maintain the urban population, and has afforded mobility necessary to enjoy the economic, social, and cultural advantages of the metropolis. But metropolitan cities have grown to the point where they threaten to strangle the transportation that helped to make them possible.

The escape to the fringes has been less than a complete success. Suburban blight is spreading into once pleasant neighborhoods from the cluttered and unsightly roadsides that have proved bad for traffic, bad for business, and bad for the community. It is the automobile that is transporting this blight to the suburbs. The natural beauty of the countryside is being jeopardized by the bulldozers. Soon the attempt to flee to the unspoiled country may be thwarted as one unplanned metropolis runs into another. Great underlying pressures are being exerted by the combination of population growth and the aggravating impact of rapid migrations made possible by the automobile.

THE WORSENING OUTLOOK

UNLESS America acts quickly to achieve comprehensive solutions, problems that seem bad today are bound to become worse in the years ahead. Some cities are starting to show the way. But their efforts hardly begin to match the problem. By 1975 we can expect another 50 million people to be living in metropolitan areas. Twenty million more workers may be added to the rush hour jam. More people and higher incomes will mean more transportation of all kinds. More jobs and more leisure will mean constantly increasing traffic. Over 100 million motor vehicles will be on the road.

If these trends are superimposed on the metropolitan hodge-podge that planless growth makes inevitable, America will be faced with an absurd paradox. In spite of the world's highest income, the majority of our people may be faced not only with poorer standards of transportation, but with deteriorating standards of living. Contrary to the comforting projections of a steady rise in national product, tomorrow's utopias may be more statistical than real.

Today cities and suburbs are forging ahead without plans, toward an inevitable day of reckoning. Many are in the midst of a building boom that is compounding congestion where the problem has already reached crisis proportions. In most cases, totally inadequate provision is being made for the additional transportation and other public services that these traffic generators demand. The headlong rush to build has left little time or thought for the esthetics and amenities of living, or for the bold concepts of urban design dictated by unparalleled economic growth and changing technology.

The whole pattern of the developing metropolis ignores how people will be living and moving in the years ahead. On the one hand vast sums are being spent for motor vehicles, highways, and other means of transportation; on the other hand these investments are being nullified to a large extent by uncontrolled urban growth that is imposing insupportable demands on transport capacity. The traffic problems of the metropolitan area continue to multiply more rapidly than transport development can meet the challenge.

To make matters worse, greater volumes of passenger and freight transport are being accompanied by shifts in method of movement, from space-saving public carriers to travel by automobile. Overwhelming preference for automobile transportation has caused a sharp reduction in the patronage of mass transit facilities by bus and rail. Prosperity for the automobile has meant depression for transit. Patronage of public carriers is down to the level of fifty years ago. The cycle of traffic losses, rising costs, higher fares, less frequent service, and further loss of business has persisted.

In the face of this worsening situation, the Congress of the United States has recently enacted the most spectacular aid program ever made available for urban areas. Under the Federal Aid Highway Act of 1956, provision has been made for the greatest roadbuilding program in history. Altogether, the expenditure of some $100 billion of federal, state, and local funds is probable over the next decade and a half. The most spectacular part of this program will be the construction of a 41,000-mile

National System of Interstate Highways to cost some $25 billion. Approximately 6,000 miles of these expressways will be located in urban areas, absorbing half the total Interstate Highway outlay. The new program adds up to the most promising opportunity yet presented to attack the growing transportation crisis in metropolitan areas.

But will the new highway program automatically solve the critical problems of traffic congestion that threaten the metropolis? And, more important, will it help to resolve the basic problems that underlie the plight of our cities?

ACHIEVING A SATISFACTORY URBAN ENVIRONMENT

THERE are grave doubts that the program as presently conceived can achieve these goals. Though the automobile reaps the full blame for urban congestion and decay, cities were already suffering from blight and to some extent from traffic troubles long before the automobile choked the highways. If the auto alone were the culprit, building more roads or substituting transit would solve the problem.

But building new roads often attracts more traffic than the newly provided capacity can accommodate, and even where mass transit is highly developed, the results have been far from satisfactory. The difficulties of the metropolis are as great in New York, with its subways, as in Los Angeles with its freeways. And though the problem is more intense in the United States, cities all over the world are struggling with similar problems of urban living and moving.

Since urban congestion has persisted no matter what the method of moving, there must be some other remedy than trying to build enough highways to keep pace with traffic growth, or attempting to persuade motorists to ride on buses.

When the metropolitan area is analyzed, it becomes apparent that there is, in fact, another approach, and that it lies outside the field of transport. Transport as such cannot solve its own problems, nor left to its own devices can it be the means of rehabilitating our cities.

The reason is that there are two sides to the transportation problem, and to date attention has been directed exclusively to one of them—the supply side. The supply side of the problem involves the facilities to move traffic: the highways, the public transit system, the railroads, terminals, parking, and other related transport facilities.

The other side is the demand side—the traffic generated by the various uses of urban land.

The transportation problem is essentially the problem of achieving a reasonable balance between the two. The task is to assure that traffic generated in urban areas does not place an impossible burden on available transport capacity.

The transportation problem in metropolitan areas, then, is really only half a transportation problem. Half the problem is building additional transport facilities. The other half is creating an environment in which the transportation system can work.

Vertical transportation by elevator illustrates the point. It is the best example of a conscious effort to relate population and economic activity to movement. Passenger and freight elevators are designed as an integral part of office buildings and apartments. They are built to carry the loads expected from the volume and type of activity to be served. But if the building is subsequently converted to a different type and density of use, the relationship between elevator capacity and traffic generated is destroyed. Congestion and disruption of service are the results.

In today's urban environment the same basic problem underlies traffic congestion: too many people and too much economic activity in relation to available transport capacity.

We have failed to measure and take into account the traffic-producing potentials of various land uses as an index of transport needs. And conversely, we have failed, despite the limitations of transport, to impose appropriate restraints on the types and intensities of permitted land uses as a means of avoiding insupportable transport demands.

The situation has been made worse by the excessive transportation resulting from haphazard arrangements or urban land uses that multiply travel requirements and force large numbers of people to go the same places at the same times. The typical arrangement is the high-density center for working and shopping, with surrounding low-density residential suburbs for living. The resulting pendulum movement from home to work poses a challenge that the best conceivable system of transportation could never hope to meet. And now, added to this basic pendulum movement, is the reverse movement of traffic from close-in residential areas to outlying employment centers, and the criss-cross movement of people from one outlying area to another.

The helter-skelter of today's urban sprawl has us moving on a treadmill. We are attempting at great cost to increase the speed at which we move. At the same time we are constantly increasing the time we need to travel to get where we want to go. Modern transport technology is being nullified by the urban environment in which it must serve.

The motor vehicle that should have helped to free the city has helped to destroy it. We have failed to adjust to the automotive age and have frequently surrendered to it instead. Obsolete streets are jammed with traffic and lined with parked cars and trucks. Pedestrians have all but lost their rights. The accident toll is a national disgrace. The noise and fumes of traffic have downgraded large areas of the city. Along the streets and highways, gas stations, used car lots, auto graveyards, hot dog stands, and billboards often mark the beginnings of uncontrolled blight.

Even if the highway program succeeded in relieving traffic congestion, this result by itself would have to be considered a failure. An expressway system that simply moves us more expeditiously through areas of urban decay would miss the mark. We need better transportation, but we also want better cities. Whether or not we will have the vision and the courage to insist on both is the multi-billion dollar question that the highway program poses for urban America.

THE KEY: LAND USE PLANNING

THE first step in transportation planning, then, is land use planning. The big hope for moving around in urban areas is to move the urban areas themselves around. We will have to attack the congestion of moving by overcoming the congestion of living. Metropolitan mobility depends on regional planning that creates a more orderly arrangement of urban living and working. New communities will have to be built and old ones rebuilt in a way that makes it possible for people who live in them to move in them.

The highway program, combined with urban renewal, is offering us the chance. Transportation problems could be alleviated if cities would restore close-in areas and make them fit to live in. It might be possible to reduce the volume and concentration of home-to-work travel if residential areas and places of work were made more compatible. The new highways can make feasible the establishment of new employment centers beyond the radius of maximum congestion. They may also help to compensate for congested living if the acquisition of rights-of-way can be combined with land purchase for badly needed park and recreation space.

The job cannot be accomplished overnight, but it can and must be started now. Consider that in the next decade, with or without plans, we will be building and rebuilding urban facilities equivalent to 50 cities the size of Boston, simply to provide for urban growth and replacement. The longer we discount the possibilities of planning a better urban environment, the more staggering will be the task when we finally realize that there is no other choice.

There are many questions that will have to be answered. For example, should a community set specific limits on total population to balance growth potentials with acceptable standards of living? What densities of population are to be permitted? What space and locations should be devoted to residential, industrial, and commercial uses, and to parks, schools, and public buildings? What are the traffic-generating characteristics of these different uses of land?

To what extent should centers of employment be moved out to reduce the influx of commuters and to make room for more appropriate uses of close-in land? What activities are most desirable for downtown locations?

How can we accomplish and effectuate for the entire metropolitan region the comprehensive land use plans that are the indispensable basis for better communities and better transportation?

Can we provide open space within the urbanized area to help balance the traffic generation of developed land? Would it be possible to reserve closely situated land for agricultural and recreational uses and at the same time to establish limits to urban sprawl? Is it feasible in this way to control the area of urbanization, to insulate one community from another, and to keep open country accessible for urban dwellers?

The vastness of our country has led us to the mistaken belief that land is plentiful and its conservation unimportant. But will land of the desired quality be accessible to our predominantly urban population if metropolitan sprawl continues at present rates? Should nearby open space be allowed to disappear when it is so badly needed to break the urban monotony?

These are questions that we know too little about, primarily because they are seldom asked. We must learn the answers as quickly as possible because without a reasonable land use plan there can be no lasting transport solutions. Good transportation, as well as good housing, education, recreation, and other services, depend on a reasonable balance between the availability of facilities and the demands imposed on them.

HIGHWAYS AND THE COMMUNITY

FORTUNATELY, the highway program itself can help to achieve the environment that is essential to its success. Highways are, in fact, one of the most potent tools of the planner.

The highway system forms the skeleton of the giant metropolis. In addition to providing circulation, it can delineate areas of different functions, serve as buffers for residential neighborhoods, and consolidate areas of related land use. Land acquisition for new highways needs to be combined with land assembly for a variety of public purposes as well as for planned industrial areas and shopping centers.

Highways can be landscaped to add beauty to the surrounding area instead of contributing to blight. Redesign of urban road systems can eliminate ineffective gridiron streets, making land available for more appropriate uses. Roads built through areas of urban decay can provide the means of clearing out obsolete sections of the city and razing substandard buildings.

The new highway program, as it now stands, may wind up attacking the transportation problem in a vacuum. It is isolated by law from the rest of the transportation system and from the urban area it is designed to serve. Under these circumstances a multi-billion-dollar investment in highways may actually intensify rather than alleviate the difficulties of the metropolis. The result may be to compound rather than relieve congestion, and to retard the development of better communities rather than seize upon the opportunity for real accomplishment.

The controlling principle for the highway program must be an improved urban environment. At times this will necessitate new rights-of-way because there is no existing route to follow. In such cases the new route can be designed to eradicate slums and blighted sections. But in many instances the alternative will be offered of rebuilding along existing roadways, and this will often be the best course from the standpoint of community development, despite higher right-of-way costs.

It would be a mistake to allow road costs alone to dictate highway policy when there are the possibilities of combining roadbuilding and renewal to achieve the most economical total program.

In some cases, then, the highway program can make a frontal attack on roadside blight by retaining and widening existing rights-of-way and thus eliminating unsightly development. In other cases new rights-of-way may be obtained through areas destined for ultimate renewal in any event. The objective in either case would be to restore wherever possible an environment in which transportation, commercial enterprises, and residential areas all can prosper.

This attack on traffic congestion and urban blight can be accomplished through a joint highway-urban renewal program designed to achieve both objectives simultaneously. What appears to be extravagance when viewed solely as a highway project may become economical in terms of transportation and urban renewal combined. The cost of eradicating blight is not avoided by ignoring the problem, but only postponed.

LOOKING AT THE TOTAL TRANSPORT PICTURE

BUT highways are only one part of the transportation system. Urban mobility depends on a wide variety of freight and passenger facilities including railroad and air transport, rail rapid transit, taxi, bus, parking, and other terminal facilities.

For many car owners the principal problem is not highways but parking; and for millions of commuters the principal transportation problem is transit: antiquated rail facilities, overcrowded buses, and sub-standard service. The success of any program of highway construction depends to an important degree on the adequacy of solutions in these other sectors of the transportation system.

The fact is, however, that the isolation of highway policy from transportation policy has made it impossible to develop a satisfactory total transportation system. How are we to assure that the principal objective of carrying traffic through and around the metropolitan area, as part of the task of building a national system of highways, will at the same time contribute to the maximum relief of local traffic congestion?

What steps must be taken to be certain that parking facilities and bus and truck terminals are provided to accommodate the increase in motor traffic that these new highways will create? Will they be designed and located as part of a total plan, or will they be left to chance?

Can the new highways be designed to help meet the mass transit requirement of the metropolitan area? What consideration will be given to rapid transit, by rail or bus, on the expressway system?

What of the imbalance between heavy investment in new highways and the scarcity of capital for transit? What measures should be taken to modernize transit equipment and improve public carrier services, so that a balanced transportation system can be developed that makes the best use of both?

What role can mass transit be expected to play in the years ahead? Why do people select one mode of transport rather than another? Will improvements in transit help to attract greater patronage? What are the technological possibilities in this area?

Answers to these questions imply a total transportation plan to match a total community plan. But today the task of keeping the metropolis on the move is divided so many ways that no one is responsible for the results. Metropolitan areas leave the task to dozens of independent highway departments, transit authorities, port authorities, toll authorities, railroads, and taxi companies. Building a transportation system under these conditions is like trying to build a house with the carpenters, bricklayers, and plumbers going it alone. A piecemeal approach has doomed the urban resident to piecemeal relief.

Today's approach suffers from the added fact that no unit of local government is big enough to encompass the problem. Local governments are attempting to supply the very transportation services that have rendered these governments obsolete.

The fact remains that good transportation made America's urban economy possible—and poor transportation must not be allowed to destroy it. Without drastic measures to overcome the administrative, financial, and legal bottlenecks, neither moving nor living in urban areas will be worth the struggle.

ORGANIZING TO DO THE JOB

How can the multi-billion-dollar investment made possible through the new highway program make the most effective contribution to better communities and better transportation?

The previous discussion has pointed out that the two goals are inseparable, that effective solutions for metropolitan transportation depend on a major replanning and redevelopment of the metropolis itself. But it has been noted at the same time that the highway program can serve as a primary tool in arriving at transportation and planning solutions, and that the combination can mean not only more satisfactory methods of moving, but more satisfactory ways of living.

One fact is obvious: that while the money is available for the highway program, new administrative, financial, and legal tools are needed to permit the full potentials of the program to be realized.

Metropolitan communities do not yet have the comprehensive plans that can furnish an urban environment in which the highway program can most effectively serve. And the highway program cannot be used to its maximum potential as a tool for building better communities until federal legislation insists on this objective.

How can the highway program be revised to make it an integral part of the total task of replanning and redeveloping metropolitan areas? Should the urban planning and renewal provisions contained in housing legislation be expanded and strengthened? Or is new legislation needed to provide a fresh attack on the total problem with which the federal government now deals in separate and unbalanced parts? Should planning and renewal programs be made comparable in magnitude to the highway program?

At the executive level federal action in urban affairs is being administered in a series of vacuums. The federal Bureau of Public Roads in the Department of Commerce is responsible for carrying out the highway program. It operates through the highway departments of the states. The Housing and Home Finance Agency administers the housing program through which urban planning and renewal activities are carried on. Here the federal contact is with the cities. There are encouraging instances of an integrated approach by these two groups, but many legal and administrative details stand in the way of a satisfactory united effort. How can the interests of the federal government in urban affairs be managed more in keeping with the realities of the urban problems they seek to treat?

At the local level the problem focuses on the inability of existing governmental machinery to cope with the problems of metropolitan areas that have expanded far beyond the old city boundaries.

What kind of metropolitan arrangements are needed to accomplish the land use planning that is basic to the solution of metropolitan problems? What role can the states play in this area? How could a unified approach to highway and transportation problems be accomplished? Should transportation be provided through a metropolitan transport agency, or through a multiple-purpose regional agency? Or does the answer lie in some form of metropolitan government?

It is clear that neither federal, state, nor local governments are organized to carry out an effective attack on transportation and land-use planning problems. A satisfactory solution is not likely to be reached short of a complete overhaul of the administrative machinery affecting the metropolis at all levels of government.

THE PROBLEM OF FINANCE

A PROGRAM to provide satisfactory standards of urban transportation for today's metropolitan areas calls for new financial devices as well as administration innovation. Progressive thinking in the field of finance is essential to solutions that encompass the whole transport problem, that encourage the renewal of cities, and that assure the planning of desirable suburbs.

The problem of financing an effective frontal attack on urban transportation is not going to be solved by the new highway program alone. The new road legislation provides only part of the total highway network needed in urban areas, and it takes into account none of the other transportation facilities and services required for a balanced transport system.

What financial arrangements would make a concerted attack possible? Would it be desirable to pool motor vehicle fees, gas taxes, transit and parking revenues, and other transport revenues to finance a total transportation system? Should transportation be self-supporting through user charges or supported out of general taxes? Could the "prices" charged for transportation—tolls, parking fees, transit fares, and similar charges —be used to regulate traffic and influence the choice of transport method?

How can transportation and urban renewal funds be jointly applied to achieve over-all community objectives?

[247]

In addition to questions of public finance, many new financial problems arise with respect to private facilities directly related to the highway program. One of these is the development of shopping centers involving joint action by many private owners, including questions of design and land acquisition in relation to new highways. The building of these facilities introduces many opportunities for business and government to operate as partners in an enterprise that requires the participation of both.

LEGAL PROBLEMS

IMPORTANT legal obstacles stand in the way of a comprehensive attack on metropolitan problems and prevent the use of available funds to launch such an attack. The objective is in many respects frustrated by the shortcomings of federal legislation dealing with highways and urban planning and renewal.

How can federal law be strengthened to assure that roads in urban areas conform with local area planning and promote its realization? How can local planning efforts be accelerated to provide the aid that highway engineers need now? What changes need to be made in state highway laws to achieve more satisfactory understanding and consideration of urban requirements?

Can right-of-way be acquired in connection with expressway construction to provide for related development of parking areas, shopping centers, industrial districts, recreation areas, park lands, and related facilities?

What are the possibilities of reserving land in metropolitan areas for agricultural and forestry, to assure a better balance between rural and urban development?

These and other questions require prompt answers if the extraordinary federal highway program now under way is to provide the long-awaited relief that metropolitan living demands. As the United States has become progressively more urbanized and motorized, a closer relation between transportation and urban development has become essential. We will have to plan transportation facilities to achieve better communities, and community planning will have to be designed to achieve better transportation. The new highway program, broadly conceived, can launch a revolutionary attack on metropolitan problems that is long overdue.

CHAPTER 7

Mass Transportation

As THE DECADE OF THE 1950s drew to a close, it was obvious to many observers that the American city was in a state of crisis on many fronts. The flight of middle-class Americans to the suburbs was under way in full force. The old central city in large metropolitan areas was fast becoming a ghetto for the lower socio-economic classes. Suburban shopping centers wooed shoppers away from central-city stores; many firms relocated or established suburban branches to be within reach of their former customers. As a result, business activity was in a state of stagnation in downtown areas.

The move to the suburbs brought financial woes to the central city. As the need soared for city services to meet the requirements of a relatively poorer population, those firms and individuals that had provided the major source of tax revenues were moving steadily into outlying communities and out of the reach of the city tax rolls. In a not so facetious sense, the American city could be likened to a doughnut: all the dough was on the outside and there was nothing in the middle.

As might be expected, urban transportation in general was in trouble. The drift of population to the less densely populated suburbs had moved an increasingly large proportion of the metropolitan population beyond effective, economical reach of existing public-transportation facilities and operations. The transport needs of this population had to be met largely by increased use of the automobile for all transport purposes. This added to the burden of inadequate outlying highway systems and created chaos in older parts of the metropolis where streets had been laid out prior to the advent of the automobile.

Highway programs continued apace, but despite ever-increasing highway expenditures by all levels of government, there never seemed to be enough roadspace to meet the avalanche of automobiles, especially at the commuting peaks. While the highways were marvels of engineering skill in many cases, they were very expensive in terms of the cash and land that had to be given up for their construction. And, sadly enough, they did not alleviate congestion to the extent it had been promised they would.

For its part, urban mass transportation had its own particular crisis. There had been no end to the generally deteriorating condition of mass transportation that had set in at the end of the Second World War. The companies which had accrued surpluses as a result of heavy wartime traffic had used up their resources, and by the late 1950s they were generally living a hand-to-mouth existence. Many public transit concerns went out of business, especially in smaller cities. The situation was hardly better in larger metropolitan areas. Even where transit companies managed to keep their heads above water, earnings were slim and it was difficult to secure funds for new facilities, for improvement of facilities, and for the replacement of equipment.

Added to the burden common to most U. S. cities, those metropolitan areas that enjoyed the benefits of commuter railroad transportation were shaken by the train-off provisions of the Transportation Act of 1958. Before the passage of this act, railroads wishing to abandon passenger train service had to plead their cases with the various state regulatory authorities —bodies which typically were highly reluctant to allow train service to be dropped. Although commuter railway service was a millstone around the neck of any railroad operating it, state agencies usually met attempts to reduce these deficit operations with a stone wall of refusal. Under the Act of 1958, however, the ICC could be petitioned when state procedures had been of no avail. The chances were now excellent that after only a year or two it would be possible for railroads to abandon large chunks of commuter service.

Launching an attack on urban transport woes was no easy task for metropolitan areas, faced as they were with a host of transport problems. As the process of metropolitanization had occurred, the suburbs and satellite cities that formed around the major central cities continued their strong economic and social ties, but they remained politically separate. In the minds of most suburban politicians and residents, this separation was a thing to be most jealously guarded. These fragmented political entities were difficult to organize for any sort of unified approach aiming at solution of the transport problems that plagued the whole metropolis; whatever transport interest existed was likely to be quite local in nature. The political fragmentation meant that there was also fiscal fragmentation. In short, there was no way to bring the full resources of the metropolitan area to bear on a problem that was common to the whole.

There was pressure from the cities for action from higher levels of government to help them in their quest for a solution to the problem. The desired solution was most often a financial one. Funds were available for highways, of course, but under the transport policy of that time there was nothing available for mass transportation.

Little help was available from state governments. These bodies had their own financial problems and were often as badly in a fiscal bind as were the municipalities within their borders. A vacuum existed on local and state levels. If improvement was to be sought in the condition of mass transport, it was obvious, as the 1960s arrived on the scene, that the spark had to come from the federal government.

Joint Policy and Procedural Statements on Improved Coordination of Highway and General Urban Planning, 1960

U. S. TRANSPORTATION POLICY, as well as many other aspects of federal policy, has been plagued for years by lack of coordination. It is almost inconceivable, for example, that the Interstate Highway program could have been formulated and undertaken, in view of the proposed expenditure of tens of billions of dollars over a period of less than two decades, without a rigorous analysis of the effect of such a program on non-highway-oriented modes of transportation. Yet this is exactly what happened. Likewise, there was no thought given to the impact of federal transport programs—principally highway programs—on urban areas. It was as if the various federal programs were carried on quite separately, with none expected in any way to affect any of the others.

The material that follows is a precedent-shattering as well as precedent-setting statement. In it we find the beginnings of coordinated efforts between highway and urban-renewal programs. We also find the admission of the powerful role that transport can play in city life. It is a tacit admission that merely building highways is not a solution to transport problems in American cities. There is no mention of federal participation in programs benefiting mass transportation. But the call for coordinated effort and the demand for comprehensive urban planning to cover all aspects of transport indicate encouragement of mass transport to a point at which, in conjunction with sound highway programs, the needs of the public may best be met.

A NEW STEP in government coordination to bring about joint planning of highways and urban development in our metropolitan areas was an-

"Joint Policy and Procedural Statements on Improved Coordination of Highway and General Urban Planning," Housing and Home Finance Agency—U.S. Department of Commerce, November 1960. The reading is introduced by the Housing and Home Finance Agency news release of November 29, 1960.

nounced today by Secretary of Commerce Frederick H. Mueller and U. S. Housing Administrator Norman P. Mason.

The two officials announced an agreement by which methods will be developed, under a Joint Steering Committee, to make highway and urban planning funds available for joint use in comprehensive urban and metropolitan planning.

Federal highway legislation authorizes the use of 1½ percent of total program funds for planning and research work in connection with the Federally-aided highway program. Such funds are allocated through the Bureau of Public Roads in the U. S. Department of Commerce to the states for highway planning.

At the same time, the Housing and Home Finance Agency makes grants for planning in metropolitan areas, as well as for comprehensive programming of urban renewal activity on a community-wide basis in individual localities. Coordination currently is carried on largely through procedures providing for case-by-case consultation between the Federal, State, and local bodies involved.

The new agreement provides for an experimental approach to the use of highway and urban planning funds jointly in an urban area where local and state bodies are prepared to establish coordinated planning that will embrace both highway and general urban plans, such as land use controls, community facilities, and housing and other growth.

A Joint Steering Committee will be appointed representing the U. S. Department of Commerce and the Housing and Home Finance Agency which will have overall responsibility for encouraging joint projects and will review and evaluate progress of experimental joint planning that is undertaken in metropolitan areas.

Regional Joint Committees from the two agencies will be set up to encourage and assist in the joint use of highway and urban planning funds in metropolitan areas prepared to carry on such comprehensive undertakings. Either state or local agencies may initiate a proposal for a jointly financed planning project, but the project must be jointly sponsored by a State, metropolitan, or regional planning agency eligible for urban planning grants, and a State highway department.

It is emphasized that this will be a demonstration operation at this point to develop experience in practical planning operations. It will not substitute for present procedures in regular program operations.

POLICY STATEMENT

THE Federal Government is vitally interested in encouraging and assisting the sound growth and redevelopment of our cities and their surrounding urban areas. More and more of our rapidly growing population will live in urban areas, particularly in metropolitan areas. Future changes in the physical characteristics of these urban complexes will profoundly influence the health, happiness and prosperity of all our people and the strength of the nation.

The States also have substantial and even more immediate interest in the sound future growth of their metropolitan areas. State highway departments and planning agencies are already concerned with municipal planning. The highway departments are spending substantial Federal and State funds for both planning and construction in urban areas and are legally responsible for initiation and execution of Federal-aid highway projects. State interest has been expressed by the Conference of State Governors which has recognized that better coordination of State activities is needed both to assure economical use of State and Federal funds and to enable metropolitan planning and development programs to be fully effective.

Local people must reach a working agreement upon what they want their communities to become since they should be the ones to initiate and carry out the plans. Many urban areas are making progress in this direction and a few are on the way to outstanding success. Successful planning in the larger metropolitan areas, however, is heavily dependent upon the active cooperation of almost all the political jurisdictions involved and of most private individuals and groups whose decisions will influence the pattern of future development and redevelopment.

The Federal Government assists various types of development which contribute significantly to the physical character of the urban environment, and it has a responsibility to see that these aids are used efficiently and economically.

. . .

Federal and State highway officials have recognized this problem and have encouraged planning which meets both the objectives of sound community development and the purposes of the Federal-aid highway program. The availability under Federal highway legislation since 1934 of 1½ per cent of total program funds for planning and research has been invaluable. These funds have facilitated planning aimed at assuring a highway system compatible with sound community development.

The various programs administered by HHFA have a continuing major impact on the character and direction of urban development. Urban renewal operations are beginning to transform our cities. The recently authorized program of grants for community renewal programming will help cities assess their total urban renewal needs and determine the best ways to satisfy them over a period of years, taking into account local land use objectives, prospective financial capacity, and other community development programs such as water, sewer and transportation systems. The FHA system of mortgage insurance, the public housing program, and advances and loans for the planning and construction of community facilities also directly influence the shape and quality of urban development.

The HHFA also provides matching grants for comprehensive planning of metropolitan areas in their entirety and of smaller cities and towns. The program authority is very broad. It is helping localities to look at their over-all development problems and possibilities. It assists them to do the necessary planning and programming for future development.

While much has been done by both agencies, much more needs to be done by them and by other Federal agencies administering programs of Federal aid for community development. It is of the greatest importance that the impact on the community of all Federally-assisted programs be harmonious and that the timing, character and location of all Federally-assisted improvements be compatible with desirable community development goals.

To assist in meeting these requirements, the Secretary of Commerce and the HHFA Administrator are establishing an experimental procedure for the joint financing, through Federal-aid highway planning funds and urban planning grants, of the planning required for a cooperative and comprehensive approach to metropolitan area development. The purpose of this undertaking is to stimulate a continuing process of planning and development coordination which will:

(a) Give consideration to all forces, public and private, shaping the physical development of the total community.

(b) Cover land uses and controls as well as plans for physical development and combine all elements of urban development and redevelopment into a clear-cut, comprehensive plan of what the citizens want their community to become.

(c) Cover the entire urban area within which the forces of development are interrelated.

(d) Involve in the planning process the political jurisdictions and agencies which make decisions affecting development of the metropolitan area.

(e) Link the process of planning to action programs.

The objective, then, is not merely a planning process but the development of effective cooperation and coordination both among the local governments within a metropolitan area, and between these governments and the State and Federal agencies involved in area development activities. This process must be continuing if it is to serve its purpose effectively as the areas grow and change. In the beginning, this joint activity may be limited to metropolitan areas where the need is greatest and the prospects for significant accomplishment are most promising. If local interest warrants, this effort will be extended as quickly as staff and funds permit.

PROCEDURE FOR COORDINATING JOINT FINANCING OF COMPREHENSIVE PLANNING IN METROPOLITAN AREAS

Joint Steering Committee. The Secretary of Commerce and the Housing and Home Finance Administrator shall appoint a Joint Steering Committee consisting of equal representation from both agencies to supervise and review this experimental program for coordination of the use of HHFA urban planning grants and 1½ per cent highway planning funds. The Joint Committee will have responsibility for (a) developing procedures, (b) putting these procedures into effect, (c) evaluating the effectiveness of this experimental program, and (d) recommending modifications based on experience.

Regional Joint Committee. The Joint Steering Committee, in cooperation with the heads of the Regional Offices of HHFA and the Bureau of Public Roads, shall appoint Regional Joint Committees consisting of an equal number of persons from each agency who have responsibility for urban planning and highway planning activities, respectively. The duties of these committees shall be to (a) explore the interest and the capacity of agencies in any metropolitan area to carry on comprehensive planning for the entire area; (b) encourage the joint financing procedure in areas where it offers the greatest promise of constructive results; (c) advise and assist State and local planning agencies and State highway departments in the development of proposals for jointly financed planning projects; (d) review and make recommendations with respect to applications for such assistance; and (e) provide advice and assistance during the operation of an approved planning project.

Project Initiation. Any State or local agency may initiate a proposal for a jointly financed planning project, but such a project must be jointly sponsored by a State, metropolitan, or regional planning agency eligible for urban planning grants, and a State highway department. The Regional Joint Committees will provide advice and assistance to any agency wishing to initiate such a project, and will work with the sponsoring agencies to develop an approvable project.

Proposals for coordinated planning will be approved for joint financial assistance only when the following conditions are met:

(1) The proposal aims at achieving a unified process of planning covering all relevant aspects of development and land use;

(2) Planning will cover the entire urbanized area involved;

(3) There are prospective problems in planning or locating Federal-aid highways in the area.

(4) Planning is to be conducted under the policy guidance of a metropolitan coordinating committee broadly representative of the governing officials of the local jurisdictions within the area and including representatives of major State planning and development agencies.

This procedure is an alternative to rather than a substitute for existing procedures for initiating comprehensive urban planning projects for Federally-aided highway planning projects for metropolitan areas. The possible need for coordinated planning under joint financial assistance should be considered, however, by the Regional offices of the respective agencies in reviewing applications for either type of project. When such a need is believed to exist, the application should be referred to the Regional Joint Committee for consideration.

Cost-sharing arrangements will be developed by agreement among the sponsoring agencies on the basis of the planning project prospectus, subject to the approval of the HHFA and the Bureau of Public Roads. The regular eligibility requirements of the urban planning grants and highway planning programs will continue to apply.

Federal Laws: Assistance to Mass Transportation

JOHN F. KENNEDY became President in large part because of his appeal to urban voters. He was the first candidate for the nation's highest office who really appeared to have a good grasp of the problems of an increasingly urbanized society. It seemed at his election as if the atmosphere were ripe for federal action to alleviate many urban problems.

By the beginning of 1961 a bright spot was badly needed. The situation was growing rapidly more desperate throughout the nation. Motorists and automobiles fumed away together in seemingly endless peak-hour traffic jams. Mass transportation was reaching new postwar lows in the number of passengers handled; profits were practically nil; and there were severe cutbacks in the quantity and quality of service offered. The situation was particularly severe in the area around New York City. Under the terms of the Transportation Act of 1958, the ICC had given permission to the New York Central Railroad to abandon its West Shore commuter railway and ferry service; many other rail carriers in the area were threatening to go out

Excerpts from the Housing Act of 1949, the Housing Act of 1954, and the Housing Amendments of 1955, as amended through June 30, 1961.

of the commuter passenger business. In other large cities the story was the same. The U. S. Conference of Mayors and the American Municipal Association began desperately to step up their lobbying for federal legislation to aid mass transport.

The first fruit of the effort for improvement came in the Housing Act of 1961. Amendments to existing housing legislation provided for expansion of coordinated planning that would include consideration of mass transport, and for a program of loans for the purchase of new equipment. Most important was a provision encouraging experimentation and research in urban transport. Mass transportation demonstration projects were to be aimed at finding out how to increase passenger appeal. Following are the relevant parts of the legislative package that began the revitalization of mass transport in American cities.

GRANTS FOR MASS TRANSPORTATION DEMONSTRATION PROJECTS*

Capital Grants

SEC. 103.

(a) (1) THE ADMINISTRATOR[1] may make capital grants to local public agencies in accordance with the provisions of this title for urban renewal projects: . . .

. . .

(b) The Administrator may, with the approval of the President, contract to make grants under this title aggregating not to exceed $4,000,000,000: *Provided,*[2] That of such sum the Administrator may, without regard to other provisions of this title, contract to make grants aggregating not to exceed $25,000,000 for mass transportation demonstration projects which he determines will assist in carrying out urban transportation plans and research, including but not limited to the development of data and information of general applicability on the reduction of urban transportation needs, the improvement of mass transportation service, and the contribution of such service toward meeting total urban transportation needs at minimum cost. Such grants shall not be used for major long-term capital improvement; shall not exceed two-thirds of the cost, as determined or estimated by the Administrator, of the project for which the grant is made; and shall be subject to such other terms and conditions as he may prescribe. The Administrator is authorized, notwithstanding the provisions of section 3648 of the Revised Statutes, as amended, to make advance or

* Excerpts from the Housing Act of 1949, as amended through June 30, 1961; Title I—Slum Clearance and Urban Renewal; Public Law 171, 81st Congress, 63 Stat. 413, 414; 42 U.S.C. 1453.

progress payments on account of any grant contracted to be made pursuant to this section. The faith of the United States is solemnly pledged to the payment of all grants contracted for under this title, and there are hereby authorized to be appropriated, out of any money in the Treasury not otherwise appropriated, the amounts necessary to provide for such payments: *Provided,* That any amounts so appropriated shall also be available for repaying to the Secretary of the Treasury, for application to notes of the Administrator, the principal amounts of any funds advanced to local public agencies under this title which the Administrator determines to be uncollectible because of the termination of activities for which such advances were made, together with the interest paid or accrued to the Secretary (as determined by him) attributable to notes given by the Administrator in connection with such advances, but all such repayments shall constitute a charge against the authorization to make contracts for grants contained in this section: *Provided further,* That no such determination of the Administrator shall be construed to prejudice the rights of the United States with respect to any such advance.

GRANTS TO ASSIST MASS TRANSPORTATION PLANNING*

SEC. 701.

(a) In order to assist State and local governments in solving planning problems resulting from the increasing concentration of population in metropolitan and other urban areas, including smaller communities; to facilitate comprehensive planning for urban development, including coordinated transportation systems,[3] on a continuing basis by such governments; and to encourage such governments to establish and improve planning staffs, the Administrator[4] is authorized to make planning grants to—

(1) State planning agencies, or (in States where no such planning agency exists) to agencies or instrumentalities of State government designated by the Governor of the State and acceptable to the Administrator as capable of carrying out the planning functions contemplated by this section, for the provision of planning assistance to (A) cities, other municipalities, and counties having a population of less than 50,000 according to the latest decennial census, (B) any group of adjacent communities, either incorporated or unincorporated, having a total population of less than 50,000 according to the latest decennial census and having common or related urban planning problems resulting from rapid urbanization, and (C) cities, other municipalities, and counties, referred to in paragraph (3) of this subsection and areas referred to in paragraph (4) of this subsection;

* Excerpts from the Housing Act of 1954, as amended through June 30, 1961; Urban Planning; Public Law 560, 83d Congress; 40 U.S.C. 461.

(2) official State, metropolitan, and regional planning agencies, or other agencies and instrumentalities designated by the Governor (or Governors in the case of interstate planning) and acceptable to the Administrator, empowered under State or local laws or interstate compact to perform metropolitan or regional planning;

(3) cities, other municipalities, and counties which (A) are situated in areas designated by the Secretary of Commerce under section 5(a) of the Area Redevelopment Act as redevelopment areas or (B) have suffered substantial damage as a result of a catastrophe which the President, pursuant to section 2(a) of "An Act to authorize Federal assistance to States and local governments in major disasters, and for other purposes" has determined to be a major disaster;

(4) to official governmental planning agencies for areas where rapid urbanization has resulted or is expected to result from the establishment or rapid and substantial expansion of a Federal installation; and

(5) State planning agencies for State and interstate comprehensive planning (as defined in subsection (d)) and for research and coordination activity related thereto. Planning assisted under this section shall, to the maximum extent feasible, cover entire urban areas having common or related urban development problems. The Administrator shall encourage cooperation in preparing and carrying out plans among all interested municipalities, political subdivisions, public agencies, and other parties in order to achieve coordinated development of entire areas. To the maximum extent feasible, pertinent plans and studies already made for areas shall be utilized so as to avoid unnecessary repetition of effort and expense. Planning which may be assisted under this section includes the preparation of comprehensive urban[5] transportation surveys, studies, and plans to aid in solving problems of traffic congestion, facilitating the circulation of people and goods in metropolitan and other urban areas and reducing transportation needs. Funds available under this section shall be in addition to and may be used jointly with funds available for planning surveys and investigations under other Federally-aided programs, and nothing contained in this section shall be construed as affecting the authority of the Secretary of Commerce under section 307 of title 23, United States Code.

(b) A grant made under this section shall not exceed two-thirds[6] of the estimated cost of the work for which the grant is made: *Provided,* That a grant may be made under this section to a city, municipality, or county described in clause (A) of subsection (a)(3), or to a State planning agency (as provided in clause (C) of subsection (a)(1)) for the provision of planning assistance to such a city, municipality, or county, for not more than 75 per centum of such estimated cost. All grants made under this section shall be subject to terms and conditions prescribed by the

Administrator. No portion of any grant made under this section shall be used for the preparation of plans for specific public works. The Administrator is authorized, notwithstanding the provisions of section 3648 of the Revised Statutes, as amended, to make advances or progress payments on account of any planning grant made under this section. There is hereby authorized to be appropriated not exceeding $75,000,000[7] to carry out the purposes of this section, and any amounts so appropriated shall remain available until expended.

(c) The Administrator is authorized, in areas embracing several municipalities or other political subdivisions, to encourage planning on a unified metropolitan basis and to provide technical assistance for such planning and the solution of problems relating thereto.

(d) It is the further intent of this section to encourage comprehensive planning, including transportation[8] planning, for States, cities, counties, metropolitan areas, and urban regions and the establishment and development of the organizational units needed therefor. The Administrator is authorized to provide technical assistance to State and local governments and their agencies and instrumentalities undertaking such planning and, by contract or otherwise, to make studies and publish information on related problems. In extending financial assistance under this section, the Administrator may require such assurances as he deems adequate that the appropriate State and local agencies are making reasonable progress in the development of the elements of comprehensive planning. Comprehensive planning, as used in this section, includes the following, to the extent directly related to urban needs: (1) preparation, as a guide for long-range development, of general physical plans with respect to the pattern and intensity of land use and the provision of public facilities, including transportation facilities,[9] together with long-range fiscal plans for such development; (2) programming of capital improvements based on a determination of relative urgency, together with definitive financing plans for the improvements to be constructed in the earlier years of the program; (3) coordination of all related plans of the departments or subdivisions of the government concerned; (4) inter-governmental coordination of all related planned activities among the State and local governmental agencies concerned; and (5) preparation of regulatory and administrative measures in support of the foregoing.

(e) In the exercise of his function of encouraging comprehensive planning by the States, the Administrator shall consult with those officials of the Federal Government responsible for the administration of programs of Federal assistance to the State and municipalities for various categories of public facilities.

(f) The consent of the Congress is hereby given to any two or more

States to enter into agreements or compacts, not in conflict with any law of the United States, for cooperative efforts and mutual assistance in the comprehensive planning for the physical growth and development of interstate, metropolitan, or other urban areas, and to establish such agencies, joint or otherwise, as they may deem desirable for making effective such agreements and compacts.

Approved August 2, 1954.

LOANS FOR MASS TRANSPORTATION FACILITIES AND EQUIPMENT*

Declaration of Policy

SEC. 201.

It has been the policy of the Congress to assist wherever possible the States and their political subdivisions to provide the services and facilities essential to the health and welfare of the people of the United States.

The Congress finds that in many instances municipalities, or other political subdivisions of States, which seek to provide essential public works or facilities (including mass transportation[10] facilities and equipment), are unable to raise the necessary funds at reasonable interest rates.

It is the purpose of this title (subject to the limitations contained herein) to authorize the extension of credit to assist in the provision of certain essential public works or facilities by States, municipalities, or other political subdivisions of States, where such credit is not otherwise available on reasonable terms and conditions.

Federal Loans

SEC. 202.

(a) The Housing and Home Finance Administrator is authorized (1) to purchase the securities and obligations of, or make loans to, municipalities and other political subdivisions and instrumentalities of States (including public agencies and instrumentalities of one or more municipalities or other political subdivisions in the same State), to finance specific projects for public works or facilities under State, municipal, or other applicable law, and (2)[11] to purchase the securities and obligations of, or make loans to, States, municipalities and other political subdivisions of States, public agencies and instrumentalities of one or more States, municipalities and political subdivisions of States, and public corporations, boards, and commissions established under the laws of any State, to finance the acquisition, construction, reconstruction, and improvement of facilities and

* Excerpts from the Housing Amendments of 1955, as amended through June 30, 1961; Title II—Public Facility Loans; Public Law 345, 84th Congress; 42 U.S.C. 1492.

equipment for use, by operation or lease or otherwise, in mass transportation service in urban areas, and for use in coordinating highway, bus, surface-rail, underground, parking and other transportation facilities in such areas. The facilities and equipment referred to in clause (2) may include land, but not public highways, and any other real or personal property needed for an economic, efficient, and coordinated mass transportation system. No such purchase or loan shall be made for payment of ordinary governmental or non-project operating expenses.

(b) The powers granted in subsection (a) of this section shall be subject to the following restrictions and limitations:

(1) No financial assistance shall be extended under this section unless the financial assistance applied for is not otherwise available on reasonable terms, and all securities and obligations purchased and all loans made under this section shall be of such sound value or so secured as reasonably to assure retirement or repayment, and such loans may be made either directly or in cooperation with banks or other lending institutions through agreements to participate or by the purchase of participations or otherwise.

(2) No securities or obligations shall be purchased, and no loans shall be made, including renewals or extensions thereof, which have maturity dates in excess of forty years. Subject to such maximum maturity, the Administrator in his discretion may provide for the postponement of the payment of interest on not more than 50 per centum of any financial assistance extended to an applicant under this section for a period up to ten years where (A) such assistance does not exceed 50 per centum of the development cost of the project involved, and (B) it is determined by the Administrator that such applicant will experience above-average population growth and the project would contribute to orderly community development, economy, and efficiency; and any amounts so postponed shall be payable with interest in annual installments during the remaining maturity of such assistance.

(3) Financial assistance extended under this section shall bear interest at a rate determined by the Administrator which shall be not more than the higher of (A) 3 per centum per annum, or (B) the total of one-half of 1 per centum per annum added to the rate of interest paid by the Administrator on funds obtained from the Secretary of the Treasury as provided in section 203(a).

(4) No financial assistance shall be extended under clause (1) of subsection (a) of this section to any municipality or other political subdivision having a population of fifty thousand or more (one hundred fifty thousand or more in the case of a community situated in an area designated as a redevelopment area under the second sentence of section 5(a) of the Area Redevelopment Act) according to the most recent decennial census, or

to any public agency or instrumentality of one or more municipalities or other political subdivisions having a population (or an aggregate population) equal to or exceeding that figure according to such census.

(c) In the processing of applications for financial assistance under clause (1) of subsection (a) of this section the Administrator shall give priority to applications of smaller municipalities for assistance in the construction of basic public works (including works for the storage, treatment, purification, or distribution of water; sewage, sewage treatment, and sewer facilities; and gas distribution systems) for which there is an urgent and vital public need. As used in this section, a "smaller municipality" means an incorporated or unincorporated town, or other political subdivision of a State, which had a population of less than ten thousand inhabitants at the time of the last Federal census.

(d) No loans may be made for transportation facilities or equipment, pursuant to clause (2) of subsection (a) of this section, unless the Administrator determines (1) that there is being actively developed (or has been developed) for the urban or other metropolitan area served by the applicant a program, meeting criteria established by him, for the development of a comprehensive and coordinated mass transportation system; (2) that the proposed facilities or equipment can reasonably be expected to be required for such a system; and (3) if such program has not been completed, that there is an urgent need for the provision of the facilities or equipment to be commenced prior to the time that the program could reasonably be expected to be completed: *Provided,* That no such loan shall be made, except under a prior commitment, after December 31, 1962.

Financing

SEC. 203.

(a) In order to finance activities under this title, the Administrator is authorized and empowered to issue to the Secretary of the Treasury, from time to time and to have outstanding at any one time, notes and other obligations in an amount not to exceed $650,000,000: *Provided,* That of the funds obtained through the issuance of such notes and other obligations, $600,000,000 shall be available only for purchases and loans pursuant to clause (1) of section 202(a) of this title and $50,000,000 shall be available only for purchases and loans pursuant to clause (2) of such section. Such obligations shall be in such forms and denominations, have such maturities and be subject to such terms and conditions as may be prescribed by the Administrator, with the approval of the Secretary of the Treasury. Such notes or other obligations shall bear interest at a rate determined by the Secretary of the Treasury which shall be not more than the higher of (1) 2½ per centum per annum, or (2) the average annual interest rate on all interest-bearing obligations of the United States then forming a part of the public debt as computed at the end of the fiscal year next preceding the issuance by the Administrator and adjusted to the nearest one-eighth of 1 per centum.

The Secretary of the Treasury is authorized and directed to purchase any notes and other obligations of the Administrator to be issued hereunder and for such purpose the Secretary of the Treasury is authorized to use as a public debt transaction the proceeds from the sale of any securities issued under the Second Liberty Bond Act, as amended, and the purposes for which securities may be issued under such Act, as amended, are extended to include any purchases of such notes and obligations. The Secretary of the Treasury may at any time sell any of the notes or other obligations acquired by him under this section. All redemptions, purchases, and sales by the Secretary of the Treasury of such notes or other obligations shall be treated as public debt transactions of the United States.

(b) Funds borrowed under this section and any proceeds shall constitute a revolving fund which may be used by the Administrator in the exercise of his functions under this title.

General Provisions

SEC. 204.

In the performance of, and with respect to, the functions, powers, and duties vested in him by this title the Administrator shall (in addition to any authority otherwise vested in him) have the functions, powers, and duties set forth in section 402, except subsection (c)(2), of the Housing Act of 1950. Funds obtained or held by the Administrator in connection with the performance of his functions under this title shall be available for the administrative expenses of the Administrator in connection with the performance of such functions.

. . .

SEC. 206.

As used in this title, the term "States" means the several States, the District of Columbia, the Commonwealth of Puerto Rico, and the Territories and possessions of the United States.

SEC. 207.

The Administrator is authorized to establish technical advisory services to assist municipalities and other political subdivisions and instrumentalities in the budgeting, financing, planning, and construction of community facilities. There are hereby authorized to be appropriated such sums as may be necessary, together with any fees that may be charged, to cover the cost of such services.

Approved August 11, 1955.

NOTES

1. Housing and Home Finance Administrator.

2. Section 303 of the Housing Act of 1961, Public Law 87–70, approved June 30, 1961, 75 Stat. 149, 166, inserted this proviso and the next two sentences of this subsection.

3. The provisions relating to transportation were inserted by sec. 310, Housing Act of 1961, Public Law 87–70, approved June 30, 1961, 75 Stat. 149, 170.

4. Housing and Home Finance Administrator.

5. See note 3.

6. Sec. 310, Housing Act of 1961, Public Law 87–70, approved June 30, 1961, 75 Stat. 149, 170, substituted "two-thirds" for "50 per centum."

7. Sec. 310, Housing Act of 1961, Public Law 87–70, approved June 30, 1961, 75 Stat. 149, 170, substituted "$75,000,000" for "$20,000,000."

8. Sec. 310, Housing Act of 1961, Public Law 87–70, approved June 30, 1961, 75 Stat. 149, 170, inserted provisions relating to transportation.

9. Ibid.

10. Sec. 501, Housing Act of 1961, Public Law 87–70, approved June 30, 1961, 75 Stat. 149, 173, inserted provisions relating to mass transportation facilities and equipment.

11. Ibid.

The Federal Urban Transportation Demonstration Program

JOHN C. KOHL

THIS ARTICLE BY JOHN C. KOHL is perhaps the clearest available statement of the thinking behind the federal urban-transport demonstration grant programs carried on under the Housing Act of 1961. It is based on his experience as Assistant Administrator in charge of transportation programs for the Housing and Home Finance Agency (now part of the U.S. Department of Housing and Urban Development).

The role of the federal government in such programs is not that of initiator. As the 1961 law is written, this is the exclusive function of local

"The Federal Urban Transportation Demonstration Program," *Traffic Quarterly*, July 1964.

governments and of transport agencies. The federal government simply assists demonstration projects, which are initiated at the local level and for which local participants are willing to pay one-third of the cost. One of the most interesting parts of the following article is the section on federal evaluation of demonstration proposals.

It should be noted that while Mr. Kohl's article considers specifically only demonstrations carried on under the provisions of the Housing Act of 1961 (the Urban Mass Transportation Act of 1964 had not yet been passed at the time this article was written), the discussion applies as well to subsequent demonstration programs financed under the provisions of the 1964 Act.

THE DEMONSTRATION has long been a useful device for achieving an effective linkage between research efforts and their practical application. The demonstration project is being increasingly recognized as a significant element in the research world when it is a professionally organized activity carried on under well-defined field conditions for purposes of illustrating, interpreting, testing or validating specific technical developments and their operational consequences.

Federal interest and support of such demonstration programs stems, apparently, from 1903, when the Department of Agriculture was faced with the problem of gaining widespread acceptance of measures designed to control the boll weevil, then ravaging the cotton crop. Even though their entire production was threatened with devastation, farmers were reluctant to employ new and unfamiliar techniques proved only in the laboratories of the Department and of state agricultural colleges.

To encourage popular adoption of essential measures, a plan was devised to have the "scientific way" actually tried out by a representative farmer. Technical assistance was provided, but the convincing aspect was the promise of compensation to the farmer in the event of crop loss. The Department had persuaded some local businessmen, willing to take a small risk in the interest of preserving their local economy, to contribute to a guaranty fund. There was no statutory authority, even for the mere nine hundred dollars required, for any commitment of public monies to such a fund.

At the end of the crop season, when the cotton was picked, the record showed not only that boll weevil damage had been averted but also that the farmer's yield was far above even the most optimistic of normal expectations. The demonstration had been spectacularly successful. Word spread so rapidly that more than 7,000 cotton farmers were reported to have volunteered their cooperation the following year. Research recommendations were no longer doubted as harmful or impractical and the control program was launched.

Thus, demonstration approaches were introduced and became firmly established in agricultural technology. Gradually, other federal agencies, drawing upon the experience of the Department of Agriculture, have utilized demonstration programs to augment their research with substantial returns, both in more effective application and in sharpened research efforts themselves.

Where there is a broad public involvement in utilizing research applications, as in agriculture, health, welfare and other public services, demonstrations provide an invaluable means for introduction of improvements and innovations. They permit desirable periods of adjustment during which reactions can be ascertained and evaluated before commitments are made to fixed courses of action. Equally important is the feedback of demonstration findings to research programs where new guidelines and bases for establishing priorities of effort are constantly being sought.

Legislative Authority

AMONG the most recent federal demonstration activities is the program authorized by the Congress in the urban transportation provisions of the Housing Act of 1961. In several respects, this program was the most important element of the three-part effort initiated by the Congress, yet it is much less known and understood than the provisions for urban transportation planning, or for financial assistance through loans, which have been widely discussed.

Section 103 (b) of the Housing Act of 1949 as amended by Section 303 of the Housing Act of 1961 provides the statutory authority for the current urban transportation demonstration program:

> . . . The Administrator (of the Housing Agency) may contract to make grants aggregating not to exceed $25,000,000 for mass transportation demonstration projects which he determines will assist in carrying out urban transportation plans and research, including but not limited to the development of data and information of general applicability on the reduction of urban transportation needs, the improvement of mass transportation service, and the contribution of such service toward meeting total urban transportation needs at minimum cost. Such grants shall not be used for major long-term capital improvement; shall not exceed two-thirds of the cost, as determined or estimated by the Administrator, of the project for which the grant is made; and shall be subject to such other terms and conditions as he may prescribe. . . .

Although not specifically written into the law, there is evidence of clear legislative intent to require that grants by the federal government under this section be made only to public bodies. The record of hearings held in 1961, when urban transportation legislation was under consideration, and before it was combined with the Housing Act of 1961, indicates not only such intent but also the reasons supporting this little-understood condition attached to demonstration grants.

Senator Harrison A. Williams, Jr., of New Jersey, in his testimony before the Housing Subcommittee of the House Committee on Banking and Currency at its hearings in May 1961 said:

> By extending the assistance to governments and public bodies rather than to private carriers, it will encourage the involvement and participation of state and local governments to come to grips with the problem —financially and otherwise. Perhaps, our greatest need is getting people studying and working on the problems of urban transportation at the local level, which would not happen if the federal government deals directly with the private carriers.

Private carriers—the transit operators—and other private or public groups which might be locally appropriate and necessary to a project, would, it was made clear, participate through contractual arrangements with the public sponsor receiving the federal grant. No arrangement necessarily favoring all-public organization of projects and excluding private interests was countenanced by the record of legislative hearings.

The subcommittee indicated endorsement of this concept—a public channel for federal assistance with broad participation of other public agencies and private organizations under contract with the local sponsor. It was heeded by the administrator in his development of guidelines for conducting the urban transportation demonstration program so authorized and circumscribed.

ADMINISTRATIVE INTERPRETATION

FUNDAMENTAL to the formulation of administrative criteria for the operation of the program is the recognition of the important role of local interests in solving urban problems. Both the stipulation that demonstration projects must "assist in carrying out urban transportation plans and research," and the requirement that the federal participation "shall not exceed two-thirds of the cost," along with the legislative intent of the use of "the public channel," all reinforced the interpretation that this program should be locally sponsored and managed. The federal role is not that of initiating and operating demonstration projects but is, instead, that of assisting local groups technically and financially.

In other words, the Housing Agency conceives its activity as primarily that of responding constructively to locally initiated efforts, rather than promoting any centrally conceived and directed program concentrating upon urban transportation research.

The added statutory stipulation pertaining to the "development of data and information of general applicability" has been interpreted to exclude projects solely concerned with uniquely local transportation problems. Obviously, the results of any demonstration project must benefit not only the community participating in the project, but also other communities having similar problems. To insure the dissemination of project results, then, is a principal federal responsibility in this program and requires considered attention to project reports and their distribution.

Further, the emphasis of the law upon "carrying out urban transportation plans and research" has been interpreted to mean that demonstration projects should be oriented to operational problems and the practical evaluation of techniques or methodology, rather than to preparation of specific plans or the prosecution of basic transportation research.

Where a particular plan or research finding is the incidental result of project efforts directed toward the testing and evaluation of procedures or operations, there is, seemingly, no conflict with demonstration objectives. In fact, it is recognized that the prospect of such specific results may well be the inducement for local participation, while the broadly applicable evaluations justify the federal participation. Introducing and maintaining a legitimate balance between local and general objectives has been one of the more difficult aspects of project development.

Finally, the prohibition of the use of demonstration grants for "major long-term capital improvement" has been conscientiously applied because the principal and sometimes, sole objective of some proposals was the construction of a permanent transit facility for which regular financing had proved impossible. Rentals and other recognized charges for the use of capital equipment or facilities during the term of a demonstration was, however, recognized as a proper use of funds insofar as the particular items could be shown to be essential to the attainment of project objectives. Provision for crediting the project with any remaining capital value at its conclusion has been a mandatory requirement in these cases.

These interpretations have imposed upon the demonstration program a character substantially unlike the centrally directed, scientifically oriented research programs of many technical agencies—government, university and private. The major objective of encouraging and stimulating local initiative and support has, of necessity, modified many projects which could have been technically more elaborate had emphasis been concentrated upon scientific considerations alone.

[269]

Importantly, also, the specified ceiling upon federal participation in project costs has resulted in the failure of several technically desirable demonstrations to materialize because local resources were inadequate to produce matching funds. Public transportation is not a "lush" industry. Thus, neither technical nor geographic factors could be brought into balance as dictated by any nationally projected outline of urban studies.

Program Organization

Responsibility for the administration of the initial phases of this new federal transportation program was lodged by the Congress in the Housing and Home Finance Agency. This decision, it might seem at first, runs counter to the federal policy of concentrating responsibility for transportation, generally, within the Department of Commerce. Local transportation, however, was determined to be so intimately related to the complex field of urban problems—housing and community development in all their aspects—as to heavily outweigh the purely transportation issues. Close coordination was, nevertheless, ordained between the Housing Administrator and the Secretary of Commerce, who were made jointly responsible to the then President Kennedy for the study of the longer-range federal role in urban transportation. It should be noted that liaison has been continuously maintained.

With responsibility for operation of the preliminary program and for the joint study with the Secretary of Commerce authorized by the Housing Act of 1961, the Housing Administrator, Dr. Robert C. Weaver, undertook the development of an organization to administer and carry on the necessary functions. Three alternatives were considered: first, an assignment to one of the existing constituent agencies of HHFA for operation as part of an already established program, such as that of the Urban Renewal Administration, which has had jurisdiction over urban planning assistance (the so-called "701 Program"); second, an assignment to the existing regional organizations of HHFA with minimum central operation; and third, the organization within the Office of the Administrator of a compactly specialized staff.

After weighing the advantages and disadvantages of these alternatives, in the light of the tentative nature of the federal effort, the Administrator decided in favor of a small technical and administrative unit on his immediate staff—the third alternative.

Accordingly, an HHFA Office of Transportation was established in October 1961, shortly after the passage of the Housing Act. An assistant administrator (transportation) was assigned as its director, and four divisions—legal, planning, engineering and economics—were manned by professional specialists. In addition to the operation of the newly authorized programs, the Office was directed to render transportation advice to the administrator, as might be required, and technical service to the Urban Renewal Administration, to facilitate transportation planning as a part of the comprehensive urban planning assistance ("701") program.

In this manner, specialized professional skills in transportation, local transportation particularly, were brought into close contact with the broad range of professional talents involved in the widely varied programs of community development. While there have been some, and not unexpected, difficulties in intra-organizational communication, these have been judged minimal. Over-all, the problems of urban transportation are being considered as integral parts of the physical and social complex of urban growth and change; they are not treated as isolated technical problems, to be solved entirely by transportation considerations.

The demonstration program has, thus, been organized to take full advantage of a situation in which qualified professional personnel has been in exceedingly short supply, and to gain the maximum utilization of available technical talents.

EVALUATION OF PROJECT PROPOSALS

WITH the early indication that the demonstration concept would be generally unfamiliar to local communities and their transit operators, and that program activity would be slow to develop for this reason (and because of difficulties in obtaining local matching funds), original ideas for an elaborate processing procedure with extensive formal reviews of project proposals were discarded. Instead, a simple procedure of direct staff review and discussion of each proposal, as received, has been adopted.

To insure an adequate and comprehensive scope for these reviews, a series of questions has been evolved from experience and is now being utilized in developing a staff consensus. Such questions are also utilized in discussions with applicants for projects; they have proved invaluable in formulating workable demonstration proposals.

Basic to every review are questions centered on the objectives or purposes of a proposed demonstration. Are the objectives clearly stated? How does the proposal fit into local regional-planning studies and, if successful, would the demonstration objectives probably become an on-going part of local transit practices? Will their attainment contribute useful answers to problems of urban transportation planning or research?

Closely related in importance is the focus of the objectives. Is the "general applicability" of sought-for results positively established? This must be answered affirmatively; a loose implication of broad interest is not considered sufficient to establish eligibility of a proposal with a strongly local emphasis.

A third general question emphasizes the need for detailed design of a project by the proposed sponsor—a function which the limited staff of the Office of Transportation cannot assume. Are the various elements of the proposed demonstration logically and practically arranged and related to indicate a reasonable attainment of the stated objectives?

Here, it should be remarked, considerable attention is directed toward the duration of project operations. Is it sufficiently long to permit a stabilization of variables, and, particularly, will it allow enough time for public habits to be influenced? Experience in transit operations has revealed that the public is often slow to react to changes and that an uncertain time period is still involved in communication. Also, seasonal variations must be bridged in many cases. In general, therefore, "quickie" projects, curtailed through obvious limitations on local resources, have been discouraged.

Next, answers are sought for the question: What technical information and statistical data is the project expected to develop, and is there indicated adequate and competent professional guidance and control to assure reliable findings? Is responsibility for reporting results soundly defined and assigned?

If the foregoing questions can be answered satisfactorily, the proposal is deemed of technical substance. There still remains a group of practical questions pertinent to its financial aspects.

First, are the estimated costs reasonably consistent with the scope and magnitude of the stated objective and expected activities? Are the various divisions or allocations of cost firmly established on a unit basis so that total costs can be determined and supported? What provisions are set up for budgetary control, progress payments, records, final settlement and audit?

With these questions clearly answered, the costs of project operations would seem to be soundly established. There remains, then, the other side of the financial coin to be examined. How is the non-federal support, or the local matching fund, to be obtained? Is it reasonably assured, in adequate amount, to carry the project to its expressed objectives?

Beyond the total amount of the matching fund, there needs to be some definition of the financial responsibilities of the various participants. How are the individual obligations to be met, and how are these funds to be combined so as to be applicable to project needs?

There are, also, the legal questions. Does the applicant qualify as an eligible public agency with the necessary legal authority to carry on the project and to receive and disburse the funds involved? Have the various regulatory agencies, such as a public service commission which may have jurisdiction, given their approval, or indicated otherwise their clearance of the proposal? Is obstructive litigation pending?

No particular scale of priorities in rating projects has been applied to the answers from this battery of questions, and no project has been evaluated entirely on an initial submission. More importantly, such questions are helpful in discussion with sponsors who seek advice in refining or modifying their proposals. Seldom has the first draft of a proposal been adequate to provide more than a few of the necessary answers.

Out of exchanges between HHFA staff and proposed demonstration project sponsors, and then from staff discussions of project details, including a review by the HHFA Research Coordinating Committee (to insure against duplicating or conflicting efforts), a firm evaluation of the merits of the individual proposal is established. Any recommendation which then goes forward to the administrator for final action represents a consensus of engineering, planning, economic and legal participation in this largely informal process.

Project Activities

Experience gained in the very early stages of program development led to what has become an essentially three-stage process of project negotiation. By such staging, local officials are spared embarrassment resulting from any rejection of a formally prepared and submitted application, and the Office of Transportation is relieved of a pyramiding load of routinely unproductive processing.

The first stage is, typically, an informal inquiry about the demonstration program and its possible usefulness in an interested local area. Such inquiries have been received from a large number of individuals representing public and private organizations in almost three-hundred communities. Many were private transit companies, seeking to finance new equipment or facilities; others were seeking federal support of all sorts of transportation research and development promotions. Many inquiries were, thus, ineligible.

Where the inquiry indicated the possibility of an eligible project being developed, because a desirable objective had been cited, and eligible participants could be involved, the HHFA response suggested that an informal proposal be prepared. A proposal was expected to cover the information called for in a list outlined in an official bulletin which describes the process for submission of a proposal. In the period from November 1961 through March 1964, a total of forty-four proposals was submitted to the Office of Transportation for consideration.

In the same period, ten of these proposals were ultimately found inappropriate to the program, or were withdrawn by their potential sponsors, usually for lack of local matching funds—a persistent transit problem. Nine proposals were, as of March 1964, still pending, or awaiting further local action.

The remaining twenty-five proposals progressed to the third stage, in which formal application for demonstration grant support is submitted, accompanied by the approvals of official bodies involved and a proposed project budget. Of these applications, nineteen have received approval by the Housing Administrator, five are still under active consideration and one has been withdrawn by its sponsor for extensive revision.

Of the nineteen approved projects, two have been completed and final reports distributed; seventeen are active. The nineteen projects represent a total aggregate cost estimated at nearly $31 million, of which the federal share represents a commitment of slightly more than $20 million, or two-thirds of the total estimated cost. Since the duration varies from six months to forty-eight months, no single completion date can be cited.

Most of the approved projects can be classified into two general categories: experimental changes in transit services and fare structures; and testing and evaluation of new equipment and operating techniques. Their duration varies from six to forty-eight months, as necessitated by project objectives.

The active projects are inspected periodically by the HHFA transportation staff to assure conformance to objectives and to the purposes of the federal grant. Technical and procedural questions are reviewed with sponsors to insure a sound basis for final reports.

While most of the current demonstrations represent no radically new or completely untried activities, they do incorporate much more broadly based objectives and a level of professional involvement experienced in only very few transit efforts prior to the establishment of the federal urban transportation program.

The transit industry and the local communities it serves had long recognized the need for more adequate research, development and demonstration efforts, but had been unable to secure financial resources necessary to mount adequate programs. Numerous trials of attractive, new ideas were frustrated simply for lack of money and, as a consequence, there were no new inputs to transportation planning on behalf of public transportation. In far too many transportation studies, transit was either ignored or relegated to a very minor role, despite a sustained feeling, among planners and public officials alike, that it deserved greater consideration because it provides a continuing, essential public service.

Already the resources of the federal program, and the demonstrations encouraged thereby, have produced a broader interest among transportation planners. Transit is again gaining recognition in the planning process as a result of the attention generated by the demonstration projects. Although it will be some little time in the future before significant findings become available, there is ample evidence that one demonstration purpose has been achieved in many metropolitan communities—responsible public officials, planners, highway engineers and transit operators have again been brought together in intelligently directed efforts to improve and solve critical situations in urban transportation.

Three Experiments in Urban Transportation

GEORGE M. SMERK

INFORMATION REGARDING THE OUTCOME or the findings of the various demonstration programs is public information because public money was spent and because the purpose of the demonstrations is to make results available. It is desirable that as many communities as possible take advantage of the findings. However, neither the U. S. Department of Housing and Urban Development nor the Housing and Home Finance Agency, which preceded it, publish any compilation or evaluation of findings. The particular demonstrator must be contacted for information, a process that is more than a little cumbersome.

The following article was written to make some of this material more generally available. It is the first of what the author hopes will be a series of papers and monographs describing and evaluating the various demonstrations that have been carried on. This particular paper, written in 1964, deals with only the first three experiments for which any considerable amount of information was available. The motherlode is much richer now, and what follows should be considered as merely a scratch on the surface.

THE concept embodied in the magic words "research and development" has been accorded a hallowed position on mankind's list of priorities. The majority of the nation's industries annually invest sizable sums in research of all types. New methods and processes are investigated, new products

"Three Experiments in Urban Transportation," *Business Horizons,* Summer 1964.

tested and analyzed; the public pulse and psyche are regularly plumbed and mapped to find the proper nuance to guarantee at least a modicum of success for the huckster's tub-thumping. For its part, the federal government spends billions on R&D, ranging from NASA's exploration of outer space to the Department of Agriculture's determination of the best way to pack peaches in a refrigerator car. At our colleges and universities, academicians indulge themselves in thousands of research projects ranging from the esoteric to the pedestrian.

Strangely missing from this lineup has been a serious effort directed at solving the urban transportation problem. While we are rapidly approaching a time when we may land a man on the moon and can apparently already wash our clothes in cold water, we still suffer from monumental traffic jams and sick cities. In most of our metropolitan areas, the business of simply getting to work remains tedious at best, and is usually a vexing and expensive struggle with automobiles and people that worsens each month. Despite all the funds directed toward research since the end of World War II, the contusions of urban transport remained for the most part untreated until the summer of 1961.

ACTION AT LAST

ALTHOUGH June 30, 1961 probably passed by without arousing the undue notice of most urban dwellers, this date may take its place in history as a red letter day for the future of American cities. On that date Congress enacted the Housing Act of 1961, which included provisions for certain types of federal aid to mass transportation research in urban areas. This legislation has been the most concrete step yet taken by the federal government to help find a realistic solution to the devastating and devitalizing crush of traffic congestion, and climaxes a long period of activity on the part of urban areas to get help in finding their way out of the transport quagmire.

The path leading to the Housing Act of 1961 has been a thorny one. By the end of the immediate postwar period—around 1950 or 1951— the larger urban areas had become seriously alarmed about increasing traffic congestion and the concurrent decline of public mass transportation. The postwar move to the suburbs and the daily automotive inundation of downtown metropolitan areas had begun with a vengeance. Attempts to solve the problem with new and improved highways were under way, but some observers were unimpressed by the efficacy of a largely one-dimensional approach. It struck the critics that solving congestion problems in the city center by making it easier for motorists to get there was not unlike a plumber trying to cure a stopped-up drain by seeing how much further he could open the faucets.

As the decade of the fifties moved on, larger cities belatedly came to understand that they could not solve their problem with highways catering to an ever increasing load of automotive traffic. As downtown areas and central cities began to decline and decay in the grip of traffic strangulation, those concerned with revitalizing the city saw that the solution depended largely upon upgrading mass transport.

But upgrading, requiring construction and expansion of rapid transit and rail commuter service, is expensive. Considering the financial state of the urban transport industry, new construction or R&D programs are out of the question. Moreover, metropolitan areas in the United States suffer from acute political and financial fragmentation, which makes it impossible for them to bring the area's full resources to bear in solving problems, whether they relate to transport, education, or air pollution. The states offered relatively little help, either because of financial difficulties of their own or because of the general animosity of rurally dominated state legislatures toward projects aimed at aiding urban areas. As a final resort, the cities appealed to the federal government. Their pleas were finally answered by a Congress slowly becoming more urban minded during an administration that was attempting to get at the heart of many of our most crucial domestic problems.

Under the provisions of the Housing Act of 1961, funds were channeled through the Housing and Home Finance Agency for three programs related to mass transport: to aid in planning coordinated urban transportation systems, to provide equipment loans, and to provide demonstration grants for research and experiment with new methods, ideas, and approaches. At long last, the federal government saw fit to encourage means of urban transport other than the private automobile. The appropriation of $42.5 million is hardly a drop in the bucket compared to the more than $1.0 billion spent on urban highways the same year. However, the "conventional wisdom" of federal aid directed only toward highway construction had been shattered. Alternative approaches had a foot in the door at last.

The demonstration grant program is the most important, arresting, and dramatic part of the three-pronged attack on urban traffic strangulation. The program can be criticized for trying to do too much with limited funds; only $25 million was earmarked for this program—hardly enough to buy a mile of good urban freeway. However, the requirement under which local agencies had to pay one-third of the total cost of the project stretched the effectiveness of the federal funds and ensured genuine interest on the part of given localities. Even though the funds were limited and were scattered among fourteen projects, this widespread pilot program for urban transport relief offers considerable long-range possibilities and payoff.

The principal aim of the demonstration research projects is to provide better knowledge of urban transport of all types through experiments in service improvement, fare adjustments, new and improved technology, and coordination of the efforts of urban transport agencies. The projects seek to discover how mass transport may be made to appeal to an automobile-minded, affluent society; they are probing to find the features of mass transport that are most potent in attracting riders away from their cars. The fact that mass transport can move substantial numbers of people in and out of larger cities, at a lower cost to society than is possible with automobiles, has no intrinsic appeal. Some factor or factors other than social costs clearly must be considered, especially in a free society where consumers exercise a free choice. Most of the demonstrations, therefore, experimented with consumer reactions to various aspects of service, pricing, and technology, and investigated the ability of these approaches to be supported out of farebox revenues.

THREE EXPERIMENTS

ALTHOUGH most of the demonstration research projects are still being carried on, three of them are either completed or have produced sufficient results to be useful and thought provoking.

Detroit

The first demonstration grant was awarded to the city of Detroit for making substantial increases in the bus service along the fourteen-mile Grand River Avenue route. The cost of the experiment was $336,600, of which the federal government contributed $224,000. The experiment was conducted during April, May, and June, 1962.

The issue in the Detroit experiment was whether or not stepped-up bus service would produce significant gains in riders. During the experimental period, frequency of service was increased 70 per cent during rush hours, and during off-peak hours as well as on Saturdays and Sundays. As a result, the headway (the time interval between vehicles) was considerably reduced. In the early morning hours from midnight to 6 a.m., headways were shortened from 20 minutes to 15. In peak periods (6 a.m. to 9 a.m. and 3 p.m. to 6 p.m.), headways were cut from 3½ minutes to 2. The headway was reduced from 6 minutes to 3½ in the off-peak daytime hours between 9 a.m. and 3 p.m., and, in the evening hours between 6 p.m. and midnight, they were cut from 15 minutes to 10. Similar reductions were made on Saturdays and Sundays.

It was found that increased service during certain time periods resulted in significant increases in patronage. Sampling during the experimental period indicated an average daily increase of almost 3,000 passengers, or about 12 per cent above the average of similar periods in previous years. The greatest percentage of increase came during the off-peak times. Sundays, for example, enjoyed an increase of patronage averaging 34 per cent, and Sunday evening patronage increased 63 per cent.

The average weekly increase in revenue was 3.79 per cent. As the experiment continued, farebox receipts showed a progressive increase from 0.42 per cent the first week to 8.6 per cent for the final week, as compared with comparable pre-experimental periods.

Perhaps the results would have been more meaningful had the demonstration continued for six months or a year; nevertheless, it indicates clearly that, even in a relatively short time, improvements in service do indeed boost patronage. It should be noted that increased frequency was the only change made. Standard buses and existing fare structures were maintained, and there was no speedup in the scheduled running time. It was easier to maintain schedules, however, because more frequent operation meant that fewer people were waiting at bus stops and that less time was required for loading.

Seattle

The second demonstration project was in some ways the most dramatic of all, because it involved the monorail built to link downtown Seattle with the Century 21 world's fair held in that city during the summer of 1962. For this project, the Housing and Home Finance Agency granted $10,000 to the University of Washington, which put up $5,000. The object of the study was to determine the initial cost of operation, various operating and structural characteristics, and—most important—public reaction to the new mode of urban transport.

Tests conducted during the experimental period showed the monorail to be definitely inferior in riding quality as compared to conventional trains; on the other hand, it was far superior to either the bus or private automobile under ordinary operating conditions. Traction difficulties similar to those on highways were experienced on the concrete beamway during slick rainfall. As had been expected, businessmen along the street where the elevated monorail beamway structure was built were somewhat less than enchanted. From a cost and operational viewpoint, monorail technology has been shown by subsequent studies in San Francisco to be less desirable than conventional two-rail equipment for complete transit systems. But for a shuttle-type service of a specialized nature such as the Seattle monorail, this technology seems to offer some potential.

The most important result of the demonstration was the analysis of the overwhelming public acceptance of the monorail. Unlike any of the other demonstrations, the Seattle study was not confined to an alteration or improvement in an existing service; instead, it examined an entirely new concept of urban transportation. The highly specialized use of the monorail and the aura of the world's fair may have influenced the findings related to public acceptance. However, the possibilities of mass rapid transit were revealed to the citizens of an area never served by any form of such a system. Perhaps the most meaningful part of the monorail demonstration involved a questionnaire survey of persons residing far enough away from Seattle's central core to make rapid transit facilities a feasible urban alternative. The investigators sought to compare the attractiveness of automobile and rapid transit travel under varying relative cost and time expenditures. The possible shift from automobile to rapid transit was estimated first on the basis of potential journey time. The questionnaire tested consumer reaction under hypothetical conditions in which a proposed rapid transit system took 50, 75, 100, 125, 150, and 200 per cent as much total elapsed time for a given journey as did automobile travel. Another test was made concerning the reaction to rapid transit on the basis of fare 50, 100, and 150 per cent of the individual's estimated cost of using his car.

The respondents indicated that they would be swayed more by the amount of time involved than by the cost. Cost factors, in terms of transit fare compared to out-of-pocket expenses for driving, were less important where travel time by the transit system was proportionately less than that by automobile. Again, as the hypothetical travel time by rapid transit exceeded the time by auto, the number of commuters by automobile who expressed a preference for rapid transit dropped off sharply, even where the hypothetical cost of rapid transit was substantially lower than the cost of auto travel.

Massachusetts

The third demonstration project was perhaps the most ambitious and informative of all. This grant was made on Oct. 6, 1962 to the Mass Transportation Commission of the Commonwealth of Massachusetts. Its purpose was to finance two-thirds of the cost of a year long experiment involving the Boston, Fitchburg, Worcester, and Pittsfield areas. The total estimated cost of the project was $5.4 million, of which the federal share was $3.6 million and Massachusetts' share was $1.8 million.

The aim of the project was to analyze the effects of service improvements and fare reductions on the public use of all available forms of mass transportation. The commission contracted for alterations in service and/ or pricing with the commuter railroads in the vicinity of Boston, the Metropolitan Transit Authority of Boston, and local bus companies serving the other cities. The Boston & Maine and the New York, New Haven & Hartford railroads were involved in the commuter railway research.

Bus Service Research

In the experiments with bus service in communities outside Boston, carefully planned increases in service plus modest extensions of some routes definitely increased patronage. However, Revenues in many cases were not sufficient to cover the costs involved, and a number of these experiments were phased out as the subsidy money came to an end.

Feeder buses to railway stations operating in the outer suburban areas around Boston were only slightly used, although the trains were heavily patronized. However, feeder buses serving areas of dense population located close to downtown were generally successful in moving passengers and generating revenue. Improved bus service and stepped-up schedules in suburban areas where the population density was too low to warrant rail service into Boston proved to be quite successful in attracting new riders. A number of these suburban lines continued the service after the conclusion of the experiment.

In Boston and the immediate vicinity, bus experiments conducted by the Metropolitan Transit Authority had generally good results. Improved services, new services, and some route extensions showed a steady growth in public acceptance. Approximately 6,700 riders used the new and improved services daily (most had been using their cars).

The transit authority's reduced fee parking lot experiments were successful when operated in conjunction with rapid transit lines; substantial increases in the use of both parking and transport facilities were realized. This was not the case, however, where low cost parking was combined with bus service between peripheral parking lots and the downtown section. There seemed to be little incentive, the commission study noted, to leave the stream of traffic, park the car, and then board a vehicle that plunged right back into the same stream of traffic.

The Railroad Experiment

The most important part of the Massachusetts experiment was that conducted with the Boston & Maine and New Haven railroads. The largest scale of experimentation was carried on with the B & M, which currently moves approximately 5.9 million commuter passengers per annum. This is but a shadow of former patronage. In the six-year period from 1956 to 1962, annual passenger volume had dropped 60 per cent—about 8 per cent per year—from the 1956 total of 14.4 million riders. Under the commission experiment, 70 per cent more service was offered while fares were initially reduced 30 per cent.

The results are most significant. The secular decline in passenger use was replaced by a steep upswing. The experiment began in January, 1963 with a sharp traffic increase during the first week. By the end of October, the average number of passengers had risen over 32 per cent from the pre-experimental average, and continued to move steadily upward. Nor was the gain in traffic confined only to peak hours; off-peak ridership increased by almost 70 per cent. This gain is particularly important, since off-peak revenue contributions are vital in breaking even on commuter operations.

The effect of a fare increase during the course of the experiment provided an important bit of knowledge. The reduced fares were eliminated at the end of July; on Aug. 1, higher peak hour fares were introduced at about the pre-experimental level. The improved service was continued. Despite the fare rise, patronage mounted steadily. Furthermore, when the Aug. 1 peak hour fare increase went into effect, special low off-peak fares were instituted, but off-peak patronage did not respond. Use did not increase above the already substantial levels of the first phase.

Results from the experiments involving the New Haven, which got under way about two months after the B & M program, were similar. Service increased somewhat on two of the six New Haven commuter lines, but fare reductions of 10 per cent were in effect on all operations. Modest but encouraging gains in patronage were realized, primarily on the lines with increased service. None of the New Haven lines had as great a percentage increase in patronage as the B & M services, although operations with increased off-peak service showed significant growth in off-peak patronage. A fare increase in September, similar to the B & M boost in August, had no effect on ridership.

The reasons for the difference in passenger growth between the New Haven and B & M experiments are not hard to figure out. New Haven fares on a per mile basis were much higher to begin with than those on the B & M; in addition, the fare cut was more modest. Furthermore, the B & M offers modern, air-conditioned, self-propelled Budd Rail-Diesel-Cars, while the New Haven uses older and less attractive equipment. Again, the New Haven demonstration was carried on with a relatively small amount of publicity in comparison with the B & M experiment, and tended to be overshadowed by the earlier project.

Some Conclusions

What useful conclusions may be drawn from these three experiments? The major finding has been that the public will accept mass transportation where the quality of service has been improved.

The Importance of Time

Quality of service has many dimensions; it may include vehicle comfort, schedule reliability, speed, amount and frequency of service, improvement of stations and other fixed facilities, ease of transfer, route relocation, and any number of lesser factors. The success of the Detroit experiment and the B & M segment of the Massachusetts Transportation Commission study indicates the importance of increasing the number of units of service—buses or trains—and thereby rendering more frequent service. This service reduces waiting for the passenger and allows him to choose desirable departure and arrival times. Furthermore, increased frequency of service coupled with some schedule speedups can result in a mass transport service that considerably reduces travel time for the commuter.

Travelers want to spend as little time as possible making their trips; therefore, the attractiveness of a mode of transportation appears to depend on time required to arrive at a destination. The findings of the Seattle questionnaire bear this out; rapid transit was considered an acceptable substitute for the automobile where it was considerably less time consuming.

Equipment and Price

Other quality factors tend to be intertwined with one another and the time factor. However, the quality of the equipment probably has a substantial effect on the acceptability of travel modes. For instance, the gains in acceptance during the New Haven Railroad experiment may have been affected greatly by the antiquity and general condition of the cars. Comfort is difficult to measure, since it has aesthetic and psychic as well as physical aspects, but frequent breakdowns and outdated and uncomfortable equipment are certain to affect patronage.

The cost of driving one's car is viewed by most urban travelers to be about equal to that of using mass transport; in the quality of the service, however, the edge is generally on the side of the private automobile. Where the cost is equal, the form of transport with the best service will be used. A lowered price alone may have a slight effect on the acceptance of mass transport, but seems to have a stimulating effect when coupled with a decided improvement in service. Dramatizing the improved operation by both raising the quality and lowering the price gives added publicity and appeal to improved operations. In stimulating the use of mass transport, therefore, it appears that the greatest initial impact can be gained by improved service that results in less journey time, plus sharp cuts in fares. Once the service has gained acceptance, fares may be raised once more.

The pricing problem is, of course, intimately related to the question of mass transport systems supported out of the farebox. This point was recently brought into the limelight by the B & M's announcement that it intends to apply for permission to abandon all commuter service. Even with the sharp increase in traffic resulting from the demonstration program, revenues did not cover costs. Those interests hostile to urban mass transport have jumped on this situation with both feet, claiming that it is proof that mass transport, even under subsidized demonstration programs, is a failure. The increases in traffic resulting from the experiment would seem to indicate otherwise; nevertheless, the subsidy question and self-support are matters that demand attention.

Financing Transit Systems

Without a doubt, these projects show that greatly improved mass transportation is needed in our cities and that it will be used if provided. The importance of the quality factor points toward some form of grade-separated, rail rapid transit. This will cost a considerable amount of money. Should these new and improved facilities be paid for out of the farebox? Clearly, if improvements on existing facilities cannot pay for themselves, we should not expect expensive new facilities to be self-supporting. Moreover, we cannot expect private enterprise to continue services at great loss to itself, even though those services may benefit the public considerably.

It is this public benefit that is at the heart of the problem. The benefits of improved transportation in a metropolitan area accrue to those who use the improved transport facilities and, indirectly, to everyone in the metropolis. For example, if a constantly increasing number of people rode the commuter trains of the New Haven and B & M, those who had to use their cars would be benefited. If more suburbanites used the trains to come downtown to shop, retail establishments would benefit. If enough persons use the trains, it may not be necessary to enlarge a highway or build a new one, thus saving the cost of construction as well as the monetary and social costs of displacing individuals and businesses from the path of the new road.

These benefits are a direct result of improved commuter railroad service; they accrue to the community at large, but cannot be reflected in the form of fares paid to an institution that performs public transport service. Looked at in this way, urban transport becomes a community service like public education, smog relief, or sanitation. When benefits to the public are broad and when that value cannot be precisely pinpointed or the costs allocated to particular beneficiaries, the usual way to pay for them is through tax assessment of the general public.

With transport, there is the opportunity to recapture from patrons a sizable proportion of the costs from the recognizable benefits bestowed on users, with the remainder made up through subsidies. This in no way differs from the situation with urban highways. Experts generally agree that the high costs of highways are not met by collections from gas and license taxes in urban areas, and deficits must be met from the general tax revenues. For instance, the city of Philadelphia one year subsidized motorists to the tune of $28 million. This appears to be a common occurrence in American cities, so there should be no ethical objection to mass transportation sharing in the same source of funds as the private users of highways. In fact, most urban areas in the United States that enjoy rapid transit service subsidize those operations to a degree; subsidy ensures continued operations and is cheaper than highway construction.

This does not mean that every improved mass transportation project must be subsidized initially, or that subsidies once begun must be continued for eternity. Local conditions play a large part in determining the need for public support. If mass transport service is made attractive enough, chances are good that, in the long run, it could be self-sufficient in most metropolitan areas. But to expect self-sufficiency in a short span of time is like expecting an infant to run the hundred-yard dash before he has learned to walk.

It is impossible to make any broad statement about all of the demonstration research projects financed under the Housing Act of 1961. It will be several years before all the returns are in, and it is likely that the information and understanding gathered from the first three research programs will be substantiated by forthcoming results.

All in all, the demonstration projects indicate that a significant increase in public acceptance of mass transport will occur if the quality of the service is sufficiently improved. This improvement, which appears to be stepping up the speed and frequency of service, will be expensive—but not so expensive as continuing to muddle along as we have, obsequiously pandering to the insatiable and costly needs of the motor car.

Time, effort, and research are needed to make mass transportation more competitive with the private automobile in those areas where mass transport involves less cost to society. The strongest efforts of local, state, and federal governments, coupled with private enterprise, are necessary. If we hope to make life tolerable within our great metropolitan areas, we must act swiftly to make those vital improvements in transportation that will loosen traffic congestion and help make our cities more livable.

Joint Report to the President by the Secretary of Commerce and the Administrator of the Housing and Home Finance Agency, 1962

THE JOINT REPORT of the Secretary of Commerce and the Administrator of the Housing and Home Finance Agency is a crucial document to study if one is to understand the attitude of the federal government in subsequent action related to urban transportation. This report submits the fact that American cities must have a blend of private and public transportation if they are to hope for sound land-use, the improvement of traffic flow, the availability of transport to all segments of the population, and the provision of urban transport at minimum cost.

The report calls for a continuation of the demonstration grant program to increase present knowledge of urban transport and to provide information on means to operate it in a more attractive and efficient manner. More important, however, it goes beyond the federal role under the Housing Act of 1961 in that it calls for the use of federal funds to help finance capital improvements. Recognition is thus given to the inability of local areas to finance needed mass-transport improvements. There is also strong emphasis on comprehensive and coordinated planning, with highway, mass-transport and urban-development programs being taken as part of a whole rather than as separate, distinct, and unrelated elements.

DEAR MR. PRESIDENT: We have the honor to transmit herewith a report on urban transportation prepared jointly by the Department of Commerce and the Housing and Home Finance Agency. This report was prepared pursuant to your instruction to undertake a study of urban transportation problems and the proper role of the Federal Government in their solution. In carrying out this survey we have drawn heavily upon the excellent reports earlier prepared by committees of the Congress, and staff research conducted over the years by the Bureau of Public Roads and the Housing and Home Finance Agency. In addition, we commis-

"Joint Report to the President by the Secretary of Commerce and the Housing and Home Finance Administration," *Urban Mass Transportation—1962* (Hearings before a Subcommittee of the Committee on Banking and Currency, United States Senate), March 28, 1962.

sioned the Institute of Public Administration to do a special study involving field investigations in some 40 representative urban communities in various parts of the country.

Transportation is one of the key factors in shaping our cities. As our urban communities increasingly undertake deliberate measures to guide their development and renewal, we must be sure that transportation planning and construction are integral parts of general development planning and programing. One of our main recommendations is that Federal aid for urban transportation facilities should be made available only when urban communities have prepared or are actively preparing up-to-date general plans for the entire urban area which relate transportation plans to land-use and development plans.

The major objectives of urban transportation policy are the achievement of sound land-use patterns, the assurance of transportation facilities for all segments of the population, the improvement in overall traffic flow, and the meeting of total urban transportation needs at minimum cost. Only a balanced transportation system can attain these goals—and in many urban areas this means an extensive mass transportation network fully integrated with the highway and street system. But mass transportation has in recent years experienced capital consumption rather than expansion. A cycle of fare increases and service cuts to offset loss of ridership followed by further declines in use points clearly to the need for a substantial contribution of public funds to support needed mass transportation improvements. We therefore recommend a new program of grants and loans for urban mass transportation.

Even as we undertake this new program for mass transportation, we must press forward with our Federal-aid highway program. Effective mass transportation systems can significantly reduce the need for additional close-in highways, especially at peak hours. But even with extensive reliance on mass transportation and corresponding reduction of highway construction in the central city, total urban highway requirements in the next two decades will be considerably greater than the capacity that will become available if current levels of Federal outlays are sustained.

As you stated last year in your special message to the Congress on highways, we must not allow the progress we make in urban transportation to come at the expense of unnecessary personal hardship to American families. Those displaced by new highway and mass transportation construction should be given relocation assistance comparable to that required under the Federal urban renewal law. Such help becomes all the more imperative as the tempo of needed public construction is stepped up.

[287]

We are convinced that the program proposed herewith will contribute significantly to the welfare of our people and the sound growth of our economy.

Respectfully yours,

Luther H. Hodges,
Secretary of Commerce
Robert C. Weaver
*Administrator, Housing
and Home Finance Agency*

Conclusions

1. Urban transportation is a major determinant of how people live and work in an urban setting. The type and quality of transportation bears heavily upon questions of concentration versus dispersion of urban populations, growth or decline of central business districts and core cities, the success or failure of urban renewal, housing and public improvement programs, recreational and cultural opportunities, and the relationships of suburbs and smaller outlying cities to the central city and to each other.

2. The different means of urban transportation are closely interrelated. Action on any one mode will affect the others. For example, decisions respecting suburban railroads serving large cities affect the level of automobile use, which in turn affect the efficiency of surface transit. Despite spectacular progress in highway facilities, in no metropolitan area has a freeway system yet been completed. There is need for improvement in coordination and increasing efficiency of transportation in urban areas.

3. Our highways play a vital role in urban transportation and will continue to do so. They provide for the movement of both people and goods by private vehicle; and the roadbed for a substantial portion of public mass transportation.

The Bureau of Public Roads will in the future (a) permit the reservation of highway lanes for the exclusive use of specific types of motor vehicles when comprehensive transportation plans indicate this to be desirable, and (b) encourage the development of rail transit and highway facilities in the same right-of-way whenever more effective transportation will result.

4. Increased emphasis on mass transportation is needed because only a balanced system can provide for:

(a) The achievement of land-use patterns which contribute to the economic, physical, and social well-being of urban areas.

(b) The independent mobility of individuals in those substantial segments of the urban population unable to command direct use of automobiles.

(c) The improvement in overall traffic flow and time of travel within the urban area.

(d) Desirable standards of transportation at least total cost.

5. Comprehensive planning is the first step in achieving good urban transportation. Planning should be a continuing process and should include all of the interdependent parts of the urban community and all agencies and jurisdictions involved, and should be coordinated with policymaking and administration. Transportation planning should be a part of systematic land use and development planning. It should be for the system as a whole rather than for its individual components—private vehicles, buses, or rail transit.

The Bureau of Public Roads will, in the future, emphasize that highway planning must include the planning of adequate traffic control systems, parking facilities, and circulation systems on city streets commensurate with the volumes and composition of traffic anticipated on freeways and major arterial streets.

6. To make transportation plans effective will require coordinated direction of construction and operations for all parts of the transportation system. The form of direction or coordination will vary from one area to another because of the diversity of political jurisdictions and operating responsibilities for transportation.

7. Mass transportation must be viewed as a public service and often cannot be a profitmaking enterprise. While mass transportation is provided on a more or less limited scale in hundreds of localities, it is generally not possible to support a large-scale investment program from the fare box. But the price to the community and the Nation of inadequate mass transportation can be uneconomic uses of land and higher than necessary costs of public facilities, excessive travel, and increasingly aggravated congestion at peak hours.

The most compelling need for mass transportation is during peak periods of movement to and from work. In many areas, it can meet this need better than other forms of transportation. But the offpeak slack means insufficient revenues to cover total operating expenses and needed capital investment. Efforts to cover total costs by increasing fares and decreasing service have proved self-defeating: those who can afford to pay are increasingly impelled to use autos; and the aged, low-income people and others heavily reliant upon public transportation are unduly penalized.

8. In view of the importance of mass transportation for urban develop-

ment and the impossibility of financing a large capital improvement program from the fare box, a public contribution is clearly needed. Because of the fragmentation of local government in urban areas and their limited means for raising tax funds, substantial Federal financial participation is called for. Without Federal help the most that can be expected are piecemeal efforts which cannot be effective. Federal assistance on a substantial scale for mass transportation along with continuation of the needed highway program would encourage rational local investment decisions leading to better balanced urban transportation systems. Federal aid for capital improvements would also facilitate levels of services and fares which will attract sufficient users so that mass transportation can make its potential contribution to urban growth and renewal.

9. Every urban community that seeks Federal aid must want good transportation enough to make a substantial contribution of its own. This will give the local people a stake in a sound capital investment program and a pocketbook concern with sound management and efficient operations.

10. Construction of highways and mass transportation facilities frequently causes great hardship to families and businesses which are displaced. Location decisions should take full account of effects on established neighborhoods, and when people and businesses must be displaced, their moving expenses should be paid from public funds and families should be assured of relocation in suitable housing.

11. Long-range progress in urban transportation, as in other fields, must be encouraged by a large and sustained research effort. Through extensive technological and economic research we can look forward to the creation of improved transportation systems which will serve the needs of future urban growth and renewal at minimum total cost.

RECOMMENDATIONS

General

1. To improve competence in the urban planning process, both the Bureau of Public Roads and the Housing and Home Finance Agency should be enabled to offer to the States and local governments more guidance, increased technical service, and training for personnel in the technical aspects of planning.

2. Suitable relocation housing should be assured to families displaced by Federally assisted construction of highways and transit facilities. Also the moving expenses of families and business should be met from Federal funds. Legislative provisions for such assistance should parallel the provisions for the urban renewal program.

[290]

Recommendations for Urban Mass Transportation

1. Mass transportation projects which are parts of comprehensively planned urban transportation systems should be eligible for Federal grants covering two-thirds of project cost which cannot reasonably be financed from expected net revenues. Local or State contributions would have to cover the other one-third of net project cost.

2. For an emergency 3-year period, Federal grants of one-half net project cost should be made available where there is an urgent need to preserve an existing facility or service that otherwise probably would cease to be available for transportation purposes; where an official program for a coordinated transportation system is being actively prepared; and where the assisted project can reasonably be expected to be required for such a system.

3. An authorization for grant contracts of $500 million should be made available over a 3-year period, with $100 million authorized in fiscal 1963.

4. Federal loans should continue to be available where private funds cannot be obtained on reasonable terms for financing mass transportation projects. Where a Federal grant is involved, the loan could cover the portion of capital outlay financed from revenues where financing is not otherwise available on reasonable terms.

5. Long-term Federal assistance should be made available only (a) where an organization exists empowered to plan for substantially all of the urban area to be served, (b) where transportation planning as a part of comprehensive areawide development planning is being conducted as a continuing process, and (c) where the assisted project will be administered through a public agency as a part of a unified or officially coordinated transportation system for all or substantially all of the urban area.

6. Federal grants and loans should be made only to qualified local public agencies. Such agencies, however, could lease facilities and equipment or make other arrangements for private operation of assisted mass transportation systems.

7. In order to encourage and help finance needed economic and technological research in mass transportation, the $25 million authorized for the demonstration grant program should be made available for these purposes and an additional $10 million a year should be authorized for the next 3 fiscal years.

8. Legislative provisions should be made in advance for interstate compacts for the establishment of agencies to carry out transportation and other regional functions in urban areas extending across State lines.

Recommendations for Urban Highway Programs

1. Federal-aid secondary funds should be made available for expenditure on extensions of that system in urban areas.

2. Use of Federal-aid highway funds should be permitted for the construction of highway facilities for the exclusive use of specific types of motor vehicles whenever comprehensive transportation plans indicate this to be desirable.

3. Funds for highway research should be augmented by providing that an additional one-half of 1 percent of the funds apportioned to the States for the Federal-aid primary system, the Federal-aid secondary system, and extensions of these systems in urban areas be available for this purpose.

4. The use of Federal-aid highway funds made available for planning and research purposes should be required rather than permissive; the matching of such funds by the States should be required in accordance with statutory matching requirements; and the funds not used for planning and research should lapse.

5. Beginning no later than July 1, 1965, approval of Federal-aid highway programs for projects in any metropolitan area should be made contingent upon a finding by the Secretary of Commerce that such projects are consistent with adequate, comprehensive development plans for the metropolitan area or are based on results of a continuing process carried on cooperatively by the States and local communities and that the Federal-aid system so developed will be an integral part of a soundly based, balanced transportation system for the area involved.

SUPPORTING INFORMATION

Urban Growth Trends

The rate of the urbanization process in the United States in recent decades has been spectacular: 70 percent of the Nation's population now lives in urban areas. For these urban areas, transportation problems have been complicated not only by the tremendous population increase but by the changing pattern of urban growth. In the last decade (1950–60), metropolitan area growth constituted 85 percent of the total national population increase, but more than three-fourths of this growth in the metropolitan areas took place outside of the central cities.

Economic prosperity, coupled with improved mobility, have enabled an increasing number of American families to live in suburban areas. This residential outflow from the central cities has been accompanied by extensive commercial and industrial decentralization, and as a result urban travel patterns have changed materially from those of former years. There has been a relative decrease and sometimes an absolute decrease, in the numbers of trips to the central business district, while the numbers of crosstown trips have risen rapidly.

These changes, in turn, have greatly affected modes of travel. Since World War II, automobile usage has been increasing while transit patronage has been declining steadily. From 1956 to 1960, the number of revenue passengers carried by buses and street cars declined by about 22 percent, while the number carried by grade-separated transit declined by only 4 percent. Today, in most urban areas, over 85 percent of the total daily travel is by automobile. On the other hand, at peak hours 40 to 90 percent of the travel to the central business district in our larger cities continues to be made by public mass transportation.

By 1980 the total population of the United States is expected to reach 250 million, and it is anticipated that 3 out of every 4 persons will be living within urban areas. Occupying only about 2 percent of the Nation's land area, the urban areas will contain not only a great concentration of the total population but of commerce and industry as well. Over half of the total population in 1980—some 140 million people—are expected to be living in 40 great urban complexes, each with a population exceeding 1 million.

By the year 2000, less than 40 years hence, the Nation's total population may well reach 350 million. If present trends continue, 85 percent of these people will live in urban areas; more than 50 urban complexes will have attained the million population mark.

These estimated increases and concentrations of population clearly indicate the tremendous demand for transportation facilities for which we now need to plan.

Urban Transportation Planning

Urban planning assistance program (sec. 701). The purpose of the urban planning assistance program (sec. 701 of the Housing Act of 1954, as amended) is to assist State and local governments in dealing with planning problems in metropolitan and other urban areas; to facilitate comprehensive planning for urban development on a continuing basis; and to encourage these governments to establish and improve planning staffs.

Planning grants may be made to State planning agencies for planning assistance to smaller cities and communities either singly or in groups with a population of less than 50,000. Agencies empowered to perform metropolitan or urban regional planning may receive grants directly or through State agencies. Special provisions are made for officially designated redevelopment areas, disaster areas, and federally impacted areas. Finally, grants are available for State and interstate comprehensive urban planning and for related research and coordination.

Emphasis is given to encouraging planning for entire urban areas. Needed technical assistance for planning and organizing to carry out plans on a unified metropolitan or regional basis may be provided by the Housing Administrator.

Under the law, comprehensive planning which may be assisted

includes the following, to the extent directly related to urban needs: (1) preparation, as a guide for long-range development, of general physical plans with respect to the pattern and intensity of land use and the provision of public facilities, including transportation facilities, together with long-range fiscal plans for such development; (2) programing of capital improvements based on a determination of relative urgency, together with definitive financing plans for the improvements to be constructed in the earlier years of the program; (3) coordination of all related plans of the departments or subdivisions of the government concerned; (4) intergovernmental coordination of all related planned activities among the State and local governmental agencies concerned; and (5) preparation of regulatory and administrative measures in support of the foregoing.

The Housing Act of 1961 made two major additions in the basic authority. The first was to explicitly encourage the planning of "coordinated transportation systems" as a part of comprehensive planning. Such planning includes comprehensive urban transportation surveys, studies, and plans to aid in solving problems of traffic congestion, to facilitate the circulation of people and goods in the metropolitan and other urban areas, and to reduce transportation needs. Second, the authorization for appropriations was increased from $20 million to $75 million, and the amount of the grant permitted was increased from one-half to two-thirds. The funds may be used jointly with funds available for planning surveys and investigations under other federally aided programs such as the 1½-percent funds of the highway program.

As of December 31, 1961, section 71 grants had assisted comprehensive planning for 1,922 small communities, 123 metropolitan or regional areas, and 16 States. Grants totaling $22,285,000 had been approved to that date.

Highway planning and research program (1½-percent funds). The annual authorizations made by the Congress for Federal aid for highways are apportioned among the States by methods prescribed by law. Under the Federal-aid legislation, 1½ percent of the funds so apportioned annually to each State are earmarked for highway planning and research.

This provision, as initiated in legislation of 1934, applied to planning only; research was added by legislation of 1944. As now codified in section 307(c) of Title 23—Highways, United States Code, the legislation provides that:

Not to exceed 1½ percent of the sums apportioned for any year to any State . . . shall be available for expenditure upon request of the State highway department, with the approval of the Secretary [of Commerce], with or without State funds, for engineering and economic surveys and investigations, for the planning of future highway programs and the financing thereof, for studies of the economy, safety, and convenience of highway usage and the desirable regulation and equitable taxation thereof, and for research necessary in connection with the planning, design, construction, and maintenance of highways and highway systems, and the regulation and taxation of their use.

While no specific proportion of the 1½-percent funds is designated for urban planning, it will be noted that both planning and research in planning are included in the descriptive list of work for which the funds may be used. The States are responsible for initiation of programs of planning and research projects to be undertaken with the 1½-percent funds, and the overall needs in each field in each individual State are the basic criteria used by Public Roads in reviewing the programs for approval.

In recent years the 1½-percent funds have been used to great advantage in many States in conducting a variety of studies related to urban highway planning. Many of the studies have ultimately produced actual capital improvement programs which are now under construction.

While the Federal-aid legislation does not require each State to use all of the 1½-percent funds allotted to it, for planning and research, nor is statutory matching required (10 percent State matching for Interstate funds; 50 percent State matching for ABC funds), it has been Public Roads' policy in the past to urge them to do so.

As with the Federal-aid funds for highway construction, the 1½-percent funds are not advanced to the States prior to use. The Federal-aid share of the cost of projects is claimed by the States on a reimbursement basis, subject to Public Roads audit.

Joint efforts. The Department of Commerce and the Housing and Home Finance Agency have agreed to the use of highway and urban planning funds jointly in an urban area where local and State bodies are prepared to establish coordinated planning. Both agencies are pledged to stimulate and cooperate in a continuing process of planning and development coordination which will:

[295]

1. Give consideration to all forces, public and private, shaping the physical development of the total community.

2. Cover land uses and controls as well as plans for physical development and combine all elements of urban development and redevelopment into a clear-cut, comprehensive plan of what the citizens want their community to become.

3. Cover the entire urban area within which the forces of development are interrelated.

4. Involve in the planning process the political jurisdictions and agencies which make decisions affecting development of the metropolitan area.

5. Link the process of planning to action programs.

The objective of this joint effort is not merely a planning process but the development of effective cooperation and coordination both among the local governments within a metropolitan area, and between these governments and the State and Federal agencies involved in area development activities. In this way it can be assured that transportation will play its proper part in serving and helping to shape the community in the form its citizens desire.

Interagency committees have been set up at the national and regional level to promote better understanding of the cooperative approach and to aid in working out necessary arrangements. Although these arrangements have been in force for only a short time, excellent joint planning programs have been initiated in key areas and an increasing number are in the negotiation stage. Joint planning programs are underway in 16 areas, and consideration is being given to the initiation of programs in 22 additional areas.

The Federal-Aid Highway Program

The Federal-aid highway program is contributing substantially to the solution of the urban transportation problem. Construction of the 41,000-mile Interstate System is well underway. Financing of the 90-percent Federal share of its total $41 billion cost has been assured by Federal legislation which has provided sufficient revenue to the highway trust fund for both the interstate and the regular Federal-aid highway programs. Over 5,000 miles, or 13 percent, of the Interstate System are in urban areas, and they will account for 45 percent of the total expenditure —the latter figure closely paralleling the proportion of total system travel generated in the urban areas.

On the Federal-aid primary and secondary systems the urban portions total 33,000 miles of city streets and expressways. Federal-aid funds for the improvement of these systems (commonly called the ABC program) are traditionally authorized biennially by the Congress, the latest provision being $925 million for each of the fiscal years 1962 and 1963. These funds are matched 50-50 by the States. Under the Federal legislation, 45 percent of the ABC Federal aid is for work on the primary system (either rural or urban portions), 30 percent for the secondary system, and 25 percent specifically for the urban portions of the two systems. Projects costing $1.5 billion were completed in fiscal year 1961 under the ABC program, and 29 percent of this was spent in urban areas.

The construction of new highways and the improvement of existing streets and highways is an essential part of the urban transportation program. New and improved facilities are needed to provide for the movement of goods as well as for personal travel by automobile. In addition, freeways, with improved feeder routes, make possible the development of freeway bus systems to serve public mass transit needs.

It is essential that the Federal-aid highway programs, including the provisions for urban highway construction, continue undiminished. No increases in authorizations are recommended at the present time. However, greater flexibility in the use of Federal-aid highway funds to meet urban transportation needs can be provided by amending the Federal-aid highway legislation to permit the State highway departments to use Federal-aid secondary funds on extensions of that system in urban areas. Federal participation in projects on such extensions is now generally limited to urban funds. This will be particularly helpful in certain States containing many individual and grouped urban areas that are finding it increasingly difficult to improve the extensions of Federal-aid secondary routes into urban areas because the improvement of arterial streets in larger cities has a greater priority for the use of available urban funds.

Studies have indicated that under certain conditions the reservation of highway lanes for the exclusive use of specific types of motor vehicles will assist in solving urban transportation problems.

Also, in some instances, more effective urban transportation will result from the development of rail transit and highway facilities in the same right-of-way. However, the additional cost occasioned by the rail facilities could not be borne by highway funds; moreover, many rail rights-of-way needed for a balanced system will require corridors separate from freeways.

Present Mass Transportation Programs

As recommended by the President in his special message on our Nation's housing, national concern with the importance of mass transportation for urban development was first recognized in Federal law by the enactment of the Housing Act of 1961. That act provided for two new assistance programs for urban mass transportation to be administered by the Housing and Home Finance Administrator. These were in addition to strengthening the urban planning assistance program, as discussed in an earlier section.

First is a program of loans for financing the acquisition, construction, reconstruction, and improvement of mass transportation facilities and equipment. Loans may be made to State and local public agencies where such financing is not otherwise available on reasonable terms. Where economically warranted, loans may have maturities as long as 40 years, and they must be of such sound value or so secured as reasonably to assure repayment. The facilities and equipment acquired with such loan may be operated by the borrowing agency or by private firms or other public agencies under a lease or other approved arrangement.

In order to assure that proposed improvements are in conformance with sound planning, the law requires that there is being actively developed (or has been developed) for the whole area served by the applicant, a program for the development of a comprehensive and coordinated mass transportation system and that the proposed facilities or equipment will be required for such a system. There is a further administrative requirement that the mass transportation program shall be a part of a comprehensively planned transportation system, including highways, to serve the urban growth and renewal needs of the area. These requirements may be waived where there is an immediately urgent need for the provision of facilities or equipment to be commenced prior to the time that the planning program could reasonably be expected to be completed.

Loans up to a total of $50 million are authorized. Loan commitments under the present program cannot be made after December 31, 1962.

The second new program provides contract authority of $25 million in Federal grants for mass transportation demonstration projects. The Federal grant may cover two-thirds of the cost of projects which will assist in carrying out urban transportation plans and research. They may include the development of data and information of general applicability on the reduction of urban transportation needs, the improvement of mass transportation service, and the contribution of such service toward meeting total urban transportation needs at minimum cost. Federal grants may not be used for major long-term capital improvements.

The purpose of the program is to stimulate fresh thinking and experimental undertakings which will bring about improved service and greater efficiency in the mass transportation field. Small as well as large cities all over the country are interested in experimenting with changes in levels of service and fare structures, technological improvements, and improvements of the relations of mass transportation to other parts of the urban transportation complex. They have difficulty in raising their one-third contribution to the cost, however, since the demonstrations are expected to have general applicability to similar localities. The exclusion of major long-term capital improvements from eligibility for Federal assistance also makes many worthwhile projects ineligible.

A combined appropriation of $42.5 million is available in the fiscal year 1962 for both the new mass transportation demonstration grant program and the loan program.

Capital Requirements and Financing for Urban Mass Transportation

Total capital requirements for mass transportation in the next decade are estimated at $9.8 billion by the Institute of Public Administration in its report to the Secretary of Commerce and the Housing Administrator. The estimates are rough approximations and probably on the conservative side, but they are based on intensive study of published information and on-the-spot investigation in 26 urban regions.

In the smaller cities, a recent survey by the American Transit Association revealed that 69 percent of their membership responding to a questionnaire indicated that replacement of buses was their most pressing problem, and 42 percent indicated that an outright subsidy was the only form of assistance which could be effective because of their condition.

The major purposes to be served by the estimated $9.8 billion total investment requirements are presently planned new systems, $2.8 billion; extensions of existing systems, $1.7 billion; rehabilitation and replacement, $4.3 billion; new projects now being considered for initiation in the next decade, $1 billion. For all purposes, right-of-way and structures are estimated at $6.4 billion and rolling stock at $3.4 billion.

It is not possible at this time to estimate precisely the amount of Federal grant and loan assistance that will be needed in the next decade to enable urban areas to make the investments that will be required if mass transportation is to make its proper contribution to sound urban development and renewal. As the first stage in a long-range program, we recommend that $50 million in Federal grants be made available over the next 3 years, that the present $50 million loan authority be made permanent, and that adequate funds be provided from grant authorizations for undertaking and stimulating badly needed economic and technical research and development in urban transportation. The progress that cities and urban regions can make in the next 3 years in planning and programing their comprehensive transportation systems and the experience gained in analyzing applications for Federal assistance will give a greatly improved basis for estimating long-term needs.

The recommended program of Federal grants would cover two-thirds of the net cost of capital outlays for mass transportation projects. Any net revenues which can reasonably be expected from transit operations would be used to support as much as possible of total project cost. The amount that fare collections can reasonably be expected to exceed operating costs depends on detailed analysis of each situation.

Many bus systems can meet most of their equipment costs from revenues if they can obtain loan funds on reasonable terms. To make their proper contribution to urban transportation, however, service of many systems must be improved and offered at reasonable fares. Such service improvements may cost more than the fare box will carry. There may also be requirements for substantial investment in fixed facilities such as separate rights-of-way and boarding facilities which cannot be fully amortized from revenues.

Net receipts also may cover a large part of the cost of rolling stock for urban rail systems, depending on the total position of the system. But experience indicates that in most circumstances the heavy investments now required for rights-of-way, rail installation, and subway construction cannot be covered from the fare box.

Except in truly emergency situations, the investment of Federal, State, or local public funds in mass transportation is justified only where the facilities are part of a comprehensive transportation system which is designed to serve the prospective growth and renewal needs of the whole urban area and is administered on a fully coordinated basis. This kind of planning, programing, and organization takes time to develop. Many areas have undertaken the process, but only a few are well advanced in making it truly comprehensive.

Federal planning assistance through the section 701 urban planning assistance program and the use of 1½-percent highway research and planning funds is stimulating a great increase in State and local urban planning efforts. Mass transportation will not receive proper attention in planning action programs, however, unless local officials see the realistic possibility of installing and effectively operating the systems which would be called for in good planning. Such a possibility usually is doubtful if the urban areas must look forward to covering the total public cost of good mass transportation from their own limited tax resources. This is the basic reason for recommending a Federal program to cover two-thirds of such cost.

The demand for Federal grants probably will be moderate in the early years of the program because of essential planning and administrative requirements, but, if these requirements for sound urban development are to be met, local communities must have reasonable assurance that

Federal support will be available when needed for investments in mass transportation.

Assistance for Displaced Families and Businesses

Thousands of families and businesses are caused great hardship by the construction of highways, mass transportation routes, and other public improvements. The Bureau of Public Roads estimates that about 15,000 families and 1,500 businesses will be displaced each year in the next 6 to 8 years by the completion of the Interstate Highway System. Family displacements by federally assisted urban renewal activities are running about 30,000 a year and are expected to average more than 35,000 a year over the next decade. Around 4,000 businesses are being displaced annually by urban renewal. Another 30,000 to 35,000 families a year are estimated to be displaced by other public actions in urban areas. This means that some 85,000 urban families have to move each year because of public action, much of it assisted with Federal funds.

Under the federally assisted urban renewal program, families must be assured the availability of decent, safe, and sanitary housing when they are displaced by demolitions, code enforcement, and other urban renewal activities. Also the moving expenses of families and businesses are paid from Federal urban renewal program funds. For families needing such assistance, the average payment is about $65. The average payment to business is about $1,150.

In order to alleviate hardship caused by public action and to provide equity in treatment, provisions similar to those for urban renewal should be made in the Federal-aid highway program and also in other federally assisted programs causing displacements.

Urban Transportation Research

Extensive research must be undertaken to improve the technology of urban transportation and to furnish public officials and industry dependable information on the relations among different forms of transportation and the rest of the urban economy. As summarized by the Institute of Public Administration:

> Topics on which work is needed include improvement of vehicles, roadbeds, power systems, traffic control systems, and other technology; methods of projecting demand for urban transportation; influence of different modes of transportation on urban development and land use; determinants of individual transportation behavior; costs and pricing of different transportation modes; and administering and financing urban transportation systems.

Highway research. The Bureau of Public Roads, since its very beginning in 1893, has had an important influence in highway research, both through the efforts of its own staff and through its leadership and guidance to others. With the authority for use by the States of the 1½-percent funds for research, since 1944, the Bureau's influence has been broader than ever.

In addition to studies related to the physical problems of roadbuilding and maintenance, a great deal of Public Roads research in more recent years has been directed toward the problems of planning, design, and operation of highways. Mathematicians, geographers, city planners, and psychologists are now included in the Public Roads staff. Work accomplished or underway, either directly or by sponsorship, varies broadly. As examples may be cited studies of human behavior as related to driving; evaluation of economic and social effects of highways; methods of forecasting highway usage, tax revenues, and needs; correlation of travel with such factors as land use and employment; and evaluation of electronic controls for driver and vehicle guidance. Much of this research is oriented directly toward urban transportation problems.

Since 1944 the Bureau of Public Roads has participated with the State highway departments in conducting travel habit studies designed to provide factual data needed for urban transportation planning. The early studies were pioneering efforts and their analyses left much to be desired, especially in projecting future travel desires. However, these studies continue to be a basic planning tool, and analyses of the data collected and tabulated in one city after another have led to the establishment of quantitative measures of the basic relations between travel desires and land use and other social and economic factors of the metropolitan area. The establishment of these quantitative measures has made possible the integration of transportation and general land use planning, which is now deemed essential for realistic planning. It is now possible to study the interaction that exists between transportation and economic development and land use.

It is essential that research be continued and expanded to provide more precise planning study techniques; to search more deeply into the factors affecting urban development; to quantify more accurately the relationships between land use and travel; and to learn more about the attitudes and desires, with regard to all aspects of urban living, of the individual citizen.

Research is also essential in transportation technology—both of the vehicle and of the roadbed—if planning is truly to prepare for the future.

It is believed that the Federal Government has a responsibility to stimulate additional highway research activities in the Federal-State cooperative area. To accomplish this, an additional one-half of 1 percent should be made available from funds apportioned to the States for the Federal-aid primary system, the Federal-aid secondary system, and extensions of these systems in urban areas (the A-B-C program) for highway research purposes. This additional one-half of 1 percent, together with State matching funds, would amount to almost $10 million annually. This sum would be in addition to the present 1½-percent which is currently being used for highway planning and highway research.

Reasearch in mass transportation. Work is needed to improve transportation facilities and equipment including model and prototype construction, with emphasis on transit vehicles and power systems, traffic signaling, automatic controls, and methods of construction. It is essential to stimulate and support experimentation with new equipment and systems to test their practicality and demonstrate their effectiveness in improving and reducing the total cost of urban transportation.

Outstanding among the many studies which need to be made of the economics of urban transportation are questions of why groups of people choose different means of urban travel under various conditions and how their choices would be affected by changes in the quality and cost of different kinds of private and public transportation that might be made available. Planning and investment decisions for highways and mass transportation are profoundly affected by what people believe about the answers to these questions. But there is little systematic knowledge on which to base these beliefs. The administration, therefore, has requested the Congress to appropriate funds for a substantial study of these problems by the Housing and Home Finance Agency. This study would start with analysis of information which has been developed in the course of urban transportation planning and would be coordinated with related studies supported by the Bureau of Public Roads.

The Housing Administrator should be given broad authority to conduct urban transportation research and development projects. Depending on what is most appropriate for the particular project, the studies and research should be carried on by agency staff or be made under agreement or contract with other Government agencies, universities, the National Academy of Sciences, nongovernmental research agencies, State and local governments, or individuals. It is recommended that the funds authorized last year for mass transportation demonstration grants be made available for those purposes by modifications of present legislation. An additional $10 million a year for the next 3 years also should be provided from the capital grant funds proposed for the new mass transportation assistance program. Such broad authority and substantial financing are required to make a good start toward basic improvements in urban mass transportation technology and economics.

A Message from the President of the United States, 1962

PRESIDENT KENNEDY'S TRANSPORTATION MESSAGE gained prominence initially because it was the first time a chief executive had sent a special message to Congress on the subject of transportation. Moreover, it called for a considerable rethinking of U. S. policy toward transportation regulation in that it recommended a much increased reliance on competition and a consequent lessening of regulatory strictures. Because of the hue and cry which was raised about the portion of the message that dealt with intercity transport, somewhat less notice was given to the portions of the message that dealt with the problems of urban transportation.

Reproduced below is the portion of the President's message dealing with urban transportation. The reader will find in President Kennedy's recommendations to the Congress a close parallel with the major points made in the joint report of the Secretary of Commerce and the Administrator of the Housing and Home Finance Agency.

It should be noted that the President strongly implies the policy of the federal government to be to preserve existing urbanized areas and to guide future growth along similar lines. This is not to suggest that the urban growth patterns of the past are faultless, but rather that it would be unwise and uneconomic to alter radically such form and substance as has proved essential to urban vitality. Academic arguments that the city as we know it—with a strong core and relatively high density--should be allowed to wither away in exchange for purposeful urbanization on the pattern of Los Angeles, are thus by implication laid to rest as being strictly the province of ivory towers and not the policy of the federal government.

I HAVE PREVIOUSLY EMPHASIZED to the Congress the need for action on the transportation problems resulting from burgeoning urban growth and the changing urban scene.

Higher incomes coupled with the increasing availability of the auto-

"The Transportation System of Our Nation," message from the President of the United States, 87th Congress, 2nd Session, House of Representatives Document No. 384, April 5, 1962.

mobile have enabled more and more American families, particularly younger ones with children, to seek their own homes in suburban areas. Simultaneously, changes and improvements in freight transportation, made possible by the development of modern highways and the trucking industry, have reduced the dependence of manufacturers on central locations near port facilities or railroad terminals. The development of improved production techniques that require spacious, one-story plant layouts have impelled many industries to move to the periphery of urban areas. At the same time the importance of the central city is increasing for trade, financial, governmental, and cultural activities.

One result of these changes in location patterns has been a change in the patterns of urban travel. Formerly people traveled mainly along high density corridors radiating to and from downtown. Today traffic patterns are increasingly diverse. Added to traditional suburb-to-city movements are large crosstown flows which existing mass transportation systems are often not geared to handle. Also, the increasing use of automobiles to meet urban transportation needs has resulted in increasing highway congestion, and this has greatly impeded mass transportation service using those highways.

This drastic revision of travel patterns in many urban areas has seriously impaired the effectiveness and economic viability of public mass transportation, which is geared to the older patterns. A steady decline in patronage and a concomitant rise of unprofitability and financial problems have occurred. This has been particularly true of rail commuter and streetcar services limited to particular routes by fixed roadbeds.

To conserve and enhance values in existing urban areas is essential. But at least as important are steps to promote economic efficiency and livability in areas of future development. In less than 20 years we can expect well over half of our expanded population to be living in 40 great urban complexes. Many smaller places will also experience phenomenal growth. The ways that people and goods can be moved in these areas will have a major influence on their structure, on the efficiency of their economy, and on the availability for social and cultural opportunities they can offer their citizens. Our national welfare therefore requires the provision of good urban transportation, with the properly balanced use of private vehicles and modern mass transport to help shape as well as serve urban growth.

At my request, the problems of urban transportation have been studied in detail by the Housing and Home Finance Administrator and the Secretary of Commerce. Their field investigations have included some 40 metropolitan and other communities, large and small. Their findings support the need for substantial expansion and important changes in the urban mass transportation program authorized in the Housing Act of 1961 as well as revisions in Federal highway legislation. They give dramatic emphasis, moreover, to the need for greater local initiative and to the responsibility of the States and municipalities to provide financial support and effective governmental auspices for strengthening and improving urban transportation.

On the basis of this report, I recommend that long-range Federal financial aid and technical assistance be provided to help plan and develop the comprehensive and balanced urban transportation that is so vitally needed, not only to benefit local communities, but to assure more effective use of Federal funds available for other urban development and renewal programs. I recommend that such Federal assistance for mass transportation be limited to those applications (1) where an organization, or officially coordinated organizations, are carrying on a continuing program of comprehensive planning on an areawide basis, and (2) where the assisted project will be administered through a public agency as part of a unified or officially coordinated areawide transportation system.

LONG-RANGE PROGRAM

SPECIFICALLY, I recommend that the Congress authorize the first installment of a long-range program of Federal aid to our urban regions for the revitalization and needed expansion of public mass transportation, to be administered by the Housing and Home Finance Agency. I recommend a capital grant authorization of $500 million to be made available over a 3-year period, with $100 million to be made available in fiscal 1963. Only a program that offers substantial support and continuity of Federal participation can induce our urban regions to organize appropriate administrative arrangements and to meet their share of the costs of fully balanced transportation systems.

This Federal assistance should be made available to qualified public agencies in the form of direct grants to be matched by local, non-Federal contributions. For rights-of-way, fixed facilities, including maintenance and terminal facilities, and rolling stock required for urban mass transportation systems, grants should be provided for up to two-thirds of the project cost which cannot reasonably be financed from expected revenue. The remaining one-third of the net project cost would be paid by the locality or State from other sources, without Federal aid. The extension and rehabilitation of existing systems as well as the creation of new systems should be eligible. In no event should Federal funds be used to pay operating expenses. Nor should parking facilities, except those directly supporting public mass transportation, be eligible for Federal grants.

While it is expected that the new grant program will be the major Federal support for urban mass transportation, it is important to have Federal loans available where private financing cannot be obtained on reasonable terms. I therefore recommend removal of the time limit on the $50 million loan authorization provided in the Housing Act of 1961. Federal loans would not be available to finance the State or local one-third contribution to net project cost.

Although grants and loans would be available only to public agencies, those agencies could lease facilities and equipment or make other arrangements for private operation of assisted mass transportation systems. The program is not intended to foster public as distinguished from private mass transit operations. Each community should develop the method or methods of operation best suited to its particular requirements.

A community should be eligible for a mass transportation grant or loan only after the Housing Administrator determines that the facilities and equipment for which the assistance is sought are necessary for carrying out a program for a unified or officially coordinated urban transportation system as a part of the comprehensively planned development of the urban area.

The program I have proposed is aimed at the widely varying transit problems of our Nation's cities, ranging from the clogged arteries of our most populous metropolitan areas to those smaller cities which have only recently known the frustrations of congested streets. There may, however, be some highly specialized situations in which alternative programs, for example, loan guarantees under stringent conditions, would be better suited to particular needs and the Congress may, therefore, wish to consider such alternatives.

EMERGENCY AID

TIME will be required by most metropolitan areas to organize effectively for the major planning efforts required. Even more time may be needed to create public agencies with adequate powers to develop, finance, and administer new or improved public transportation systems. Meanwhile, the crisis conditions that have already emerged in some areas threaten to become widespread. Mass transportation continues to deteriorate and even to disappear. Important segments of our population are thus deprived of transportation; highway congestion and attendant air pollution become worse; and the destructive effects upon central business districts and older residential areas are accelerated.

In recognition of this serious situation, I also recommend that the Congress, for a period of 3 years only, authorize the Housing Administrator to make emergency grants, (a) where there is an urgent need for immediate aid to an existing mass transportation facility or service that might otherwise cease to be available for transportation purposes, (b) where an official long-range program for a coordinated system is being actively prepared, and (c) where the facilities or equipment acquired under the emergency grant can reasonably be expected to be required for the new long-range system. This emergency aid should not exceed one-half of the net project cost. Upon completion of an acceptable area-wide transportation program within 3 years, these emergency projects, if a part of the ultimate system, should qualify for the balance of the regular Federal assistance available under the long-range program.

<h2 style="text-align:center">ROLE OF HIGHWAYS</h2>

HIGHWAYS are an instrumental part of any coordinated urban transportation program, and must be an integral part of any comprehensive community development plan. Accordingly, I have requested the Secretary of Commerce to make his approval of the use of highway planning funds in metropolitan planning studies contingent upon the establishment of a continuing and comprehensive planning process. This process should, to the maximum extent feasible, include all of the interdependent parts of the metropolitan or other urban area, all agencies and jurisdictions involved, and all forms of transportation, and should be closely coordinated with policymaking and program administration.

Progress has already been made in coordinated transportation planning for metropolitan areas through the use of funds made available under both Federal highway and housing legislation. To increase the effectiveness of this effort, I recommend that the Federal-aid highway law be amended to increase the percentage of Federal funds available to the States for research and planning. Legislation will be submitted to effectuate this change and to provide that (a) these funds should be available for planning and research purposes only; (b) the funds be matched by the States in accordance with statutory matching requirements; and (c) any funds not used for planning and research lapse.

In addition I recommend that the Federal-aid highway law be amended to provide that, effective not later than July 1, 1965, the Secretary of Commerce shall, before approving a program for highway projects in any metropolitan area, make a finding that such projects are consistent with comprehensive development plans for the metropolitan area and that the Federal-aid system so developed will be an integral part of a soundly based, balanced transportation system for the area involved.

Highway planning should be broadened to include adequate traffic control systems, parking facilities, and circulation systems on city streets commensurate with the traffic forecasts used to justify freeways and major arterial roadways. Provision for transit and highway facilities in the same roadway, permissible under present law and already tested in several cases, should be encouraged whenever more effective transportation will result. Moreover, I have requested the Secretary of Commerce to consider favorably the reservation of special highway lanes for buses during peak traffic hours whenever comprehensive transportation plans indicate that this is desirable.

To permit the State highway departments greater flexibility in the use of Federal-aid highway funds to meet urban transportation needs, I further recommend that the Federal-aid highway law be amended to permit more extensive use of Federal-aid secondary funds for extensions of the secondary system in urban areas.

I have asked the Secretary of Commerce and the Housing and Home Finance Administrator to consult regularly regarding administration of the highway and urban mass transportation programs, and to report to me annually on the progress of their respective programs, on the needs for further coordination, and on possibilities for improvement.

RELOCATION ASSISTANCE

LAST year in a message to the Congress on the Federal-aid highway program, I called attention to the problems of families displaced by new highway construction and proposed that the Federal highway law be amended to require assistance to such families in finding decent housing at reasonable cost. The need for such assistance to alleviate unnecessary hardship is still urgent. The Secretary of Commerce has estimated that, under the interstate highway program alone, 15,000 families and 1,500 businesses are being displaced each year, and the proposed urban mass transportation program will further increase the number of persons affected.

To move toward equity among the various federally assisted programs causing displacement, I recommend that assistance and requirements similar to those now applicable to the urban renewal program be authorized for the Federal-aid highway program and the urban mass transportation program. Legislation is being submitted to authorize payments of not to exceed $200 in the case of individuals and families and $3,000 (or if greater, the total certified actual moving expenses) in the case of business concerns or nonprofit organizations displaced as a result of land acquisitions under these programs.

MASS TRANSIT RESEARCH AND DEMONSTRATIONS

FURTHER, I believe that progress will be most rapid and long lasting if the Federal Government contributes to economic and technological research in the field of urban mass transportation. These research activities should be an integral part of the research program described later in this message. Important parts of this program should be carried out by the Housing Administrator directly, through contract with other Federal agencies, private research organizations, universities and other competent bodies, or through the allocation of funds to local public agencies for approved programs.

To facilitate this approach, I recommend that the $25 million authorized last year for demonstration grants be made available for broad research and development undertakings, as well as demonstration projects, which have general applicability throughout the Nation. That amount, plus an additional $10 million from the proposed capital grant funds for each of the years 1963, 1964, and 1965 should suffice for these purposes. These funds, together with research funds available under the Federal-aid highway program, can contribute to substantial advances in urban transportation.

INTERSTATE COMPACTS

FINALLY, since transportation in many urban areas is an interstate problem, I recommend that legislation be enacted to give congressional approval in advance for interstate compacts for the establishment of agencies to carry out transportation and other regional functions in urban areas extending across State lines.

Urban Mass Transportation Act of 1964

AFTER A LONG LEGISLATIVE BATTLE between urban and rural forces, notably in the House of Representatives, the Urban Mass Transportation Act of 1964 was signed into law by President Johnson on July 9, 1964. With the passage of this legislation, the federal government launched a broader program to aid the improvement of mass transportation in American cities than had ever before been the case. This program was to be achieved

"Urban Mass Transportation Act of 1964," Public Law 88–365, 88th Congress, 2nd Session.

through federal grants for capital improvements. The Act of 1961 had confined the activities of the federal government to provision of funds for demonstration purposes, along with a limited program of equipment loans. The 1964 Act continued these programs and allowed the federal government to contribute up to two-thirds of the cost of new equipment and facilities.

This legislation gives added strength to two facets of federal policy toward urban transportation. Of first importance is planning: a continuing program of comprehensive planning is necessary in any given city or metropolitan area in order for it to qualify for the capital grants. If the planning process is complete or is completed within a specified period, up to two-thirds of the net cost of the project may be obtained; otherwise only fifty percent of the cost of capital projects may be recouped from federal coffers. This financial incentive reinforces the new federal policy of coordinating transport programs with other aspects of urban development.

Second, the projects must be initiated and partially financed on the local level. Thus local initiative, as in the 1961 Act, is again a prime requisite. This is in keeping with the prevailing federal attitude that it is the role of the national government to provide hospitable conditions—plus some financial aid—to encourage local solutions to local problems. Since only a portion of the cost is provided to any one place, moreover, the limited amount of available federal money can cover more ground.

An Act

To authorize the Housing and Home Finance Administrator to provide additional assistance for the development of comprehensive and coordinated mass transportation systems, both public and private, in metropolitan and other urban areas, and for other purposes.

Be it enacted by the Senate and House of Representatives of the United States of America in Congress assembled, That this Act may be cited as the "Urban Mass Transportation Act of 1964."

Findings and Purposes

Sec. 2.

(a) The Congress finds:

(1) that the predominant part of the Nation's population is located in its rapidly expanding metropolitan and other urban areas, which generally cross the boundary lines of local jurisdictions and often extend into two or more States;

(2) that the welfare and vitality of urban areas, the satisfactory movement of people and goods within such areas, and the effectiveness of housing, urban renewal, highway, and other federally aided programs are being jeopardized by the deterioration or inadequate provision of urban transportation facilities and services, the intensification of traffic congestion, and the lack of coordinated transportation and other development planning on a comprehensive and continuing basis; and

(3) that Federal financial assistance for the development of efficient and coordinated mass transportation systems is essential to the solution of these urban problems.

(b) The purposes of this Act are:

(1) to assist in the development of improved mass transportation facilities, equipment, techniques, and methods, with the cooperation of mass transportation companies both public and private;

(2) to encourage the planning and establishment of areawide urban mass transportation systems needed for economical and desirable urban development, with the cooperation of mass transportation companies both public and private; and

(3) to provide assistance to State and local governments and their instrumentalities in financing such systems, to be operated by public or private mass transportation companies as determined by local needs.

FEDERAL FINANCIAL ASSISTANCE

SEC. 3.

(a) In accordance with the provisions of this Act, the Administrator is authorized to make grants or loans (directly, through the purchase of securities or equipment trust certificates, or otherwise) to assist States and local public bodies and agencies thereof in financing the acquisition, construction, reconstruction, and improvement of facilities and equipment for use, by operation or lease or otherwise, in mass transportation service in urban areas and in coordinating such service with highway and other transportation in such areas. Eligible facilities and equipment may include land (but not public highways), buses and other rolling stock, and other real or personal property needed for an efficient and coordinated mass transportation system. No grant or loan shall be provided under this section unless the Administrator determines that the applicant has or will have (1) the legal, financial, and technical capacity to carry out the proposed project, and (2) satisfactory continuing control, through operation or lease or otherwise, over the use of the facilities and equipment. No such funds shall be used for payment of ordinary governmental or non-project operating expenses.

(b) No loan shall be made under this section for any project for which a grant is made under this section, except grants made for relocation payments in accordance with section 7(b). Loans under this section shall be subject to the restrictions and limitations set forth in paragraphs (1), (2), and (3) of section 202(b) of the Housing Amendments of 1955. The authority provided in section 203 of such Amendments to obtain funds for loans under clause (2) of section 202(a) of such Amendments shall (except for undisbursed loan commitments) hereafter be exercised by the Administrator (without regard to the proviso in section 202(d) of such Amendments) solely to obtain funds for loans under this section.

(c) No financial assistance shall be provided under this Act to any State or local public body or agency thereof for the purpose, directly or indirectly, of acquiring any interest in, or purchasing any facilities or other property of, a private mass transportation company, or for the purpose of constructing, improving, or reconstructing any facilities or other property acquired (after the date of the enactment of this Act) from any such company, or for the purpose of providing by contract or otherwise for the operation of mass transportation facilities or equipment in competition with, or supplementary to, the service provided by an existing mass transportation company, unless (1) the Administrator finds that such assistance is essential to a program, proposed or under active preparation, for a unified or officially coordinated urban transportation system as part of the comprehensively planned development of the urban area, (2) the Administrator finds that such program, to the maximum extent feasible, provides for the participation of private mass transportation companies, (3) just and adequate compensation will be paid to such companies for acquisition of their franchises or property to the extent required by applicable State or local laws, and (4) the Secretary of Labor certifies that such assistance complies with the requirements of section 10(c) of this Act.

LONG-RANGE PROGRAM

SEC. 4.

(a) Except as specified in section 5, no Federal financial assistance shall be provided pursuant to section 3 unless the Administrator determines that the facilities and equipment for which the assistance is sought are needed for carrying out a program, meeting criteria established by him, for a unified or officially coordinated urban transportation system as a part of the comprehensively planned development of the urban area, and are necessary for the sound, economic, and desirable development of such area. Such program shall encourage to the maximum extent feasible the participation of private enterprise. Where facilities and equipment are to be acquired which are already being used in mass transportation service in the urban area, the program must provide that they shall be so improved (through modernization, extension, addition, or otherwise) that they will better serve the transportation needs of the area. The Administrator, on the basis of engineering studies, studies of economic feasibility, and data showing the nature and extent of expected utilization of the facilities and equipment, shall estimate what portion of the cost of a project to be assisted under section 3 cannot be reasonably financed from revenues— which portion shall hereinafter be called "net project cost." The Federal grant for such a project shall not exceed two-thirds of the net project cost. The remainder of the net project cost shall be provided, in cash, from sources other than Federal funds, and no refund or reduction of that portion so provided shall be made at any time unless there is at the same time a refund of a proportional amount of the Federal grant.

(b) To finance grants under this Act there is hereby authorized to be appropriated at any time after its enactment not to exceed $75,000,000 for fiscal year 1965; $150,000,000 for fiscal year 1966; and $150,000,-000 for fiscal year 1967. Any amount so appropriated shall remain available until expended; and any amount authorized but not appropriated for any fiscal year may be appropriated for any succeeding fiscal year. The Administrator is authorized, notwithstanding the provisions of section 3648 of the Revised Statutes, as amended, to make advance or progress payments on account of any grant made pursuant to this Act.

EMERGENCY PROGRAM

SEC. 5.

Prior to July 1, 1967, Federal financial assistance may be provided pursuant to section 3 where (1) the program for the development of a unified or officially coordinated urban transportation system, referred to in section 4(a), is under active preparation although not yet completed, (2) the facilities and equipment for which the assistance is sought can reasonably be expected to be required for such a system, and (3) there is an urgent need for their preservation or provision. The Federal grant for such a project shall not exceed one-half of the net project cost: Provided, That where a Federal grant is made on such a one-half basis, and the planning requirements specified in section 4(a) are fully met within a three-year period after the execution of the grant agreement, an additional grant may then be made to the applicant equal to one-sixth of the net project cost. The remainder of the net project cost shall be provided, in cash, from sources other than Federal funds, and no refund or reduction of that portion so provided shall be made at any time unless there is at the same time a refund of a proportional amount of the Federal grant.

RESEARCH, DEVELOPMENT, AND DEMONSTRATION PROJECTS

SEC. 6.

(a) The Administrator is authorized to undertake research, development, and demonstration projects in all phases of urban mass transportation (including the development, testing, and demonstration of new facilities, equipment, techniques, and methods) which he determines will assist in the reduction of urban transportation needs, the improvement of mass transportation service, or the contribution of such service toward meeting total urban transportation needs at minimum cost. He may undertake such projects independently or by contract (including working agreements with other Federal departments and agencies). In carrying out the provisions of this section, the Administrator is authorized to request and receive such information or data as he deems appropriate from public or private sources.

(b) The Administrator may make available to finance projects under this section not to exceed $10,000,000 of the mass transportation grant authorization provided in section 4(b), which limit shall be increased to $20,000,000 on July 1, 1965, and to $30,000,000 on July 1, 1966. In addition, notwithstanding the provisions of section 4 of this Act or of section 103(b) of the Housing Act of 1949, the unobligated balance of the amount available for mass transportation demonstration grants pursuant to the proviso in such section 103(b) shall be available solely for financing projects under this section.

(c) Nothing contained in this section shall limit any authority of the Administrator under section 602 of the Housing Act of 1956 or any other provision of law.

RELOCATION REQUIREMENTS AND PAYMENTS

SEC. 7.

(a) No financial assistance shall be extended to any project under section 3 unless the Administrator determines that an adequate relocation program is being carried on for families displaced by the project and that there are being or will be provided (in the same area or in other areas generally not less desirable in regard to public utilities and public and commercial facilities and at rents or prices within the financial means of the displaced families) an equal number of decent, safe, and sanitary dwellings available to those displaced families and reasonably accessible to their places of employment.

(b) Notwithstanding any other provision of this Act, financial assistance extended to any project under section 3 may include grants for relocation payments, as herein defined. Such grants may be in addition to other financial assistance for the project under section 3, and no part of the amount of such relocation payments shall be required to be contributed as a local grant. The term "relocation payments" means payments by the applicant to individuals, families, business concerns, and nonprofit organizations for their reasonable and necessary moving expenses and any actual direct losses of property, except goodwill or profit, for which reimbursement or compensation is not otherwise made, resulting from their displacement by the project. Such payments shall be made subject to such rules and regulations as may be prescribed by the Administrator, and shall not exceed $200 in the case of an individual or family, or $3,000 (or if greater, the total certified actual moving expenses) in the case of a business concern or nonprofit organization. Such rules and regulations may include provisions authorizing payment to individuals and families of fixed amounts (not to exceed $200 in any case) in lieu of their respective reasonable and necessary moving expenses and actual direct losses of property.

COORDINATION OF FEDERAL ASSISTANCE FOR HIGHWAYS AND FOR MASS TRANSPORTATION FACILITIES

SEC. 8.

In order to assure coordination of highway and railway and other mass transportation planning and development programs in urban areas, particularly with respect to the provision of mass transportation facilities in connection with federally assisted highways, the Administrator and the Secretary of Commerce shall consult on general urban transportation policies and programs and shall exchange information on proposed projects in urban areas.

GENERAL PROVISIONS

SEC. 9.

(a) In the performance of, and with respect to, the functions, powers, and duties vested in him by this Act, the Administrator shall (in addition to any authority otherwise vested in him) have the functions, powers, and duties set forth in section 402, except subsections (c)(2) and (f), of the Housing Act of 1950. Funds obtained or held by the Administrator in connection with the performance of his functions under this Act shall be available for the administrative expenses of the Administrator in connection with the performance of such functions.

(b) All contracts for construction, reconstruction, or improvement of facilities and equipment in furtherance of the purposes for which a loan or grant is made under this Act, entered into by applicants under other than competitive bidding procedures as defined by the Administrator, shall provide that the Administrator and the Comptroller General of the United States, or any of their duly authorized representatives, shall, for the purpose of audit and examination, have access to any books, documents, papers, and records of the contracting parties that are pertinent to the operations or activities under such contracts.

(c) All contracts for construction, reconstruction, or improvement of facilities and equipment in furtherance of the purposes for which a loan or grant is made under this Act shall provide that in the performance of the work the contractor shall use only such manufactured articles as have been manufactured in the United States.

(d) As used in this Act:

(1) the term "States" means the several States, the District of Columbia, the Commonwealth of Puerto Rico, and the possessions of the United States;

(2) the term "local public bodies" includes municipalities and other political subdivisions of States; public agencies and instrumentalities of one or more States, municipalities, and political subdivisions of States; and public corporations, boards, and commissions established under the laws of any State;

(3) the term "Administrator" means the Housing and Home Finance Administrator;

(4) the term "urban area" means any area that includes a municipality or other built-up place which is appropriate, in the judgment of the Administrator, for a public transportation system to serve commuters or others in the locality taking into consideration the local patterns and trends of urban growth; and

(5) the term "mass transportation" means transportation by bus or rail or other conveyance, either publicly or privately owned, serving the general public (but not including school buses or charter or sightseeing service) and moving over prescribed routes.

(e) There are hereby authorized to be appropriated, out of any money in the Treasury not otherwise appropriated, the funds necessary to carry out all functions under this Act except loans under section 3. All funds appropriated under this Act for other than administrative expenses shall remain available until expended.

(f) None of the provisions of this Act shall be construed to authorize the Administrator to regulate in any manner the mode of operation of any mass transportation system with respect to which a grant is made under section 3 or, after such grant is made, to regulate the rates, fares, tolls, rentals, or other charges fixed or prescribed for such system by any local public or private transit agency; but nothing in this subsection shall prevent the Administrator from taking such actions as may be necessary to require compliance by the agency or agencies involved with any undertakings furnished by such agency or agencies in connection with the application for the grant.

LABOR STANDARDS

SEC. 10.

(a) The Administrator shall take such action as may be necessary to insure that all laborers and mechanics employed by contractors or subcontractors in the performance of construction work financed with the assistance of loans or grants under this Act shall be paid wages at rates not less than those prevailing on similar construction in the locality as determined by the Secretary of Labor in accordance with the Davis-Bacon Act, as amended. The Administrator shall not approve any such loan or grant without first obtaining adequate assurance that required labor standards will be maintained upon the construction work.

(b) The Secretary of Labor shall have, with respect to the labor standards specified in subsection (a), the authority and functions set forth in Reorganization Plan Numbered 14 of 1950 (15 F.R. 3176; 64 Stat. 1267; 5 U.S.C. 133z-15), and section 2 of the Act of June 13, 1934, as amended (48 Stat. 948; 40 U.S.C. 276c).

(c) It shall be a condition of any assistance under this Act that fair and equitable arrangements are made, as determined by the Secretary of Labor, to protect the interests of employees affected by such assistance. Such protective arrangements shall include, without being limited to, such provisions as may be necessary for (1) the preservation of rights, privileges, and benefits (including continuation of pension rights and benefits) under existing collective bargaining agreements or otherwise; (2) the continuation of collective bargaining rights; (3) the protection of individual employees against a worsening of their positions with respect to their employment; (4) assurances of employment to employees of acquired mass transportation systems and priority of reemployment of employees terminated or laid off; and (5) paid training or retraining programs. Such arrangements shall include provisions protecting individual employees against a worsening of their positions with respect to their employment which shall in no event provide benefits less than those established pursuant to section 5(2)(f) of the Act of February 4, 1887 (24 Stat. 379), as amended. The contract for the granting of any such assistance shall specify the terms and conditions of the protective arrangements.

AIR POLLUTION CONTROL

SEC. 11.

In providing financial assistance to any project under section 3, the Administrator shall take into consideration whether the facilities and equipment to be acquired, constructed, reconstructed, or improved will be designed and equipped to prevent and control air pollution in accordance with any criteria established for this purpose by the Secretary of Health, Education, and Welfare.

STATE LIMITATION

SEC. 12.

Grants made under section 3 (other than grants for relocation payments in accordance with section 7(b)) for projects in any one State shall not exceed in the aggregate 12½ per centum of the aggregate amount of grant funds authorized to be appropriated pursuant to section 4(b).

Passed the Senate April 4, 1963.
Attest:

FELTON M. JOHNSTON
Secretary

Passed the House of Representatives with an amendment June 25, 1964.
Attest:

RALPH R. ROBERTS
Clerk

1966 Amendments to the Urban Mass Transportation Act of 1964

FEW PIECES OF LEGISLATION are by any means perfect when they are first placed in the Congressional hopper. And when finally enacted into law, what emerges is a product of considerable give and take. Little of the law

"An Act to Amend the Urban Mass Transportation Act of 1964," Public Law 89–562, 89th Congress, 2nd Session, September 8, 1966.

of the land is free from compromise or oversight or from misunderstanding of its potential ramifications. If legislation is to meet the needs of the people as times change and experience grows, it must constantly be reevaluated and amended. Even though federal programs concerning mass transportation are relatively new, a very obvious and necessary strengthening process is already evident. Plugging the gaps began with the Urban Mass Transportation Act of 1964, when the capital-grant program was added to the programs in force under the Housing Act of 1961.

By 1966 more gaps were in need of filling. The Amendments to the Urban Mass Transportation Act of 1964, signed into law by President Johnson on September 8, 1966, are evidence of increasing maturity in Congressional thinking with regard to mass transportation. In addition to renewing and providing funds for the continuation of the existing programs, the Amendments established four new programs. One of these gave recognition to the fact that highly expensive engineering and planning work is often needed before a city or metropolitan area can comply with the law regarding the capital-grant portion of the Act of 1964; it made federal money available, on a matching basis, for the technical studies that are required before application for a federal capital grant can be initiated. Such expensive planning is especially necessary for construction of new or additional rapid-transit facilities.

Aid was also provided for a new program of management-training grants, thus recognizing the vital need to improve the calibre of management in the mass-transit field. While there were restrictions in the number who might qualify for these loans in any one year, this aid was certainly a move in the right direction. Aid programs to colleges and universities were also provided for research and training to foster comprehensive studies on urban transportation problems. Finally, the Secretary of the Department of Housing and Urban Development was given a mandate to work with the Secretary of Commerce in backing research efforts aimed at developing new transport modes and systems.

The Amendments were not a complete victory for those hoping for a substantial reinforcement of federal urban-transport programs. The funds that were authorized were not all that might have been desired, nor were they sufficient to launch a large-scale offensive on urban transportation. Nevertheless, those interested in the future of mass transportation in the United States are generally encouraged by this legislation.

An Act

To amend the Urban Mass Transportation Act of 1964.

Be it enacted by the Senate and House of Representatives of the United States of America in Congress assembled,

AUTHORIZATION

SEC. 1.

(a) The first sentence of section 4(b) of the Urban Mass Transportation Act of 1964 is amended by striking out "$150,000,000 for fiscal year 1967" and inserting in lieu thereof $150,000,000 for each of the fiscal years 1967, 1968, and 1969."

(b) Section 6(b) of such Act (redesignated section 6(c) by section 3 of this Act) is amended by striking out "and to $30,000,000 on July 1, 1966" and inserting in lieu thereof "to $30,000,000 on July 1, 1966, to $40,000,000 on July 1, 1967, and to $50,000,000 on July 1, 1968."

ASSISTANCE FOR CERTAIN TECHNICAL STUDIES
AND TRAINING PROGRAMS

SEC. 2.

(a) The Urban Mass Transportation Act of 1964 is amended:

(1) by redesignating sections 9 through 12 as sections 12 through 15, respectively; and

(2) by inserting after section 8 the following new sections:

"GRANTS FOR TECHNICAL STUDIES

"SEC. 9.

The Secretary is authorized to make grants to States and local public bodies and agencies thereof for the planning, engineering, and designing of urban mass transportation projects, and for other technical studies, to be included, or proposed to be included, in a program (completed or under active preparation) for a unified or officially coordinated urban transportation system as a part of the comprehensively planned development of the urban area. Activities assisted under this section may include (1) studies relating to management, operations, capital requirements, and economic feasibility; (2) preparation of engineering and architectural surveys, plans, and specifications; and (3) other similar or related activities preliminary and in preparation for the construction, acquisition, or improved operation of mass transportation systems, facilities, and equipment. A grant under this section shall be made in accordance with criteria established by the Secretary and shall not exceed two-thirds of the cost of carrying out the activities for which the grant is made.

"GRANTS FOR MANAGERIAL TRAINING PROGRAMS

"SEC. 10.

(a) The Secretary is authorized to make grants to States, local bodies, and agencies thereof to provide fellowships for training of personnel employed in managerial, technical, and professional positions in the urban mass transportation field. Fellowships shall be for not more than one year of advanced training in public or private nonprofit institutions of higher education offering programs of graduate study in business or public administration, or in other fields having application to the urban mass transportation industry. The State, local body, or agency receiving a grant under this section shall select persons for such fellowships on the basis of demonstrated ability and for the contribution which they can reasonably be expected to make to an efficient mass transportation operation. Not more than one hundred fellowships shall be awarded in any year. The grant assistance under this section toward each such fellowship shall not exceed $12,000, nor 75 per centum of the sum of (1) tuition and other charges to the fellowship recipient, (2) any additional costs incurred by the educational institution in connection with the fellowship and billed to the grant recipient, and (3) the regular salary of the fellowship recipient for the period of the fellowship (to the extent that salary is actually paid or reimbursed by the grant recipient).

"(b) Not more than 12½ per centum of the fellowships authorized pursuant to subsection (a) shall be awarded for the training of employees of mass transportation companies in any one State.

"(c) The Secretary may make available to finance grants under this section not to exceed $1,500,000 per annum of the grant funds appropriated pursuant to section 4(b).

"GRANTS FOR RESEARCH AND TRAINING IN URBAN TRANSPORTATION PROBLEMS

"SEC. 11.

(a) The Secretary is authorized to make grants to public and private nonprofit institutions of higher learning to assist in establishing or carrying on comprehensive research in the problems of transportation in urban areas. Such grants shall be used to conduct competent and qualified research and investigations into the theoretical or practical problems of urban transportation, or both, and to provide for the training of persons to carry on further research or to obtain employment in private or public organizations which plan, construct, operate, or manage urban transportation systems. Such research and investigations may include, without being limited to, the design and functioning of urban mass transit systems; the design and functioning of urban roads and highways; the interrelationship between various modes of urban and interurban transportation; the role of transportation planning in overall urban planning; public preferences in transportation; the economic allocation of transportation resources; and the legal, financial, engineering, and esthetic aspects of urban transportation. In making such grants the Secretary shall give preference to institutions of higher learning that undertake such research and training by bringing together knowledge and expertise in the various social science and technical disciplines that relate to urban transportation problems.

"(b) The Secretary may make available to finance grants under this section not to exceed $3,000,000 per annum of the grant funds appropriated pursuant to section 4(b)."

(b) Such Act is further amended:

(1) by striking out "section 10(c)" in section 3(c) and inserting in lieu thereof "section 13(c)"; and

(2) by striking out "under this Act" in section 13(c) (as redesignated by subsection (a)) and inserting in lieu thereof "under section 3 of this Act."

RESEARCH, DEVELOPMENT, AND DEMONSTRATION PROJECT

SEC. 3.

Section 6 of the Urban Mass Transportation Act of 1964 is amended by redesignating subsections (b) and (c) as subsections (c) and (d), and by adding after subsection (a) a new subsection as follows:

"(b) The Secretary shall, in consultation with the Secretary of Commerce, undertake a project to study and prepare a program of research, development, and demonstration of new systems of urban transportation that will carry people and goods within metropolitan areas speedily, safely, without polluting the air, and in a manner that will contribute to sound city planning. The program shall (1) concern itself with all aspects of new systems of urban transportation for metropolitan areas of various sizes, including technological, financial, economic, governmental, and social aspects; (2) take into account the most advanced available technologies and materials; and (3) provide national leadership to efforts of States, localities, private industry, universities, and foundations. The Secretary shall report his findings and recommendations to the President, for submission to the Congress, as rapidly as possible and in any event not later than eighteen months after the effective date of this subsection."

STATE LIMITATION

SEC. 4.

Section 15 of the Urban Mass Transportation Act of 1964 (as redesignated by section 2 of this Act) is amended by striking out the period and inserting in lieu thereof the following: ": *Provided,* That the Secretary may, without regard to such limitation, enter into contracts for grants under section 3 aggregating not to exceed $12,500,000 (subject to the total authorization provided in section 4(b)) with local public bodies and agencies in States where more than two-thirds of the maximum grants permitted in the respective State under this section has been obligated."

Approved September 8, 1966.

"Message from the President of the United States, 1986"

WILFRED OWEN

WHEN IT CAME TO SELECTING a final reading for this volume, it seemed obvious that two objectives should be met to end the book on a proper note. The material should afford some relief to readers who have dutifully chugged through many pages of material taken from sober and rather formal government documents. In addition, the item chosen should provide the reader with a look into the future.

The problem is happily solved in this final selection. No one writes with more wit, wisdom, and imagination on the subject of transportation than does Wilfred Owen. On this occasion he takes a look into the future by giving us the text of a Presidential Message to Congress on the subject of urban transportation—dated 1986. While the tone is often light, the import of the message is most serious, for if the steps outlined are not taken, the transportation problem in our cities may worsen to the point of substantially reducing the quality of American life.

ONE OF THE MAJOR TRANSPORTATION PROBLEMS in Washington is drafting Transportation Messages for Presidents to send to Congress. The difficulty is that transportation covers so much more territory than transportation specialists cover. It is not easy to find an expert whose insights range all the way from ship subsidies and supersonic planes to locomotive boilers and rates on interstate spinach.

As a consequence the Brookings Institution has prepared a series of

"Transportation and the City," Twelfth Annual Wherrett Lecture on Local Government, Institute of Local Government, Graduate School of Public and International Affairs, University of Pittsburgh, 1966.

instant transportation messages as a public service for hard-pressed Presidents. One need only feed into a computer the date and subject of the message, the name of the President, statistics from the Interstate Commerce Commission and the Corps of Engineers, and other irrelevant inputs. What comes out is unbelievable.

For this evening's presentation we have programmed a sample message on urban transportation. Its purpose is to commemorate the twentieth anniversary of two Federal Departments established in 1966: the Department of Housing and Urban Development and the Department of Transportation. The message has not been cleared with the White House, and there is no reason to believe that it ever will be.

To the Congress of the United States:

Throughout the history of this Nation the wheel has had a profound influence on cities, on their accomplishments and on their problems. We have passed through four stages.

To begin with, wheels that glide on rails made big cities physically and economically possible. They supplied the metropolis with food and drink, and they moved large numbers of people from peripheral homes to central work places.

Second, it was wheels moving on the highways of the motor age that spread cities all over the landscape and transported the slums to the suburbs.

Third, it was the multiplication of these wheels that transformed the new mobility into an advanced state of immobility in which cities with too much transportation eventually had almost none.

Fourth, with urbanization now intolerable, it was the wheel that helped us escape from outmoded patterns of city life to embrace entirely new concepts of urban design and urban living.

This devastating cycle turned out all right in the end because of two events of the greatest good fortune. One was the establishment in 1966 of the Department of Transportation, which permitted us for the first time to view transportation as a system of transportation. The other was the launching of the Department of Housing and Urban Development, which showed us that urban transport was really part of a larger system of urban settlement.

Many of you will recall the lamentable situation that confronted us in 1966 when we first made a comprehensive attack on transportation and cities. According to the statistics, we were the richest nation in the world. But we lived in a dingy way, and had failed miserably to achieve minimum standards of urban living. It was not just that buses were crowded, subways antiquated, highways congested, and pedestrians forgotten. The Washington *Post* reported in February 1966 that there were more rats in American cities than there were people. [No one knows exactly how the count was made.] The World Health Organization announced that very same moment that when rats were subject to noise and overcrowding they began to suffer severe tensions and eventually resorted to eating each other.

It was concluded by analogy that people were also suffering. At least six to seven million families were living in substandard housing in 1966. There was extensive overcrowding. Five thousand communities had un-filled sewage disposal needs and two thousand had neither disposal nor collection systems. Forty percent of all communities had inadequate water systems. All of them lacked useful open space and play space. The major problem in the cities was not moving but living.

Under these circumstances the projected addition of another 100 mil-lion people by the year 2000, and presumably an equal number of rats, suggested an extremely agitated urban environment. President Johnson had stated in 1965 that in view of this growth we would have to build as much new urban plant in the remainder of the twentieth century as we had built in the entire period since the first colonists arrived on these shores.[1] In thirty-five years we would have to duplicate all of urban America. Either there would not be room to move, or else, if we con-tinued to expand the area devoted to urban settlements, the bulldozers would destroy what was left of the countryside. The only question seemed to be whether the chaos would be high-density or low-density.

The nightmare was described in the *New York Times* early in 1966:

An additional 100 million people will undermine our most cherished traditions, erode our public services and impose a rate of taxation that will make current taxes seem tame. The new masses, concentrated (as they will be) in the already strangling urban centers, cannot avoid creating conditions that will make city life almost unbearable.[2]

Fortunately this was not the way events were to take us. Today we pay homage to those leaders in business, in the universities, and in state and local governments, who, with the assistance of a new and purposeful pair of Federal Departments, met the problems of urban society head on. In a joint communique dated April 1, 1967, the Secretaries of Transportation and Urban Development arrived at a historic meeting of minds. No matter how bad a city's transportation, they said, it was not as bad as most other aspects of urban living. The basic ills were blight and slums, poverty and unemployment, poor health and poor education, the absence of amenities, and the pollution of the air, the water, and the land. All the fuss about whether transportation would be provided on rubber tires or on steel wheels was diverting attention from the basic problems.

The goal was to improve the conditions of urban life, to envision the urban future that was in our powers to achieve, and to use the tools of urban and regional planning and of science and technology to realize a better life. Transportation was critical, but it was also too important to be viewed simply as a means of moving traffic. Transportation would have to be thought of as a means of designing a more satisfying environment. In the process, urban mobility would be well served. For much that would be done to improve the urban environment would also help improve transportation. This two-way relationship between transportation and urban structure has proved to be the key to the urban revolution.

TRENDS IN TRANSPORT

LET us look first at the accomplishments of the Department of Transportation. It took 26 years and 5 Presidents to get this one off the ground. One of the most significant impacts resulting from it was that people began to look at transport not in separate pieces but as a whole. Transportation trends suddenly assumed fresh meaning. When we began to look at the whole picture, it became clearer what a mess we were in. First, while the number of people in urban America had doubled in forty years, public transit riding had declined by 7,000 million customers. Transit riding in 1966 was less than it had been in 1907. The volume of commuting had expanded enormously as employment passed the 70 million mark, yet the volume of railway commuting was cut in half and travel by rapid transit stayed right where it was for 45 years.

This was indeed a strange combination of events. Urbanization had crowded us into one percent of the nation's land. Home-to-work travel had risen to unprecedented peaks. Yet transit patronage was plunging. People had chosen mass living but had rejected mass moving!

Naturally these trends could not have occurred if there had been no changes in cities themselves. Much of the population had moved to suburbia to avoid unpleasant living and to take advantage of the space that motor vehicles had made plentiful. Industries moved outward for elbow room, where employees came by car, power was delivered by wire, and materials moved by truck.

Yet a revival of mass transit was inevitable. Highway traffic in big cities was critically congested. It was painfully obvious that a combination of autos and buses, both using the same highway system, could not provide the service demanded. The fact that gasoline and diesel engines were polluting the air and threatening the health of whole cities was an added problem. Motor vehicles were splashing 50,000 corpses over the landscape every year. The excessive time and energy spent for home-to-work travel and the unsightliness of an automobile society were added reasons to look for new high-speed public transit systems.

The impetus for something better was already there. In San Francisco, after a long struggle, the Bay Area Rapid Transit District finally built the most advanced transit system in the world: the first completely automatic trains, with operations governed by computer. Today these pioneer facilities still provide service at top speeds of more than 70 miles an hour.

Washington had also begun the first 25 miles of another rail rapid transit system, and other major cities had similar plans. These developments were the natural outcome of a balanced approach to urban transportation.

But how many people foresaw in 1966 the other dramatic development that was to take place in public transit? Almost unnoticeably, the airplane had begun a revolution in travel that was destined to be the outstanding transportation breakthrough of that generation. In retrospect we could have seen from travel between cities what could ultimately be expected of transportation within the cities themselves.

In 1916, intercity travel by public carriers was substantial—all of it by rail. By 1940, the railways had lost more than one-fourth of their patrons despite the increase in population. The trends suggested that the day would come when intercity public carriers would be out of business altogether.

But what happened was exactly the opposite. The downward trend in intercity public carriers was suddenly reversed, and by 1966 total travel was three times the 1940 figure. And all of the gain was accounted for by the airplane!

The revolution in intercity air transport was to take on a new urban complexion. Up to the mid-sixties, aviation developments had focused on long-distance movement between major cities. A reliable jet-powered air bus had not yet moved onto the local scene. But the history of intercity transport was destined to repeat itself in the urbanized areas of America. Conventional aircraft in the New York metropolitan area in 1966 were already providing air service from the major air terminals to 24 local airports. Commuter flights were being provided among a large number of cities, big and small. Helicopter service from the roof of the Pan American Building to New York's major airports had reduced travel time on congested highways from an hour to seven minutes. The roof-top helicopter service already carried peak loads of over a thousand passengers a day to furnish a preview of the next generation of commuters.

As the design and performance of air vehicles and the potentials of vertical flight were perfected, the line between intercity and urban travel began to be blurred. Commuting came to include a growing volume of longer trips by air. Public transit was revived not simply by the ability of trains to move faster, but by the ability of aircraft to move slower.

The growth of short-haul air transport and its impact on the city could not have taken place without other technological changes which favored a dispersed pattern of urban living. These included nuclear power, new methods of energy distribution, satellite communications, new methods of waste disposal, automation, combination telephone and television, shorter hours of work, and higher personal incomes. These forces in combination undermined most of the age-old reasons for central cities. Together they remade the map of America. The whole country shrank into a figuratively smaller space, the fabric of urbanization was loosened, and urban settlements were dispersed throughout the country in new urbanized regions.

All forms of transportation reinforced these new patterns of urbanization. Innovations included the jet helibus, the automated highway bus, and modern rail lines both on the surface and in subways. The private automobile, with turbine power and electronic controls, continued to dominate the transport scene, but with dignity.

As the Congress well knows, we were fortunate, in these rapidly changing times, to have the services of a Department of Transportation. As soon as the new agency began to function, transportation systems planning quickly found its way from space transport to earth transport. The process led to a coordinated system that has successfully overcome congestion, poor service, air pollution, high rates of accident occurrence, and the neglect of physical coordination. Technical progress during the past two decades has helped save the lives of half a million Americans.

One of the most important pieces of legislation passed by the Congress during these pioneer times was the so-called Transportation Book Writers Protection Act, which made it a federal offense to follow an author instead of his ideas. This led to a flood of new ideas. All over America people who had never thought about writing began writing about what they were thinking.

With the help of these suggestions, we undertook a variety of other steps that were to prove equally effective in leading to satisfactory transportation solutions. City governments became aware for the first time that to increase the supply of transportation was only half the job. The other half was to reduce the demand for transportation.

The importance of attacking the demand side of the problem was obvious from what we observed around the globe. Cities in all parts of the world were being plagued by congestion regardless of methods of moving.

[329]

Commuters in New York and Tokyo in the 1960's were just as frustrated with railways and subways as their counterparts in Los Angeles were with the freeways. The five o'clock crush in Istanbul, with its streetcars, was no different from the muddle in Bangkok, with its bicycles and buses.

There were obviously universal factors contributing to urban congestion around the world, and the most obvious was the global tendency to crowd too many people and too much activity into too little space. Urban areas were being defeated by simple geometry. The city of the late twentieth century could no longer survive on the theory that to be bigger was to be better.

Fortunately being bigger was made unnecessary and being better was made possible largely because our mobility made overconcentration obsolete. At the same time we were learning through regional planning and through imaginative urban design how to avoid the underlying causes of congestion.

RENEWING THE CITY

UNDER the leadership of the new Urban Department a new generation of city builders has done more to solve urban transportation problems than transportation technology itself.

The accomplishments that we commemorate tonight are the more remarkable when it is remembered that the Presidential Message recommending a Department of Transportation in 1966 made what seemed to be the fatal mistake of dividing urban transport responsibilities between that Department and the Department of Urban Development. Fortunately the error, which historians ascribe to a practical joker in the Government Printing Office, was detected in time. Obviously all urban transport needed to be under the jurisdiction of the Department of Transportation, subject to the policy guidance of the Department of Urban Development.

In the revolutionary development of a national program for rebuilding our cities the Bureau of the Budget played a vital role. The Bureau announced publicly in February 1966 that it was thinking five years ahead. It was finally dawning on the American public that if private enterprise prospered through planning, the planning of public enterprise should not be considered an act of aggression. Second, by insistence on program planning and budgeting systems, the Budget Bureau forced us to ask the fundamental questions: what kind of urban environment did we want, and how could transportation help to achieve it?

As a result of some soul-searching, agreement was reached on a series of basic guidelines for America's urban renaissance:

(1) The principal problem of cities is not how to move, but how to live.

(2) Whenever we improve the conditions of urban living, we do more than anything else to overcome the problems of moving.

(3) Transportation is not only a means of moving, but a means of creating the urban environment we seek.

(4) We need no longer look at transportation as a problem, for modern technology has made it a solution.

What these rules say is that systems concepts could not stop with urban transportation, but had to be extended to urban living. Otherwise, we might have succeeded in traveling faster, but without even thinking of where we were going. For as Lewis Mumford had written a quarter century earlier, mechanical solutions to transportation problems were pure deception as long as nothing fundamental was done to improve the city itself.

Let us review what has been accomplished toward this end since 1966. At that time the central core was typically crowded with commercial activities. People who worked there in the day had to make their escape at night to find the space and quiet to sleep.

In those days new buildings were erected to accommodate more and more people without regard for the additional public services that had to be provided. Investments in housing and business were always welcomed by the city fathers, while tax-supported schools, play space, transportation, and other public services got debated later. We had architects for buildings, but no architects for cities.

Urban America needed open space to look at and to sit in, interspersed with developed land, so that parks and playgrounds could be enjoyed frequently and without the need for transportation. For some cities the task of introducing park land was not easy. The biggest addition to recreation space in New York during the decade of the sixties was 100 feet long by 42 feet wide. This oasis off Fifth Avenue cost a million dollars, including a set of mirrors to give the illusion of not being cramped.

Other problems included the ancient gridiron pattern of city streets, the crosshatching of asphalt that made a desirable use of land for living and working impossible. The gridiron system failed to serve the needs of transport and also made safe and pleasant neighborhoods impossible. A sensible solution was the campus-like development of urban land that we see today, in which the buildings turn their backs to the street and citizens can move on foot, free from the threat of being mowed down.

The mistake of designing highways simply to move traffic became evident when cities began building expressways in the air. We had no sooner torn down the elevated railways than we began elevating the highways. Boston turned its back to the sea and built an elevated inner loop that largely destroyed the opportunity to redevelop the waterfront. Hartford, Connecticut, having launched a successful downtown renewal program, created a new nightmare of elevated roadways that intruded on the ground of the Capitol itself. If these roads had been built to improve the urban environment as well as to move traffic, they would have been designed as parkways with appropriate landscaping, or as depressed roads or tunnels.

Parking on the streets was another primary cause of traffic congestion. Although street capacity was limited, a few parked cars were permitted to destroy the investment in an entire lane of expensive street. Double parking compounded the trouble. Truck loading at the curb made it worse. These uses of the streets also made urban neighborhoods unsightly. It was therefore of key importance that public parking be provided as an integral part of the road system. In the private sector, of course, all new buildings are being provided with their own off-street vehicle storage.

A major threat to the success of anything done to improve the urban environment was the indiscriminate and tasteless commercial structures that blighted almost every American roadside in the sixties. The greatest offenders were the automotive and petroleum industries: the pennant-bedecked gas stations, automobile graveyards and used car lots. These and other commercial outcroppings littered the public highways all over the United States and created America's longest slums.

When it was made illegal to locate billboards close to the new Interstate Highway System, many corporations circumvented the ban by erecting signs off the road but big enough and high enough to be visible to motorists. Travelers could still see part of the countryside by peering underneath the advertising. But these towering signs became increasingly hazardous to air navigation, and their removal in the interest of air safety was one of the first practical examples of transport coordination.

Many other errors were overcome through enlightened transport policies. Roads and streets were designed specifically to assure desirable sites for shopping centers, housing developments, recreation areas, playgrounds, and industrial parks, and to serve as buffer areas between incompatible land uses. Land was acquired for roads and other community projects at the same time. For example, slum clearance provided the opportunity to eliminate a large mileage of unnecessary streets and to provide walkways for pedestrians.

Still another victory over congestion was achieved through the reduction of peak hour traffic. As machines took over routine office work, fewer people were employed downtown. Automation also resulted in a shorter work day and work week, which significantly reduced the concentration of travel. With a five-hour day, staggered hours could be extended from eight o'clock in the morning to noon. The so-called "rush hour" was eliminated.

THE NEW URBAN AMERICA

YET it was obvious that making over the old cities could not succeed without providing additional urban developments to house the rising population and to accommodate those displaced by eradication of slums. The choice was either to let existing metropolitan areas spread without restraint, or to channel growth into new urban communities. Fortunately for America the latter course was chosen.

What we were seeking, as Clarence Stein had first named it, was the new regional city—a whole region that included the countryside as well as the more densely built-up urban areas. The farmer and the urbanite who had been separated through all of history could finally be brought together in the regional city. There the rural resident could find the same benefits of education, medicine, and cultural activities as the city dweller, and city people could enjoy the country. The old idea that a dense city center was necessary for men to come together for work and cultural activity was technologically obsolescent.

To realize the regional city, as Lewis Mumford had stated, we needed a balanced development for the whole region. We had to protect good agricultural lands, preserve landscapes for their beauty, and surround built-up areas with greenbelts of farmland or woodland. The task was not one for planners alone, or for government alone. Industry, business enterprise, and cultural institutions of all kinds joined in the exciting adventure. We were on the way to a kind of decentralization that would consist of many moderate-sized communities joined in a much larger urban association. The advantages of city and country could be shared, thanks to the availability of modern transportation. The new mobility was a new state of mind in which we began to live without boundaries in the twilight of big cities.[3]

This is the concept of urban America that was being created in 1966. We found ourselves rejecting both overconcentration in the old-fashioned central city and monotony and disorder in the suburbs. We were on the threshold of an era in which a great network of new urban communities and planned spillover areas would become a reality through federal, state, and local cooperative arrangements, through new tax policies and financial incentives, and by the teamwork of the public officials, businessmen and the academic community. Our wealth, our leisure, and our mobility transformed the vision of the regional city into reality.

The American people refused to be crowded into one percent of the nation's space when so much land was available. They looked at the map of the United States and spotted many places where climate and topography were agreeable, where there was easy access to outdoor recreation, and where there was land. They staked out the best areas for urban settlement, and the natural areas to be preserved. A national plan for urban development assured us that a nation "born of farms" would not "die of cities."[4]

At one time limited means of transport dictated where cities had to be. This was the major constraint that kept us from taking advantage of the land. But now transport would permit urban settlements wherever they were considered desirable.

For urban man, Charles Abrams told us long ago, there was no shortage of space.[5] With living space of one acre per 50 persons, the entire population of the world in 1966 could have settled in West Germany. At the same density, everyone in the United States could have lived on the West Coast, with a view of the Pacific. The problem was not lack of space, but how we used it. In the Netherlands, people had learned to use what little land there was in ways that created a satisfactory environment. There the population was 800 per square mile in 1966, compared to 100 persons per square mile expected in the United States by the year 2000.

There was indeed enough room in America. But this did not mean that 300 million people left to their own devices could not despoil 3 million square miles. It meant rather that we had to begin giving thought, as a nation, to how the inheritance of a continent could be used wisely.

Wolf Von Eckardt, writing in *Harpers Magazine* in 1966, proposed how this could be done. We should build 350 new communities of 100,000 persons, to house 35 million people—half the expected increase in population over a period of two decades. The need, he said, was partly to respond to the growth of urban population, but it was also to accommodate those displaced from high-density slums as urban rehabilitation redesigned the old cities. New communities were also necessary to permit workers to move closer to their jobs. Since industry was moving to the suburbs, workers should also be permitted to do so. And they should not be denied the freedom to move either because they were too poor or because they were Negroes.

The practicability of a new urban America was already being demonstrated twenty years ago by forward-looking architects, businessmen, and planners who undertook to build the pioneer new cities. The most prominent of these was Reston, Virginia. It was 350 years between Jamestown, the first urban settlement in America, and Reston, the first of the planned settlements. This community of 7,000 acres provided a wide variety of housing, industry, public facilities, and recreation opportunities. There were single-family houses, townhouses, and rental units in low, medium, and high-rise buildings, all with close access to open land. The seven villages making up the city were linked together by park lands and by a common town center.

The new community of Columbia in Maryland was also being built at that time. This suburban city of 150,000 close to Washington emphasized industrial and commercial employment opportunities to assure the city's economic vitality. New architectural design and land use planning assured esthetic quality, good public services, open space, and convenient recreation and transportation.

Here in 1966 were the previews of the kind of urban life that millions of Americans would enjoy in succeeding years. We soon learned, however, that even 350 of these new settlements would be unequal to the task of housing the urban population. A thousand new planned communities would be needed, and we set our sights in the last third of the twentieth century to building them. It was in no small measure the work of the Department of Urban Development and the help of the Department of Transportation that set the stage.

Eventually the new urban fabric and the old were brought into close association with each other through a rapid transit network—partly on the ground and partly in the air. The new transport technology, including vertical flight aircraft as well as electronic guidance for road and rail transport, created the planned dispersal that is the basic design for today's urban living. The new settlements made overcrowding obsolete and offered an alternative to sprawl. They minimized the need for moving and at the same time maximized the ability to move. All forms of transport shared in the victory over time and space, and in the creation of a satisfying urban civilization.

These accomplishments were made possible at the local level through the establishment of government agencies responsible for all methods of transportation, and through the pooling of transportation revenues to finance complete transportation systems, and through subordinating transport engineering to community desires.

In summary, the Secretaries of Transportation and of Housing and Urban Development have earned the gratitude of all Americans as we commemorate the twentieth anniversary of America's effort to redesign and rebuild urban society. We have resolved transportation problems improving urban life, and we have used transport technology as a tool for community development.

What we have accomplished would have been beyond man's reach had it not been for those pervasive changes that today provide the underpinnings of the Grateful Society: the increased availability of public funds through disarmament; the increase in wealth achieved through automation; the elimination of poverty through a guaranteed annual income; the solution of complex problems through the use of computers; and the improvement of transport and communications through unprecedented technological innovation. These have been the primary factors that have permitted us, in two momentous decades, to proceed much of the way toward rebuilding all of urban America.

This Message on Urban Transportation was programmed for the 99th Congress. There are other transportation messages that might be more appropriate twenty years from now. It is still possible that we will put the mechanics of moving ahead of the satisfactions of living. In that case we will have resigned ourselves to the material and esthetic poverty of much of urban America today. The shambles that this implies has inspired other messages of a different kind for 1986. We are keeping them in the computer memory. For unless this country launches a massive attack on urban ills, future Presidents will need to have a message of despair in reserve.

NOTES

1. "The Problems and Future of the Central City and Its Suburbs," Message from the President of the United States to the Congress, Doc. No. 99, 89th Congress, 1st sess. (March 2, 1965), p. 2.
2. David E. Lilienthal, "300,000,000 Americans Would Be Wrong," *New York Times Magazine,* Jan. 9, 1966, p. 25.
3. E. A. Gutkind, *The Twilight of Cities,* 1962, p. 187.
4. Elmer T. Peterson, ed., *Cities are Abnormal,* 1964, p. v.
5. Charles Abrams, "The Uses of Land in Cities," *Scientific American,* September 1965, p. 151.